Plantation Societies, Race Relations, and the South: The Regimentation of Populations

Plantation Societies, Race Relations, and the South: The Regimentation of Populations

Selected Papers of

EDGAR T. THOMPSON

Duke University Press
Durham, N.C.
1975

© 1975, Duke University Press

L.C.C. card no. 75–728

I.S.B.N. 0–8223–0336–1

PRINTED IN THE UNITED STATES
OF AMERICA BY KINGSPORT PRESS

To My Father and Mother
John Sanders and Annie Smith Thompson

Contents

III. The South: A Morally Sensitive Society

Foreword

Edgar Thompson says somewhere that he became conscious of the plantation when he left it to go to college. A childhood on a plantation, followed by conscious study of it from some distance, and then living in plantation country, visiting plantations in other parts of the world, and continued study of this peculiar institution made this book. The plantation began as an "enacted institution"; it was planted, the people as well as the crops. It became "crescive." As a matter of fact, W. G. Sumner, who made the distinction between enacted and crescive institutions, went on to say, "Pure enacted institutions which are strong and prosperous are hard to find. It is too difficult to invent and create an institution, for a purpose, out of nothing." (*The Folkways*, Boston, 1904, p. 54.) It is of the plantation growing, changing, declining, but persistent, that Thompson tells. In roughly similar conditions colonies have been planted in many parts of the world in modern times; they have developed along somewhat different lines. Yet there are features of social structure common to all of them. Thompson concentrates on the American institution, in which African imported laborers and their descendants worked for European men. The two parties lived close to each other—the two parties, physically so close that the biological frontier became blurred while the social frontier was cut deep and barricaded. The Africans thus became black, and the Europeans became white. The races, in the modern sense, were thus invented, complete with histories and qualities. As Montesquieu noted and ironically described in the eighteenth century, the black man had already been given his God-ordained place in the world without a soul.

In America the black got a shouting, singing and weeping soul—he got SOUL. Outsiders never quite understand the peculiar combination of closeness and distance of the plantation society. Thompson is perhaps the last of a generation that will have experienced the plantation in that form, and the last scholar to be able to write of it over a period of forty adult years. Once social change sets in, the generations never repeat each other nor match again.

But it is not only the plantation which grows (is crescive) and changes. The two races who form the major part of the population also change. The colored race with its octoroons, quadroons, mulattoes, and other fractions and shades was not imported to the American South. It was bred here out of African and European components as well. The ruddy so-called whites did their share, in the meantime developing some locally bred types as well; some are called "red-necks." But that epithet became the designation of a group with its distinguishing marks and its standing. The races which Thompson deals of are, some of them, products of the plantation itself. Again the plantation is crescive; it breeds races. These are the races which sociologists and historians study. Geneticists and some psychologists study a different kind of race, abstracted from complex combinations and sortings of variables. Intelligence quotient is apparently assumed to be of paleo-historic origin, and race is an entity whose characteristics were developed in some distant pre-time. It is odd to see race as some immutable variable become current again, this time in the word of the scientist rather than that of the apologist for the racial status quo. The races Thompson talks of are the living ones of the American South.

Thompson is of that generation who studied with Robert E. Park at the University of Chicago in the 1920's and 1930's. Some had racial experience on which to build the more systematic and thorough study encouraged by Park. Some then went to study race relations and institutions in various parts of the world. Among them E. Franklin Frazier and Thompson stand out. Both went back to their native region, the South. Both studied Southern institutions—the family, religion and the plantation among others. Both branched out to study similar institutions in other parts of the world.

The work of these two men forms a solid part of the corpus of sound and understanding work on the institutions of race relations. Thompson's present collection is an important addition to the corpus.

Everett C. Hughes

Boston College

Preface

The American South has been a subject of study from many different points of view, usually in terms of its particular regional setting and historical antecedents. There is a considerable body of literature on its geography, its economy, its politics, its literature, and its history. Much more research is currently in progress. Right now our intellectuals and commentators appear to be deeply involved in an effort to reduce the South to "problems," social problems, especially those inherited from the "gloomy wrongs" of the past, rather than to stand apart and use it as an object of detached investigation.

The utilization for study of a society within a traditional geographical locus, such as that of the South, may serve in some measure to break down categorical and dogmatic distinctions too narrowly maintained by the separate academic disciplines. The study of a region invites an interdisciplinary approach. The papers that follow suggest that the South may profitably be viewed as a social laboratory and studied comparatively. From this point of view, students of race relations, of rural economics and sociology, of social institutions, of the history and sociology of the South, and of geographic and ecological regions generally may find in these papers something of interest in their study and teaching.

There is overlapping, but most of the papers seem to fall naturally into three groups: (1) the plantation institution and its system, (2) race as an ideology functioning to bring people of diverse backgrounds and complexions in plantation situations into orderly caste-like relations with each other, and (3) the South as a more or less representative plantation society where men in the course of trying to control nature for private economic ends seek also to control other men as means to these ends.

Although the American South signifies an area in the southern and southeastern part of the United States it has never been merely a geographical expression. Rather it is and has been an historical synthesis fashioned by an interplay of unity with, and difference from, its regional neighbors as well as by activities and happenings within itself. The Europeans who settled along the long eastern American seaboard differentiated north and south along economic and institutional lines. Those to the south came to know themselves and to be known as "Southerners," and the South became that territory occupied by a people who, along with their special institutions, defined it as something more than an area which simply lies south of some point of reckoning. It did not become South in the sense in which Americans have understood that word until the institutions developed, spread over the land, and imposed themselves upon the society. The essential South is drawn from its culture and especially its institutions, not primarily from its geographical location. Chief among these special institutions was the plantation.

American historians and novelists have long sensed an organic connection among things, people, and events in Southern society and have sought explanations in such themes as climate, types of agriculture, agrarianism, the race problem, Cavalier descent, and others. The quest for a "central theme in Southern history" was first formally stated by Ulrich B. Phillips in 1928 who found it in the determination of whites to insure that the South remain forever "a white man's country." About this theme as well as others David Potter commented, "The quest for a central theme . . . is likely to continue. For the South remains as challenging as it is baffling, which is about as challenging as a subject can be."

The search for a "central theme" among historians may shift to a search for context among social scientists. The two conceptions, theme and context, are, of course, related, but the difference between them may have significant consequences in the outlook and for the methods of each type of investigator. A theme threads through a process of change to bring seeming dissimilarities into a substantial degree of coherence; indeed Phillips spoke of a "climate of coherence" in support of the principle of maintaining white racial superiority. A context, on the other hand, is a setting directing attention to the relational aspects of a matrix. In the case of a society, such as that of the South, it is a cultural matrix associating people and their institutions in a system outside of which they are imperfectly understood or misunderstood. Each institution in the system is in considerable measure a function of each of the other institutions. They each reinforce one another.

In no society, no matter how homogeneous and well integrated, will the segments or items of a culture fit together perfectly. In the South there were from the beginning discrepancies, imbalances, and incongruities, but this only means that it was never as changeless as sometimes it appeared to be. It was unstable enough to effect change, and with each change came some shift in the relational fabric, but to a remarkable extent it maintained a high degree of consistency among its parts from one generation to another. Conventional understandings and expectations were too regularly verified in everyday experience to excite many people to examine the nature of the social order in which they lived. It was a sturdy culture whose strength and persistence fashioned that social type called "Southerner." The type was more self-consciously in evidence after the Civil War than before.

A contextual situation invites comparison with other societal situations which appear comparable. One might ask if similar forms, structures, systems, or institutions characterize other times and places and with what likenesses and differences—if one assumes, as I do, that a society, any society, is best understood in the perspective of other societies and their histories. To paraphrase Kipling, what do they know of the South who only the South know? There have been other Souths with similar institutional frameworks.

The student of society is required to place the object of his investigation in a situational context. It is the central thesis of the papers in this book that the position of the plantation institution in Southern society has been pivotal, that the society must be understood in considerable measure as an elaboration of that institution, and that the institution itself must be understood in the context of the general social order which formed around it and which it dominated. It was not always so, however, even after the region had become well populated, and it is not so now. Nevertheless, for many decades it did powerfully regularize the activities of Southerners and other institutions in an extensive economic, political, and social network from Maryland to eastern Texas. They might very well have been called Southerners in some other societal complex, just as in a directional sense we speak of Westerners and Northerners, but without the presence of the plantation and its system, they most assuredly would have been Southerners of a very different kind.

The plantation has been present in many other societies around the world. It appears to have been very influential if not dominant in many of these but not in most. From each of these societies, however, we have something to learn if only by abstracting institutions and qualities from other historical and cultural complexities commensurable enough to reward comparative investigation. The principal abstraction has to do with the plantation estate itself. The further we go with these investigations, the more we have to learn about the South and its people. Preoccupation with the North-South contrast may make us "good" Southerners, even professional Southerners, but it will be most helpful now, I think, if we turn for insight and understanding to those agrarian societies in other parts of the world, especially just north and south of the equator, where labor problems and race problems have tended to merge.

The Introductory paper and the short paper on "The Little Races and Racial Theory" included in this collection have not hitherto been published. The publication of the other selections extends over a period of forty years or more in a variety of different books and journals and intended for different audiences. This may help to explain, even though it may not justify, why there may be a vexing amount of repetition. I am persuaded that there may be some virtue in repetition. There are some minor omissions and deletions, but for the most part I have left the papers very much as they appeared originally even though I am aware of some of the gaffes which time and other students have subsequently brought to light. For each selection readers should note the date of original publication and make whatever allowances they feel should be made. In many libraries some of the papers are not now accessible.

To more than anyone else I am indebted to the late Robert E. Park, my teacher at the University of Chicago, who during my graduate student years and even long after that, aroused my interest in plantation societies and in race relations. I owe much also to the late Romanzo Adams at the University of Hawaii. Dr. Everett C. Hughes, my classmate and friend at Chicago, has continued to influence me where Dr. Park left off and has contributed a Foreword to this book. Many of the papers, especially the Introductory paper, have been read by Drs. Ida Simpson, Arlin Turner, and Joseph Spengler of Duke University and by Dr. Herbert Blumer of the University of California. Dr. Dan Chirow, now at the University of Washington, provided valuable criticism, more of which I should have accepted. My obligation to each of these as well as to many others is great, but they are, of course, in no way responsible for my failure to take greater advantage of their wisdom. Mr. Theodore Saros, Associate Director of the Duke University Press, encouraged publications of these papers and saw the process through to completion. Mrs. Josephine Stipe of Chapel Hill reproduced the map and made the drawings from old prints. Mr. Richard Franck, my student assistant, prepared the bibliography. Miss Nancy Miller and my wife, Alma Macy Thompson, assisted in the proofreading.

Edgar T. Thompson

Duke University
February, 1975

Plantation Societies, Race Relations, and the South: The Regimentation of Populations

Cane cutters on an Hawaiian plantation

The Plantation: Background
and Definition

I

The inception of a research problem, as well as the course and results of the investigation itself, may formally be separated from the published report; personal bias, misconception, and experience, in the physical as well as in the social sciences, may lurk behind the scenes to add as well as to detract from the quality of the study. Perhaps readers have a right to be told what these personal influences are and have been insofar as the investigator himself is aware of them.

The series of papers that follow developed from a long-time interest in an institution, the plantation, which in considerable measure gave shape and meaning to a certain body of experiences in my life. I grew up on my father's plantation in South Carolina, but during the years of my residence there I took for granted what I was unwittingly assimilating. I raised no questions of my own and heard few if any questions raised by others. Everything was so overwhelmingly obvious. Nothing about that experience was then intellectually problematic.

My conscious interest in the plantation began when I left it to enter the university. I had to leave it in order to discover it. I never returned except during vacations or later as an occasional visitor, but at some point sentiment began to attach itself to memories of the life I had lived there with members of my family, our neighbors, and our friends on the plantation both black and white. The black ones and some of the white ones were or had been sharecroppers. Not yet had I risen above the common assumption of all of us, when occasionally we came to compare Southern and Northern life styles, that the plantation was something uniquely Southern. We had never heard of plantations anywhere else. It probably was not slavery alone that John

C. Calhoun had in mind when he spoke of "our peculiar institution" for which he demanded special consideration; it was the plantation and the plantation system of the Southern States. To the question, What is Southern about the South? the answer would have been, had anyone bothered to answer it at all, the plantation and its system of connecting and supporting institutions.

The question became a serious one for me when I began to realize that I am part of the history of that system, that it is part of me, that in studying it I am in effect acting as historian of my own life. It is a history which goes rearward over a period of three hundred years or more, uniting me with a continuing institutional tradition. This tradition literally gave and continues to give shape and content to people, events, and even certain agricultural staples of that part of the United States we call "the South." For long my ancestors and predecessors in this massive society took their way of life for granted, as I did, and raised very few questions about it. Before the "War of Northern Aggression," as some Southerners still call the Civil War, Southerners took relatively little interest in their history for, as Baudet puts it, "history does not begin in Paradise." It begins when its people have to leave it, "when there is a past to remember, to lament, to idealize." [1] The tremendous expansion of Southern historiography, now the leading expression of social scholarship in the South,[2] got underway after the devastation and losses incident to the Civil War when that catastrophe brought what most Southerners regarded as an ideal state to an end, when old plantation mansions were burned or began to crumble, and the past became a golden age.

During my undergraduate years I avidly read much of this literature and, in so doing, relived the life of the Old South and refought the battles of the Civil War in which my two Confederate grandfathers were engaged. Still steeped in the pathos of that South, I entered the University of Chicago as a graduate student in sociology where I came under the influence of a great teacher, Robert E. Park, who asked the questions I had not thought to ask. For one of his courses, I undertook to write a term paper on the subject of the plantation which was one item in his course outline. It was an easy assignment, I thought, because I knew all about the subject already. I have never known so much about it since (and, incidentally, I have never finished that term paper). As I went along, I realized I knew less and less about some aspects of the institution and more and more about other aspects I didn't know I knew. I became consciously aware of much I had unconsciously taken for granted. At any rate, I was led to move outward to study other plantation societies throughout the world. I had not given much thought to the fact that there were others, but there they were in what has been called "the golden belt of plantations" around the tropical and semitropical world— "golden" because of the rich profit the belt has yielded the planters.[3]

Awareness of the existence of numerous plantation societies invited comparative analysis, and in responding to this invitation I lost much of my subjective bias and became somewhat more detached and objective. It appeared that my own experience as well as the experience of others in Southern plantation society is much more durable, repetitive, and accessible to others than I had supposed. In my thinking, I began to see that the plantation is an institution subject to objective study, an entity to be talked about, named and identified. It became the thematic context for most of my later work.

I suppose there have always been two sorts of investigators. In a given framework of interest, one sort is fascinated by the differences between one thing and another, and the other sort, by the resemblances. Contrast and comparison, points of difference on the one hand and points of resemblance on the other, always go together, but the run of attention following preoccupation with the one as opposed to the other is not the same. In general, history emphasizes the particular and the different; science, including social science, searches through comparison for recurring likenesses on the basis of which generalizations and scientific laws may be established. In the first instance, one is impressed with the great multiplicity of Nature, its richness and diversity, and undertakes to describe and interpret it; in the second, one is impressed with its unity and undertakes to explain it.

Efforts toward the comparative study of whole societies or national entities, aside from the metaphors of "growth" or "development," have yielded very few rewarding generalizations, but the promise is infinitely greater when a student of the history of a country seizes upon an institution or a situation within it. The historian Frederick Jackson Turner, for example, came to focus upon the American frontier, the Wisconsin part of which had consciously influenced his own life, but his students and followers continued to investigate, define, and type frontiers all over the world.[4] Geographers and sociologists, as well as historians, now take frontiers into account in their studies as a matter of course.

My intellectual development followed a similar path. My undergraduate major was in history, and I tried to teach the subject later in a Florida high school. When I discovered plantations in other parts of the world my attention turned from North-South contrasts to the comparison of the institution in the South, in the West Indies, in South America, in Africa, and in Asia and the Pacific. Comparative study, of course, is endless; one constantly encounters new situations where the institution, or something very much like it, is or has been present. There is always more beyond so that the search for the irreducible core of the plantation, or any other institution or object, can go on forever. Of course, there will be differences within the category, but the recognition of these differences only leads to an effort to formulate a typology.

My own effort to do this beyond the obvious classifications on the criteria of agricultural staples produced, forms of labor control, patterns of management, and the like has been slight. I realize that such obvious principles of classification tend to harden into fixed molds just as stereotypes do and tend to preclude efforts to get beyond them. More fundamental principles will be required and no doubt will turn up as the comparative study of plantation societies continues. Some work on the differences between aspects of the Southern plantation and the institution in the West Indies, in Brazil, and elsewhere has appeared in the literature, but, in the absence of basic classification principles going well beyond the ethnocentrism of national historians, such work has not progressed very far. Comparison becomes more and more complex: every plantation is in some ways like every other plantation, every plantation system is in some ways like every other plantation system, and every plantation and every plantation system are in some ways like no other plantation or plantation system and like no other institution or system of any kind. But the word *plantation* synthesizes all into one commanding image.

II

When the study of an institution becomes comparative, the problem of identification and definition becomes a matter of first importance. What, aside from terminology, is the *thing* one is investigating? Certain landed units may be called plantations in the South, *fazendas* or *engenhos* in Brazil, or estates elsewhere. Examination of the characteristics of each thing or institution differently named may lead us to place them all in a single category. I shall call this category "plantation" while recognizing that this term derives mainly from an English historical experience which may be very different from other historical experiences leading to an almost identical institution but differently named. The name objectifies a historical experience and asserts its existence; it is based upon the popular expectation of regularities in behavior and function of the institution so named. For my purpose this is "plantation," or "the plantation."

So, what is the thing named "plantation" that we are investigating? Not only is definition a matter of initial importance, but often it is the purpose of the whole investigation, not to be answered until the final sentence is written, if then. In the absence of definition there cannot be a scientific investigation at all. It marks a difference between popular and scientific concern. Consider the manner in which an ordinary lay conversation changes when someone asks the seemingly irrelevant question of definition. Here we sit glorifying the romantic grandeur of old plantation mansions and society or, more likely, because it is chummier, excoriating it for the evils associated with it, when some pedant asks, What is a plantation? The rest of us sit in pained silence because of this inconvenient and inconsiderate disturbance of the peace until someone changes the subject. Or we may be moved to contemplation, to discussion, rather than just idle talk. Either an interesting conversation has been wrecked or a deliberation pitched upon a more or less value-free level ensues. It no longer is a chatty conversation; curiosity may take over, and we may become somewhat more objective. This attitude, however, may actually place one on the side of the critics since objectivity is so often popularly regarded as attack. It may lead to dangerous thoughts. Invariably the number of participants in the initial conversation will dwindle and those who remain or come to join the company will change character. In effect we now have a salon or a seminar.

When the question of definition arises in the conversational stage, the usual practice is to turn to a dictionary or an encyclopedia. From such sources, e.g., the *Oxford Dictionary,* we learn that the word *plantation* derives from the Latin *plantare,* to plant, and *plantatio,* the act of planting. The metaphor "plantation" progressively signified (1) a migration or transplantation of plants, trees, institutions, or people from one habitat or country to another; a migration implying settlement but without a designated form of settlement ("Ascanium . . . carrying forth a plantation of men . . . found a white sow"); (2) that which is planted (an indigo plantation); (3) the place planted; a migration with a designated form of settlement (a community such as Plymouth plantation); and (4) a tropical or semitropical estate; the terminus of a migration with a designated form of settlement *and* economy vesting jurisdiction in some established authority ("In Virginia every estate is a plantation . . . with its servants and slaves."). In the sense "the settlement of persons in some locality, especially the planting of a colony; colonization," the word dates from 1586. With the meaning "a settlement in a new or conquered country; a colony," the word dates from 1614. Probably the earliest use of the word to mean "an estate or farm, especially in a tropical or semitropical country" was in 1706.

The plantation type of colony was a form of settlement whose relations with the metropolis were not culturally derivative merely, such as the Greek colony was, nor yet simply administratively and politically bound to the metropolis, like the Roman military colony, but were connected with a center which was primarily a market, a source of capital and credit, and initially of labor. It was expected to be self-supporting. Political and cultural relationships between the metropolis and the plantation type of colony were not superseded by the market relationship. On the contrary: economic, political and cultural relationships were mutually reinforcing, but the economic connection was dominant. Behind plantation, however, was an ideology similar to that of the Crusades. Indeed, plantation might almost be considered an extension or transformation of the crusading spirit. Perry Miller said of the plantation of Virginia that it exhibited "a set of principles for guiding, not a mercantile investment, but a medieval pilgrimage." [5]

From these statements it appears that a social movement which was also a migration terminating in overseas settlement evolved in certain New World areas, such as the American South, into a landed estate specializing in the production of an agricultural staple for export. As such it developed a tradition and a structure which were transmitted through a succession of generations whose members forgot, or never knew or cared, how it all came about. Its continuity was vested in an upper planter class which controlled the system and gave the plantation its standing as an institution.[6] The planter class gave it form and imposed that form upon the larger society. How did it all come about?

III

During and following the Middle Age, Europe, that continental peninsula of angry storms, seethed with national, provincial, and sectarian rivalries and wars arising out of, and in turn giving rise to, numerous social movements. Social movements have been called "minor slow-burning revolutions" generated by social disorganization and unrest. Some of these movements resulted in new institutions in England and in the rest of Europe; others took the form of migration to overseas territories and, in time, some of these also resulted in new institutions. In any event, they were composed of participants capable of being reshaped and remoulded. The movements focused attention upon particular objectives, some of which had to do with aspirations in New World utopias. A migratory movement which envisaged a new home in a new country and a new start with new opportunities must surely have been appealing. Unlike individual migration from country to city, from routine monotony to excitement and glamor, which also requires no great urging, back-to-the-land movements have to be set in motion by fresh-air and ample-space propaganda and some collective ideal. They generally have been organized and actively promoted by governments, religious or business organizations, and other agencies. Plantation as migration or—better perhaps—migration as plantation obviously was such a movement and as such was sponsored by English landed and commercial interests.

The migratory impulse of which plantation was a part resulted in one of the great historical chapters of all time. For over 450 years after the discovery of the New World Europe expanded into every continent, rearranging populations and economies almost everywhere. The period was a focal point in a great historical movement, a vast mobilization of human energy and action and ideas. It was as though Europeans by design set out to farm the world and to utilize the people of other lands and races as part of that design. More interesting than mankind at rest is mankind in motion, and the story of this tremendous continental overflow, including accounts of explorations and discoveries of strange peoples with strange customs, has since become the very stuff of historical romance. Plantation as migration and settlement has been a part of that story.

The drive to move outwards during this period centered on Spain, Portugal, Holland, and especially England. England, perhaps more than the others, was disorganized and unstable enough to respond sensitively and vigorously to the new opportunities presented by an expanding world.[7] Circumstances prepared the English to move, through popular and private enterprise coupled with governmental encouragement, in new directions and to experiment with new techniques. But there was much to learn from the prior experience of other pioneering countries, especially Portugal.

Professor J. A. Williamson has suggested that the early plans for the plantation of North America were shown in the various patents of Henry VII which contained a good deal of well-developed theory, much of it probably derived from Portuguese practice in the fifteenth century. The origin of the term "plantation" as applied to a settlement may be found in the reign of Mary (Queen of Scots) when English and Scottish settlers were planted in Ireland. Here the English technique of plantation and settlement was worked out.[8] The technique was soon applied to the plantation of Virginia; the two "plantations" were so contemporary that attitudes toward the natives, the "wild Irish" of Ireland and the "Red Indians" of Virginia, were not very far apart.[9] It is worthy of note that both Sir Humphrey Gilbert and Sir Walter Raleigh had large Irish interests and also were involved in plantation enterprises in the New World.

The diacritical differences in the pronunciations of the word "plantation" suggest something about a change in meaning from English migration to Southern estate which should be noticed. American Southerners have pronounced it as "plant-a′-tion"; the

English and dictionary accent is "plan-ta'-tion." The two pronunciations, distinguishing between the movement and the institution which grew out of it, are useful and might very well be
retained. The first has reference to a land unit where crops not
grown in Europe, commercial agriculture as opposed to folk
agriculture, such as cotton and tobacco, are planted; the second
has reference to the planting of people. The plantation of Ulster
in Ireland and of New England in America were directed migrations which displaced populations with new settlers, but which
were not institutionalized into estates as was the case in tropical
and semitropical America.

It may be suggested that migration as plantation took the form
it did in England because the Irish Sea and the wide expanse of
the Atlantic Ocean made individual and family migrations, such
as the American gold rush and the South African trek, difficult
if not prohibitive. Roman colonization could proceed northward
by degrees; the Southern plantation estate, once established,
could advance westward without assistance; but transoceanic migration from Europe had to be promoted, directed, and controlled by interests outside those who actually migrated. To this
end capital in amounts beyond the means of such individual
adventurers as Gilbert and Raleigh was required. It was not until
men of means could combine fluid capital and transoceanic transportation for both goods and people that stock companies interested in trade and production for trade could be organized to
promote significant plantation migrations strong enough to survive. "Adventurers of the purse" combined to send "adventurers
of the person," or plantationites, to those parts of the New World
which promised ultimate profit.

In his essay "Of Plantations," Lord Francis Bacon, a share-
holder in Guy's plantation in Newfoundland, compared the art
of establishing plantation settlements in the New World with the
art of forming forest plantations in England. In either case, he
told those promoting such undertakings, "you must take account
to lease twenty years profit, and expect your recompense in the
end; . . . (there must be no) base and hasty drawing of profit in
the first years." [10] A great deal of capital—wealth combined with
patience and waiting power—would be required. The plantation
of America was no mere military or political conquest; in view
was the annexation of mineral, forest, and land resources essen-

tial to the life of a growing world economy centered in Europe, especially in England. Each enterprise was an "imperialistic" venture at a time when that expression was not well known, but when (as probably always since) the colonizing force was purposeful capital, not just the migration of an individual or a collection of individuals. Plantation was something more than the abstract flow of people as settlers or as labor; it was no less than a transplantation of *purposes, wills, energies,* and *capital.* The Spaniards in Mexico and in Peru expected and got quick returns in the form of gold and silver from their conquests, but English plantations in North America had to wait long before the resources of the areas planted, especially agricultural products, could become profitable. The time interval in the English instance required capital, and capital was a controlling force at every stage in the evolution of the plantation from migration to estate. As finally established as estate, the plantation was at one and the same time both a capitalistic and a feudal institution. But much more than this is involved: in the larger context of economic history the story of plantation from migration to institution to institutional system to vital regional interdependence around the world is a chapter in the origin and development of capitalism itself.

More immediately relevant, however, is an interesting sidelight on plantation as a social movement. Social movements tend to control future actions by reference to the way they proceeded before. The Crusaders of the Middle Ages came to learn how to carry on a crusade and developed techniques for doing so. Plantation also became patterned; men learned so well how to organize and conduct a plantation that Sir Peter Colleton could say, "Planting [the settling of new lands] is my trade and I think I may say without vanity that I understand it as well as any man." [11]

The dominant motive in English overseas plantation generally manifested itself in a variety of ways, whether in Ireland, Newfoundland, New England, Virginia, or certain islands in the West Indies. But always the thrust was basically economic. Very much the same sort of promoters with similar economic motives backed the plantation of both Massachusetts and Virginia; [12] the differentiations came later. Settlers in the Puritan tradition were planted in New England and developed town communities. (The official name of Rhode Island is still "Rhode Island and Providence Plantations" and in Maine a plantation is a loosely organized and thinly settled division of a county.) They also settled on the island of Old Providence off the coast of Nicaragua and there developed slave plantation estates.[13]

There is good reason to believe that the *fondaco* of Italian merchants in the Mediterranean which became the trading factory of the English in the Orient furnished a model for settlements in Brazil and in Virginia. In the earliest English plantation at Jamestown in Virginia the head of the local council was designated "president" as in the English factories in India. The settlers, or factors, were expected to trade with the Indians on behalf of the Virginia Company, throwing all the earnings into the common store as was done in the trading factories in India. An American historian of this period, John Fiske, misunderstanding the origin and nature of the practice, called the system "communism" and condemned it as evil.[14]

The old British Empire did indeed possess a dual nature. In the East it became and remained an active commercial empire; in the West it became a plantation (settlement) empire. Those two sides of imperial economy, trade by sea and plantation by land, together were administratively embraced by the "Lords of Trade and Plantations." In the East, the natives were ready and eager to trade in easily available commodities; in the West one party to what initially was planned as a commercial relationship made economic demands which the productive organization of the native American Indians was unable to meet, except in the northern fur-trade and skin-producing country, and even there it was a passive commerce. Both factor and planter-entrepreneur were, of course, motivated by the prospect of the profitable exchange of goods, but with an important difference. Along that type of frontier which attracted the planter more than the trader, or factor,[15] a labor supply had to be found, organized, and controlled. Into these areas the planter-entrepreneur had to muster an industrial army of occupation, usually by importation; people as well as goods had to be transported. Thus began the age of free trade in labor which since has expanded to global proportions. The result was the contact of people of different origins, different cultural traditions, and different levels of culture.

After an inevitable period of turmoil a new society grew up

with new traditions, a new social order, based not on kinship but
on the territory occupied. In the South and elsewhere this new
order rested upon the mutual accommodation of diverse peoples
defined by the plantation, now become a landed estate, and its
system. Such an outcome was of course not unique to the South
or even to other plantation societies; it was and is a process of
politicization from which the state and other sorts of formally
disciplined societies have emerged around the world. According
to Teggart, the state initially appeared at the termini of routes
along certain favorable frontiers.[16] The plantation as a little state
appeared along overseas frontiers hugging the sea and other
avenues of low-cost access to the markets of Europe and of the
world for the purpose of bringing favorable lands into new and
presumably higher uses. It was and is not now, of course, the only
institution having and achieving such a purpose.

IV

But to return to plantation as migration and its institutionalization as landed estate in the South: Among the immediate profit-
making motives in the settlement of Virginia there were, in addition to trade, the lure of gold which failed to materialize, and the
need to supply wood-starved England with timber. The sight of
a rim of mighty virgin forests along coastal North America and
the unavailability of other articles of export aroused hopes of
extensive exploitation which, however, could not be realized
because of the great labor involved and the very high cost of
transportation to England. Nevertheless, timber shipments of
masts for ships, especially selected King's Trees, began about as
soon as a settlement was made. More important, however, than
shipments of timber and certain by-products of timber was the
fact that some areas of land were cleared of trees. They were
cleared by dint of very hard labor, a gauge of the back-breaking
tasks later to face other settlers who moved into the thickly
forested West and took up farming. Slavery initially was perhaps
as important in these tasks as it later was to become in the cultivation of the staples of plantation agriculture; it figured mightily
in the process of settlement as well as of agricultural production.
Clearing "new ground" remained a feature of plantations well
into the present century.

Land cleared was land cleared for action. Land cleared was land cleared as potential private property. The trend toward the development of private property in land in Virginia was directly connected with the discovery of the delights and profits of the cultivation of tobacco. There had been some haphazard agriculture before, but with tobacco, agriculture was systematically pursued and the plantations multiplied. Settlements to the north of Virginia and Maryland discovered no important export crop, but in tobacco the planters of Virginia realized a market connection with England and Europe, and tobacco traded to the outside world was the stimulus which led to the tobacco plantation and to the acquisition of private property in land. From a convivial and peaceful usage among the Indians, among the individuated English settlers tobacco became an addictive vice. That "bewitching vegetable," as William Byrd called it, transformed Virginia into a colony founded on smoke, as the disappointed and disapproving King of England characterized it. Tobacco was not altogether new to England, having arrived there earlier from the West Indies, but thenceforth almost all New World tobacco ordinarily was called "Virginia tobacco." It was an ideal crop from the point of view of shipping and marketing since it had small bulk and high value and, like many drug products generally, supplied a steadily expanding market in England and on the continent. It was the first and, for almost two centuries, the most important cash crop of the Southern plantation economy, falling only much later before the competition of cotton for land use in the lower South.

Certain folk or traditional crops of English and European agriculture were transplanted and cultivated in North America, especially in areas of temperate climate, but the cultivation of the crops of plantation agriculture was not known in Europe.[17] Their cultivation in America had to be learned, organized, and directed by a new type of entrepreneur. In Brazil this man became a *senhor de engenho,* later a *usineire,* and in the British plantations a planter, something more than a mere farmer, or a type of farmer who did not really like to farm or intend to do the work of farming.[18] Nevertheless, he was better able to appreciate and respond to market and other news affecting his agricultural interests than others. The crops which the planter-entrepreneur initiated in Virginia and elsewhere, such as drug

crops (tobacco) and dessert crops (sugar and spices), were exported to Europe as luxuries for the rich which in time became necessities for the proletariat as well. These and others to follow were commodities that had to go immediately into the channels of commerce, since they could not be extensively consumed on the producing plantations. By 1618 the trading factory in Virginia, as originally intended, was giving way to the plantation as estate, and the planters were granted the right to export goods for themselves. A system of society was growing up around the cultivation of tobacco, a botanical annual but on its way to becoming what Zimmerman has called an "institutional perennial." [19]

The stage had earlier been set for such a societal development when Virginia, itself the original plantation, dissolved into a number of "particular plantations." [20] As a result of a new policy formally adopted in 1616–1617 specific tracts of land were granted to individuals and organized groups of Englishmen. Within a few years, fifty or more such grants were made, each providing for the transportation and planting of from one to four hundred men. Each "particular plantation" retained both the political and economic motives and powers present in the original plantation enterprise.[21] This development occasioned a distinction between "colony" and "plantation." [22] With the distinction once established, there was no longer need to speak of any plantation as "particular" since all were. With the emergence of Cavalier Virginia after about 1642 a society popularly identified with such well known names as Carter, Byrd, Mason, Beverly, Randolph, Pendleton, and Washington—men destined to become great planter-statesmen—took form and flowered. Such men had no intention of working the land with their own hands; the lordly tradition they inherited from England predisposed them only to supervise the labor of others and attend to affairs of state, and to this end they and their successors imported white indentured servants from England and black slaves from Africa. Getting and settling labor on the estates, and perfecting devices and laws for its control, became the chronic problem of Virginia and of the South for the next several hundred years.

V

Taking off from dictionary definitions of the use of the word "plantation" at earlier and later periods of its history, I have tried

to outline, omitting considerable detail, the process of institution-alization whereby the plantation as migration became, in Virginia and in the South, plantation as estate. It was an estate with its own identifying architecture set in the midst of ample space. A principle of settlement, of agricultural production, and of public order was established, standardized, and socially sanctioned. As the social order which it imposed began to sink deeply into the habits of individuals and into the customs of the South, it created divergent sentiments on the part of those who wanted to preserve and humanize it and on the part of others who sought to escape from, overthrow, or replace it with some other system. The ideal "other system" in America was the family farm system; the family farm has been to the plantation what the church has been to the saloon. It was because one class of Americans regarded it as a vested interest and as good, and another class regarded it as evil and sought to destroy it, that the plantation and its system had sufficient instability to permit change at all, or at least the kind of drastic change instituted by the Civil War.

Students of institutions generally seem not to have paid much attention to that class of institutions I choose to call "settlement institutions." They are those institutions which cannot exist apart from certain territorial assumptions and landed necessities; they are institutions which connect land and people in a special way and exist in this very connection. When the connection is broken the institution becomes only a state of mind or a memory. The living institution not only covers land with the visible signs of its presence, signs which reflect its nature and power of action, but the land itself is an intrinsic part of it. Settlement institutions cannot be transplanted to the city, for they require not just naked space upon which to operate but land to operate upon.

It is probably true that men rarely if ever live directly upon nature's land as the animals do. Men live in culture and in institutions, and the institutions in their turn, particularly the kind of institutions I am calling settlement institutions, interact with the natural habitat and the market to define the terms upon which men may live and work on the land. Apart from institutional and cultural contexts, the so-called man-land ratio is a very unreal concept. Now, land as it appears in nature is continuous except when it comes to the water's edge. Settlement institutions impose upon the land some principle of discontinuity which may be expressed by fences and other man-made boundaries. They operate to break up the land into nameable and countable units which then may be recorded and transferred or transmitted as property in formal ways as well as in public understanding. Settlement institutions sort out, classify, and give meaning to the colors and shapes of the land and movements upon the land to which names are assigned. What are the distinguishing characteristics of that institutional unit we call the plantation?

It was Spinoza, I believe, who held that all definition is negative which is another way of saying that we best define a thing in terms of what it is not. The plantation is not a great many things, but it is significantly not a relatively few things to which it is allied by the land connection but from which it otherwise differs. The results of a comparison of the plantation with other institutions along such a continuum go beyond school-book definitions into bodies of meaning as experienced by the members themselves of each institution or as stereotypes by others outside. We call the plantation a settlement institution, a habitat embodying both land and people, and there are quite a number of other such institutions to compare it with. It is identified with, but at the same time distinguished from, other forms of settlement institutions. An incomplete and brief comparison with a few others may serve to call attention to some of its more significant features.

VI

To begin with, the plantation is not just a big farm. It is not a family farm, perhaps the simplest settlement institution. Some years ago Warren Wilson described the family farm as a "human unit of land," that is, a piece of land which the farmer and his family have domesticated and made a working partner along with the horses, the cows, and the dog. It is not just so many acres. The family farm is a unit of land which one family can handle without much help from the outside. Traditionally, especially in New England, the outside help was "the hired man, a type of farm laborer which is peculiarly American, and of the nineteenth century." [23]

Agriculture is the only primary form of industrial organization common to colonies of all latitudes, but the units of agricultural production appear to bear some relation to climatic zones. Plantations are characteristically located in tropical and semitropical areas, whereas family farms, with some important exceptions, tend to characterize the agriculture of temperate zones. On various frontiers both institutions have functioned to bring land into new and presumably higher uses, but history as well as geography and climate must supply explanations for their different distributions. Where the land is occupied by conquest, by migration, or by the importation of labor, the effect is to break up the familial and traditional organization of society and to create a proletarian labor class. This occurs in plantation settlement where the laboring class tends almost everywhere to be set off as racially different. On the other hand, where the invading people, the settlers, are able and willing to supply the labor themselves, where the land occupied is used, in the first instance, to produce goods for immediate consumption, there settlement may be achieved with free labor, with the labor of the settler and his family. The result is the family farm. The settler brings his culture with him and does not impose it, to any great extent, upon native peoples presumably of more elementary culture. Instead he supplants them. Here proletarianization does not take place.

The family farm has a history, a history not yet fully told so far as I know. Where agriculture had to be carried on under the threat of hostile action by outsiders, families were compelled to live closely together for protection. Peasant villages were the rule, and isolated homesteads, the exception. In Europe this pattern seems originally to have been most strongly developed in the Mediterranean countries, giving place to irregularly distributed farms further north. There appear to have been some isolated farmsteads in England. Early English settlements in America, however, were modeled after the village pattern, especially in New England, even to the extent of establishing the Common.

In America the isolated farm, like the log cabin, may have been due to early Swedish influence. If so, it was a powerful influence along the forested frontier as settlers streamed down the Ohio Valley and pushed the Indians aside. Sims tells us that it was not until the settlement of the American Middle West that scattered homesteads made their "first appearance on a large scale." [24] These isolated homesteads probably stemmed from that "in-

dividualistic Southern element" of which Frederick Jackson
Turner speaks in *The Frontier in American History* rather than
from the community and congregation-minded New Englanders
who occupied the more northerly parts of Ohio, Indiana, and
Illinois.

These Southerners, who probably were the original "squatters," originated in part as white indentured servants who had
served out their time on the plantations of Virginia and further
south. Many of them moved individually and in family groups
into unoccupied lands in the Piedmont. They or their descendants pushed across the Appalachians into Tennessee and Kentucky. From these territories they crossed the Ohio River and,
as was the customary practice, squatted on lands to which they
had no legal title.[25] Instead neighbors recognized and respected
popular titles such as "tomahawk rights," "cabin rights," or "corn
rights." The system moved westward into the prairie states
beyond Illinois and took deep root there. Political agitation
throughout this larger Middle West resulted in 1862 in the passage by Congress of the Homestead Act which gave legal sanction to the holdings of the squatters.

The traditions of squatter democracy pervade Middle Western
society to this day. It was an order of society in which there were
neither lords nor vassals, a society of prideful farm ownership,
the spiritual as well as the geographical center of middle class
America. In it appeared something not duplicated in the Old
Plantation South until well after the Civil War—the growth of
numerous small towns each nucleating the surrounding farms
into a local community unity. Here was an approximate realization of the agrarian ideal of Jefferson and of the later reformers
with whom Horace Greeley was associated. Here was the cradle
of the Republican Party, which has placed the protection and
prosperity of the family farm in each of its political platforms
ever since.

The family farm in both the upland South and the Middle West
was integrated into a social order against which the plantation
society of the South waged a duel during the greater part of its
pre-Civil War history. That war itself was a chapter in this duel.

Two additional apparent differences between the Middle
Western farm and the plantation should be noted. First, the
squatter and homesteader entered into an orderly relationship

with a market subsequent to established settlement *after* which the farm was transformed into the larger and specialized machine operation characteristic of the wheat and corn belts today. The plantation, on the other hand, was sparked into life by the market relationship itself. Again, there often appears to be an organic evolution from the household industry of family farm areas to large-scale manufacturing industry in the same areas. In plantation areas manufacturing industry may be said to be "instituted," that is, transplanted, from the outside almost overnight, but not without conservative opposition.[26]

VII

The term generally in use for large landed estates is *latifundia* of which plantations are, of course, a subtype. But the *latifundium* as a term used to name an extensively farmed property in post-Hannibalistic Italy was, more narrowly, also a subtype of large estate. Latifundia in Italy apparently arose with the decay of the existing system of peasant proprietorships. Pliny the Elder complained that "latifundia ruined Italy," and Goldsmith later in England lamented the destruction of a "bold peasantry" when the Enclosure Movement there consolidated small holdings into large landed properties. Enclosure movements under one name or another seem to have occurred with almost cyclic regularity with similar results in many societies before and since Pliny and Goldsmith. Latifundia uproot a rural population; plantations settle populations on the land. To some extent, the Enclosure Movement in England supplied a part of the population planted in America. However, the plantation institution, once established, may swallow up small farms in its path of advance.[27]

The term *latifundium,* in its general sense, frequently is extended to include that institutional form called in England a "manor," and by other names elsewhere. This form grew up in Europe with the decline of the peace and trade organized and protected by Roman legions when semibarbarous peoples from the north invaded, conquered, and pushed back the Roman frontier into Italy itself. A vast area was reorganized under new and quarrelsome authorities into thousands of manors and other bits of sovereignties between which war was a normal and inevitable condition. The later coming of the national state expanded peace areas, but the principles of local self-sufficiency, political authority, and immunities from the laws of the king, as well as feudal loyalty of peasant to lord, remained. A high degree of economic self-sufficiency was not only a fact, but became an ideal as well. Notwithstanding the ideal, however, the manor was bound to be economically incomplete as is every state which occupies only a portion of the earth's surface. There are incipient threads of trade which traced their way further and further outward, leading to town, to national, and then to international trade. As town life arose there was offered a market and a contrasting way of life against which the manor could not compete. Its decline came first in England which was especially favored by access to cheap water transportation and whose foreign trade steadily expanded in consequence. With trade the manor was transformed into other forms of economy. For the market relationship holds in it a different principle of organization.

The plantation is based upon this principle, and the essential difference between it and the manor lies in this fact. The plantation clings to the cheaper transportation of coastlands, islands, and archipelagoes and is not to be found in the landlocked parts of the earth where the manorial form continued longest, as in Russia. The manor produces to consume and is therefore organized around a variety of agricultural and animal goods yielded up to the lord as rent or as feudal dues; the plantation is organized around the production of a staple crop in which it specializes, and self-sufficiency is a fact mainly to the extent that supplies cannot be imported economically from elsewhere. The lord of the manor is a rent and tax collector; the planter is a manager and entrepreneur. The planter produces to sell, and in line with this purpose he devises strategy to improve and increase production and to get his staple to market. On the manor there is an organization of classes differentiated from within, while the plantation tends to become an organization of races brought together from without.

In the seventeenth century Lord Baltimore succeeded in erecting some sixty manors in his Maryland grant, but the ready availability of land to the west rendered his effort precarious and finally impossible. The provisions of Locke's "Fundamental Constitutions" for Carolina in 1669, like the Dutch patroonships along the Hudson River, failed to take root. Martin's Hundred and similar grants in Virginia failed for the same reason; an institution dependent upon scarcity of land could not succeed where land was abundant and open so long as settlers were free to settle upon them. In the absence of a system of labor control, at once both mobile and locally concentrated, such as could be obtained either from coerced natives or by the importation of indentured, contract, or slave labor from abroad, manorial agriculture was impossible. In the South the manor became a plantation. In a situation foreign to both blacks and whites two sets of people impinged upon each other to produce a new institution, also foreign to each as well as to the native Indians. It was an institution which transformed all parties participating in it, particularly the black man who lost so much and assimilated so much that he became in fact the original American with fewer cultural survivals than either the Indian or the white man. The plantation, particularly in the South and in the West Indies, became something much more than "a mechanical mixture of borrowed elements." [28] It gave rise to new mixtures, to new peoples, and to new cultures.

There are other important differences between the manor and the plantation and there are also other important similarities. Both lord and planter exercised judicial functions and both tended eventually to become officials of the larger state. Both manor and plantation are political institutions, that is, institutions based upon the principle of authority, which in both cases implies the existence of an aristocracy. Titled aristocrats, as opposed to plutocrats, appear to evolve in societies based upon landed estates, and if Southern plantation society developed no genuine titled aristocracy, as the manor did, it did develop a gentry with aristocratic pretensions. It was the planter gentry that held the South together and gave it such meaning and purpose as it had. The feudal attitude, or something close to it, seems invariably to accompany the kind and duration of the relationships which a manorial or plantation peasantry has with its gentry. On neither the manor nor the plantation was the feudal attitude present to begin with; feudalism, however, became part and parcel of the manorial system and, with the development of personal relations and sentiments, came also to characterize the moral order of plantation societies, especially the older ones. The plantation as it existed in the South, in Brazil, and in Old Hawaii assumed that proprietors lived on the land and personally directed the affairs of the estate. But there is a marked tendency, under corporate ownership, for the political and racial organization of the plantation to change its character. There is little or no sentiment attached to the large rubber plantations of Southeast Asia and to the type of life developed on them. They appear to make no claims on anyone based upon the old customs.

While plantation society in the South, and especially in the Old South, as elsewhere, provided an ordering or regimentation by race, class, domestic, and sex relationships of a large proportion of the population in a manner similar to that of manorial society, it never achieved so perfect a form. But the outlines of the form were there. Black slaves at the bottom of the pyramid upward to free blacks, to poor whites, to yeoman whites, to small and large planters at the top, the system came to form a symbiotic structure whose strata were differentiated according to the prevailing standards of status, family connections, land holdings, income and skill. Not only yeoman farmers but ministers, lawyers, teachers, and doctors aspired to the status of planter, and small planters strove to become great planters. By virtue of their white skin poor whites, yeoman whites, members of the professions, and lesser planters participated in the force and significance of the status symbolized by the great planters. To some degree the entire society of the old plantation South was cast in the image of the great planters.

VIII

The ranch, as we have commonly understood and named this mobile farm in the United States, represents another distinctive orientation to the land and another distinctive style of life. On the ranch the relations of men to the land are mediated, not through crops, but through such marketable and self-transporting animals as cattle and sheep. This institutionalized form is or has been found in Central and South America, especially Argentina, Hawaii, North and South Africa, Australia, and elsewhere as well as in the United States. The mature age of ranches in this country spanned a period of not more than twenty years after 1861,[29] but the form began as an undifferentiated aspect of tidewater plantations on uncultivated forest lands in the early

colonial South. Cowpens, as they came to be called when differentiated from plantations proper, later occupied Piedmont
areas west of plantation and farming areas. Farmers and planters
moving westward pushed them still further into forested lands
beyond the mountains until finally they came to a line roughly
following the ninety-eighth meridian where the Great Plains
begin. Beyond this institutional fault line, as Walter Webb calls
it,[30] "the ways of life and living changed. Practically every institution that was carried across it was either broken or remade or
else greatly altered." At this fault line the cowpen was transformed into the ranch in what was for it an ideal set of circumstances. Webb goes on to say (p. 207): "In the final analysis the
cattle kingdom arose at that place where men began to manage
cattle on horseback. It was the use of the horse that primarily
distinguished ranching in the West from stock-farming in the
East."

The cattle baron who owned and profited from the Western
American ranch has figured little in the ranching tradition of this
country, but there developed a veritable cult of the cowboy as
there developed a cult of the gaucho in Argentina. The work of
this man was rough, dirty, poorly paid, dull and monotonous,
solitary, and often dangerous. But he rode a horse, and, to the
extent that freedom is always freedom to move, the cowboy was
emancipated and free from the beginning, for he was highly
mobile and as such an ideal figure for romantics. A familyless
man, he knew little of the society of proper women, but possibly
with the intention of attracting the attention of females against
the competition of numerous other men, he sported showy dress
and gaudy accessories. He matched his "ten dollar horse," it was
said, "with a fifty dollar saddle."

The cowboy never "worked"; rather he "rode for" a certain
ranch. In him there was scarcely a notion that he might change
character and milk a cow. He would willingly work long and hard
hours tending cattle, but if asked to plow a field or perform any
other type of farm work, he was quick to march off and look for
another job. He worked on the land, but he would not work the
land itself and he was contemptuous of those who did, especially
of those encroaching farmers he called "nesters." What was true
of the cowboy on the western ranch in America was also true of
the Argentine gaucho. Oscar Schmeider has written: "After a few

generations of life in the Argentine plains the gaucho looked with utter contempt on any kind of agricultural work, although it had been the main occupation of his Spanish ancestors. As a consequence, cultivation of the soil was restricted to a minimum." [31]

We have only to contrast the stereotype of the cowboy or the gaucho with that of the lowly, shabbily dressed worker in plantation fields almost anywhere and everywhere, whether indentured servant, slave, sharecropper, contract laborer, or simply as a labor import into what for him is a strange land, to realize the great difference in status and life style between the two. The ranch owner is not generally understood as one who realized his status in and through those who work for him. But the dominant expression of the planter has been in terms of sovereign authority and subjection, as a realization of himself as superior to those under him. He knows himself in terms of the height to which his subordinates have raised him, and this is the conception of him held by the larger community generally. His is not necessarily the prestige of the "expert," but the prestige of authority and of his class or race. Among the workers who have supported his claim to prestige and social standing, particularly in the older plantation societies, there has been little to dramatize the work they performed aside from brute strength, cunning, good luck, religious piety, and occult beliefs and practices. There was room on the plantation for loyalty, rebellion, honor, and disgrace, but there has been no recognition to compare with calf-roping, bulldogging steers, bronc-riding, trick-riding, rope and whip work, and other heroics of the cowboy's life which have been institutionalized in the rodeo.

Finally, let it be noted that the cowboy's work in ranching and in trailing, that is, in both the production and the marketing ends of the cattle business, was not rigidly separated. The plantation laborer, on the other hand, had little or nothing to do with the marketing of the crops which he produced. Nevertheless, ranch and plantation each possessed a social organization designed to produce and another one to market. In the case of the plantation, marketing was handled through an entirely separate mechanism which, in the South before 1861, was known as the factorage system, a survival and adaptation of the trading factory. The planter of the period may well have been a good farm manager, but he seems to have been rather indifferent to business matters outside his plantation. The tobacco, cotton, or sugar factor in the port cities was at once his commission merchant, banker, bookkeeper, advisor, collector and disburser, and the one who honored checks and paid bills. The disruption of the factorage system was one of the drastic consequences of the Civil War.

IX

Large industrialized agricultural units employing substantial numbers of hand or "stoop" laborers, such as those that have characterized large areas in California, point up certain other properties of the plantation. These units have been worked by armies of migratory laborers made up of Orientals, Mexicans, and lower Middle West whites who seasonally have marched from crop to crop and from place to place.[32] They have lived in bunkhouses rather than in cabins or homesteads, and they are dependent for necessities on an employer but not necessarily upon any particular employer. Relations between workers and employer and among the workers themselves are highly secularized and contractual. The plantation, on the other hand, ordinarily is concerned to immobilize and stabilize at least a nucleus of workers into year-round settled communities, but this nucleus could be supplemented to meet seasonal crop requirements. These are not, however, communities of diverse and independent institutions, interests, and goals such as village communities normally are. Rather the plantation community is more like a company town dominated by a single company, family, or planter pursuing a unitary economic goal and subordinating schools, churches, stores, commissaries, recreation, hospitals, housing, and even families to that goal. But residence on the plantation does imply certain obligations and expenses on the part of the planter even where slavery is the worker's condition. Corresponding obligations and duties on the part of the workers likewise develop. Generations may pass, as generations have passed, and the plantation may develop a moral order, some sort of piety, some respect for tradition. This, too, will pass, as now it is passing in the South as wage or machine labor takes the place of tenant labor. Such an outcome does not develop on the agricultural factory estates of California. Instead there are inevitably unionization and strikes.

X

In that type of rationalized latifundia where there is extensive mechanization ordinarily there is a high return per unit of capital and labor and a low return per unit of land in agricultural production. We call this the power farm. Prior to the invention of the reaper practically all American agriculture was carried on by human and animal labor. The coming of the tractor, followed one after another by other machines, changed all this. The tractor served to pitch crop production, especially of grains, upon a new and very different plane and set the stage for a drastic reorganization of farming. For agricultural units tend to adjust themselves to the type of power available. The plantation generates power beyond the energy of the proprietary family by multiplying the number of human hands which, in the South, took the form of servitude, slavery, and sharecropping. These measures gave the plantation somewhat the same advantage over the small family farm that the large machine-powered farm gained over the plantation.

During the 1920's and 1930's, Americans read of the extensive operations of the Thomas Campbell Corporation in Montana on its 95,000 acre property. At that time, the corporation operated 109 tractors, 100 planting machines, 80 binders, 600 harvesters, 11 threshing machines, fleets of automobiles and trucks, and produced during this period more than one million bushels of wheat each year. To conduct this huge operation a relatively small number of technicians, skilled mechanics, and highly qualified and well-paid managers, who dressed for dinner and were free to order their leisure time as they saw fit, were employed. They were subject to company rules, to be sure, and to discipline according to their middle-class status, but they were not regarded and did not regard themselves as ordinary farm laborers. The machines they operated and maintained required fuel but no food; they drew no wages and required no rest; they did break down on occasion, but otherwise they had no uncertain habits; they did not sulk, talk back, run away, or hold resentments. They obeyed the touch of a lever blindly and powerfully.

On his plantation the planter plays two roles. In one of them he is an agriculturalist possessing the technical knowledge and skill necessary to produce the crop successfully. He must know seeds, fertilizers, soils, planting times and harvest times, and at the same time be something of a weather prophet, for on such knowledge depends his income. However, this kind of knowledge is not enough. To realize his business purposes he might very well like to reduce the human beings who work for him to the level of animals and machines. But human nature will out, and to deal with it he must play another and a much more difficult role. For the most insistent problem of the plantation stems from the fact that it is full of people who, in spite of all rules, regulations, punishments, and rewards insist upon behaving like human beings. Of all forms of property, slaves probably are the most troublesome. The human workers of whatever race or status come with an infinite variety of feelings, intentions, thoughts, weaknesses, strengths, and these have to be lived with and somehow managed. The planter knows, or is presumed to know, the ways of his people with a certain predictive accuracy.[33]

Of all forms of management supervision, agricultural supervision is perhaps the most oppressive. Because poor work may not show up until much precious time has passed, constant supervision at every stage is essential. Someone has to stand around to watch and inspect. Inevitably such close supervision gives rise to resentments and passions that must be contained, and to quarrels that must be adjudicated. The planter can be no mere landlord or farmer; he is also a chief of state and head of government.

XI

The plantation might with profit be compared with several other types of agricultural enterprises, large and small. In pre-Communist Manchuria, for instance, farmers produced an illegal but highly profitable crop, the opium poppy, in secret gardens, and organized themselves militarily to protect themselves and the crop against the police and the armed forces of the larger state. This was another form of "military agriculture."[34] On the plantation a population also is regimented, but the discipline here is directed inward in order to deal with the uncertainties of labor, weather, insects, and the vagaries of the crops within the institution itself. To be sure, there have been instances as in colonial Brazil,[35] as well as occasionally along the southern American frontier, when the plantation also had need to protect itself against outside attack. But normally this defense function is taken over by the larger state which more often than not is part of the plantation system dominated or powerfully influenced by the planter class. Tobacco in Virginia, like opium in Manchuria, was also an addictive drug, but here the colony and State were greatly concerned to forward the interests of the planters, not to attack them. I have described plantations as small states in many respects, but unlike states they do not make overt war upon one another. They do, however, collide as indicated almost everywhere by the enormous amount of litigation over boundaries.

Again there was an interesting type of large-scale agricultural operation which existed in Dutch Indonesia, particularly Java and Sumatra, between 1830 and 1870 and which has had parallels elsewhere. In Indonesia it was known as the "culture system." [36] In earlier conquests, conquerers were content to take in tribute what subjugated natives were accustomed to produce, but the Dutch added a positive condition to the system of tribute-taking when they dictated a long list of products other than traditional East Indian goods, such as rice, wanted in Holland or which promised profit when traded. To secure these they adopted a variation of the *corvée,* that is, the compulsion of native labor through village headmen working under the direction of Europeans to produce agricultural products for export. Unlike slave labor which is demanded permanently, *corvée* labor is conscripted on a temporary, though recurring, basis. After his term of work the native returns to his village to work for himself. The result in the Dutch East Indies was what Boeke called a "dual economy" [37] and the people became what Redfield called "imperialized folk." [38]

The plantation, by contrast, appears to operate as a feudal-capitalistic enterprise built up by an individual entrepreneur or by a company, not by an imperialistic state acting as such. It originally is an institution of settlement as the culture system in the East Indies and elsewhere was not. The culture system farmed out existing villages; the plantation established new habitation centers.

XV

Eric Wolf and Sidney Mintz have compared the plantation to the hacienda in Middle America and the Antilles.[39] The hacienda reaches back into colonial Spanish America and is still a characteristic feature of Hispanic-American life. The word, like the word plantation, has a variety of meanings and uses, but in the area and period covered by their study, Wolf and Mintz characterize both institutions as dominated by a landowner working a dependent labor force. Both require a market for their produce. The plantation is likely to specialize in a single crop to a much greater degree than the hacienda, but the hacienda also may feature a specialty such as pulque in Mexico, brandy in Peru, and coffee in Puerto Rico. It is, however, principally the scope of the market which serves to differentiate one from the other. Haciendas characteristically supply local markets with a variety of products, not all of them vegetable, whereas plantations characteristically produce some specialty such as sugar for distant markets. The staple specialty classifies the type of plantation that produces it, e.g., sugar or tobacco plantations. The status aspirations of haciendado and planter are similar, but the corporate plantation may produce "without reference to the status needs of the owners." [40] There appear to be no corporate haciendas.

In two of the papers included in this collection, suggestions are offered on the differences between the mine and the plantation in one and on the agricultural mission and the plantation in the other.

XVI

The series of brief comparisons between the plantation and cognate institutions offered above, as well as many others not offered, may serve to add meaning and insight to the formal definitions of the dictionaries. In lieu of attempting a summary definition derived from such comparisons perhaps we have learned enough to recognize the essential features of the institution wherever and whenever it is or has been present.

The plantation is far from being an ethereal, no-time, no-place, institution; it is an earthly institution, a place where people living closely together make things happen in a work-a-day world. Although widely distributed around the world, it is not universal. No form of latifundium is universal, but one cannot escape the impression that, where plantations are not present, some other form of landed estate-building, capital accumulation, labor control, and production for metropolitan markets probably appears.

So long as the people of the northern latitudes want and need agricultural commodities which can be produced only in the tropics or semitropics they (or increasingly the people of the newly independent states) will organize to produce them. This will be true regardless of the controlling political system and ideology; Castro has not abolished the large sugar units in Cuba.

If, from my survey of the plantation as compared to other types of agricultural institutions, no formal definition seems justified, at least four primary facets of the institutions are distinguishable:

1. *The plantation is a settlement institution.* It spreads and arranges a new population over a territory, historically a frontier territory, in a process of demographic and economic succession.[41] In the process, population clusters are formed, and an estate emerges settled on its own land and occupying its own space. This space defines a unit of authority, and the settlement on it is the institution's most obvious and visible aspect. As the plantation becomes a settled community, paths and trails multiply about the planter's residence—the "Big House" as it was called in the South—leading to the quarters or tenant cabins and connecting to the "Big Road," the plantation's outlet to other plantations or to nearby towns. These paths and roads are notations on the surface of the earth of the kind of human relationships they serve.

The growing crops are evident here, and the people move about in patterned fashion as activities appropriate to the purposes of the enterprise take place. One expects to see an interdigitation of people of different rank, race, and color as these activities are pursued. In the pursuit of these activitites, the land itself is shaped to accommodate the plantation's economic purposes and its authoritarian methods. The important consideration is not the geographic or topographic form of the land, even though this is important as it affects cultivation and access to markets, but rather the form of the institution on the land as it affects the larger society.

Although the plantation can exist as an isolate, the suitability of large-scale agriculture in an area will normally carry with it the probability of a region, e.g., the South, in which there is a multiplicity of plantations, that is, a plantation system. The multiplicity will build up its own sustaining system in which the plantation is the economic and political base of an institutional hierarchy. The plantation sends its staple far out beyond the area in which it is physically located, but its satellite institutions in the system, such as the school and the church, serve mainly the local community. The base institution in the system competes with other plantations for labor, but all have to cooperate in such matters as road-building, marketing, and policing and in such other functions in the order in which they come to be recognized as common interests. It is these matters of common interests that are likely to be taken over by the county or larger state; but, to the extent the planters control these governmental units, they too become a part of the plantation system. The forms of authority and control as worked out on individual plantations will be extended throughout the region and sanctioned in custom and in law by the larger society.

We may call the settlement of Europeans along certain frontiers of the world for the purpose of enlarging the area of trade and production for trade "positive" settlement. The expression implies "negative" settlement such as has occurred where natives have been displaced by the encroachment of farms and plantations. Natives, in such situations, have been confined to preservations or reservations. The fate of the American Indian [42] has its parallel in other parts of the world where natives have been found less desirable for plantation labor than imported foreign labor. Reservations may be designed as accessible labor reservoirs to be tapped as needed or simply as a way of setting problem-makers off in space. Put under the control of a government agent or commission and granted vocational schools, the reservation may be regarded as a sort of secular mission and its residents as wards of the state. The reservation may, and often does, become an ethnic island when finally it is surrounded by invading populations. In eastern and southern United States where Indian, white, and black blood have intermixed to form what I have called "little races" (see pp. 162-182) located in interstitial areas symbiotic to the farms and plantations nearby, remnants of the old reservation system still exist.

The so-called "poor whites" have never been confined to official reservations, but in the pre-Civil War South, when members of this class had little or no place on the plantations except as overseers, they segregated themselves in pineywood, wiregrass, sandy, or swamp lands away from black slave competition. This does not mean, however, that they were not an integral part of the Southern plantation system. Slaves and masters cannot constitute the only classes in the total population of a community; there has to be a buffer class between the slaveholders, on the one hand, and the slaves on the other—a nonslaveholding class which supports the slaveholders. In the South, white planters, poor whites, and yeoman whites together made up the larger community which supported the enslavement of blacks; they had in common the same skin color and often the same surnames. After the Civil War a large number of ex-Confederate soldiers returned to the plantations as poor sharecroppers. In the newer plantation areas of the world, such as Malaya, a class of poor whites has not appeared, but other groups have served the same buffer function.

2. *The plantation is an economic institution, an industrial dynamic exercised through agricultural rather than through manufacturing production.* The economic dynamic is built into its geographic location, its territorial expansion, its authoritarian structure, and into the way it shapes the lives of its people. It is that aspect of the plantation which orients local interests and activities to the larger world of metropolitan markets outside. If the economy of the small farm is mediated by village and small town middlemen to larger markets, plantations look to metropolitan centers, originally abroad, where the prices of their staples are set, where credit is extended and capital is available, and where supplies are purchased. As suggested earlier, these services may be mediated by coastal city factors. When market demands extend beyond certain limits the organization of production into more specialized larger units is a likely probability. Plantation and other large-scale agricultural production units, like those of manufacturing industry generally, constitute a response to increasing outside demand. The internal organization of the plantation is a function of the external situation which includes not only its major market centers, but also its competitors in other parts of the world. This surely is one factor in the plantation owner's effort to reduce the labor cost to its lowest point and to close off options that might otherwise attract his labor.

The economics of situations in which plantation enterprises develop enter powerfully into their labor requirements. Forced labor is labor required by the sole demands of another's purpose, for objectives that the laborers may not understand. They are given a wage, at a place and a time, at a speed and under penalties for the infraction of rules, all determined by the will and interests of another. But in frontier situations of much land and scarce labor the alternative presented the planter is not free labor as against forced labor, but forced labor or no labor at all. An inspection of plantation experience historically and around the world indicates that planters generally have felt it necessary to turn to forced labor of one sort or another.

3. *The plantation is a political institution,* that is, it is a miniature state or a submultiple of a larger state. The state is that supreme institution which exercises a monopoly on the use of force in a given territory. It is an outcome of what Teggart calls "politicization," which originally and essentially, perhaps, is landlordization. In the process, a society based upon the family, the tribe, and the sacred ties of kinship is superseded by a territorial organization with ties that bind people to the soil, to an estate, and finally to a mother country. Not filial piety, but the common interests of people occupying a territory become the controlling principle; the sentiment of family and kinship may rise and fall or may fade completely, but common interests persist.

One of the theories of the state which seem significantly to help us better understand the plantation as a political institution has been offered by Franz Oppenheimer. As qualified and supplemented by other scholars, the theory argues that the state arises with the subjection of one people by another resulting in the organization in the same territory of social and racial classes in addition to the usual age and sex divisions. The division of labor which existed between men and women in tribal society is extended to the classes and races making up the state. The state is a state of classes.

An early expression of the state in Northern Europe was the estate of the first of the Hohenzollerns on the German-Polish frontier of Prussia. Prussian nobles in the fifteenth century, deprived of feudal warfare as a pastime, turned from fighting as a profession to farming with subjugated Slavic peasants.[43] The state, or estate, of Joachim II probably was much smaller in area than many plantations in the South and elsewhere. The suggestion is strong here that the inception and development of the plantation, like Joachim's estate, bare the elementary processes that go into the making of the state itself. For the plantation, too, is an incident in the conquest, settlement, and exploitation of an invaded territory. Its chief of state, the planter, may exercise almost complete authority or acquire immunities from the laws of the larger state of which he becomes a part. There are and have been plantations with their own jails, police, coinage, rules and regulations, chains of command, and systems of rewards and punishments extending beyond the hiring and firing practices of modern industry. In the Old South, letters of absentee planters defining and limiting the powers of resident overseers might be regarded as something approaching constitutions.[44] Plantation workers have been slaves, indentured servants, contract laborers, sharecroppers, as well as workers subject to control over food and water supplies. The hallmark of their condition is obedience whether induced by compulsion, custom, habit, or even reverence.

In his classic study H. J. Nieboer [45] shows that slavery and other forms of forced labor are never merely symbiotic relations between one human animal and another. They are utilitarian relations, but they also are much more. Each form has to be understood in the context of a cultural or institutional order of society. In the Old South slavery and the forms of labor control that preceded and followed it become intelligible only in the context of that institution, the plantation, which was called into being in the first place by the chronic and persistent demand for labor.

The plantation represents one type of situation in which the labor problem and the race problem meet. To sanction and to rationalize a political order some kind of myth is invariably generated, and in plantation societies generally this tends to take the form of a belief in inferior and superior races. Race is a form of biological thinking. Some degree of biological thinking, that is, a disposition to account for behavior as an expression of something inborn and biologically inherited, is perhaps present in everyone, but in certain situations where strangers are brought together such a disposition may be carried to the extreme. The myth or idea of race is such an extreme expression of biological thinking and may become part of the culture itself, a part of the reality it is meant to describe. It may become not only a classificatory but also a normative idea giving the structure of a society a rigidity it would not otherwise have. It is generated out of the teeming world of change and falls back into a situation where it is recognized and found useful. The plantation society that developed in the South is an example. There are others. But plantation societies, seeking to legitimize themselves and to justify the exercise of the power of one group over another, have at times and places become the very bastions of the idea. It is an amorphous idea to begin with, but one sometimes elaborated into an ideology whose biological foundations are secondary. Its political and social advantages to the controlling classes, however, are anything but secondary. It is an idea which operates to insure a high degree of consistency and stability of class and status levels. It is an idea so deep and so pervasive as in certain societies, such as that of the South, to enter into the language itself and its assumptions, a part of the medium of communication.

In the South, the idea was born with slavery but it did not die with it, if anything it became more virile after Emancipation than before since the system then had to deal with its laboring class of another color now become increasingly mobile and competitive. The social game of the two major races, the game of imputing more and more behaviorial characteristics deemed congenitally rooted in each race, elaborated itself into a grand structure of believed-in differences. That structure now is top-heavy and in process of disintegration.

4. *The plantation is a cultural institution*, that is, in time, if there is time, it achieves a distinctive "way of life" common, up to a point, to all its members. The arms of the company in the metropolis, the laws of the larger state, even of the market, may be long, but none of these can reach out and completely determine behavior and meanings on the estate itself. Each plantation as it matures carries on a double life, like a cell, one a dependent life in an extensive and complicated economic organism, and the other a quite independent and self-contained life. This is especially true of plantations in the older New World areas such as

northeastern Brazil, the islands of the West Indies and the southern United States. There appears a strange combination of the worldly-wise and sophisticated at the upper levels of the social hierarchy and of the provincial at the lower levels. The upper level is concerned with events anywhere that enter into the pricing of the staple produced; the planter is the one most likely to keep up with and respond to the news of the larger world. The lower level ordinarily does not know or care what happens to the cotton or tobacco after these crops are gathered and leave the fields. Under the protective conditions of a high degree of physical isolation, the settled year-round, often generations-long, community establishes an individuality and a culture as a separate social unit. Life on it usually is intensely local.

To isolate is normally to continue previously formed habits and customs. But when a new settlement begins as a collection of individuals drawn from widely diverse backgrounds, as is generally true of plantation settlement and especially of New World slave plantation settlement, it becomes necessary to destroy in order to re-create. To break the wills and habits of others in the formation of a new institution, to redirect and maintain a new direction, requires a situation of isolation. The plantation, like a monastery or a military garrison, functions as an isolating mechanism through which new habits and outlooks are fashioned. Not the least of these new habits is the sheer habit of living together. This is the kind of situation in which a new culture carried by a new people is generated, and the ultimate outcome is a culture in which activity is reduced to a routine, to a more or less dull but comfortable monotony, and to settled expectations. Thus we find, as we would expect to find, plantations each with its own tradition, its own notions of what is right and what is wrong, its own body of folk products such as stories, songs, proverbs, even sermons, and its own distinctive dialect.[46] This is the plantation celebrated in popular fiction and in nostalgic literature.

The plantation as a cultural institution and system is more than a political fabric. Both the antebellum and postbellum South often exhibited in the relations between the races the extremes of kindness on the one hand and of brutal cruelty on the other, and sometimes a strange combination of both. But normally relations between all races and classes were governed by a customary ethic, by that kind of code which the Germans call *Sittlichkeit,* by what it is decent to do or not to do, the laws and morality notwithstanding. Occasionally it is actually in conflict with law and morality. Ordinarily it is not reflected upon; it is just expected as a matter of second nature. It does not involve the application of force, it is not a matter of conscience, but it has, nevertheless, a compelling quality. Those who have attacked the Southern "way of life" have not recognized its presence, and it is so far beneath the level of public consciousness that Southerners, even in their best writings and oratory, have not been able to give it adequate expression, although this is what Mark Twain tried to do in *Huckleberry Finn.*

XII

Putting these four aspects of the plantation together, the institution appears (1) as a way of settling and concentrating a popula tion of mixed origins on a frontier, a broad and moving area in transition from a lower to, presumably, a higher form of civilization; (2) as a way of producing an agricultural staple for a metropolitan market within geographical limits fixed by the means of transport; (3) as a way of disciplining a population for labor under the authority of a planter; and (4) as an institution which develops in time through collective activity a distinctive style of life or culture.

The plantation is a type of landed estate which survives under competitive frontier conditions; it has survival value in its struggle with the small farm and with other types of agricultural economies. Survival under these conditions is powerfully aided by the elaboration of a supporting system of other political, religious, and educational institutions called a "plantation system." To say that the plantation is a frontier institution is to say that, as finally organized, it is a transient institution and subject to a cycle of change as the frontier moves on, as population increases, as all qualified land is occupied and as new conditions of competition emerge. We may continue to call it a plantation long after change has completely altered its constitution and it becomes another sort of latifundium or breaks down into a system of peasant proprietorships. It may pass into the hands of a man of wealth in the city who expects to support the estate rather than be supported by it. He may evict its lower level people and trans-

form the property into a hunting preserve or into a dude plantation supported by tourists. Each of these changes has somewhere
occurred and others are in prospect.

In its final stage, the plantation becomes an invisible and
ghostly, but no less real, institution. It now is a state of mind and
not a body of people and statistics; it is a way of acting and
believing not yet outlived. In the larger society it leaves a heritage, a set of norms for those who would affirm and conform to
them as well as for those who would deny and rebel against them.
Even at those points where men in modern societies feel the
plantation mind most alien, it is necessary to understand present
behavior and attitudes in terms of what went before. The heritage helps us better understand today's white and black Americans, especially those of Southern origin, those who remain on
the land in the South as well as those who live in the counter
plantation culture of black ghettoes in the cities. All of us are both
beneficiaries and victims of that heritage.

Looking back over my effort to identify the plantation and its
system, especially in the South, I am conscious of the fact that
the institution was a somewhat different thing as it evolved
through cumulative changes over time. These changes add to the
difficulties of definition. In the perspective of the past we can
now see an institution moving inevitably from stage to stage
which the people involved in it at the time could not see or
foresee. There resulted an order of society not contemplated by
those who brought it about, which was in fact often contrary to
the motives and interests that at different times actuated them.
That order of society was the result of human action, to be sure,
but not of the execution of any human design. Men collectively
seemed to stumble upon an establishment which later they rationalized, defended, and even fought for as good. So it is with
our institutions generally.

I

The Plantation: A Chapter in the
Natural History of the State

The Big House in ruins: the passing of a symbol of continuity

• 1 •

Mines and Plantations and the
Movements of Peoples

"The organization of the plantation is much like that of a coal mine" says J. Russell Smith while discussing the characteristics of the Red River country in northeastern Louisiana, northwestern Mississippi, and eastern Arkansas. [1] The opening up of new and highly profitable veins of ore containing silver near Athens during the time of Pericles marked the beginning in Attica of hard industrial slavery. Of it Zimmern says: "It will be noticed at once how very closely this labour-system corresponds to the conditions with which we have already become acquainted on the tropical plantations." [2] In these silver mines some 20,000 slaves, "living instruments," were employed either above or below ground. Work went on without interruption night and day to produce "almost the only article for which there can be said to have been an international market and an unlimited demand." [3] These observations suggest why the large commercial mine and the plantation have built up similar reputations.

The large commercial mine and the plantation, one supplying industry with energy resources and the material for its machinery and tools, and the other supplying tropical foods and agricultural nonfood staples for manufacture, are interregional and frequently world-wide in the extent of their economic relations. It is within the context of the world community and its economic and geographical co-ordinates that these two institutions can best be studied and compared. They both specialize in the production of a commodity which is sold on a wide market. They characteristically use imported, or at least, labor introduced from some

SOURCE *American Journal of Sociology*, XXXVII, January 1932, pp. 603–611.

distance rather than indigenous labor. The special dependence which imported labor has upon the providence of the employer subjects it, perhaps even in the face of liberal legislation, to some degree of compulsion greater than that applied to native or "free" labor. All the way from slavery to vaguely felt and undefined "forced" labor, the mine and the plantation tend to get similar reputations with respect to the status of their labor forces. It is this similarity of reputation which invites a comparison and contrast of these social institutions.

This paper is limited to a consideration of some factors concerning the mine and the plantation which relate to the fundamental problem of human ecology, the problem of the distribution and redistribution of population. It is not, in and of itself, the distribution of mineral resources or of plant life which is important in human ecology. What is significant is the extent to which human association with minerals, plants, and animals in the effort to control them for human use effect a changing integration and selective distribution of people upon the earth. To this end let us consider first the mine.

The formation of mineral resources is so slow that supply, once exhausted, cannot naturally be renewed in the lifetime of the human race. The operation of a mine takes from it its capital value. One of the most important things to be observed about the mine is its fixed location. The factory may shift its location as great a distance as from New England to North Carolina but the location of the mine is fixed by the limited distribution of the mineral resources. This means that certain important links in the skeletal framework of the community—the area over which there is competitive cooperation—will be furnished by the distribution of minerals. [4] It is important to note that the distribution of mineral resources bears little relationship to other elements in the environment such as climate, soil, land forms, etc. Yet these factors, if they do not affect their distribution, are highly important in production. Say Jones and Whittlesey:

. . . . the cost of production at the mine varies with climate. Where minerals are found in regions having a climate unsuitable to the hard physical exertion common to most mining, the miners demand high wages, or short shifts, and in some cases labor must be drawn from population groups which are acclimated. In the numerous mines of the Andean Plateau, only natives, whose lung capacity is large, can work hard in the high altitudes; the tin mines of Malaya are manned by natives or by coolies from the warmer parts of China. Less direct, but just as potent, is the effect of climate on the food supply. Wherever a mining district lies in a region of climatic extremes, the production of foodstuffs is restricted or precluded. This necessitates importation of food, and the cost of transportation must be added to the price of the mineral for the sake of which the people are abiding in the wilderness. The short growing season of high latitudes makes it necessary to haul food long distances to the coal mines of Spitzbergen or the gold mines of the Yukon; the low temperature of high altitudes, such as the Andean Plateau, has the same effect, relative nearness to food-producing regions being offset by the high cost of transport over steep slopes. Scarcity of rainfall trammels mining operations. Deep wells or long and costly aqueducts may be necessary; in the nitrate desert of Chile and the diamond mines of Southwest Africa, water must be imported in ships or distilled from sea water. [5]

The cost of transporting bulky minerals, especially the prime minerals of industry, accounts, the natural environment permitting, for the displacement of populations toward them tending to create large population centers. "If the mountain will not come to Mahomet, Mahomet must go to the mountain." But the fixed and unequal distribution of other minerals makes necessary their transportation to the centers.

The transportation of minerals to regions populous and progressive enough to use them is a serious problem in many cases, for rich deposits are as likely to occur in out-of-the-way places as in well-settled regions. Thus coal is found in Spitzbergen and the Middle Rockies, gold on the Yukon, in South Africa, and in desert Australia, copper in the desert mountains and plateaus of Western America, nitrates in the barren and remote low latitude desert of Western South America, and iron, copper, silver, nickel and arsenic in the ice-scoured Laurentia. [6]

"Rich deposits are as likely to occur in out-of-the-way places as in well-settled regions." Well-settled regions are regions of well-settled movement. For a social group, like a person, develops habits of movement which become routine. "Movements of men, like those of fluids," says A. C. Haddon, "take the line of least resistance, flowing, as it were, in channels or open areas bounded by barriers." [7] The easier movements over lines of least resistance become habitual and customary and the society tends to become static. "Its members may be said to have locomotion but not mobility. They do not move on highways, but along 'routes.'" [8] Now it is adventure and exploration that direct movement away from its ordinary paths and make new ways. These new movements become most significant when they are followed up, for then new points are brought into customary relations with other points and the activities of the community are to some extent reorganized and widened. [9] As much as anything else, perhaps, has man's desire for minerals, especially gold and silver, forced him away from beaten paths and made him a geographical pioneer. Tropical luxuries he may obtain by barter from natives along the coast or he may organize production in places accessible to his ships, but to the mine he must build railways and solve the engineering problems involved.

These new custom-breaking ways result from the fixed location of mineral resources and man's unceasing efforts to effect a better integration between them and the oceans, the world's natural highways of commerce. It follows from the fact of fixed location that there is little room for competition with the countries possessing monopolies of specific minerals. South Africa is said to have about 50 per cent of the world's gold and 60 per cent of the supply of nickel. The exercise of such monopolies may lead to excessive prices, or lowered consumption, or both. If the supply is actually limited the world is at the mercy of the producing country, for it is obvious that mines cannot be located except where the minerals are to be found. In such cases competition is possible only from substitutes as of aluminum or tinware.

Not only is the mine a fixed point in the structure of the community, a nodal point in a sensitive vibrating economic system, but it functions as a more or less fixed division of labor. So long as it continues to operate in the community, it supplies one product or none at all. In times of depression there is no talk of diversification. Its operation maintains and insures division of labor in the community whose market it supplies. [10] Its own division of labor throbs unchanged and continuous, but at varying rates of intensity, throughout the interdependent world. This is why production of the more important mineral resources, such as coal, iron, and copper, is so useful an index of the prosperity of the community, that is, of the extent to which its parts and members are integrated. [11]

The fact that continuous cultivation of the soil tends to exhaust such chemical ingredients as phosphorus and nitrogen which plants need for growth, thus requiring the use of commercial fertilizers, is evidence that agriculture has a certain kinship with mining and that the two cannot be absolutely divorced. Nevertheless there are fundamental differences. Agriculture, as contrasted with mining, produces a seasonal crop. Relatively speaking, the agricultural crop is continually reproduced by man. Capital is kept intact and an income derived from it.

Now plant life, unlike a mineral resource, is closely related to factors in the physical environment such as climate, soil waters, rainfall, etc., and the natural distribution of the various forms of plant life will be limited to the areas where the combination of environmental factors makes sustenance possible. This does not mean that any certain form of plant life will be found growing everywhere that conditions for growth are favorable, but it is certain that such plant life will not be found where conditions are unfavorable. It does mean, however, that within the limits imposed by the natural environment, plant life, unlike mineral resources, can be distributed by human agencies to suit the convenience of consuming populations.

The plantation is one form in which agriculture is organized for production. It differs from the manor in that production is specialized rather than diversified and self-sufficing. It tends to differ from the family farm in the scale of its operations and in the impersonality of its human relations. When it loses specialization and impersonality it becomes something like the manorial institution. Again, plantations may be said to be instituted at points along the community's frontier, sometimes with almost catastrophic suddenness. [12] It is, for this reason, a settlement institution, an end-point of human migration. Latifundia, by contrast, arise with the consolidation of smaller farms; they emerge out of the interaction of economic factors in the community at a certain stage of its evolution and result in the uprooting of rural people from the land.

Minerals must be mined where they are to be found, but capital can call into existence a plantation to produce a salable commodity at lowered cost and have a wide range of choice in the selection of the site. The case of rubber will illustrate. Before about 1900 most of the world's supply of rubber came from wild *Hevea* trees in the deep interior of Brazil. The high cost of transporting the raw rubber to Para on the coast together with the high export taxes exacted by the government was a considerable part of the ultimate price paid by the consumer. With the rise of the bicycle and later the automobile industries an increasing demand for rubber led to attempts to lower the cost of production and win the market. In 1876 *Hevea* plants were taken to Ceylon where their cultivation was begun on the estates. Since about 1900 plantation production has spread to Netherlands India, Malaya, Borneo, India, Burma, French Cochin-China and other places in the Far East. In the competition certain advantages seemed to be held by Malaya with the result that this region rapidly became the world's most important rubber-growing area increasing from a bare 100 tons produced in 1905 to over 200,000 tons in 1922. [13] Transportation from these areas is both easy and inexpensive thus rendering rubber more accessible to the rest of the world. There are, of course, many other factors involved in the transfer of the center of rubber production from Brazil to the Far East, but this one of greater accessibility must be reckoned as highly important among them. Thus with plantation agriculture, areas may be made to produce plants not originally indigenous to them in competition with other areas where such plant life grows in the wild state.

It is, for this reason, more difficult for a country to maintain an agricultural monopoly than to maintain one over a mineral resource. In 1924, India controlled about 99 per cent of the world's jute, and, with Ceylon, about 70 per cent of its tea, but attempts to exploit such monopolies would certainly have spread production to other areas. The failure of coffee valorization in Brazil and of the effort made by British growers to control the price of rubber will come to mind in this connection.

Competition in the realm of plantation products is usually limited to similar climatic zones over the world. Bananas may be grown under hot-house conditions in Canada, but not profitably. Canada, then, is not in a position to compete successfully with Nicaragua, but Puerto Rico is. The development of the sugar beet has shown, however, that not all tropical plantation agriculture is secure against competition from northern lands. Nor is it secure against competition from the chemical laboratory as has been shown in the case of indigo and may again be shown in the case of rubber. But, on the whole, the competition of plantation products is limited to areas possessing similar physical conditions favorable to the special forms of plant life.

The tobacco plantation, and later plantations of indigo, rice, etc., were the first specialized industries in North America. As they became more specialized their position of dependence helped to call into existence other specialized and supporting industries and areas. Both beef ranches in the West and labor ranches in Africa supplied it with necessities. Then came specialization in horses in Kentucky, mules in Missouri, wheat in the West, and manufacturing in New England. Specialization demands more specialization. Nevertheless, the plantation's division of labor is not as determined as that of the mine. In periods of depression or overproduction it may diversify its products enough to feed its operating force without discontinuing operations. In plantation areas, such as cotton, there is a continuous swing in the direction of greater specialization and then back again toward some diversification.

Intermediate between mine and plantation, in certain respects, is the forest. As the natural distribution of the virgin forest is cut, or virtually mined, it recedes farther and farther away from consuming centers. Production and transport costs mount. There is agitation for conservation, then for reforestation. When the forest is planted and treated as a crop, [14] it is subject to competition with other crops for standing room. In this geographical competition it is probable that the location, or position, of the forest will, within physical limitations, tend to be determined, as the location of other crops is determined, by its market relations.

Within natural limitations our growing control over all plant and animal life is leading either to their extinction or to their geographical distribution after a more rational than natural pattern of usefulness to the human community. In a plant community the dominant species are trees, and the symbiotic relations of other species are organized with reference to them. In the "web of life" of the aggregate plant, animal, and human community, man is, in the language of the plant ecologist, the dominant species. "As the dominant species he controls the environment to such an extent as to determine what other species may live in the community." [15] In this inclusive plant, animal, and human community the culture of all plants and animals is more and more organized with reference to man. But as agriculture and horticulture find their regional locations in our competitive scheme of things they distribute their human caretakers with them.

• 2 •

Comparative Education in Colonial Areas, with Special Reference to Plantation and Mission Frontiers

We already are familiar with some of the more general and objective facts concerning white and Negro educational opportunities in the South. These facts are often and strikingly expressed in terms of the money spent in our biracial system of education. Thus it is pointed out that the average expenditure for every pupil throughout the nation in 1930 was $99.00. The average expenditure for white children in the South was less than half this amount, or $44.31, while the average expenditure for Negro children was only $12.57, or about one-fourth that for southern white children and about one-eighth that for the average of the United States. Those southern states with large Negro populations, where the average pupil in a rural school comes from a tenant family, show even greater discrepancies. In 1930 Georgia spent an average of $35.42 for each white child and $6.38 for each Negro child. Mississippi, with half her population Negro and more completely dominated by the plantation system than any other state, [1] spent more for her white children than did Georgia ($45.34 per child) and less for her Negro children ($5.45 per child). [2]

More important than these figures (and many more might be offered) are the attitudes in the southern social situation which they represent and presumably measure. All such statistics must be understood in the context of southern culture. A comparison of southern culture with American culture as seen, for example,

SOURCE In Charles S. Johnson (ed.), *Education and the Cultural Process,* University of Chicago Press, 1943, pp. 82–93.

by Clark Wissler may serve to suggest some of its essential features. After comparing American culture with the cultures of other societies, Wissler tells us that its dominant characteristics may be condensed into three sets of ideas and beliefs which, he says, actuate the American people. These are mechanical invention, universal suffrage, and mass education. [3] Now if the complex of these characteristics defines the American culture, then historically the South has not been a part of it, or at least has been only marginal to it. In fact, the South has differed so radically from the rest of the United States that it became, by the time of the Civil War, culturally and economically almost a separate nation. The establishment of the Confederacy was intended to give these cultural and economic facts a more complete constitutional sanction.

American culture is and has been characterized "by a great emphasis upon mechanical devices." Southerners have imported and used these devices in increasing degree, to be sure, but the "amiable American hobby" of tinkering with machinery has been so little an integral part of southern life that a mechanical cotton mill is still regarded by many as a "fotched-in contraption" alien to its traditions. Economic opportunities in the North have offered a constantly increasing variety of ways of earning a livelihood, whereas the South, until relatively recently, has offered only one, agriculture, and that, a particular kind of agriculture. The mechanization of southern agriculture has, in recent years, expanded rapidly, but traditionally the southern plantation has operated mainly with hand labor and with only elementary tools and machines. Negroes particularly have been outside the American mechanical tradition.

Industry in the South, and especially the textile industry, was originally developed by local interests in a sort of crusade to provide opportunities for poor whites. It came with the recognition that the section had a poor-white as well as a Negro problem, and it was sponsored as a program for the solution of that problem. These white millworkers, recruited from rural areas, have continued to speak the language and carry the mental images of the farm. Control of the industries in which they work has largely passed to outside interests; and these interests have succeeded, in large measure, only by bringing the operation of the factories into line with the paternalistic traditions of the plantation system.

Universal suffrage, or "the idea that what most of the people in the group approve will be as near to the correct solution as can be achieved for the time being," is, according to Wissler, another dominant trait of the American culture. Years ago James Bryce, in *The American Commonwealth*, likewise noted the disposition of the American people to refer every question to the arbitrament of numbers, confident that the people are sure to decide right in the long run. In the South, however, the mores have largely nullified the ideal of universal suffrage, which has been regarded as something imposed upon a defeated people by the northern victor. Since the rise of the southern white democracy the ballot box has become a symbol of class stratification based upon color. Recent southern opposition to the abolition of poll taxes serves to show that the old attitude toward suffrage as a class privilege and not as a procedure for the democratic determination of policy continues to possess considerable strength. The meeting and settling of all issues by means of the ballot has never been the practice in the South. In the United States rule by just one majority group occurs only in this section; elsewhere the membership of the majority changes from one issue to another. As far as the South is concerned there are two reasons for this. One is the presence in this region of an authoritarian tradition stemming from the planter aristocracy and woven into the general class and racial situation. The second reason is that the issues that appear as problems elsewhere in the nation have not been regarded as problems in the agrarian and feudal order of this region where they are settled in the mores. [4] Consequently, a large part of the southern population, including the greater part of the Negro population, has not been accustomed to resort to the ballot to change those conditions which constitute problems elsewhere but which in the South have been taken for granted as if they were a part of the order of nature itself.

American culture, Wissler continues, "is characterized by an overruling belief in something we call education—a kind of mechanism to propitiate the intent of nature in the manifestation of culture." But formal mass education, even for whites, certainly has never been a completely integral part of southern culture. That it is not even now is shown by the figures on the money spent in the South's educational system presented at the beginning of this paper. Upon an illiterate and agricultural laboring population in the South has rested a planter and upperclass white population whose literacy probably originated or was maintained through the necessity for keeping in touch with the affairs of the market and the city and with political and economic conditions affecting the market. With a substantial income and leisure even an illiterate planter became concerned to give an education and a certain amount of "culture" to his children. But for those who have remained more or less outside the sphere of direct market relationships no great need for education has been felt. In the past, southern agriculture has required little above a uniform grade of unskilled labor, subject to routine tasks, shaped to change on the basis of contingency alone, and one which was not required consciously to assume the risks incident to selling in a foreign market. As a result, education has not appeared to these classes as a necessity or as something having survival value, but merely as something which conferred status, and often a rather dubious status at that. For in the folk mind there was the general conviction that book learning only muddled up thinking and that ordinary gumption and common sense were sufficient for whatever problems men had to face. And to the planters and employers of labor an educated peasantry has seemed no more advantageous than an uneducated one.

The numerous towns and villages which, from the very beginning of settlement, formed a nucleus for the small farms of New England and provided favorable soil for public school education found no historical parallel in the South. Here, after the Civil War, towns and villages began to appear in greater numbers with the partial disintegration of the plantation system. The southern public school movement, which accompanied the rise of towns and villages, represented in part an adjustment to a new set of economic and social needs in a changed situation. It assumed the character of a crusade led by devoted idealists charged with pathos for the illiterate and benighted and urged on by unfavorable comparisons with the more advanced North and West. The crusade resulted in notable progress in attaining a more fundamental educational process, but, as in the educational crusades of Japan and Soviet Russia, much of the alleged advance has turned out to be spurious when the amount of rote learning it produced is considered. Learning by rote has become not only a fact but something of a tradition, especially in the rural white and Negro schools of the South.[5] The reason is that southern society, unlike a society such as that of Denmark, has not been the kind of society in which separate institutions designed for the instruction of the children of the masses were required for the integration of economic and political life. This is ceasing to be true, but the tendency from Colonial days to the present has been to regard the public school, and especially the Negro school, like the cotton mill, as a "fotched-in contraption." The schools have been tolerated and maintained by being brought into line with the class and racial traditions of the plantation system.

Accompanied by a friend, I once attended a rally at a Negro school in a Texas community. The white city-school superintendent of this community was a Scotchman from North Carolina. The rally had been organized by the colored principal acting under orders from the white superintendent, who, while making a speech, pointed his finger at the colored principal and said, "I told him if he didn't bring this school into line I would find me another principal." The setting was in a school building and there was no cotton or tobacco to be seen, but my friend and I agreed on our way home that the superintendent seemed to run the school as if it were a plantation and to regard the principal, the teachers, and the pupils as the planter regards his tenants and laborers. There was no ill will, and the superintendent seemed to have the welfare of the school at heart; but the pattern of control was the pattern of the plantation.

It should be evident from all this that we have to understand education, like almost everything else in this region of the United States, in the light of a cultural situation which is southern and not American if we accept Wissler's analysis of American culture. And it would seem that behind whatever differences there are in the southern situation lies that very quintessence of southernism, the plantation, an institution which long has ceased to be merely a large estate on which cotton or tobacco is grown but one which, like Christian Science, has become a state of mind. Within the structure of this institution and the system which has grown up around it the positions of both white and Negro education have been assigned along caste lines.

The institution of the plantation, as it developed in the South and in other colonial areas around the world, was originally and has continued to be a type of economic enterprise very unlike those other economic enterprises that developed in the laissez faire capitalism that succeeded feudalism in Europe. Unlike the "free" labor of capitalistic Europe—that is, labor free to seek and to change employers—plantation labor was sought, moved, settled, and controlled by employers. In different plantation societies the control has taken different forms, and in a single plantation society like that of the South the control has changed in form from indentured servitude and slavery to sharecropping. But always the form has served to emphasize the political, i.e., the authoritarian, character of the institution to a degree exceeding that of the economic enterprises of European and northern United States capitalism.

The plantation represents one kind of political institution which develops at points of intercultural and interracial contacts, but in the course of the long history of such contacts on the part of migrating people there have been many other kinds of latifundia. The state itself, according to Oppenheimer [6] and others, originated in just such situations. It would seem that the contact of peoples differing in race and culture nearly always results in some new institution, organized around the problems of control growing out of the new social relationships and furnishing a structure through which the motives and purposes of those who came to exploit the situation can in some measure be realized.

Thus along the world's frontiers have arisen such varied and interesting institutions of the land as haciendas, plantations, farms, missions, ranches, and the like. They are as varied and as interesting as are the immigrant institutions of the large city, but they cannot be passed in quick review by walking through forty blocks,[7] and so their range is not so apparent and comparison among them is not so easy. They are institutions of the land and of settlement, and, once established, they largely determine how people shall live on the land. But more important for our purpose here is the fact that they seem to lay bare the elementary processes that go into the making of the state; in them the competitions and conflicts of racial and cultural groups living in the same territory are brought down to their most elementary terms. And as obvious and elementary as any, in the conquest and exploitation of a pioneer region, is the process whereby the land is alienated and its resources brought under the control of invading settlers, planters, missionaries, and the like. New land or settlement institutions arise as an incident in the process of extending the range of the "political formation and economic exploitation" which Oppenheimer has conceived to be basic to state-building. The land changes hands, and those who come to possess it and to convert it to new and presumably higher uses subject those over whom they come to possess authority to new and stricter forms of discipline. To this end they make and enforce new rules and impose new conditions of life generally. The important point to be noted here is that the class which enforces the new arrangement is the same class which instructs in the new arrangement, not simply in order to indoctrinate but also to bring about a level of efficiency necessary to sustain it.

Education in a homogeneous society is normally a process of inducting the maturing individual into the social heritage. It is thus, as Dewey has emphasized, essentially a process of renewal and growth without which the group would have no continuity. As the society becomes more complex, the process by which members educate one another through their daily contacts has to be supplemented and augmented by more formal instruction in separate educational institutions, but education continues to be a matter of transmitting a tradition from one generation to another. In a situation of racial and cultural contact, however, education becomes a matter of expanding a culture from one people to another; it becomes a part of the process of acculturation. In intercultural and interracial situations, where the culture of the dominant group is regarded as the standard, the members of the lower groups must learn things from the school which members of the dominant group are presumed to learn in the home, such as rules of hygiene and of conduct. Since the adults of the subordinate group are as illiterate in these matters as their children, education often begins with the adults before it reaches their children. In any case, the task of the elementary school for the subordinate population is much more important and much more difficult than that of the elementary school for the children of the dominant group. Incidentally, it is on the elementary-school level that the education of Negro school children in the South is weakest.

The whole of European culture has never impinged equally upon the whole of a native culture. Since culture is carried in the knowledge, skills, attitudes, habits, and tools of particular individuals, European culture has worked upon native society through the medium of the purposes of trader, administrator, planter, missionary, etc. Because these purposes and programs get incorporated in plantations, trading factories, missions, and the like, the thought suggests itself at once that a comparison of the histories of these various colonial institutions, with attention to the role of education in each, might prove very rewarding. Students of southern education might in this way gain insight into and perspective toward the problems of education in a plantation society which might very well change our whole conception of them. We might, for one thing, discover just how education grows up as a natural process, how it works, how it becomes formalized and ritualized, and just why and how it undergoes change. For such a purpose no other institution of the frontier seems to promise more than a study of the agricultural mission.

Such a study is made all the more significant by the fact that the education of Negroes in the South has always had a certain missionary quality about it, even since the planter regained control from the northern missionary. The schools of the Negro in the South, unlike their churches, have always been directed and controlled from outside their own ranks. Planter and missionary have held different and conflicting points of view, but both have assumed the necessity for outside and overhead control.

In their most obvious and visible aspects the plantation and the agricultural mission appear quite similar. They both are large landed estates. They both rest upon an agricultural economy; and very often the mission, like the plantation, exports its products to foreign markets. They both import supplies from abroad. In both, the field labor is performed by a people different in cultural and ordinarily in racial origin from those who direct and manage the enterprise. The latter possess great authority, and the former may be legally or in effect slaves. But, similar as the two institutions are in their organization and in their natural interests, in their political and moral principles they are ideological antagonists. Their very different histories and original purposes have, nevertheless, resulted in a similar phenomenon.

The mission represents the working-out of motives and purposes inherent in religious proselytism. Implicit in such a religion as Christianity is the belief that it possesses a universal validity, a belief which imposes upon its followers the moral obligation to transmit its precepts. This obligation takes an organized and concrete form in the person of the missionary, who, by definition, is committed to the propagation of his faith by teaching and persuasion. And, of course, the most obvious field for propagation lies among those people most completely outside the culture in which the religion originated.

The pioneer missionary usually begins his work by carrying his message to the heathen in a direct manner. There is something typical in the picture of Charles William Eliot in early New England preaching with Bible in hand to the Indians in the snow. The Indians appeared interested in his strange behavior, at least for a while; but they did not know what he was talking about, and Eliot undoubtedly soon discovered that fact. When it is apparent that direct attempts at conversion avail little, then it is realized that conversion has to begin with civilization. Missionaries conceive of themselves as propagating a particular religious doctrine, but they are really propagating a culture. Usually coming from small communities, they soon begin to lose interest in their narrow religious doctrines and begin to interest themselves in the larger problems of cultural assimilation. What they finally seek to do is merely to educate. The immediate expression of the indirect method in missionary activity is a concentration upon agricultural, health, and domestic education as a solvent for the native's physical and mental disabilities.

There are subtle and unexpected adjustments to be made, too, in the missionaries' social relations with the heathen. What these are and how they arise is naïvely revealed in a letter written by Mrs. Lucy Thurston, wife of one of the pioneer missionaries to the Hawaiian Islands, to a friend in Boston in the year 1835. The letter was occasioned by the necessity for explaining to their supporters back home why the missionaries in Hawaii kept native servants in their households.

. . . . In our own house we have the various classes of master and mistress, of children, and of household natives. There is a native family attached to our establishment, whose home is a distinct house in our common yard. They give us their services. One man simply cultivates taro, two miles up the country, and weekly brings down a supply of the staff of life for ourselves and our dependents. Another man every week goes up the mountain to do our washing. . . . In like manner a third man, who under the old dispensation, officiated as priest to one of their gods, now, under a new dispensation, with commendable humility, officiates as cook to a priest and his family. Then, aid in the care of the house, of sewing, and of babyhood, devolves upon female hands.

We commenced mission life with other ideas. Native youth resided in our families, and so far as was consistent, we granted them all the privileges of companions and of children. Not many years rolled on, and our eyes were opened to behold the moral pollution which, unchecked, had here been accumulated for ages. I saw, but it was parental responsibilities which made me so emphatically *feel* the horrors of a heathen land. I had it ever in my heart, the shafts of sin flying in every direction are liable to pierce the vitals of my children. . . .

I reviewed the ground on which I stood. The heathen world were to be converted. But by what means? Are missionaries with their eyes open to the dangers of the situation, to sit conscientiously down to the labor of bringing back a revolted race to the service of Jehovah, and in doing so practically give over their children to Satan? . . . I could see no alternative but that a mother go to work, and here form a moral atmosphere in which her children can live and move without inhaling the infection of moral death. . . . The first important measure was to prohibit them altogether the use of the Hawaiian language, thus cutting off all intercourse between them and the heathen. This, of course, led to the family regulation, that no child might speak to a native, and no native might speak to a child, babyhood excepted. This led to another arrangement, that of having separate rooms and yards for our children, and separate rooms and yards for natives. The reason for this separation . . . was distinctly stated to household natives. . . . We are willing to come and live among you, that you may be taught the good way; but it would break our hearts to see our children rise up and be like the children of Hawaii. . . .

Dear Mrs. Bishop, who was laid in her grave six weeks before the arrival of the reinforcement, longed exceedingly to see and give them a charge from her sick couch. The purport of it was this: "Do not be devoted to domestic duties. Trust to natives, however imperfect their services, and preserve your constitutions." I needed no such warning, for I had learned the lesson by my own sad experience, and when, after years of prostration, I was again permitted to enjoy comfortable health, I availed myself of the aid of natives for the accomplishment of such domestic duties as they were capable of rendering. . . . For as one of our physicians told me, "You may as well talk of perpetual motion, as to think of performing as much labor here as you could have done by remaining in America."

As to the effects produced upon natives thus employed in our families, they have more intelligence, more of the good things of this life, more influence among their fellows than they could otherwise possess; and numbers of them, I doubt not, will be added to that great company, which no man can number, redeemed out of every kindred, and tongue, and people, and nation. [8]

A planter's wife in early Virginia might easily have written an almost identical letter to a friend in England.

Lind has shown the close affinity between the mission and the plantation in the development of the Hawaiian Islands. The early competition between them merely evidenced "the fundamental affinity between them." Later they joined forces "in urging the transition from the native system of land tenure to one more in conformity with capitalistic principles." The missionaries were among the earliest to foresee the commercial possibilities of sugar cane, especially after financial assistance from the homeland was terminated, as a means of supporting the missions and furthering the advancement of their parishioners. The mission estate of Father Bond in Kohala formulated a fixed set of rules for the government of its members. [9]

Protestant missions not only developed agricultural estates in the past but they maintain a large number of them at the present time, or did until recently, in the Orient, in Africa, in South America, and in the South Seas. In 1920 the International Association for Agricultural Missions was organized "to promote the interests of Christian agricultural work in all lands."

But the institution of the agricultural mission was carried to its most extreme development by missionary priests of the various Catholic orders operating in what is now the southwestern part of the United States, in Latin America, and in the Philippines. Perhaps no other community in the world has been so greatly influenced by the agricultural mission as has Paraguay, in South America. In the seventeenth and eighteenth centuries the unmarried Jesuit priests in Paraguay, unlike the Protestant missionaries in Hawaii, did not encounter the problem of protecting their children as they grew up among an alien population, but other forces in the situation established them as a class apart. However, their demonstration of success in the organization of agriculture, and the example of their own efforts and production, operated to set up links of influence and dependence between themselves and the natives: links which were not established forcefully or even consciously but which gave them prestige and then authority and power.

When the power of the Jesuits extended far enough to make it possible, tribal life was forcefully broken up and the Indians were "reduced," as the friars put it, to mission-village life. These

reductions grew up, Keller tells us, "in the wide regions relatively or totally unoccupied by Europeans." [10] In the missions the
Indian charges were rigorously isolated from the world, and the
missionary normally formed the only contact with the outside.

Bourne gives us a picture of mission life and points out what
the mission came to be. Under the increasing supervision of the
friars, the Indians, he says,

. . . were taught the elements of letters, and trained to peaceful, indus-
trious and religious lives. In fact, every mission was an industrial school,
in which the simple arts were taught by the friars, themselves in origin
plain Spanish peasants. The discipline of the mission was as minute as
that of a school: the unmarried youths and maidens were locked in at
night; the day's work began and ended with prayers and the catechism;
each Indian, besides cultivating his own plot of land, worked two hours
a day on the farm belonging to the village, the produce of which went
to the support of the church. The mission was recruited by inducing
the wild Indians to join it, and also by kidnapping them. Spanish
America from California and Texas to Paraguay and Chile was fringed
with such establishments, the outposts of civilization, where many thousands of Indians went through a schooling which ended only with their
lives. In the process of time a mission was slowly transformed into a
"pueblo de Indios" . . . . and the mission frontier was pushed out a
little farther. [11]

When the mission in Latin America "had been included within
the slowly expanding area of intercourse with the outside world,"
as the market came nearer and the mission became more and
more dependent upon it, it ceased to be a mission. Like the
plantation, it was a frontier institution, and when the frontier
passed on the mission went with it. But not before it had accomplished a significant transformation in the culture of the Indians.
It introduced new methods and standards of agricultural production, it taught new arts and crafts, and it left the Indians at least
nominally Catholic in religion. However, in spite of the devoted,
persistent, and strenuous efforts· of the priests, the mission left
no high and lasting educational tradition. The literacy they promoted only led to the charge that the mission Indians had
become mere apes and parrots incapable of progress and invention when left to themselves. [12]

If the mission grew up out of a background of religious fervor,
the plantation had its origin in northern European capitalism. A
plantation was originally a migration, a transplantation of people

to overseas territory; and, in certain frontier areas capable of producing a staple crop for the European market, the migration passed over into an institutional structure for the production of the staple. The plantation type of migration became, in these areas, the plantation type of estate. Where this happened the migration was not composed of family, community, or congregational groups intent on reproducing in the New World the agricultural economy of the Old. It did not, in other words, result in the kind of settlements that the Pilgrims made in New England or the Germans made in Pennsylvania and in parts of the South. The kind of migration which resulted in plantation establishments, where they were economically possible, was a migration made up of individual adventurers and traders seeking profitable investments. They did not come to make a home for their children or to convert the natives to Christianity, although these things occurred to them later. It is significant that, in the histories of the various plantation societies, the members of the initial planter class are recruited from the ranks of ship captains and traders. These are the sort of men who possess both capital and knowledge of investment opportunities in foreign places. They are likely to be unfamiliar with the folk agriculture of their home countries, and there is no reason why they should seek to reproduce it abroad. But an opportunity for profitable investment in new commodities of agriculture like tobacco, sugar cane, or rubber is in line with the commercial interests which they represent. Hence it is that the virtues of these men are not those of niceness and scholarship but of resourcefulness and enterprise, and in the areas where they operate they are too busy opening up the country and profiting from the exploitation of its resources to concern themselves overmuch with the educational welfare of the general population. [13] The South is that part of this nation where the planter has most profoundly impressed himself upon the form of society and where something of his original motives and attitudes persist.

The concern of the missionary is for the educational and spiritual welfare of the natives, but the purpose of the planter to profit through the exploitation of land and labor leads ordinarily to an unfavorable judgment of native workers. In plantation societies the native is invariably condemned as lazy and worthless. The remedy is not to improve him through education.

It is cheaper and far easier to turn to outside sources. Thus the planters of the South imported white indentured servants from Europe and then Negro slaves from Africa. The planters in Natal turned to India, and those in Hawaii to China, Japan, and the Philippines. It is a frequent observation that whereas the native is not a very satisfactory laborer in the land of his birth he is highly prized when he is transported to territory strange to him.

With imported male or family-less laborers the control situation changes in favor of the planter. It is easier to fit unattached individuals into their proper places in the organization of plantation work. They are encamped upon the land of the planter's estate, held there, and prevented from scattering out over the territory generally. It is to prevent such dispersion in areas where there is free or waste land available that slavery, indentured servitude, contract labor, and other forms of forced labor arise.

Up through this stage the plantation itself is a kind of school but not one formally and consciously organized for the purpose of teaching. Nevertheless, as Booker T. Washington said, "every slave plantation in the South was an industrial school. On these plantations young colored men and women were constantly being trained not only as farmers but as carpenters, blacksmiths, wheelwrights, brick masons, engineers, cooks, laundresses, sewing women, and housekeepers." [14] In Africa it was said that the "best school for the African is a good European estate." [15]

The situation changes again when the importation of outside labor is interrupted. This happened in the New World when the African slave trade was shut off; it happened in Mauritius, in Natal, and in some of the islands of the West Indies when India refused to allow more of her people to emigrate as laborers to these plantation areas. Now it becomes necessary to find a new source of labor; and the new source is found in the children of the laborers, for in the meantime the mass of imported and assorted individuals have gradually organized themselves into family groups and have produced offspring. Born to the situation, the children tend to accept it without question; but their very presence introduces new problems of control and changes in plantation organization.

It is when the plantation reaches this stage in its life-history, the stage of Creole or "home-grown" labor, that questions of positive educational policy begin to arise. In fact, this stage in plantation development in different areas around the world is best studied in the materials on education in colonial areas because of the close relation between labor control and educational policies. In the South, before about 1800, the idea of an education for Negroes was not rejected because it was not even entertained. Because some Negroes, however, had been gaining a sort of informal education through personal contacts with whites and because some of these Negroes, like the slave Gabriel in Virginia, were found plotting insurrections, laws were passed aimed at restricting educational opportunities for them. After the Nat Turner rebellion in 1831 legislation became even more repressive; yet in spite of the laws individual whites, especially pious women who believed that "everyone should know how to read the Bible," [16] continued to teach Negroes.

As long as the children of the laborers are slaves like their fathers, as in the ante bellum South, the public educational policy is to discourage or prevent any formal education at all. "Of what use will education be to them if they get it?" is the question which appears to answer itself as far as planters are concerned. But where the children of the laborers are free, either by virtue of emancipation or because they do not inherit the legal compulsion to work which operates against their fathers, the community is forced to accept the necessity for education in some form and to some degree. The question then becomes, "What kind and how much?"

Since education is both an instrument of control in the hands of the planter class and a means of emancipation and status for the children of the laboring classes, it is easy to understand both the hopes and the fears of the employing classes when they first begin to yield the privilege of education. Stated briefly, the educational policy of the planter class is to insure that the children of plantation laborers will remain plantation laborers. If education there must be, let it be an occupational education; but often this is not a solution from the point of view of the working-class members of the dominant race, for whom such an education may raise up dangerous competitors.

To those upon whom it is urged, a vocational and occupational education is suspect, since it appears to lead to an intensification of occupational distinctions and to a society consisting of impenetrable caste strata. Since the status of the privileged class is associated with educational attainment in the sciences, the liberal arts, and the professions, it is natural for those at the bottom to be attracted to this kind of education, the kind of education which promises to lead them out of their traditional class into a higher one. The son of a plantation laborer in Hawaii, whose attitude seems typical, wrote as follows:

My parents always told me to study hard and become a great man and not a cane field laborer, who had to go to work early in the morning, rain or sun, and work to late in the evening. They even said that they would buy anything for me if it is related to school. [17]

Regardless of the type of education, the appearance of the school at the stage of "home-grown" labor in the plantation's history precipitates two problems. On the one hand, it defines child labor as a social problem, since child labor is any kind of labor that keeps a child away from school. The recognition of the large amount of child labor in the South as a social problem is a matter of recent history. Here, as in the West Indies and in South Africa, it has led to much discussion and an agitation for the primacy of the school over the demands of employers.

On the other hand, the school tends to produce a white-collar class which the industrial and agricultural system does not absorb. Even in the South the education of the Negro has developed more rapidly than have his opportunities for wider participation in economic and political life. It is in Hawaii, however, that the contest between the educational ambitions of the sons and daughters of the plantation laborers and the labor needs of the planters is most acute. In 1882 the first annual meeting of the Planter's Labor and Supply Company defined the type of labor most ideal for plantation work with the statement: "The industrial condition of these Islands requires people as laborers who are accustomed to subordination, to permanency of abode, and who have moderate expectations in regard to a livelihood." [18]

While the sugar industry was expanding, while times were prosperous and labor continued to be imported, education did not seem to be harmful. But, under the stress of a receding price, a growing burden of taxation, and a possibility that the supply of labor from the Philippines would be cut off, there developed the conviction that education makes people unfit for common plantation labor. The planters became outspoken for a fundamental change. They would place limitations upon the schools, and such schools as remained would serve merely as training grounds for plantation workers. In his address to the annual meeting of the Hawaiian Sugar Planters' Association in 1925, the president of the association said:

> Why blindly continue a system that keeps a boy or girl in school at taxpayers' expense long after they have mastered more than sufficient learning for all ordinary purposes, simply to enlighten them on subjects of questionable value; subjects on which they could as well enlighten themselves (if by any chance their inclinations tended in that direction) and at the same time, by entering some field of employment will, besides earning wages, be gaining experience and efficiency, and above all learn to appreciate the value of a dollar by working for it. . . . The solution as I see it, is that the taxpayer be relieved of further responsibility after the pupil has mastered the sixth grade, or the eighth grade in a modified form. [19]

In Malaya, which developed rapidly into a plantation community during the past half-century, the British pursued the policy of educating principally for the needs of the planters. A few English schools were maintained to train an adequate supply of clerks; there were some vernacular schools for the natives and for the children of the Indian workers on the plantations; but the British were frankly opposed to "any ideal of education not adjusted to local wants," as it must inevitably "lead to economic dislocation and social unrest." [20]

A committee in Ceylon, appointed to inquire into the state of education in that colony, objected to a type of education which had done nothing more than to produce

> a class of shallow, conceited, half-educated youths who have learned nothing but to look back with contempt upon the conditions in which they were born and from which they conceive that their education has raised them, and who desert the ranks of the industrious classes to become idle, discontented hangers-on of the courts and the Public Offices. [21]

Similar statements from other plantation areas might be offered, [22] but these are sufficient to show that the educational problems of the South are typically those of plantation societies generally.

When the educational process in a plantation society is compared with that of a mission society, the conclusion suggests itself that, whether formal education is promoted from above, as in the case of the mission, or whether it is demanded from below, as in the case of the plantation, it achieves no higher level than the needs of the situation require. And the situation is very much the same for both institutions. The great mission establishments of the past did not develop along every frontier where missionary work was carried on. They did not grow up in New England, for instance, even though the Congregational church there had a complete monopoly of the field. The great agricultural mission estates grew up in the same kind of areas where the plantations grew up and for very much the same reason—these were the areas that could grow the *Kolonialwaren* for which there was a ready market abroad. The fact that financial support from home for missionary activities in the Colonies was not expected to last forever faced every mission sooner or later with the problem of becoming self-supporting. Thus the aims of civilizing, educating, and converting and of finding means for self-support all came to coincide; and the result was to make the mission a large landed and agricultural estate. Where there was more land than there was labor to cultivate it, where there was a favorable market for the products of the land, the mission became very much the same sort of institution that the plantation became. One traveler who had seen both institutions thought that the lot of the Indian neophytes in the California missions differed very little from the lot of the Negro slaves on the West Indian sugar plantations. [23]

The two institutions have at times become so much alike that when found together they are in a condition of competition and conflict. In colonial Brazil, planter opposition to the Jesuits resulted in the forced withdrawal of the friars as the conviction grew that the missions "were simply competing plantations worked at merely nominal cost by converts adroitly turned into slaves." [24]

To the permanent and fixed elements in the environment, elements of geography and climate, even conflicting ideologies tend eventually to make the same kind of adjustment.

Education, like other aspects of culture, is a condition for the satisfaction of the elementary needs of individuals and of groups of individuals. Like intelligence, it is in considerable measure a response to a problematical situation that requires reflection and energy and struggle. The fundamental educational process is therefore a kind of biological adaptation. As long as a group is at least maintaining its numbers at given standards it may be presumed to have an educational system commensurate with its needs. It may be that the people of the South have had about all the education they could use in the kind of world in which they have lived and competed. The situation, however, is changing radically. The star of the southern plantation is on the wane, and for the future a region of white and Negro small-farm holdings appears likely. To win their bread and protect their liberties in the new world of competition and conflict with others, the people of the South must gear their minds and hands to new levels of endeavor. New needs will bring—must bring—a new and more vital education.

• 3 •

The Climatic Theory of
the Plantation

In a very general way the South may be regarded as that part of the United States where the planter has been the chief history-making personality—as that part of the Nation where the planter has most powerfully impressed himself upon the form of society. The planter is a representative of that class of individuals who historically have possessed the land as an incident of some form of conquest and put themselves at the head of political institutions based upon the exploitation of the land. The plantation arises as the personal "possession" of the planter, and it is from the standpoint of his interests that the course of its development is directed. It is first of all a unit of authority over people which comes to be defined and expressed in terms of territory. Hence the plantation is commonly understood as a relatively large landed estate.

Plantations have never physically occupied the entire extent of the area known as the South, but in point of territory covered, the plantation society of the South is undoubtedly the largest the world has ever known. In addition to many other factors which have shaped the history of this society, the factor of sheer size alone has been a highly important one. The plantation society of the South has been big enough to have weight and mass and stability and to permit the development of a plantation "system" whose parts cooperated to maintain a certain type of agricultural economy and social organization. All other institutions within the South, like the family, the church, the school, and the state be-

SOURCE *Agricultural History,* January 1941, pp. 40–60.

came parts of this system and supported it. Millions of people grew up within the system and accepted it because they knew no other and rarely if ever came into contact with ideas inconsistent with it.

The South has not been alone in its plantation experience, but most of its students and writers appear to have written and spoken as if it had. Southern writers and spokesmen have been concerned chiefly with issues over which the South has been in conflict with the North and West. They have for this reason been led to contrast the institutions of the South with those of other sections of the United States to the point of acute consciousness of differences. An inevitable consequence of contrast is a heightened sensitiveness to outside criticism and an attitude of justification and of defense.

The existence of the plantation in other times and places, however, provides a basis for comparative study which should immeasurably increase our knowledge not only of the institution itself but of similar societies which have been based upon it.

Historically, there have been at least three important plantation epochs. The first was the ancient Carthago-Roman system which developed around the production of oil and wine. Labor was supplied by slaves captured in war.[1] The second developed in connection with the colonization and exploitation of the New World. It witnessed a rise of great tobacco, rice, sugar, indigo, and cotton plantations. These were based upon Negro slave labor imported from Africa. The third and contemporary plantation development has centered in the countries bordering the Indian Ocean and in many of the islands of the Pacific. The plantations in this area are manned by cheap coolie labor recruited from regions of closed economic resources in the Orient. These huge enterprises have brought plantation agriculture to a point of efficiency and importance not hitherto known.

Aside from the plantation areas of the South the institution today controls the lives and destinies of millions of people in many other parts of the world. In the West Indies the remnants of an old colonial plantation system exist alongside the new and highly efficient plantations organized by American capital. In the Yucatan peninsula and throughout Mexico plantation estates are being broken down into small farms by the policy of the Cardenas government. The old coffee plantations of the highlands and the newer banana plantations of the lowlands give several of the Central American states dual plantation societies in many respects very different from each other. The "mass agriculture" of the banana industry has in recent years transformed primeval jungles into active and thrifty plantation communities. In South America the Guianas, Venezuela, Colombia, Ecuador, and Peru each have plantation areas proximate to their coasts. Brazil witnessed the rise of the first plantation society in the New World, a society based upon the cultivation of sugar cane by means of Negro slave labor. Today, however, it is the coffee *fazenda* of southern Brazil which gives that country what is probably the second largest plantation area in the world.

There are many important plantations in West Africa, notably in Liberia, but the outstanding plantation societies of that continent range from north to south in the eastern half, in Natal, Mozambique, Zanzibar, Tanganyika, Kenya, and Anglo-Egyptian Sudan. About each of these societies there are special points of interest which would repay comparative study. Kenya, especially since the first World War, has witnessed the rapid rise of an aristocracy of European landowners and the proletarianization of the native population. In Natal, an English planter class has developed the cultivation of sugar cane on large estates by the use of East Indian indentured labor and Bantu native labor. The clove plantations of Zanzibar are nominally owned by the once wealthy and all-powerful Arab planters.

In Asia there are several very important plantation societies with commercial outlets on the Indian Ocean. Perhaps the oldest of these is found in the island of Ceylon where on several occasions the estates have had to respond to drastic changes in world market conditions by shifting to different agricultural staples. The tea plantation society of Assam also has had a very interesting and somewhat unusual history. One of the most important plantation developments of modern times is that connected with the production of rubber in the Malay Peninsula. When it was discovered in the first decade of the present century that this long, narrow tongue of land was excellently suited to the production of rubber, the jungle was quickly converted into industrialized forests of disciplined rubber trees. The estates of European planters and companies became points where many peoples of diverse race and culture came together. No less important are the plantations in the Dutch islands of Java and Sumatra. Between the plantations of these two islands there are interesting and significant points of comparison and contrast. In the Philippines, American capital has developed sugar plantations while the Japanese have organized the sugar industry of Taiwan into large producing units to meet domestic needs. Queensland, Australia, Fiji, and Hawaii are or have been the scenes of extensive sugar plantation enterprises. The plantation industry of Hawaii is especially significant for it has given the Territory one of the most heterogeneous populations in the world.

It is obvious from this incomplete and hurried review of plantation societies throughout the world that they are numerous enough to provide the materials for a comparative and scientific account of the institution and of the societies founded upon it. Naturally we are most interested in the South, but it is a frequent experience of science that insight into the problems of a given situation is gained only by going outside that immediate situation, and the widest and seemingly most irrelevant excursions are frequently the source of the most illuminating insights. It may be that the more we learn about other plantation societies directly the more we shall learn about Southern society indirectly.

The literature of plantations is extensive, but it is for the most part, historical rather than sociological. Historians and geographers have given us most of our facts, but they have not concerned themselves with the formulation of any theory to explain the facts. Historians and geographers very properly insist on first depicting things as they are and then inferring generalizations secondarily if at all rather than setting up hypotheses and plunging at once into a search for principles and for common processes of change.

The transformation of the unique events and the concrete facts concerning particular plantation societies which historians, geographers, and others have given us into the generalizations of social theory begins with the asking of such questions as the following: [2] What is a plantation? What are the determining characteristics of a situation in which the plantation is likely to arise? Under what conditions does it undergo change? Is there a characteristic cycle of change? Why does it continue longer in some areas than in others? When the plantation breaks down, what normally succeeds it?

It is obvious that answers to such questions as these, if there are answers, would not only give a better understanding of the history of the South and of other plantation societies, but might also contribute to any regional plan to guide and control the future of a plantation society.

Insofar as general answers to any of these questions have been attempted, they have come, for the most part, from students of colonization and colonies. The reason for this is apparent. The study of colonies, as distinct from the study of a colony, invites comparison and classification. The most obvious characteristic of colonies lending itself to comparison is the economic basis of community life and, as Albert Galloway Keller, has said:

agriculture is the only important primary form of the industrial organization common to colonies of all latitudes and altitudes, and so the only criterion of classification of adequate generality, not to mention importance.[3]

Some colonies are so conspicuously dominated by plantation agriculture and others by small-scale farming that a classification on this basis follows naturally. Keller has mentioned other students of colonization besides himself who recognized at least these two types of colonies. Keller believes, however, that the postulation of other types requires a shift to criteria of discrimination which are not common to all colonies.

The principal interest in the writings of these students of colonization is not so much in the fact that they agree in recognizing the plantation and farm colonies as two fundamental types as it is in the theory which they claim accounts for the determination of the situation in which each type is likely to arise. The explanation implicit, if not explicit, in the works of most of these men is that climate is the determining factor in the situation. This explanation is either stated or assumed in the writings of such men as A. H. L. Heeren and Wilhelm Roscher in Germany, Paul Leroy-Beaulieu in France, and H. E. Egerton and Benjamin Kidd in England.[4] The most explicit statement of this point of view is by Keller:

colonies are, at least in their beginnings, societies of relative simplicity, as yet unendowed with that accumulation of relationships, institutions, and so on, through which older human groups appear to have rendered themselves, to some extent, independent of natural conditions. If this is admitted, either through conviction or as a working hypothesis, then it should be possible to construct a useful classification of colonial societies upon the broader variations of the natural conditions to which they are or have been exposed.

Of these conditions climate is, in the present case at least, the vital and determining one. It is usually so, carrying with it, as it does, so many other factors whose variations are correlated with its own; for instance, flora and fauna, including among the latter the microscopic fauna of disease. Climate, though itself varying in accordance with several factors, and though it evades classification except by type, may still, for the purpose in hand, be broadly divided into *tropical* and *temperate*. But this distinction would be of no utility in classifying colonies, because too general, if these distinct types of climate did not condition the human struggle for existence in a manner so vital as to determine two distinct types of industrial organization, upon which in turn, as what follows is designed to show, there would regularly be developed two distinctly variant types of human society. Thus the classification based upon climate and attendant influences may be shifted over into a classification based upon the type of the industrial organization. Anticipating what is to follow, we should then distinguish the tropical and the temperate colony upon the ground of their common and basic occupation, agriculture, and might name them respectively the *plantation colony* and the *farm colony*.[5]

The temperate-zone farm colony is marked by economic and administrative independence. Since its products are likely to compete with those of the mother country, it tends toward local diversified self-sufficiency. The soil is intensively cultivated and care is given to its conservation. The unit of social organization is the family, and the population is fairly well divided between the two sexes. Hence there is little mixing with natives and no large mixed-blood population. Its democratic society is characterized by free labor.

The tropical plantation colony presents a marked contrast to the farm colony in almost every respect. Tropical products rank as luxury goods in the mother country, and the plantation colony tends to specialize in the production of one or more of them. Cultivation is extensive and exploitative. The colonists are predominantly males, and the racial unit is the individual and not the family. Consequently, relations with native women produce a mixed population. Since "vital conditions do not permit of the accomplishment of plantation labors at the hands of an unacclimatized race," laborers must be imported from other tropical regions if the natives cannot be coerced.[6]

Keller apparently thinks of the physical and meteorological environment as giving rise to local survival forms which in turn elaborate secondary social and political forms of higher complexity. The differences between the plantation colony and the farm colony grow out of differences in climate. Adjustment to varying climatic conditions along the colonial frontier results in two fundamentally different labor economies and social organizations. These statements seem to summarize the climatic theory of the plantation and the society based upon it as formulated by Keller.

In spite of the fact that most of the plantation societies in the present world community are grouped in or near the tropics, the theory is subject to some very great difficulties. In the first place, it does not account for the existence of plantation societies in areas of temperate climate. In Rhode Island, for example, after about 1650, the Narragansett planters developed "an industrial system which may fairly be compared with that of the Southern colonies."[7] The situation in eastern Germany seems to be another exception to the theory. Although the lowlands of this area have an inhospitable climate with long, severe winters, after the twelfth century this frontier developed a system of large estates which seems to conform to the plantation pattern and which has been maintained for over six hundred years.[8]

The climatic theory also fails to explain the existence of tropical colonies where small farming characterizes the agricultural economy. Saba Island in the Dutch West Indies seems to illustrate such a situation.[9] Costa Rica in Central America apparently is another exception. It is a tropical country with a native-born white population of small farmers. Originally whites of Spanish origin settled the land in family groups and today "of 58,976 real estate holdings Costa Ricans hold legal title to 47,000."[10] However, after several hundred years of existence as a small farm society the banana plantation with Negro labor is now beginning to make inroads.

A third objection to the climatic theory is that it does not account for the very great and significant differences between plantation societies. They establish themselves in a variety of ways and vary greatly from place to place and from time to time. The differences between any two plantation societies may be as great as the contrasts between a plantation society and a small-farm society. James G. Leyburn evidently believes that the differences between what he calls the "settlement-plantation" society and the "exploitative plantation" society are very great. He recognizes these, not as sub-types of plantation society generally, but as full types of frontier societies along with the farm type and the ranching type.[11]

Perhaps the most serious shortcoming of the climatic theory is its failure to account for the transition from plantation to farm, or _vice versa,_ in a single area where the climatic factor remains stable. The same area and climate maintains itself through kaleidoscopic changes in economic and social life. Vincent T. Harlow has described a change in Barbados from a colony of small farms operated by white owners to a colony of large plantations operated by Negro slave labor. On the other hand, according to Avery Craven, Virginia and Maryland had by 1860 "come largely to the small farm and the small farmer." By that time the Governor of Virginia was advertising her agriculture as no longer characterized by "the large plantation system" but one of "smaller horticultural and aboricultural farming." [12]

The fact that in the present world community plantation societies are grouped in or near the tropics, which at first seems to support the theory, may be accounted for on other than climatic grounds. It is obvious that, because of climatic conditions, most of the agricultural products characteristic of the tropics cannot be grown elsewhere. Some, like cane sugar, can be produced in temperate zone areas, but the costs are materially higher when production is attempted outside the areas of optimum natural conditions.[13] Bananas, for example, can be grown under hothouse conditions in Canada, but they can be grown profitably only in the tropics. For this reason banana plantations are found in the tropics and nowhere else. They are located by the nature of the major crop. Bananas need not be grown only on a plantation basis; they may be, and frequently are, grown and marketed by peasant farmers. In the latter case the small banana farm is also necessarily restricted to areas of tropical climate.

Although the natural distribution of particular plantation staples is determined or limited by climatic factors, it does not follow that the plantation institution itself is so determined. Plantations are largely concentrated in the tropics, not because of climate, but because, in the present world community, tropical regions constitute a highly important and accessible trade and agricultural frontier, and the plantation is always an institution of the frontier. The tropics constitute a frontier where there are exploitable agricultural resources attractive to capital and which are nearer to consuming centers in terms of transportation costs than are the vast areas of sparsely peopled but potential agricultural lands in the temperate zones. Plantations have developed along nontropical frontiers in the past and conceivably may in the future.

For these several reasons, therefore, the limitations of the climatic theory seem to be more important than its applications. It does not provide a satisfactory basis for research upon the nature and problems of plantation society. Dissatisfaction arises when an effort is made to use it. Of possible significance in this connection is the fact that after elaborating the climatic theory of plantation and farm colonies in the first chapter of his *Colonization*, Keller made very little actual use of it in the following chapters which deal with particular colonies.

The question raised by a climatic theory of the plantation is really part of the larger and more fundamental question of acclimatization.[14] The acclimatization of human beings usually is discussed in connection with white settlement in equatorial regions.[15] Many writers believe that the acclimatization of white settlers in the tropics is constitutionally impossible. Thus Benjamin Kidd is well known for his opinion that "in the tropics the white man lives and works only as a diver lives and works under water. . . . Neither physically, morally, nor politically, can he be acclimatized in the tropics." [16] Ellsworth Huntington has argued that in the tropics the white man loses his will power and gives himself up to idleness, displays of temper, drunkenness, and sexual overindulgence.[17] Madison Grant has conceded that the "Nordic race can exist outside of its native environment as landowning aristocrats who are not required to do manual labor in the fields under a blazing sun" but not if its members are compelled to support themselves by their own labor.[18] The logical consequence of such views is expressed in the conclusion of William Z. Ripley that "a colonial policy in the tropics means a permanent servile native population, which is manifestly inconsistent with political independence, or with any approach to republican institutions." [19]

It has long been assumed both in the North and in the South, that cultural differences between these two sections of the United States derive from climatic differences.[20] Many if not most students of Southern society have made this assumption. Ulrich B. Phillips, for example, began his important work on *Life and Labor in the Old South* with the statement: "Let us begin by discussing the weather, for that has been the chief agency in making the South distinctive," but he recognized the fact that "The South is nowhere tropical except at the tip of Florida." [21] More recently Clarence Cason in his study of Southern society insisted that the summer heat was and is the basic factor in all Southern culture. Conducive to inactivity under the Mississippi dictum that "only mules and black men can face the sun in July," the heat, he thought, created in the South a serenity for which all men strive.[22]

Involved in all these opinions concerning the impossibility of white acclimatization in the tropics as well as those concerning the connection between Southern civilization and the climate of the South has been the assumption that only the Negro and other nonwhite peoples were capable of doing the work necessary for agricultural production under the conditions imposed by a tropical or semitropical climate. This assumption was in large measure the economic justification for Negro slavery in the South before the Civil War. Dr. Thomas Cooper, president of South Carolina College, probably stated the opinion of most white Southerners of the period when he said: "Nothing will justify slave labour in point of economy, but the nature of the soil and climate which incapacitates a white man from labouring in the summer time." [23]

Public statements alleging a superior tolerance on the part of the Negro to the climate of the South are heard less frequently since the Civil War, but the opinion, nevertheless, is still widely held. However, the gradual realization that there are now more white than Negro tenants and sharecroppers on Southern plantations seems to have been accompanied by a tendency to shift the explanation from the climate to the hookworm in order to account for the inefficiency and low status of agricultural labor. However, many upper-class Southerners seem to assume that hookworm is only a polite name for laziness which in turn goes back to an innate mental and moral inferiority.

Popular opinion regarding the acclimatization of man has

been, for the most part, based upon two assumptions: first, that the different races of mankind are distinct species, each sprung from a separate origin in its own native habitat, and second, that climate is the principal factor in limiting or regulating the distribution of species. It is significant that the various climatic theories of human society, from Aristotle to Huntington, are closely associated with the various racial theories of society. "These two theories," according to Robert E. Park, "have this in common, namely, that they both conceive civilization and society to be the result of evolutionary processes—processes by which man has acquired new inheritable traits—rather than processes by which new relations have been established between men." [24] The climatic theories support the view that social distinctions are biological and constitutional in origin rather than the result of history and circumstances.

Tested scientific knowledge concerning acclimatization is limited and the data are very inadequate. With respect to the acclimatization of human beings, cultural factors have never been taken fully into account. Complicating factors which have to be eliminated before the single factor of climate can be isolated and its effect upon human settlement in new areas determined, include such matters as the persistence of personal habits, diet, immunity or susceptibility to disease, and race mixture. Also climate itself has to be broken down into its separate elements of temperature, humidity, monotony or variety, the chemical rays of the sun, and various other factors. The writer is not competent to discuss these complicating factors, but one consideration relative to the climatic theory of the plantation may be pointed out. The problem of acclimatization is something more than the physiological problem of the conditions that control the birth, health, and growth of individuals. It is more than a matter of the optimal and limiting temperatures, humidities, etc., for this bare physiological process. It is rather a problem of the capacity of the individual, the group, or the race to maintain itself in the struggle for numerical supremacy against others. It is the problem of the importance of a single factor, climate, as it affects an individual or a group in relation to other individuals or groups. The importance of this factor of climate is directly proportional to its selective action. Acclimatization, therefore, is fundamentally a problem of competition—of biological competition.

Acclimatization involves not merely living away from a homeland; it also involves competing successfully with the natives or with other invaders of the new area. It is a process of adjustment to a different climatic situation, but it is measured in terms of success or failure in the competition with others in the same territory, and highly important in determining the outcome is the matter of just who the others are. A European group, for example, might successfully settle a new area when its competitors are, say, Indians, but not when its competitors are Negroes or Javanese. Acclimatization is a relative matter.

It is relative because the social forces operative in a given situation at a given place and time are relative, and social forces determine to a large extent how biological forces act. The acclimatization of man is influenced by a variety of cultural factors which are nonexistent in animals below man; it is conditioned by many factors which are not included in the struggle for existence among the animals and plants. The kind of human beings which tends to prevail in an area may, for instance, be determined in large part by the general conception of their status. It is reasonable to suppose that an important factor in the failure of the white man to become acclimatized to a tropical or semitropical climate is his unwillingness to compete with the natives or with the darker races on terms necessary to success. As Earl Hanson has said: "In New York and London and on our Western plains a man is allowed to be himself and to do and live about as he pleases. In the tropics he must above all be a white man and maintain the superiority of the white race, largely by a careful refusal to do any work." [25] One of the factors which help to determine how biological forces work is a code which expressly forbids the white man in the tropics to do agricultural labor.

Another historical and social factor which influences the operation of biological forces is the practice of slavery. American slavery was to a very high degree a noncompetitive status which gave the Negro a place on the land without the necessity of competing for it. Slavery likewise is a social arrangement which operates somewhat like domestication in the relations between men and animals. Slaves and domesticated animals are naturally protected against a competition which otherwise might eliminate them. Slavery does not allow full biological competition between the races inhabiting an area, although all are exposed to the same climatic environment.

There seems, therefore, to be nothing in the facts of acclimatization, so far as we know them, to support the climatic theory of the plantation. Acclimatization, and biological competition generally, is fundamentally important in altering populations and institutions in any part of the world, but the alteration may take opposite directions in two tropical colonies or in two temperate-zone colonies. Because of its tendency over a period of time to produce a homogeneous population the process of biological competition would tend normally to establish the small family-sized farm. The plantation, on the other hand, represents an intruding force from without which is political in character. It arises as a regulator of population movements and racial contacts in the interest of a planter in connection with the exploitation of agricultural resources for market.

The contrast between plantation and farm is an aspect of the contrast between estate agriculture and peasant agriculture throughout the world generally. In many countries the latter two represent distinct and competing systems of agriculture within the same climatic area with now one, now the other, dominant. In the South the plantation and the small farm with its self-directing labor have, since the days of original settlement, existed side by side. [26] According to W. M. Daniels, the competition between them

epitomizes the greater part of the *ante-bellum* industrial history of the South. The struggle moreover was an oft-renewed fight, and not a single pitched battle. In the same territory, as, for example, in seaboard Virginia, the early supremacy of the plantation yielded later, when the soil's pristine fertility had been exhausted, to the farm. And in general, while the superior efficiency of the plantation for the raising of staples vanquished the farm system in the short run, Providence for once fought against the "big battalions" and was bent on according the final victory to the smaller contestant.[27]

The plantation is not to be accounted for by climate. It is a political institution, and has to be accounted for as the state and other political institutions based upon the authority principle are accounted for, and these institutions have never been restricted to any one climatic situation. On the contrary, they have ranged from Egypt to Iceland.

A conclusion suggested by these considerations is that the climatic theory of the plantation in its popular signification is an element in the resistance to social change. It is part of an ideology which rationalizes and naturalizes an existing social and economic order, and this everywhere seems to be an order in which there is a race problem. Popular interest in acclimatization and in the question of climatic determinism does not seem to arise except in interracial situations, and it arises in these situations as the political or conflict expression of an underlying economic and biological competition between the races involved.

A theory which makes the plantation depend upon something outside the processes of human interaction, that is, a theory which makes the plantation depend upon a fixed and static something like climate, is a theory which operates to justify an existing social order and the vested interests connected with that order. Under such a conception the problems of a plantation society can be looked upon as concerning only God who alone can control the climate, and the climatic theory turns out to be really a sort of divine-right theory of the plantation. Actually, however, the theory, like other sentiments, beliefs, and attitudes connected with the plantation system, must be understood as a product of forces working within the system itself, as an important part of that system but not as an explanation of it.

• 4 •

The Plantation: The Physical Basis of
Traditional Race Relations

I

Before the Civil War, according to an old story, variations of which are even now occasionally heard in the South, a white gentleman owned a plantation; but, unable to make a living from it, he began the practice of the law and became a very successful lawyer. On his plantation he possessed a large and beautiful mansion, a number of race horses, and more than a hundred Negro slaves. But instead of being supported by the plantation, he and the law supported the plantation. He rode the circuit, defended criminals, established titles, argued cases, and otherwise worked very hard in order to maintain his estate.

One afternoon he returned from a hard day's work to find the mules idle in the stable, the cotton in the grass, and his Negroes asleep in the barn. He shouted angrily. The Negroes scrambled to their feet and began their excuses. But the master, shaking with anger, announced his most awful verdict: "I'm going to quit practicing law and let you lazy niggers starve to death."

Of course, this is a white man's story. On the other side is a story told somewhere by Booker Washington. In a certain small Southern town an immigration agent addressed a meeting of whites. An aged Negro stopped to listen as the agent's work was under discussion.

"Boss," he finally inquired of a white man, "who is dis here emmygration man and what is dis here emmygration?"

SOURCE In Edgar T. Thompson (ed.), *Race Relations and the Race Problem*, Duke University Press, 1939, Ch. VII.

It was explained that the agent was an employee of a railroad company trying to induce more white people to locate in the South.

"But Cap'n," said the Negro, "us niggers has got mo' white folks around here now dan us kin take kere of."

Negroes and whites have always been tightly interlocked in the economic and social order of the South. Whatever the white man may think he thinks about Negroes, and whatever the Negro may think he thinks about whites, one fact is certain and that is that they are highly interdependent members of the same society. Each has played a very important part in the life of his society, and each, in its own opinion, has played a more important part in the life of the other than the other has played in its own life. Hence the stories in each group expressing belief in the almost complete dependence upon it of the other.

The existence of a color line may and does involve the isolation of whites and Negroes, and members of each racial group may and do live in separate social worlds from which the others are, in varying degree, excluded. Nevertheless, between them there is a bond resulting from a common way of life and an intertwined experience. Even conflict has established the interhuman ties more closely. For society reposes upon the fact of interlacing expectations and obligations, and the differentiation of the people of the South into two great racial "moities" has had the effect of setting up a basis for reciprocal services and obligations. Paradoxically, the very cleavage between the ruling and servant classes in the South, based to a large extent upon race, has constituted the bond which has held them together. Back of the divisions and the competitions of race are the common values of a common community.

This common society of whites and blacks, this "Southern" society, is, like every other society, a product of collective action. Individual members of the two races have found ways and means of effecting various practical working arrangements. A Negro informant told Dollard that "one of the few things Negro and white men do together is to hunt," [1] but this statement ignores the countless number of occasions when "we" is used to refer to activities and achievements in which members of both races share. Many like Huckleberry Finn and Negro Jim have shared the same crusts, smoked together, fished off the same log, and lied and stolen together in the common cause of self-preservation. Even sharecropping, in spite of its present bad reputation, is not all cropping. At its worst there is sharing not only of the crop after it has been gathered but of the equipment, the work, and the risk involved in making it.

But interracial co-operation in the South is and has been much more important and far more extensive than these statements would indicate. It was from the very beginning one of the terms of his residence in America that the Negro become a party to various schemes of co-operation for the economic exploitation of the country's resources. To be sure, "co-operation" was forced upon him, but without some sort of division of labor two peoples as different in physical appearance and in tradition as whites and Negroes originally were, would not, in all probability, have remained to live together on the land as neighbors. It was said of the Chinese coolies who were imported into the Transvaal that there were only two possible places for them, the mine and the prison. In the South, for a long period in its history at least, it is very near the truth to say that a Negro who was not on a plantation doing the kind of work he was expected to do, and having the sort of relations with whites he was expected to have, was under suspicion if not actually in prison.

The most important *modus vivendi* of interracial co-operation in the South developed in connection with the production of agricultural staples like tobacco, rice, indigo, cotton, hemp, and cane sugar for the market. Agricultural production and race relations became institutionalized in the plantation.

The plantation is basic in any analysis of race relations in the South for several reasons. Its wide distribution from Maryland to Texas has served to characterize and define a whole region and not merely a small locality. It emphasizes the connection between the economic and the political aspects of race relations. It is a unit of collective activity and hence also a unit of human relations ordinarily involving members of both races. It thus serves to center attention upon the *relations* between whites and Negroes rather than upon these two races separately. The plantation brings these relations to a focus in an elementary cell-like unit. Finally, the plantation has set the cultural norm of race relations and defined what constitutes conformity and nonconformity, racial orthodoxy and heterodoxy.

II

Separating the South from the other sections of the United States is an institutional fault line. The basic institutions—the school, the church, the family—are, of course, present in all sections, but in the South they are parts of the plantation "system" as they are parts of other societal systems elsewhere. It is the plantation which is not continuous with other sections of America, and the institutions which are a part of the plantation system are not, therefore, exactly continuous with similar institutions in other parts of America.

For this reason whatever is "different," whatever is special, about the South appears to go back to the plantation and to the system of institutions which has grown up around it. And the plantation is by no means a dead, ante-bellum institution, even though it is not as strong and as vigorous as it once was.[2]

If these statements are true, then it is of some importance to look at the institution more closely, to examine it more carefully, and to study its genesis and career. It has long been taken for granted or merely condemned or glorified. The people of the South have been so close to it, so much a part of it, so familiar with it, that even they do not know as much about it as they might. They have contrasted their institutions with those of the North and West, but they have not compared them with institutions in more comparable situations elsewhere. It may come as a matter of some surprise, therefore, to learn that the plantation is an institution widely distributed around the world and controlling the lives of literally millions of people. It not only provides so many people with occupations, but it distributes and settles them in new lands, provides them with homes, governs them, punishes their delinquencies, and controls their recreation. It differentiates rank and social classes and defines the relations between them. Always and everywhere it appears to be based upon differences of race, and the races involved are not always a white and a colored race.

As the star of the European manorial system sank, that of the plantation system, likewise involving large landed estates, arose in colonial areas overseas where some agricultural staple might profitably be grown for the world market. Adventurers seeking profitable investments for their capital marched out with captains and missionaries, and the colored and so-called primitive peoples of the world became one by one integral parts on the white man's economic order. In favorable situations adventurers with the necessary capital became planters possessing themselves of the land and seeking a way to market with their cotton, tobacco, or sugar.

Out of the wilderness they carved great landed estates, but it was not enough merely to possess the land: the great need was for labor. They turned first to the natives of the areas in the New World and later in the Orient where they were opening up plantations. But the Indian, the Negro, the Malay, and the Polynesian in the land of his birth was only with great difficulty brought under the control of the planters and made dependent upon their providence. The Indian in Virginia, says Bruce, would die, but he would not work. Everywhere the native was described as lazy and incorrigible. He was called "backward" because he did not know how to turn the resources of the country he inhabited into channels of world commerce, and he did not seem disposed to assist the planter who stood ready to perform this economic service.

The characteristic solution of the planter's labor problem at this stage was to import laborers from some other part of the world where they might be purchased, captured, or recruited. The planters of the South imported white indentured servants from Europe and then turned to the vast labor reservoir in Africa. The planters in Natal turned to India, while those in Hawaii turned to China, Japan, and the Philippines.

The planter resorted to the importation of outside laborers, not only because the native population was numerically insufficient, but more often, perhaps, because it was difficult or even impossible to obtain a satisfactory degree of control over people who were at home in the local environment. The familyless man or woman recruited in some distant place and transported to a plantation region where he found himself in strange surroundings and among strange peoples was more easily made dependent upon an employer. Thus the native Negro in many parts of Africa is regarded as a very unsatisfactory plantation laborer, but in early Virginia he was regarded as superior not only to the native Indian but also to the white indentured servant.

With imported laborers, usually familyless, the control situation changed in favor of the planter. It is easier to fit unattached individuals into their proper places in the organization of plantation work. It is easier to concentrate them upon the land of the estate, to hold them there, and to prevent them from scattering out over the country where there is waste or free land to be had. Accordingly, it was to prevent such dispersion that slavery, indentured servitude, contract labor, and other forms of forced labor arose.

The control situation changed again when the flow of outside labor was shut off. This happened in America when the African slave trade was closed. It happened in Mauritius and in some parts of the West Indies when India refused to allow more of her people to enlist as plantation laborers. Hawaii today faces a similar situation with the closing of the Philippines as a source of labor. Now it became necessary to find a new source of supply. The new source was generally found in the children of the laborers, for in the meantime the mass of imported and assorted individuals had organized themselves into family groups and had produced offspring. The children, born to the situation, tended to accept it as they found it, but their very presence introduced new problems of control. It was one of the important functions of slavery that it passed along to the children of laborers the same status held by parents. Ballagh has shown that the development of slavery in Virginia was more or less directly related to the problem of the control and the definition of the status of the second generation.[3]

When the sexes among the laboring population became fairly equalized and when children began to appear, there was a moving away from the individual to the family as the labor unit. The appearance of this stage of Creole, or "home-grown," labor usually required a fundamental reorganization of the plantation involving, at the least, the abandonment of the barracks type of housing for laborers and the substitution of separate family homes.

The Southern plantation has been in this stage of development at least since the Civil War, and further changes are now in process. The typical Southern plantation today is a group of farms operated by white and Negro tenants and nucleated about the home of the white planter. The differentiation of race and class is a basis for interaction, and the sort of feudal unity which has emerged from such interaction under the protecting conditions of some degree of physical isolation has established the individuality of the plantation as a social unit. Because it is a social unit ordinarily requiring a good deal of space, covering "not a point but a territory," the plantation has naturally isolated itself, a fact which has insured a more than ordinary degree of social separateness and independence. On the other hand, since the plantation is also an economic unit producing to sell and not to consume, it has been at the same time highly dependent upon the larger economic community in which it has found its market. There is no great amount of dependence upon other plantations producing the same staple in the same general area; there is no such mutual dependence among neighboring plantations as may be observed among neighboring small farms. Hence there is no extensive elaboration of local divisions of labor.

III

One of the first things to be noticed about the Southern plantation is that it is laid securely down on the land. It is at once a human institution and an organism adhering to the terrestrial surface, a bit of humanity and a bit of soil.

In a sense the plantations of the South are the South. Or, at least, there has been a popular tendency to describe the physical features of the South in terms of the plantations. They have shaped the very face of the earth itself, transforming forests and marshes into tobacco, cotton, cane, and rice fields. This is because the plantation was originally an institution of settlement, a form of settlement which had many of the characteristics of a camp. It represented a form of settlement which characteristically appears in certain types of frontier areas under course of development through foreign investment. Alvin Johnson has described this type of settlement as camp capitalism.[4]

To a certain extent the problem of the South in the days of early settlement was not so much to find white men to settle the land as it was to find colored laborers to support them when settled. Negro slavery proved to be a form of labor control especially adapted to rapid settlement, for by means of it the labor supply became highly responsive to agricultural opportunity along a rapidly advancing frontier. The high mobility of slavery resulted in the distribution of Negroes in those parts of the South where their labor was profitable. They were planted like vegetables and have shown a strong tendency to remain where they took root, even since emancipation.

As plantation labor in the Southern states became predominantly Negro, and with the segregation of whites of the master class and Negroes on the best lands, there was a corresponding segregation of poor whites in the more inaccessible and less fertile areas. The resulting ecological distribution of the races and the classes determined in some considerable measure the extent and sort of social relations between them.

The conditions under which laborers were originally recruited for plantation purposes were such as to promote racial, cultural, and individual diversity. It was in the settlement of such a group of assorted individuals that the peculiar features of the plantation appeared. Since a planter had to establish his plantation where he found it possible to acquire suitable land, perhaps at some remote place, it was necessary not only to clear the land but also to construct a house for himself, quarters for his laborers, stables for his work animals, and shelter for his equipment. It was necessary also to establish a commissary for the purpose of storing and dispensing rations and supplies. Often he built a church on his estate and as time passed there appeared a cemetery. In short, a frontier area was transformed into a habitat, and the planter found himself, entirely incidental to his main purpose, the owner and head of a community as well as a farmer.[5] The spatial pattern of the settlement reflected its political and social structure. The special position of the planter found expression, not only in a larger and better equipped house, but in its detachment from the quarters of the laborers. The people dependent on him lived apart. After emancipation the idea of freedom found expression in a new spatial arrangement which involved the distribution of tenant cabins over the plantation.

The settlement function of the plantation has been no less important in the history of the South than its other functions of agricultural production and political control. The plantation is responsible for the fact that whites and blacks are intermixed on land which they both claim as a common social, if not legal, inheritance. Because it is an institution of settlement, insularity is implicit in its very nature. Like a lens constricted to a narrow focus the entire lives of large numbers of white and black people have been lived within its small circle.

IV

The most obvious function of the plantation is that of agricultural production. The first planted commodity in the South was tobacco, which so monopolized the life of Virginia and Maryland that they were called the tobacco colonies. In 1694 rice was introduced into South Carolina from Madagascar, and in 1745 indigo came into the same colony from Montserrat in the West Indies. In 1794 sugar cane was introduced into Louisiana from the West Indies. In the latter part of the same century cotton, most crucial of all, began to be cultivated.

These staples were intended primarily for foreign export. Agricultural operations in the Northern colonies and states, on the other hand, were concerned mainly with the production of food supplies for domestic consumption and became, for this reason, subordinate to other forms of industry. But in the South the production of staple crops became the main business of the country.

Not only did the plantation involve the use of a relatively large number of labor units but in the situation in which it evolved in the South it required disciplined and controlled labor. The South was originally, and long remained, what Nieboer terms an area of "open resources." [6] There was more land than there was labor to till it, there was a profitable market for the products of the land, and there were men of capital competing with each other for labor. Under these circumstances the planter who succeeded in getting a laborer was disposed to hold him if he could—and as long as he could. It was in response to a situation of this sort that slavery evolved out of indentured servitude and was itself supplanted by share tenancy after the Civil War.

The authority of the planter was exercised with the production of tobacco, cotton, or sugar as the first consideration. He was concerned, first of all, with the organization and co-ordination of human energy. In a competitive situation it was necessary that the work of the plantation be carried on consistently and with some degree of efficiency. Slave labor was moved in brigades, and discipline was required for the daily drill. The planter did not think primarily of the rights of men but of how to use men, and inevitably he came to take on the characteristics of a master.

In the efficient and effective management of his estate the planter tended naturally to regard his laborers as individuals and utilities. But the workers so regarded did not cease to behave as persons and to act in certain ways contrary to the interests of the proprietor. Because human beings, even as work units, cannot help acting as persons—that is, in terms of their wishes and interests—conflicts inevitably arose which required control. For this reason the plantation became not only an economic institution but an institution of government, a political institution.

V

In no other way except through authority and law can a group whose members represent different racial and cultural backgrounds be made to act as a unit. A form of organization based upon authority and law is a political organization. The arbitrary authority of the individual enters where a customary basis of control is lacking, where custom has broken down, or where there are gaps in the network of custom. Authority is likely to assert itself during periods of change when new interests and new technologies emerge.

In the frontier situation in which it develops the plantation is likely to be remote from the central authority of the state. Bowman describes the plantation on the Brazilian frontier as "remote and feudal." [7] It is feudal largely because it is remote. In the settlement of practical problems and in the management of the affairs of a heterogeneous group of people in an isolated situation the planter arises as the chief lawgiver and the chief power behind the enforcement of his law. The close connection between the governmental functions of the plantation and the existing means of transportation and communication should be emphasized. In general, the type of organization in which authority resides seems to depend upon the character and extent of the interaction of individuals upon each other, upon the solidarity of interests, but ultimately upon the means and extent of communication. Where these means are absent or undeveloped, separate or semi-autonomous bodies grow up within the state and are recognized at least as *de facto* units of government.

On the Southern frontier the privileges of the planter devel-

oped as the result of initial superior strength—physical, economic, and political. By virtue of his position and strength he
became the ruler of a small principality with power over the most
intimate details of the lives of the laborers who were his subjects.
His relations with both his land and his subjects were expressions
of his purpose. The Southern planter has never venerated his
land as "the good earth"—erosion and soil depletion evidence
this—and his personal tie with it has been largely acquisitive, and
allied with practical ends. But in it was rooted the history of his
house and on it he left some impress of himself. While the New
England farmer thought in terms of acres, the Southern planter
often thought in terms of square miles. He was monarch of all
he surveyed, but the number of acres or square miles he
surveyed was not as important as the monarchy. In fact, the
plantation is perhaps best defined not in terms of territory or of
agriculture but in terms of the authority of the planter. The
plantation ends where this authority ends, and territory matters
only in so far as it serves to define limits.[8]

The response of the planter to activities on the part of his
laborers was such, as we have said, as to make of him something
more than a mere agriculturalist. One of the first acts of self-
interest on the part of the laborer is to move away from the
plantation. In an area of open resources where labor is scarce this
is a direct threat to the interests of the planter. For this reason
the first and most important manifestation of the planter's control was to bind the laborer to himself or to the land, at least for
the duration of the crop. In numerous other ways the conduct
of the laborer, whether slave or free, bears a close relation to the
interests of the planter. When he steals, fights, assembles "unlawfully," plots, marries secretly, indulges in fornication, has illegitimate children, spends his time in gambling, cockfighting, or
courting, the planter suffers some loss or threat of loss. The rise
of rules and regulations and punishments for their violation
have reference to all these things.

The extreme expression of political control is the exercise of
the power of life and death, *jus vitae necisque.* This power was
occasionally exercised by individual planters, never with the
open but with the tacit acquiescence of the state, in the early
days of the Southern colonies and states. On the Southern frontier neighboring planters might condemn the taking of the life
of a Negro slave, but as a rule they would feel it more expedient

not to interfere, just as parents today pursue that policy in less serious matters with reference to other parents' children.[9]

Gradually, however, the colonial or state government became strong and integrated enough to assume the power of life and death unto itself alone,[10] and with the development of communication public opinion became strong enough effectively to register its condemnation. With the passing of the extreme frontier conditions under which the plantation originated in the South, the state and the federal governments encroached more and more into the domain of the planter's authority. The Civil War and emancipation finally removed the right of slavery itself, but the planter still retains a considerable measure of personal authority and customary immunity from the interference of the state. A study of lynching says of certain counties in the South: "A tradition in these counties, respected by sheriff and peace-officers as well as by the public, leaves to the planter and his overseer the settlement of any trouble which arises on the plantation among the Negroes themselves or between them and the overseer or planter. Most crimes in these counties are looked upon as labor troubles to be settled by those who own and control the plantations. As a corollary, to all practical purposes, the sheriff and other peace-officers are the planter's agents." [11]

The Southern planter has always maintained a more or less exclusive and acknowledged control over a territory, an attribute in some degree of sovereignty in every political community from the state down. The justification for his control has rested historically on several grounds. In connection with Negro slavery the original justification was based upon religion; the Negro was an infidel or a heathen. The opinion was widely held in Europe and in European colonies that unbelievers might rightfully be made slaves by Christian people. Enslavement was an act of generosity and mercy, for through slavery large numbers could be brought to Christ. But a justification which sanctioned initial enslavement and the slave trade proved to be a boomerang when it came to be a question of continuing in slavery a Negro in whom a large sum of money had been invested but who, almost maliciously it might seem to his master, became converted to the Christian religion. Religion as a justification for slavery had the disadvantage, from the planter's point of view, of impermanence. It is possible for a man to adopt a religion to meet his needs in the situation. In the American colonies it was believed that the conversion of a Negro to Christianity entitled him to freedom and many planters, for this reason, refused to allow ministers to come near their plantations. Accordingly, it became necessary for many colonial legislatures, beginning with the legislature of Maryland in 1664, formally to affirm the principle that baptism and conversion did not entail freedom. But it was clear that a new justification was needed, and, indeed, necessary.

It was found in the idea of race. "Some of the colonial assemblies," says Jernegan, "altered the religious sanction for slavery and based its validity frankly upon race." [12] The conception that certain people coming from the same general territory overseas and possessing similar physical traits were innately and immutably "different," almost different enough to constitute a separate species, powerfully reinforced the position of slavery in America and especially in the South. The *idea* of race, wholly apart from its logical and anthropological validity, had pragmatic value and influence in social life. The idea of race in the South has been no mere academic concept; it was generated out of the interaction of men of different physical marks and it functioned as a part of the plantation situation itself. As a part of the mechanism of control the idea of race served, and continues to serve, a purpose.

The idea of race, and of enslavement based upon race, came to be thoroughly accepted by both the master and slave classes as the basis of relations between them. If the legal sanction of slavery has been destroyed the idea of permanent racial differences continues as a powerful lever of control within the plantation and in the society which is an extension of the plantation, powerful because it is taken for granted by both groups.

Perhaps even more important than the bare fact that the idea of race came into existence as a substitute for religion in justifying slavery is the additional fact that after about 1830, when revolutionary attacks against the system began to be centered in the North, the social cleavage based upon it entered the mores where, at least in the South, it has remained.[13] In so far as the idea of race was bound up with slavery, the defense of slavery was at the same time a defense of the race idea. It was the Yankee, the outsider, the white man at least suspected of being allied with the subject race against the master race, the man who seemed to stand around making uncalled-for remarks and passing adverse judgments, who forced Southerners to abandon apology and substitute aggressive defense.[14] Now it was religion, along with philosophy and pseudo-science, which was brought to the support of the idea of race and, through it, of slavery which was based upon it.

At any rate, it is true, as Phillips remarks, that "after the seventeenth century, the plantation problem was mainly the Negro problem."[15] And according to Monroe Work, speaking of the present situation in the South, "the legal attitudes of tenancy are on the basis of race,"[16] although more than half the tenants on Southern plantations today are white.

To the extent that the laborers on the plantation are distinguished by physical differences, such as skin color and other features, they are regarded as in even more fundamental respects biologically different from the class represented by the planter. For this reason when their behavior varies from that of members of the planter class there is a tendency to account for it on biological (racial) grounds. They have different kinds of instincts. They can better stand the hot sun.[17] They mate promiscuously like the animals. Their women breed like animals and give birth to offspring without pain. Indeed, they are all highly insensitive to pain. It is impossible to read the expressions on their faces. They seem to die on short notice or without any notice at all. The general idea behind plantation government is that Negroes have to be governed, and governed differently from other men, because they themselves are different. A Louisiana planter advised his fellow planters that "negroes must be governed differently from the Europeans; not because they are black, nor because they are slaves, but because they think differently from the white men."[18]

When men are regarded as belonging to a species different from that to which the planter belongs, and when their behavior does not conform to the stereotype in his mind, they appear strange and unknowable. The unknowable Negro has appeared when his master or employer has had some program which ignored his wishes or what he conceived to be his interests. The members of the master class do not ever really know those whom they are trying to control; and, as in the history of men's efforts to control women, unexpected and subtle behavior is attributed to their nature as further proof that they are immutably and instinctively different. Alfred H. Stone, a Mississippi planter, describing the failure of his experiment with a new system designed to advance the interest of the Negro tenants on his plantation, said: "I mean simply to give expression to the conviction, speaking of the average, of course, and not the rare exception, that their actions have no logical or reasonable basis, that they are notional and whimsical, and that they are controlled far more by their fancies than by their common sense." [19]

In the authoritarian community of the plantation there is normally a subtle web of mutual espionage. Exact knowledge of where the planter and the overseer are, and what they are about, is the keynote to all successful shirking and wrongdoing. This has given rise to the fact, or at least the belief among whites in the South, that Negroes know white people better than white people know Negroes. [20]

Negro slavery rested upon a public opinion sustained not only by whites of the planter class but also by the body of non-slaveholding whites, and especially the poor whites. Slavery would not have been capable of much development if it had depended upon the personal power of the planter only. It was necessary for the planter's authority to be recognized by the society of whites generally; it was necessary for the slave to live in a society that regarded him as a slave. Slavery cannot exist where there is not a society of freemen, even though the freemen are as poor as the slaves themselves. [21] The poorer white man might envy and resent the privileges of the planter who in turn often looked down on the poor white with contempt, but the prejudice the latter held toward the Negro slave with whom he came into competition and conflict was an integral part of the plantation system as it existed in the South before the Civil War. Plantation society, therefore, included the poor whites.

Geographical separation of the Negro slaves and the poor whites led to social separation and antagonistic attitudes between them. The plantation overseer, except in those instances when he came from outside the South itself, was generally a representative of the poor white class thrust into the plantation community. He occupied a place between the planter and the slaves, a very narrow and circumscribed place, which kept him apart from the planter and earned him the hatred of the slaves. "Overseer chillun," one of the terms used by Negroes to refer to poor

whites, indicated the connection between the overseer's division
of labor and the poor white areas.

Bassett sums up the role of the overseer on the plantation as
follows:

The overseer's position was central in the Southern system. The
planter might plan and incite, and the slave might dig, plow, and gather
into barns; it was the overseer who brought the mind of the one and
the muscle of the other into coöperation. As he did his work well or
poorly the plantation prospered or failed. . . .

Slight as was the respect the overseer had from the planter it was
greater than the respect he had from the slaves. To them he was the
master's left hand, the burden layer and the symbol of the hardest
features of bondage. From his decisions an appeal was to the owner who
as dispenser of mercy and forgiveness had some degree of affection
from the slaves. As a giver of food and clothing and of largesses at
Christmas time and as a protector in extreme calamity the master stood
high in the respect of the slave. If he was a man of distinction his slaves
were apt to be pleased that he and not a less prominent man was the
master. But the slave was not proud of his overseer nor boasted of his
overseer's virtues. It was the fate of this man, standing in the place of
the owner, to absorb the shock of bitterness felt by the slaves for their
enslavers and in doing so keep it away from those who were in reality
the responsible parties.[22]

It is sometimes said in admiration of a certain type of white
man in the South at the present time, "he sure can work niggers."
This was the prime quality demanded in a good overseer even
in the days before emancipation complicated the problem by
making slaves "free niggers." "A good overseer to manage mules
and niggers" was the way the planters sometimes advertised, but
such an overseer was not always easy to find and when found not
easy to keep. But good or bad, it was the overseer who, perhaps
even more than the planter, epitomized the formal and objective
aspect of the plantation as an institution of political control.

VI

The Southern plantation has always had the character of a
coercive institution. In it economic and political organization has
been identified. Southern agriculture and Southern race relations have been parts of one system. The nature of one, in large
degree, has determined the nature of the other. Negroes and
whites did not meet each other simply as tourists or as sightseers.

Members of one race, with certain cultural traditions, had some *use* for members of the other race having other cultural traditions. Agricultural production represents an economic function. Race relations represent, or tend to represent, the political or power counterpart of the economic function. In a situation of "open resources," as the South has been, the plantation became an institution for regulating racial contact in the interest of the planter.

But under the influence of daily and intimate association among its members the plantation was transformed into a cultural group. The authority and power of the planter were not required for daily use; time generated new customs, and everyone within the plantation community came to know what was expected of him and to feel some sense of obligation to meet these expectations. Alongside the personal leadership and control of the planter a form of control grew up which was not imposed from the outside by a master, a form of control which the group imposed upon itself by common consensus. The forces that controlled Negroes as slaves and later as share tenants were to a large extent within the laborers themselves. A cultural and a moral order, therefore, grew up out of the secular by the same processes that the plantation as a settlement, an industrial, and a political institution grew up under the conditions of the frontier.

Whatever is most distinctive and peculiar about a people, what they take for granted—their culture, in other words—is largely an effect of the special conditions of isolation under which they have lived with physical nature and with each other. The plantation laborer is not ordinarily a personal servant, nor is he ordinarily tied to a machine. Typically he is identified with the land, as the peasant class to which he belongs always is. He is not only tied to his job but is also tied to his locality. Redfield says, "The southern negro is our one principal folk. He has a local tradition orally transmitted; he makes folk songs. Except for him we have to search for folk peoples in the United States." [23] Upon the Negro peasant folk is imposed another group, the white planter class, which communicates with the larger literate world of the market. But the members of this class also communicate directly with the folk tradition and, like nobility classes generally, of which they have been the nearest American representative, they, too, are typically identified with the land. The result is a form of society which is highly local. The rather extreme localization of life which agricultural pursuits always foster aids in the development of a distinctive group culture.

The extent of this isolation is often alluded to in the literature of plantation reminiscence. A Southern woman writes of her experiences as follows: "Confined exclusively to a Virginia plantation, during my earliest childhood, I believed the world one vast plantation bounded by negro quarters. Rows of white cabins with gardens attached; negro men in the fields; negro women sewing, knitting, spinning, weaving, house-keeping in the cabins, with negro children dancing, romping, singing, jumping, playing around the doors, formed the only pictures familiar to my childhood." Later on "it began to dawn upon us that all the world was not a plantation. The first time I ever heard of a manner of living different from this was when it became important for my mother to make a visit to a great aunt in Baltimore, and she went for the first time out of her native state. . . . My mother was accompanied by her maid, Kitty, on this expedition, and when they returned they had many astounding things to relate." Still later when she visited New York she was "surprised to hear of 'plantation customs' said to exist among us." [24]

Even today, in spite of a high rate of tenant turnover, there are many Negroes in the South still living on the plantations upon which they were born and upon which their slave ancestors lived. Lyle Saxon reports instances in Louisiana where white gentlewomen have never left the plantations on which they live.[25] In such conditions of extreme isolation it would be quite natural for values to be associated with insularity, and inroads into this closed society to be regarded as threats. A character in Kennedy's plantation novel, *Swallow Barn*, a story of early Virginia, expressed his opposition to a measure to provide the state with good roads with the statement, "The home material of Virginia was never so good as when her roads were at their worst."

In the background of wilderness and lonely striving, from colonial days to the present, the whites and blacks who lived together on the plantation "balanced in their behavior the somewhat contrary motives of getting the most for self and of manifesting an ordinary human interest in those with whom destiny had closely associated them." [26] John Mason Brown says of the

Kentucky frontier that the association between master and slave was so very intimate because, "In the solitude of the wilderness, the intense longings for the society of human kind made the companionship of the master and his household an essential condition to the happiness and contentment of both." [27] Then as now it must be supposed that the white planter family experienced the overshadowing existence of the Negro community running parallel with its own, on a different plane, but with echoes going from one to the other.

In the small and intimate world of the plantation the assimilation of the Negro slave fresh from Africa followed rapidly and as a matter of course. "Although merchants, in selling newly imported Negroes invariably advertised the tribe or geographical section from which the Negroes came, it is interesting that none of these facts were mentioned in selling seasoned slaves. It would seem that tribal differences tended to disappear as the slaves became seasoned." [28]

The data descriptive of small farms and plantations in antebellum days are very meager, but such data as exist point unmistakably to the informality of control and to the intimacy of race relations upon them. The importance of this is evident when it is pointed out that one fourth of all the slaves in 1850 were held in groups of less than ten each and another fourth in groups of between ten and twenty each. This means that at least one half the slaves were in more or less close contact with their white masters with an opportunity to share in the cultural heritage of the master class. [29] Especially was this true in the case of Negroes adopted into white households as family servants.

Written records went with the more formal and efficient control of the large slave plantations, about which our knowledge is greater but which were not nearly as numerous as the small plantations. In the areas dominated by the large estates, where the contacts between the whites and blacks were notably less, assimilation was naturally less complete. Consequently, in such areas as the seaboard of South Carolina and Georgia the Negro population early impressed visitors as decidedly "different" from Negro populations in other parts of the South, especially in Virginia and in upland districts where the plantations were smaller. These "differences in the Negro population which existed before the Civil War," says Park, "are still clearly marked today. They are so clearly marked, in fact, that an outline of the areas in which the different types of plantation existed before the War would furnish the basis for a map showing distinct cultural levels in the Negro population of the South today." [30]

When it is remembered that the ante-bellum plantation was usually a small and closely knit community in which individuals, both white and black, were brought up with a prospect of lifelong association with each other, then it is realized how the plantation offered very much the same sort of human experience that the family represents. It was an association lasting not for just a few years, as in modern industry with its high labor turnover, nor even so few as the years of association between parents and children before the latter go off to establish homes of their own, but usually for life. The content of such an experience was bound to be very personal and intimate, the sort of experience of unique relationships which gave a sense of "belonging." One "belonged" to this group to a degree that made conspiracy and concerted revolt exceptional. It was a sense of belonging which even came to be expressed in terms of kinship. The impression one gets from talking to old Negroes who have known slavery is that this was really the sense in which slaves commonly regarded themselves as belonging to a master. It was not "belonging" as the law defined it.

It was a sense of the sort of belonging which also gave the slave a feeling of proprietorship over the master and his family as expressed in the idea of "our white folks." It was an idea expressing feudal reciprocity and protection, a relationship still effectively functioning between whites and Negroes. In the Mississippi Delta, says Cohn:

Every plantation Negro—and many Negroes of the towns—has his "white folks" to whom he looks for protection when he violates the law. "Whose nigger are you?" is frequently the first question asked by a magistrate when a Negro is brought before him. If he is Mr. Brown's nigger and Mr. Brown is an important man in the community, the Negro may be let off lightly or not be sentenced at all. If he is Mr. Black's nigger and Mr. Black is a man of no importance, the Negro will receive harsher treatment. If he has no white folks at all his fate is in the lap of the gods. [31]

Paralleling the tendency on the part of the slaves to laud their "white folks" there was a tendency on the part of members of the master family to excuse the faults and delinquencies of their Negroes. Thacker says, "In our part of the world, a mistress became offended if the faults of her servants were alluded to, just as persons become displeased when the faults of their children are discussed." [32] Evidently in such a situation as this the slave was an integral part of the master's life. Within the plantation there was a reciprocal accommodation of the races, and what prejudice existed was expressed toward the free Negro rather than toward the slave. The masterless Negro was a dangerous Negro, just as the dangerous dog is the dog without a master. The free Negro, like the present-day Negro in the South without "white folks," or without some white patron, represented that vague and feared category *the* Negro. For it has never been true that the white man in the South knows the Negro; it is more exact to say, as James Weldon Johnson has pointed out, that the Southern white man knows Negroes: "that is, he knows Jim and Dan and Uncle Eph and Uncle Mose and Aunt Chloe and Aunt Sue." These Negroes are "darkies"; male Negroes without white folks are "buck niggers."

VII

Not physical and social isolation merely but co-operative activity within the physical structure of the plantation determines its culture and its social organization. Social organization is the organization of distances and of differences between individuals and groups. It exists for the purpose of controlling and directing the activities of individuals in order to bring about corporate action. Teggart speaks of culture as the result of a process of "cultivation." [33] When applied to a plantation community the expression is peculiarly appropriate for it links together land, agriculture, and culture. By the process of cultivation, or the cultural process, is meant the process by which the people who compose a community acquire, not so much opinions, as folkways and mores. It is a process which goes on beneath the level of public consciousness in the more intimate contacts and conflicts of persons and groups.

Day by day, season by season, and year by year the object of common activity and a chief bond between the various elements on the plantation is the crop. From seedtime to harvest, each season brings its round of activities.[34] Individuals, of course, develop the habits appropriate to their divisions of labor in connection with these activities, but what is more important is the fact that co-operative activities deposit in individuals a common experience. Originally of different race and culture these individuals are united for the immediate purpose at hand, and the result is, eventually, a new and common culture. It is the sort of experience for which "we" and "our" are the appropriate expressions. Writing of the plantation upon which she grew up, Page Thacker speaks of "the manner of our servants [slaves] identifying themselves with the master and his possessions, always speaking of 'our horses,' 'our cows,' 'our crop,' 'our mill,' 'our blacksmith shop,' 'our carriage,' 'our black people.' " [35]

An essential part of human culture is a language held in common and evolved by those who have to deal with others in carrying on a common life. Indeed, the culture may be said to be contained in a language whose meanings are the same for all. "Communication by spoken word," says Malinowski, "is indispensable for any concerted activity and enters into all aspects of culture as a working element." [36]

Now the sort of language that arises to meet the needs of the individuals originally representing different language groups who have come together, or have been brought together, must be understood against the background of the particular sort of activities in which they are engaged. These activities depend, of course, upon the purpose for which the individuals concerned have come together. Where the purpose is to buy and to sell, there may result a language of business, like Chinook or Pidgin, adapted to the activities and embodying the meanings of buying and selling. But where the purpose is industrial rather than commercial, where production requires the co-ordinated efforts of numbers of men, language becomes an even more important instrument for securing unified action. In a political organization like that of the plantation there is the further fact that purposes and directions have to be communicated from a higher class to a lower class, from a planter to a laborer. In this, the plantation situation resembles that of a military organization. Unified action is secured in a situation in which officers are accustomed to give orders and common soldiers are accustomed to take them. On Southern plantations the language in which orders were given, modified and simplified, became the language in which orders were received. It was a language of command, and it resulted in what students of language have called a Creole language.[37]

A Creole language arises in politically controlled groups in colonial areas, in an atmosphere of authority and obedience, where masters "talk down" to those under them. Of one such language, a dialect spoken by Negroes along the coast of South Carolina and Georgia, Johnson writes: "This strange dialect turns out to be little more than the peasant English of two centuries ago, modified to meet the needs of the slaves. From Midland and Southern England came planters, artisans, shopkeepers, indentured servants, all of whom had more or less contact with the slaves, and the speech of these poorer white folk was so rustic that their more cultured countrymen had difficulty in understanding them. From this peasant speech and from the 'baby talk' used by masters in addressing them, the Negroes developed that dialect, sometimes known as Gullah, which remains the characteristic feature of the culture of the Negroes of coastal South Carolina and Georgia." [38]

"It is not generally known," says Whitney, "that in some parts of the South, 'befo' de wah,' every large plantation had its own individual dialect. So distinct were these that a planter, by engaging a Negro in conversation, could tell at once who was his owner, or, as he would be likely to express it, whether he belonged to Poshee, Indian Field, Woodlawn, Saracen's, Mexico, etc., these being the names of some of the plantations where the dialects were distinct." [39]

During the period of the foreign slave trade, and for a long time after, all the Negroes on Southern plantations must have spoken a language very similar to Gullah or to Gombo, the Creole dialect of Louisiana. But where the plantations and farms were smaller than they were in the rice and sugar areas and where relations between whites and blacks were closer, language assimilation became much more complete, and purely local dialects were more or less destroyed.

More important than dialect, however, is the fact that the language of the situation was a language of command. Fanny Kemble and other observers from outside the South have noted the whites' "habitual tone of command." This fact becomes very important when it is recognized that language not only expresses thought but also determines thought because, as Mead often pointed out in his writings, through language we address ourselves "in terms of the common ideas and functions which an organized society makes possible." [40] This means that language is bound up with the system of social control. With its acquisition there tends to develop at the same time an acceptance of the situation. The meanings of the terms of the language develop in the general atmosphere of authority and against the background of cooperative activity involved in agricultural production. As this takes place, authority and obedience are determined more by moral and less by material factors. Henceforth the force which controls is that which those ẁho are controlled themselves in large part supply. The plantation gets a *Sittlichkeit* wherein the relations between planter and laborer come to be regarded by both as an entirely normal and even inevitable condition of things. Inequality is assumed as part of the established order and both planter and laborer acquiesce in the arrangements and accommodate themselves to them.

It is in the sort of literature in which the slave plantation's fundamental quality of naturalness is revealed that some insight into the culture of plantation society is gained. Its culture is suggested, for example, so far as the Negro slave element of that society is concerned, in such a document as that written by "Monk" Lewis, an Englishman, on the occasion of his visit in the early part of the nineteenth century to his plantation in Jamaica which he had never seen. The following passages are quoted from his *Journal:*

After reaching the lodging-house at Savannah la Mar, a remarkably clean-looking negro lad presented himself with some water and a towel: I concluded him to belong to the inn; and, on my returning the towel, as he found that I took no notice of him, he at length ventured to introduce himself by saying,—"Massa not know me; *me your slave!*" —and really the sound made me feel a pang at the heart. The lad appeared all gaiety and good humor, and his whole countenance expressed anxiety to recommend himself to my notice; but the word "slave" seemed to imply, that, although he did feel pleasure then in serving me, if he had detested me he must have served me still. I really felt quite humiliated at the moment, and was tempted to tell him. "Do not say that again; say that you are my negro, but do not call yourself my slave."

As I was returning this morning from Montego Bay, about a mile from my own estate, a figure presented itself before me, I really think the most picturesque that I ever beheld: it was a mulatto girl, born upon Cornwall, but whom the overseer of a neighboring estate had obtained my permission to exchange for another slave, as well as two little children, whom she had born to him; but, as yet, he had been unable to procure a substitute, owing to the difficulty of purchasing single negroes, and Mary Wiggins is still my slave. However, as she is considered as being manumitted, she had not dared to present herself at Cornwall on my arrival, lest she should have been considered as an intruder; but she now threw herself in my way to tell me how glad she was to see me, for that she had always thought till now (which is the general complaint) that *"she had no massa"*; and also to obtain a regular invitation to my negro festival tomorrow. By this universal complaint, it appears that, while Mr. Wilberforce is lamenting their hard fate in being subject to a master, *their* greatest fear is the not having a master whom they know; and that to be told by the negroes of another estate that "they belong to no massa," is one of the most contemptuous reproaches that can be cast upon them.[41]

In much of the literature of plantation society what is actually said is usually not nearly so interesting or so revealing as what is taken for granted; the culture is most significantly shown by what can be read between the lines. It is for this reason that such a document as "The Diary of a Young Man of Fashion in 1850" is so important.[42] It is the diary of Lestant Prudhomme, a young man who lived on his father's plantation near Natchitoches, Louisiana. While studying law he kept a diary in order to train himself to write fluently in English as his family was of French descent. Behind his gossipy remarks, his comments on the weather, and the goings and comings of his daily life, one can glimpse a culture in which there was a strong sense of house, of kinsmen, and of firm ties that went back, ultimately, to the land. It was a society where cousins counted, and where there was a great deal of visiting back and forth. A member of one of these families was almost as much at home in the home of a cousin as he was in the home of his parents. But especially noticeable was the absence of any definite interracial mood. Lyle Saxon says of young Prudhomme:

He has lived on a plantation all his life, and is so accustomed to the goings and comings of the negro slaves that he never mentions them, except in the most casual way; one would think he did not see them at all. And yet we know that he had his own personal servant, a body-servant so-called, who awakened him in the morning by bringing coffee to his bed, who did the thousand and one things which he wished done, and who accompanied him frequently on his trips over the country. Never once does he tell us of this man. . . . The negroes did not exist, as far as he was concerned, any more than the furniture around him. They were part of the picture. One would never know that they were there, except for the occasional mention of buying or selling them.[43]

Prudhomme's diary discloses the planter's assumption of superiority and mastership with a patrician's quietude. These assumptions were the overtones of his type and character.

The quality of naturalness appears again and from another direction in the letters and reports of the succession of overseers on the slave plantation of President Polk in Mississippi. Of the letters of one of these overseers Bassett says:

We have gone far enough into the plantation life as depicted in Beanland's letters to understand that slavery was just slavery. It was neither the thing of horror the abolitionists thought nor the benign institution its defenders depicted. It was a relation whereby men who had work to be done got workers to do it. From the standpoint of the laborers it was a form of service in which men worked and got the sustenance that their masters decided necessary for their wants. Beanland had no delusions about slavery. He seems to have had no idea that it was an institution. With him it was only a question of Jack, Ben, Caesar, and Gilbert. For them he did what good mastership demanded, make them obey, fed and clothed them, and tried to get them "to make a crop" for his employer, contending all the while against the uncertainties of season and health.[44]

Of course not all planters and overseers took their positions and their relations with their Negro slaves for granted. And, of course, not all slaves accepted their lot without protest. They did sometimes plot, rebel, and run away. The plantation system produced its disturbing elements which could neither be assimilated nor thrown out. But the documentary evidence points clearly to the fact that before the Civil War a plantation culture had been achieved. As a result of that war, slavery was swept away, but the habits and attitudes of racial accommodation implicit in the slave system have not entirely been destroyed. In spite of the fact that economic and social changes in the plantation South since emancipation have been many and of great consequence, these changes must not be exaggerated. Underneath all, the old plantation pattern continues on in the so-called New South. Even the divergent tendencies have to be understood against the background of this pattern.

VIII

The isolation of plantation life and activities established social and personality types such as that of the planter, the overseer, "Uncle Remus," "Uncle Tom," the driver, the mammy, the field hand, etc. The traits of the type were possessed by individuals who were, on the whole, not dissatisfied or ashamed of their roles. Otherwise they would not have constituted types. After the abolition of slavery, however, as an incident of mobility and freedom, Negroes began to depart from type, a change which whites resented and tried, in various ways, to prevent. It was because of this departure that the old type was idealized. In the Jeff Davis Museum in Richmond, Virginia, there was formerly an exhibit dedicated to the "old-time Negro who is rapidly passing away." It was a scene on a plantation where Negroes were going about their business and were happy and content.[45]

However, the old-time Negro, or at least the characteristics of the old-time Negro, persisted in the post-bellum South. After the Civil War and the abolition of slavery those Negroes who had been slaves moved around a good deal but remained, for the most part, on the land and formed a class of peasant farmers. Those Negroes who had been free before the War, or who in other ways had been favored by reason of education or natural ability, assumed racial leadership and gravitated to the cities of both the South and the North if they were not already in them. These urban Negroes have since been joined by a rather considerable migration of Negroes from rural areas and from villages and towns. As they entered new trades, occupations, and professions in the cities, and as they became a factor in industry, they developed new conceptions of themselves and acquired new personalities and new so-called racial traits. With the coming of these new types, the Negro who remained on the plantation became, by contrast, "the plantation Negro."

At a time when urban Negroes were becoming sophisticated and race conscious and developing the mannerisms that go with city life their brothers, engaged on the plantations in the crudest forms of unskilled labor, remained naïve and unsophisticated. That is, they continued to behave more or less without consciousness of the comment which their folk behavior excited in the minds of others. They have continued to behave in such a way as to reveal immediately the isolated world of the plantation to which they belong. This is not merely the behavior of the rustic; it is also the behavior of a member of a race who knows and accepts his place and conducts himself deferentially toward his "betters" of the other race.

Even in the heart of the plantation South, observers have noticed the difference between the Negroes in the towns and the Negroes on the plantations, a difference sufficient to make town Negroes appear to one observer as almost "of another race."

The "town Negroes" are markedly different. In Vicksburg I know of Negroes acting successfully as ministers, teachers, physicians, and dentists to their own race, and to both races as trained nurses, cooks, nursemaids, plumbers, carpenters, plasterers, dressmakers, store clerks, mail carriers, chauffeurs, mechanics, painters and paperhangers, brick masons, and truck drivers. . . .

One of my cooks was an interesting example of the difference between "field Negroes" and "town Negroes." Effie had been born on a plantation, but at the age of six she was taken to Vicksburg by the daughter of the planter for whom her mother worked, and brought up as the playmate of a little white girl. This meant that she was kept seasonably and neatly dressed, shared the meals of her little charge, played with the same toys, learned to read and write at the same time, had attention paid to her speech and manners, and for ten years was exposed to all the influences of a refined and pleasant home. I sometimes saw Effie's mother and sisters when they trudged in from the country, typical, dull, awkward, ugly, slovenly field Negroes. But Effie was immaculate in her person and clothing, dainty and attractive in appearance and carriage, intelligent, courteous, able to read simple books, and to write and spell fully as well as the average ten-year-old public-school child, an advanced degree of erudition for a Mississippi Negro. The difference in environment and training made Effie seem of another race from her "cornfield relations." [46]

The plantation as an institution, like every other institution, tends to pass over into, and become a part of, the personal life of its individual members. It becomes a state of mind. As a state of mind, a feudal attitude, and a pattern of race relations, the plantation may live on apart from its physical structure long after its legal and constitutional foundations have been radically changed. T. S. Matthews contributes an authentic story which exhibits the plantation in the heart of New York City.

Two old darkies, a man and his wife, have come to New York to look for a job. They have lived on a Southern plantation all of their lives and the city and its ways are strange to them. Someone has told them that the best thing to do is to go to an employment agency.

They stand before the desk in the office, and give their names and addresses. The man is asked what kind of work he is accustomed to.

"Well, suh," he says, "mos'ly I looks foh Massa's specs."

The employment agent stares at him, and then turns to the old woman.

"What can you do?"

"Mos'ly I shoos de flies off Missus." [47]

For whites and Negroes who have once been a part of the plantation tradition the past is an involuntary foundation and on it, whether they wish to or not, they have to build.[48] Both the white and Negro types of the present appear to be outgrowths and transformations of earlier types. They range all the way from the white so-called "professional Southerner," who believes that the past was better than the present and who is most in character when outside the South where there are none over whom he can be master, to the so-called New Negro who is in conscious rebellion against the stigma of everything associated with the plantation. The New Negro is not merely a different but an opposite Negro, opposite from the "plantation Negro," or at least struggling to become so.[49] Unlike the plantation Negro, who in his relationship with whites ordinarily acts in terms of personal expectations and obligations, the New Negro, living in a more formal and secondary world, is concerned about his rights. He is concerned about his rights because rights are connected with status and his status is uncertain and precarious. In various social and race movements he is trying to achieve another primary order in which he can again feel at home. In the meantime he is taking the struggle for his rights back to the plantations of the South and making fresh attacks upon a system which already is upon the defensive.

II

Race: A Situational Emergent

The planter in the West Indies stereotype

• 5 •

The Plantation as a Race-Making
Situation

The plantation is a form of organization producing staple crops for an outside, usually an overseas, market. Severe international competition has tended to press heavily on production costs, especially labor costs, and plantation labor has been recruited halfway around the world. Almost every plantation society has put some new combination of men to work—generally, but not always, under white planters or overseers. Thus, one characteristic of the plantation is a labor problem which tends eventually to be defined also as a race problem. The plantation is a race-making situation.

When the planter begins to import an industrial army of occupation and to settle it upon the land, the characteristic outlines of the plantation begin to appear. The plantation is first a settlement institution; it is a form of camp capitalism on an island or at the edge of a settlement where free land is to be had but which is still accessible to the market. In the South the planter imported his labor first from England, then from Africa, and did with it about as he pleased without reference to the native mores. In Hawaii, on the other hand, he had to take the wishes of the monarch into account and bring in only what were called peoples "cognate" to the Hawaiian peoples, i.e., Gilbert Islanders and then Chinese. In such places as Hawaii where the planters were unable to continue their original contractual controls over imported laborers, such laborers left the plantations upon the expiration of their contracts and set up intermediate businesses in the

SOURCE In Leonard Broom and Phillip Selznick, *Sociology: A Text With Adapted Readings.* Harper and Row, 1955, pp. 506–7.

towns and cities, businesses too small for members of the planter class to bother with. Their ranks were filled by new importees, perhaps from another country.

In Virginia there was a succession from white indentured servants from England to African Negroes, but here the succession of ethnics stopped. The African slave trade was never large enough to satisfy the demand, and after 1808 by provision of the Constitution the legal importation of Negro slaves was forbidden. Under the circumstances the supply of plantation labor had to be maintained, if it was to be maintained at all, by preventing the children of the Negroes from responding to the ordinary opportunities for upward mobility presented by the frontier. Lifelong servitude began with the second generation. Slavery was calculated to keep a Negro in a state of perpetual childhood, to keep him tied to a master wherever the master might go rather than to a particular piece of land, and to keep him and his offspring in their place forever. Slavery was the Southern analogue of Hawaii's labor succession.

Slavery, and other forms of forced labor similar to it, brought with it problems of control which the idea of race measurably solved so far as the planter was concerned. The naked force of the planter was never sufficient to keep men working at low place. There had to develop some kind of myth, like race, which not only those who ruled but those who are ruled accepted. It was not sufficient to assert the superiority of the white man and the inferiority of the black man; it was much more important to persuade the black man to accept the allegation of his own inferiority. This is what the idea of race achieved. In the situation the idea of race did not exist merely to effect a separation between peoples; it did this incident to its major function of control. As the cultural differences between whites and Negroes receded, visible physical differences loomed larger to become the chief marks around which to organize doctrines and beliefs of deeper biological differences.

Before World War II Japanese plantation authorities and planters in Taiwan [Formosa] had a very low opinion of the Chinese laborers on the large sugar estates there. "They were lazy, they were untrustworthy, they were irresponsible." These are the same statements that white planters in the South make about their Negro tenants and sharecroppers and have long made about Negroes generally. In Taiwan the principal parties were neither white nor Negro. Instead they were people whom we in America are disposed to classify together as Orientals. All this suggests that conceptions of race, under whatever name, are not conceptions necessarily brought to the situation out of the white man's culture and put into force by the white planter. The suggestion is strong here that *the idea of race is a situational imperative;* if it is not there to begin with, it tends to develop in a plantation society because it is a useful, maybe necessary, principle of control. In Virginia the plantation took two peoples originally differentiated as Christian and heathen, and before the first century was over it had made two races.

• 6 •

Language and Race Relations

I

Consideration of the connection between language and race immediately calls to mind the work of Friedrich Müller during the second half of the nineteenth century on the Aryan tongues.[1] Müller indirectly and unwittingly helped establish, particularly in Germany, the idea of an Aryan race by accepting language as a basis of racial classification because it seemed to him other criteria had proved unsatisfactory. Even without such scholarly support, however, the assumption that "of one tongue" is the same as "of one blood" was and continues to be a rather widespread one. It is very natural that this should seem to be so, for the observation of speech regularities in different human groupings is one of the most elementary of all observations. "Habituation to a given type of speech," said Veblen, "comes to do duty as a conventional mark of racial derivation. A certain (virtual) uniformity of habit is taken to mean a uniformity of hereditary endowment." [2] The ear classifies and gives unity to the speech that is heard as the eye classifies and gives unity to the physical traits that are seen.

The symbolizing of group membership is a normal function of language but otherwise it has, since Müller's day, been found to be as unsatisfactory as many other criteria for the scientific classification of race. It is, however, becoming more and more important in the study and understanding of race relations. In his various writings and lectures Robert E. Park implicitly if not explicitly raised the question as to the extent to which the prob-

SOURCE In J. Masuoka and Preston Valien (eds.), *Race Relations: Theories and Problems*, University of North Carolina Press, 1961, pp. 228–51.

lems of sociology, many of them at any rate, result from an inadequate analysis of the nature of communication, language, and thought. Park shared with Dewey, Mead, Cooley, and others the view that human society is dependent upon the development of communication, especially language, for its distinctive form of organization, but he seemed to feel that in its group-defining and relation-defining function language went far beyond this general discovery. This paper attempts to bring together some of what I remember from Dr. Park's lectures, the work of my own students and friends,[3] and materials I have gathered from an interesting body of literature on the so-called expediency languages [4] to suggest what seems to be the real nature of the connection between language and race relations.

In most general texts on language there will be found a chapter or a few pages on what are variously termed emergency, helping, make-shift, mongrel, *sabir*, auxiliary, compromise, mixed, bro kendown, bastard, minimum, marginal, hodgepodge, automatic, pidgin, or creole languages. The chapter or pages usually will be found toward the back of the book, and often the reader feels that some discussion of this "baby talk of mankind" is included only in the interest of comprehensiveness rather than from a sense of its importance. Often it is not mentioned at all. It may be, however, that a clearer conception of the nature and function of language can come through the back doors by way of these low status tongues rather than through the established and respectable literary languages such as Greek and English. For these tongues are not mere linguistic freaks with quaint and curious ways of saying things. On the contrary, they seem to lay bare elementary processes of communication and group formation. Moreover, they contribute to, if they do not actually determine, the differentiation of peoples in contact *into* opposing groups identifying each other as racial groups. They should, therefore, enable us better to understand the process of sociological race-making.

For convenience, and because the term is as good as any, I propose to refer to these languages as emergency languages.[5] Some general statements can be made about them. They are languages of the frontier where men of different physiognomies, cultures, and vocabularies meet for the first time and for some practical purpose. They have to be simple and inclusive enough to be learned by everyone subject to a situation which is new to them and perhaps new to the world. Their formation thus becomes an expression of, and a device for, social change. They are not, therefore, "complete" such as are the languages of the metropolis which must serve the needs of numerous occupational groups and social classes living close together.[6] There is in the emergency languages relatively little connective tissue between the words, and in this respect they differ markedly, of course, from the "tapeworm languages," as Rudolf Flesch calls them, such as English, German, and Latin. They are not originally languages of state, school, or church and are likely to be opposed by the authorities in these institutions. However, under the influence of nationalism, they later may officially be accepted and even encouraged.

The emergency languages are not originally literate languages since those who use them are not consciously concerned with transmitting a record of their traditions and achievements to posterity. They are the languages of men who talk rather than write, of men who must communicate with each other under stress of necessity. They serve the needs of the immediate present and are not oriented as yet toward a past and a future. Hence they are languages of action stressing quick, short words used in the present tense. Unlike the eyebound languages of the literate peoples, those who use the emergency languages catch them on the fly by ear. They are not just local dialects of the established languages. They are not fossil languages such as Latin or Sanskrit, and they are not hot-house languages such as Basic English, Esperanto, or Volapük. On the contrary, they are living languages at work, and each has to be understood in terms of the situation in which it arises and which it in turn helps define. An important consideration is the fact that they sometimes grow up within the lifetime of single individuals who later are able to tell the story of their formation and growth. The origin of the established languages, on the other hand, may be lost in antiquity.

II

Languages have been classified by scholars in several different ways and for several different purposes. There are genetic classifications and there are morphological classifications, each more or less adequate for the purposes of those linguists and philologists who study language apart from social situations and apart from its users, but not adequate for the purposes of sociologists who are concerned with language in the context of society. The sociology of language will develop its principle or principles of classification from the standpoint of the place and function of language in society. Dr. Park was fond of quoting Dewey's statement that "society not only continues to exist *by* transmission, *by* communication, but it may fairly be said to exist *in* transmission, *in* communication." [7] Communication establishes community in the sense that the members of the group come to understand things in the same way. Communication, according to Dewey, is the experience of meaning, and meaning is the common property which a symbol acquires when it is significant in the same way to all who use it. Thus what the sociologist has to discover is: What are the conditions under which consciousness of meaning attaching to certain vocal gestures and symbols arises? What are these meanings or systems of meanings? Using meaning as a principle of classification, what significant distinctions not exhibited by linguistic and philological classifications can be arrived at? [8] A consideration of language in relation to collective action and to the situation in which collective action is framed may suggest answers to these and similar questions.

"Action is first," Dr. Park said in one of his papers, "but the effect of action is to create an action pattern." [9] It may be suggested that action gets patterned as it gets into the language or as the language gets into it. Permanence of the pattern necessarily means that there has to be machinery for making each member of the group continually aware of the expectations of other members upon him and for inducing in him some sense of obligation to meet these expectations. Grace DeLaguna was one of the first to make clear the place of language as "the great medium through which human cooperation is brought about," [10] for the terms of the language signal the expectations of others and cue the performance of one's own obligations. Language thus orchestrates the different behaviors of individuals toward the achievement of common goals and purposes. The process was documented by Malinowski in his account of the activities of a fishing expedition in the Trobriand Islands. I think the account is worth quoting at length:

. . . Let us follow up a party of fishermen on a coral lagoon, spying for a shoal of fish, trying to imprison them in an enclosure of large nets, and to drive them into small net-bags. . . .

The canoes glide slowly and noiselessly, punted by men especially good at this task and always used for it. Other experts who know the bottom of the lagoon with its plant and animal life are on the lookout for fish. One of them sights the quarry. Customary signs, or sounds or words are uttered. Sometimes a sentence full of technical references to the channels or patches on the lagoon has to be spoken; sometimes when the shoal is near and the task of trapping is simple, a conventional cry is uttered not too loudly. Then, the whole fleet stops and ranges itself—every canoe and every man in it performing his appointed task —according to a customary routine. But, of course, the men, as they act, utter now and then a sound expressing keeness in the pursuit or impatience at some technical difficulty, joy of achievement or disappointment at failure. Again, a word of command is passed here and there, a technical expression or explanation which serves to harmonise their behaviour towards other men. The whole group acts in a concerted manner, determined by old tribal tradition and perfectly familiar to the actors through life-long experience. Some men in the canoes cast the wide encircling nets into the water, others plunge, and wading through the shallow lagoon, drive the fish into the nets. Others again stand by with small nets, ready to catch the fish. An animated scene full of movement follows, and now that the fish are in their power the fishermen speak loudly, and give vent to their feelings. Short, telling exclamations fly about, which might be rendered by such words as: "Pull in," "Let go," "Shift further," "Lift the net"; or again technical expressions completely untranslatable except by minute description of the instruments used, and of the mode of action.[11]

It is apparent that what we have reached in our argument is consciousness of meaning attached to vocal gestures for the purpose of enabling individuals to coordinate their activities. "Each utterance," Malinowski goes on to say, "is essentially bound up with the context of situation." Indeed it is, but what makes possible the use of meaning as a principle of language classification is the observation that communication requires or involves some shift in meaning with each shift in the "context of situation." It is the situation that presents the background against which men are set to act together, but the situation, as Thomas taught us long ago, requires definition. Men must have a more or less clear conception of the conditions they have to cope with as they undertake to act together for particular purposes. The terms of the language acquire meaning in terms of the situation and meaning in turn helps complete or "define" the situation.[12] Is it possible to identify types of meaning-situations each with its appropriate language?

Some of them have been identified and named, but the classification and analysis are far from complete. Without presuming to close the list I wish to call attention to three types of meaning-languages to which reference is made under one name or another in the literature.[13] I shall call them we-languages, trade languages, and command languages. All three of these languages may utilize the vocabulary of a single national tongue—English, for instance—in, say, the conversation in the family circle, the impersonal business letter, and the military order of a regimental commander. It is conceivable that many of the same words may be used in these three situations but their meanings in context are so different that they may be said to be three different languages. Much the same vocabulary may be used but there may be no effective intersituational communication; as we say, people "talk past" each other. On the other hand, speaking the same "language" is not necessarily the same thing as speaking the same tongue, that is, using the same vocabulary. The common meanings and feelings of friendship, kinship, and other relationships of intimacy may be expressed, of course, in countless vocabularies. However, the meaning-languages do tend to become separated into different vocabularies when people of different cultural and speech backgrounds come together in the same territory and have to cooperate to carry on a common life.

There is an interesting example of this in the *Reminiscences* of Carl Schurz in which this eminent German-American compared the language of his fatherland with that of his adopted country:

I have often been asked in which language I preferred to think and write. I always answered that this depended on the subject, the purpose, and the occasion. On the whole, I preferred the English language for public speaking, partly on account of the simplicity of its syntactic construction, and partly because the pronunciation of the consonants is mechanically easier and less fatiguing to the speaker. I have preferred it also for the discussion of political subjects and of business affairs because of its full and precise terminology. But for the discussion of philosophical matters, for poetry, and for familiar, intimate conversation I have preferred the German. And beyond this, I have found that about certain subjects, or with certain persons who understood both English and German equally well, I would rather speak in English or in German, as the case might be, without clearly knowing the reason why. It was a matter of feeling which cannot be exactly defined.[14]

Of course, Carl Schurz preferred his native German for the discussion of philosophical matters, for poetry, and for familiar intimate conversation, and he preferred English for public and business affairs, but perhaps not for the reasons he gave. If the situation had been reversed, if he had been an American of English-speaking parents who adopted Germany as his homeland, he probably would have viewed the comparative uses and advantages of German and English differently. In an analogous situation Henriqueta Chamberlain, during her childhood in Portuguese-speaking Brazil, viewed English in very much the same way Schurz regarded German. She wrote: "I was convinced that English was a sacred language. I heard it spoken only by my missionary parents and friends. It was quite a shock to me when I first heard an American businessman casually speaking English." [15]

III

These statements suggest that the prototype of the we-language is the *lingua madre,* the language of one's mother. One has only one real mother-tongue as one has only one real mother. Bilingual individuals such as Carl Schurz and Henriqueta Chamberlain in the personal and intimate situation are inclined to revert to the vocabulary in which the earliest block of memories and sentiments is stored, that is, to the language learned in the bosom of the family. It is the language into which many bilingual persons find it pleasant to fall back into for rest after prolonged and tiring use of the second speech. It is particularly worthy of note that language in this situation is, in addition to the active, referential function it possesses and which Malinowski's account illustrates, also in some considerable measure, an end in itself. Man is a chattering animal, and his chattering is not only a sociable kind of noise, "the grateful sign of kindred presence," but in the family it comes to be charged with sentiment and with pathos. Pronunciation, or the tune of the language, is important here. In their helpless way children cannot avoid naïvely and literally imitating both the words and the tune of the language model set before them by their parents and elders. This pronunciation and intonation tends to become the folk norm of correct speech and to become linked with the warmer feelings of trustfulness, devotion, and gratitude toward one's parents.

Any small group, if its members are squeezed together tightly enough and over a long enough period of time, will tend to reproduce the roles and behaviors of family members regardless of age and sex composition and to generate a meaning-language appropriate to primary group relationships. As the group sets itself against other groups its members discover in their shared experiences something valuable which they wish to preserve. They tend to think of themselves in terms they do not ordinarily apply to others out there. "We" have spiritual and human qualities and needs; "they" have only physical and material qualities and needs. Individuals in our group are particularized and treated as ends in themselves, and our language expresses the subtleties and nuances of the relationships between them. It is not just *a* language; it is *our* language, the language of human beings. The language of those outside, or what they call a language, is the language of people who babble and answer to silly names; they are barbarians even when they use much the same vocabulary. But in our language we know ourselves as brothers and sisters or as comrades or as fellow countrymen. In it we make love and say our prayers,[16] and in it, too, is written our poetry, our oratory, and our history. It is a common observation that the sentiment of nationalism and the sentiment of language go together. At the time we discover our people, we discover at that same time the language of our people, and the continuing life of one is bound up in the continuing life of the other.

One may resent the use of the we-language on the part of an outsider regarded as an inferior person, a servant or a slave, thus making it a snob language and using it as a principle of exclusion. In Indonesia it formerly "was considered an impertinence for a native to speak Dutch," [17] and in South Africa, according to Maurice S. Evans, "many English-speaking colonists seem to have a repugnance to hearing the natives using the English language, and go so far as to decline to carry on a conversation in it." [18]

The attitude of the Christian missionary on the frontier is just the opposite. Desiring to extend into native tribal life the high values of his faith, he faces a language problem very different from that of the administrator, planter, or trader. How can he translate the abstract concepts and values of his religion into terms comprehensible to the natives? He can organize schools for religious instruction in English, French, German, or Spanish and he has done this but at the cost of considerable effort, time, and money. He can try to put his message into the emergency language of the area but, as Margaret Mead has pointed out, "the gentler doctrines of Christianity, in pidgin, become obscured or smothered under words which are coined by missionaries and have no native equivalent to give them body. . . . When the missionaries preach and translate the Bible into pidgin, they make some effort to smooth out the crudities of the language, but in the hands of the boys these all crop up again." [19] So the fundamental solution of the problem requires the missionary to move into the native speech, into the heart of the we-language. Bridging the vocabulary gap missionaries everywhere have been in the forefront of the movement to reduce local and native tongues to writing, and as a by-product a considerable amount of prime ethnological material has come from their efforts.

IV

These remarks on the language problems of the missionary bring us back to the various meaning-situations of the frontier and to the emergency languages which these situations generate as meaning-languages. The we-language begins in the interaction between parents and children in the family. Trade and command languages, on the other hand, develop in adult relationships. I address myself first to the trade language.

What are the characteristics of trade and of the trading situation? Perhaps I cannot do better than to quote Park in answer to this question:

The conditions under which men buy and sell, have undoubtedly had a profound influence on human relations and upon human nature. Not all that is characteristically human is the product, as Cooley seems to say, of man's relations in the primary group. Men go to market and women too, not as they go to church, namely, to revive a sense of their social solidarity and of their participation in a common destiny. One meets at the market place, not friends merely, but strangers, possibly enemies. They have all, each motivated by interests presumably personal to himself, come together because they need one another and because, by an exchange of goods and services, they hope not only to satisfy their own needs but also profit by the needs of others. Besides, the market place, aside from the mere social excitement of being a member of the crowd, offers the prospect of hearing the latest news, and that is always an interest that is as intriguing to primitive as to more sophisticated peoples. There is, also, the consideration that in the market one may have, among strangers, a better chance to drive a bargain since it is always difficult to bargain with friends and relatives. On the other hand, it is notoriously easy and interesting to trade with strangers. It is even possible, under certain circumstances, to carry on a rather brisk trade with the enemy.

. . . The situation in which men bargain and chaffer is psychologically complex and tricky, and for that reason, perhaps the capacity to trade is one of the last of the fundamental human traits that mankind has acquired. Among the many definitions of man that seek to identify him with, but at the same time distinguish him from, the other animals is that which describe him as a trading animal. Man is the only animal that has learned to dicker and trade. But trade is necessarily a complex affair since it requires that one know, at the same instant, both his own mind and that of the other party. Each must understand the need of the other in order that each may make for himself the best bargain. This is inevitably the case because in this unique form of cooperation one man's necessity is another man's opportunity. But at the same time one does not wish to know the other party and his necessity too well either. One must, if possible, remain objective. It is for this reason, among others, that trade has so frequently gotten into the hands of foreigners. It is easier to be objective if one maintains the normal distances.[20]

The trader is the active agent in the situation. He comes to the trading frontiers without family attachments and leaves behind him a progeny born of native women. Often he finds it to his business advantage to take a native wife,[21] and he endeavors to acquaint himself with some of the terms of the native speech for the same reason. That old rule of the market, let the buyer beware, comes to figure in the conception of the trader, as it does also of the money lender, as a born cheat and liar, and it is easy to extend this conception to include traders and their families as a class. It is a class of people stereotyped as one given to fraud and deception as an attribute of its original nature. It is a criminal tribe, a race of swindlers. The Metics in ancient Greece, the Scotsman in early America, the Yankee in later America and in present-day Latin America, the Indian in Africa, and the Armenian in the Near East gained reputations for extraordinary shrewdness, cleverness, and mastery of commercial manipulation. Throughout Europe, as well as in America and elsewhere, the Jew has felt the force of this attitude as have the Chinese in Southeast Asia. Where these traders have insinuated themselves into peasant and tribal worlds hostile to them, they have become races apart, particularly when the traders in their turn come to characterize their peasant customers as people of low and cunning habit. Moreover, it is well to have members of an alien race in middleman occupations for they can more easily be blamed for wild price fluctuations and attacked more readily.

It is surprising how few words are required to effect trade. The Plains Indians of America traded by means of a sign language and the so-called silent trade of other primitives seems to have required little more than signals exchanged at a distance.[22] When trade becomes highly standardized it is possible to employ vending machines dispensing with vocal language altogether. Such words as are needed in the trading situation may be almost as characterless as the money used in the transaction itself; both are mere media of exchange. But the trade language has to be sufficient to effect the reciprocal activities incident to buying, selling, or bartering and it has to contain the basic meanings having to do with economic value, money, price, number, weight, quality, the various wares, services of trade, etc. The particular vocabulary embodying these meanings does not much matter.

The people of two speech communities may use the vocabulary of a third as a trade language. It is interesting to note that *lingua franca,* a term now used almost exclusively to denote any interlanguage, seems originally to have arisen as a trade language between European and Moslem traders and seamen. It is said that the English regarded the Dutch of New Netherlands as only a speech for merchants and traders. In other parts of the world the English vocabulary at times has been similarly regarded by the trade rivals of the English.

There seems to be a disposition in the literature to designate all the various trade languages as "pidgin" languages. Pidgin is said to derive from the Chinese mispronunciation of the English word "business," and the jargon which developed around Canton before 1842 came to be known as pidgin-English. Canton bookshops sold a booklet entitled *Devil's Talk, or a Vocabulary of Words in Use Among Redhaired People.* On the cover of the booklet was a picture of one of the "redhaired," that is, an Englishman. Of the trade or pidgin languages generally, Reinecke says:

They vary from artificial and clean-cut languages such as the Chinook Jargon and Cantonese-English to partial simplifications as the Nahuatl-Spanish. They may last centuries, or they may be useful only for one season. There is a minimum cultural limit to their formation: they cannot arise where the people are too fragmented, low in culture and mutually hostile or suspicious to carry on a fairly regular intertribal trade. But on the other hand they are current in trade between men of very advanced nations: Italians and North Africans, Norwegians and Russians, English and Chinese, formerly, it is said, English and Dutch, and Low Germans and Scandinavians. . . . Widespread literacy on both sides is less favorable to their formation than is general illiteracy. The essential conditions for their formation are the absence of interpreters, the absence of manuals of either language, a pressing need to establish communication before a systematic study can be made of the language of the other group, and a commerce simple enough to be carried on in a jargon. Where the commerce has become continuous, extensive, and complex, an effort is generally made to learn the most useful of the two languages, or both, or some lingua franca.[23]

V

The third meaning-language I mentioned and the one perhaps most important in defining the kind of social relationships out of which the sociological race is differentiated is the masculine language of command.

The language of command originated as a formal concept in nineteenth-century Europe when, along with the rise of the great modern nations, civilian armies were conscripted from illiterate peasant and unskilled laboring populations to replace mercenary armies. But these peasants and laborers, coming as they did from different parts of the nation and usually understanding only the local dialect—and there were a great many of these local dialects—were often unable to understand each other to say nothing of their officers. It became obvious that to have a national army it was necessary to have a national language. To the peasant conscripts from Breton, the Basque country, the Provence, French was presented as a national language in the form of a language of military command. In Germany after the war with France in 1870 the problem was much the same, but it was in the old Austro-Hungarian Empire that the problem was most acute. In that country the question of the tongue to be designated as the language of command was debated in military circles, in parliament, and in the press until World War I. The point at issue in the debate was the vocabulary in which military orders were to be given and received. The essence of the language of command, however, is not to be found in vocabulary or grammer; rather one might almost say that it is in the manner of speaking and the tone of voice in which the words are spoken. There are certain forms of collective action, war, for instance, which progress best when pushed back to the bare form of ordering and forbidding communication. Hence it was out of the nineteenth-century discussion of the problem of effective military organization that the term emerged and the concept was distilled.

But there are other forms of corporate action approaching that of the military operation, such as those connected with various expressions of state-building and industrialization, which also progress best when communication is conducted in the imperative mood. This is particularly true when these developments occur, sociologically if not geographically, "somewhere east of Suez," or along some frontier where men have little or no reverential feeling for the customs and obligations of the social orders from whence they come. For the language of command is the language that functions in a situation of authority and in turn defines the situation as one of authority. Like every other social situation this is one in which a society exists because some sort of pattern of collective activity exists. In order to exploit the situation successfully the people in it must evolve a division of labor and a system for coordinating the activities of the members of the group. Where the group is more or less homogeneous the words of the language operate as cues or signals to set off the appropriate activities of each member. But when the group is heterogeneous, that is, lacking in a common body of expectations and obligations, the words of the leader or coordinator are not signals merely; they are commands.

Some authorities hold that this is the situation in which the state originally is formed. When two or more peoples of different physical and cultural traits are intermixed on the same territory, that is, in a situation where some degree of cooperation is inescapable in spite of diversity of origin or purpose, some form of organization based upon the authority principle is perhaps inevitable. Between the various people in contact in the same territory there probably never is an even balance of power and status. Some men of clear purpose, greater strength, and superior resourcefulness from the class of greatest power seize their opportunities to carve out estates for themselves even if they have to redesign the physical and social environment in order to do so. We are accustomed to speak of a situation of this kind in terms of sovereignty and we are accustomed to say of the sovereign that he is master of the situation.

The state in our day has become vast and complex, and the language in which the state mobilizes and regiments its civilian and military personnel, enacts its laws and levies its taxes, and judges and punishes its delinquents is an equally vast and complex affair. But simpler and more elementary political institutions have appeared and continue to appear along the world's frontiers in the form of mines, ranches, factories, plantations, and the like. These institutions do, in a measure, what the states originally did when they bring together people of incommensurable cultures and put them to work at tasks new to them and at levels of discipline more severe than those to which they have been accustomed. Simpler and more elementary vocabularies likewise appeared and continue to appear through which the language of command is expressed in the areas which these institutions dominate.[24]

VI

Perhaps no one of these institutions throws the authority situation and the language of the lash into clearer relief than the plantation and the large number of emergency jargons associated with the plantation at one time or another around the world. They include Gullah on the South Carolina coast, gombo in Louisiana, papiamento in Caraçao, Taki-Taki in Surinam, Creole in Mauritius, Creolese in British Guiana, kitchen-kafir in the Province of Natal, South Africa, and many others. Beche-la-mer began as a trade jargon but later became a plantation speech in Melanesia and Papua. What is called pidgin in Hawaii became much less a trade language than a command language. The designation of these jargons as "creole" languages in French, Spanish, and Portugese plantation areas, particularly in the West Indies, "the *locus classicus* of plantation slavery," has led several scholars to apply the term as a class name to the plantation expression of the language of command generally.[25]

The plantation is an organization originating in a frontier region to produce an agricultural staple for sale in a distant market. As an institution for bringing and settling people of different origins upon the same soil, the plantation originally has something of the characteristics of a camp. But with time it develops the appearance and traditions of a well-settled community assimilating itself to the land. The planter family assumes the character of a dynasty as control passes from father to son and, especially in the case of the slave plantation, several generations of workers may die upon the same estate on which they were born. The plantation cemetery registers the fact that social relationships in the community may be as enduring as circumstances allow them to be anywhere. From this it is understandable why creole or plantation jargons are much more tenacious and enduring than trade jargons and why they come to characterize large areas and regions.

The active agent in the situation is the planter, and the plantation is his lengthened shadow. He is not, originally, a gentleman. Gentlemen go out to the frontier as governors, judges, and officials of various sorts, but the man who becomes a planter goes there to build up an estate for himself—and the ways of gentility are not essential, may even be detrimental, to this end. His evolution into the role of planter is a function of the social situation in which an authoritarian personality is built. The possession of authority is not entirely determined by the will of the man who becomes a planter; those to whom an order is directed also have much to do with determining whether or not the one who issues it has authority. Beliefs and myths of various sorts, other than those of mere gentility, develop in the situation to confirm the privileges of the man who becomes planter and aid in effecting the subordination and obedience of the laborers. The myth of membership in a race deemed superior, a myth which confers prestige upon the planter outside as well as inside the immediate situation, has been a most important factor in securing acceptance of authority.

With the acceptance of his authority the planter becomes, in a sense, the plantation itself. He might have said, had not Louis XIV allegedly had the idea first, "La plantation, c'est moi," since he symbolizes in his own person the purposes and the structure of the institution. The maintenance of himself as a prestige symbol requires that he live more or less apart from those below him. But this does not prevent him from becoming something of a *patron* to his people to whom he must grant favors in time of misfortune and from whom he expects loyalty and support. These are the familiar relationships of paternalism. Out of the goodness of his heart he will undertake to improve the condition of those who labor for him and who recognize his authority just so long as they do not get the notion that they have any right to improve their condition for themselves.

The personality structure that ruling brings exhibits itself in the planter's assumptions of superiority and speaking. Fanny Kemble described ante-bellum Southern planters as "men brought up in the habits of peremptory command over their fellowmen" and noted in their speech a "habitual tone of command." [26] Unlike the missionary, and to a lesser extent than the trader, the planter does not ordinarily move into the speech of the groups which have been recruited for labor on his plantation. The speech of an inferior people must be an inferior speech and without dignity upon the lips of a civilized person. Nor is the planter consciously interested in transmitting the values of his culture to his laborers. Hence he expects the members of these groups to come to him linguistically as well as otherwise, and so the vocabularies of the creole languages are more often than not lifted from the national speech of the planter class. However, the planter will make one concession: he is willing to simplify the tenses, inflections, gender, and number of the words and sentences he uses into a kind of "baby talk" for the benefit of the workers who are striving to understand him. This is a way of "talking down" to those whom he regards as his inferiors, but there is in his speech something that does not belong to "baby talk" as we ordinarily understand it in the family—and this is profanity. The planter, like Byron's fellow who "knew not what to say and so he swore," learns that these vocal explosions can communicate something of his will when ordinary words do not. Violent language seems to be an integral part of the plantation situation as it is of authoritarian situations generally.[27] If an order is shouted loudly enough the vocabulary in which it is given may be regarded as relatively unimportant.

The grammatical and vocabulary peculiarities of a creole language, as opposed to other types of language, are not, for our purposes, very important. What is important is the fact that its basis is the speech of the master class which, in the form in which it comes to the subordinates, is a language of command. The core ideas of this language have to do with the levels of authority and subordination, worker and management categories, individual assets and liabilities, aptitudes and efficiencies, rules and regulations, punishments and rewards, starting and stopping times, particular work operations, etc. With the acquisition of the meanings of the language there tends to develop at the same time an acceptance of the situation. These meanings and acceptances develop in the general atmosphere of authority and obedience and against the background of cooperative activity involved in agricultural production. As this takes place authority and obedience are determined more by moral and less by material factors. Henceforth the force which controls is that which those who are controlled themselves in large measure supply. In the plantation situation through the medium of the meanings of the language a *sittlichkeit* arises wherein the relations between the upper and lower classes and races come to be regarded by both as a more or less normal and inevitable condition of things.

VII

By means of the creole jargons men of different culture do manage to break through to each other and effect enough communication to coordinate the work of the plantation. From the point of view of race-making, however, what is important is not so much what the jargons communicate as what they fail to communicate. It is inevitable, especially in the early stages of its development, that the creole speech should permit the communication of only a limited range of meanings; they do not and cannot make intelligible the total behavior of the individual. In a situation where people cannot reach quick understandings through linguistic material and ideas that are not readily accessible to all, it is perhaps inevitable that most behavior will be attributed to biological nature, that is, to race. There is nothing else to attribute it to. The point involved here is not simply that there is a barrier to communication between people of different existing "races"; it is that the barrier is constitutive of the races. In the situation men cannot deal with each other as man to man. Race is a major form of isolation characterized by a high degree of tenaciousness. But the outsider of whatever sort is always more or less a barbarian whose speech to us, as to the Greeks, is not well understood. They are stupid who cannot understand our tongue and it is plain for all to see that the stupidity is born in them. Racial apartness is institutionalized in the meanings of the command language.

Now people who have not the ability or the means of expressing themselves, stupid people that is, are ripe for slavery or some degree of un-freedom. From the external and insensible point of view of those in authority over them they cannot be completely human. Despite, or even because of, their labored efforts to express themselves the members of the lower race are regarded as strange and inscrutable. Those who visibly and without doubt belong to one or the other race may come to accept the relationships and attitudes of the situation as these are wrapped up in the language. It is tho man in the middle, however, the man Dr. Park called the marginal man, who most realistically reveals the race problem as fundamentally a problem in communication. It is not sufficient to describe the problem, as it has been described, in terms of blood mixture, cultural hybridity, or status dilemma. More than anyone else in the situation this man is suffocating under an inability to communicate an overwhelming experience, an experience which it is exceedingly difficult for the rest of us to understand. He is trying in one way or another to say "I am human, too," but as he senses that our attention is not upon what he is saying but upon him as some kind of racial freak, he begins to scream and to scream louder in an effort to get across the barrier of our indifference or curiosity. "I ain't kin make my feelings known," the illiterate mulatto boy told E. C. L. Adams. The highly literate and acomplished Jewish writer, Ludwig Lewisohn, had the same difficulty.[28] If the marginal man cannot adequately make his feelings known he may get some relief by cursing the rest of us for our obtuseness. But we are not impressed with what he says, and the louder he screams and the more he curses the more convinced the rest of us are that he is queer and racially different.

The disposition to impute the cause of behavior to biological nature must be a continuing disposition if a system of race relations is to be established and given permanence in a society. To achieve this it is not sufficient for the dominant classes merely to assert the natural inferiority of the subordinate classes. Simple ethnocentrism will effect this attitude anyway. What is necessary is that the people of the subordinate classes accept and act out some measure of belief in their own inferiority. The psychological mechanism which Mead suggested as basic to the establishment of this or any other kind of social organization is that of communication through language involving the appearance of the other, the one at the other end of the relationship, in the definition of the self. Mead reminds us that we exist for ourselves as we are regarded, or think we are regarded, by others and as we appear in the speech of others.[29] The taking of the role of the other one leads the individual to control his own responses in the interest of cooperative group activity. This analyzes a function of language noticed earlier. Self-control takes place with reference to other selves, but otherwise there is no hard and fast line between self control and social control. Language is bound up with the system of social control, and the language of command is at the center of that kind of society, such as a plantation society, in which there is likely to be a racial hierachy. One takes that form of the self which appears in the values and meanings of the speech of others regarding him. In the authoritative situation one raises himself to superiority or condemns himself to inferiority in the language that others use to elevate or condemn him. One issues orders in the language and from the point of view of those to whom orders are issued. One asks for favors in the language and from the point of view of those who grant or reject favors. When the line between those who issue orders and grant favors and those who carry out orders and petition for favors is stabilized and more or less coincides with some physical or behaviorial hallmark which is accounted for in biological terms, we have race and race relations.

The conception of race implies abstractness of social relations, for the person dealt with as overlord or as subordinate and from whose point of view the other one regards himself, tends to become a type. The language of command, more than any other meaning-language, perhaps, functions to categorize experience and in so doing develops a system of marks and tags which, in the case of mixed bloods, may become very elaborate. Then when individuals of a given class of marks get a name in common, conceptual selection operates to endow all of them with certain attributes deemed hereditary and to withhold from them certain other attributes also deemed hereditary. The meanings contained in the terms and words for alleged racial types tends to fix perceptions of these individuals and, derivatively, thought and behavior toward them. Thus are races made, named, tagged, endowed, and imprisoned in the meanings of the language.

VIII

For how long? For as long as the creole language continues to be, as it begins, a language of command, until such time as those who speak it, originally enemies or else with very little in common, begin to detach themselves from the fate of their local groups and by a new and inner reorientation become a part of a larger society. In such a society they get new selves and become new men. See what has happened in New Guinea. The plantations there were initiated by the Germans who recruited labor for them from numerous native tribes. Then with World War I white Australian planters took over and continued the recruiting practices of the Germans. Both German and Australian planters preferred "work boys" brought together from many localities in New Guinea so there would be no "one talk" and all must speak the same jargon. Margaret Mead describes the situation as follows:

It is safer to recruit a boy for work in the Admiralties from the Solomons and a boy for New Britain from the Admiralties than to take a local boy who is continually being drawn back to his village by the claims of local ceremony—feasts or fasts or village feuds. And from the needs and wishes of the master has grown a counter feeling among the boys, a desire for the adventure of working in new islands, under new masters. . . .
To become a work boy far afield is the great adventure of lives that from childhood have been bounded by the lagoon or the two hills that walled in the valley where the village lay. At home the boys have

spoken a language known to perhaps a hundred, in rare cases a thousand, people; they have followed ways of life peculiarly their own and recognized as unlike those of their neighbors of the next inlet. From the narrowness of their own little communities they can escape for a few years into this wider community, where human relations are differently patterned, where a language is spoken in which they can converse with boys several shades lighter or six inches taller than themselves. . . . They will speak a language that even the white man understands and learn to give commands in the same insolent and arrogant fashion as white masters. When they return to their villages, they will be newly armed with a language of rebuke and contempt which they can shower at will upon their less traveled "Marys". . . .[30]

The creole speech, in New Guinea as elsewhere, grows up among the assorted members of the plantation's labor force out of the necessity for understanding the orders of the planter. Incidentally, however, it almost inevitably becomes a *lingua franca* for communication between the laborers themselves.[31] It is not just a speech of mixed vocabulary any more than it is just a speech of mixed-bloods. It is a speech characteristic of areas where a great deal of tribal intermarriage and racial miscegenation is going on. In those families where neither parent is able to communicate without difficulty in the mother tongue of the other the stage is set for the creole jargon to become a *Familiensprache*, the medium of intimate intercourse within the family and, in general, the language of human nature. Widespread participation in speech used in this way operates to lift natives from tribe to nation, engenders among them common interests and feelings, awakens among them a conception of a larger community, and in time brings with it a spirit of nationality or race-consciousness. This is the way African tribesmen have been transformed into American Negroes and the process is being repeated today in other frontier situations. In New Guinea there is going on what Stephen Reed calls a "Kanaka revolution" with de-tribalized, plantation, creole-speaking work-boys coming to constitute a third group between the members of the old tribes on the one hand and the Europeans on the other.[32] This composite group of "Kanakas" is changing the creole speech from a command language into a we-language as they become a new people.

• 7 •

The Idea of Race and
the Race Problem

This *Reader* belongs to that class of books which seeks to gain
perspective. "In the absence of perspective," Whitehead said,
"there is only triviality." Here we seek perspective on the problem of race from a large number of authors and from a wide
range of documentary material dealing with lore, myths, rationalizations, doctrines, poetry, and social fiction as well as from
serious scientific studies and reports.

The race problem is a problem so immediately in the minds
of so many people, a problem so insistently demanding action,
even drastic action, right now, that a sense of balance and proportion is not easily come by and held to. When men are caught in
the meshes of racial feeling it is next to impossible to view the
matter with the degree of objective consideration necessary to
understanding and rational action. On the other hand, those who
have not experienced the emotions of race probably are not in
the best position to understand and to act upon the race problem
either. For all of us some method for gaining greater depth and
distance is needed.

The readings in this book are organized around the race problem. What is this problem? There have been many answers. Here
it may be suggested that, fundamentally, it is the problem of
understanding and dealing with an idea, the idea of race. In
particular areas the race problem is identified with relations of
tension between two or more specific peoples, but this is only a
local expression of the problem. In every region where race

SOURCE In Edgar T. Thompson and Everett C. Hughes (eds.), *Race: Individual and Collective Behavior*, The Free Press, 1958, pp. 1,2.

relations are problematic they are implicated in concrete social, political, demographic, and biological problems, but these same problems can and do exist where there is no racial involvement. The race problem is everywhere accompanied by charges of discrimination, segregation, and injustice, but these same charges are made where the idea of race is absent. The idea is not limited to men of ill-will; in the same community it is entertained by men regarded by their fellows as well as by themselves as men of good-will and responsibility. Neither is it limited, where it exists, to members of only one race; men of the "inferior" race will not agree to many things done in its name, especially when done to them, but they may be almost as completely possessed by the idea as the men of the "superior" race. The people of the community can divide themselves into different races only because they all hold the idea of race in common. And not only do they hold it but they believe in it, and believing in it, are moved to action by it. Thus the problem becomes a race problem, and ceases to be some other kind of social and political or demographic problem, when it becomes implicated in "a way of life" or "a civilization" which, of course, must be defended at all costs. When this happens the ordinary problems of a society have been pushed down into its deeper structure where they have become a part of its constitutional organization.

The idea of race is only one of many schismatic myths which have divided mankind into warring groups throughout history. But in perhaps no other form of ethnocentrism have the divisions been regarded as so wide and so deep as the divisions that are believed to be based upon race. Here the separation is not to be bridged by learning a new language, or by conversion to a different religion, or by changing to another costume, or by professing loyalty to another ruler or set of laws. Race does not result in a mere estrangement of peoples; it is presumed to effect nothing short of an abysmal separation. The idea of race is present, says Yves R. Simon, "the moment one admits that there exists, apart from individual and sociological causes of infamy, a mark of degradation which is properly biological, permanent, transmissible by physical generation, inherent in the chromosomes, independent of all good will and all good conduct, ineffaceable, fatal in the way death is fatal." [1] Race is ultimate and final.

It is a terrible idea. Europe, which has given the world so many energizing ideas, gave this one too, but Europeans seem not to have fully realized the drastic quality of their contribution. It might almost be said of Europe as a whole, as Vidal de la Blache said of Germany, that it came to represent "above everything else an ethnic idea." [2] Yet no matter how full of error, the idea has been a source of tremendous energy within Europe itself as well as along the frontiers of European colonization and trade. It still is powerful, but almost everywhere it is at least beginning to decline and to assume a defensive position. The facts of biology and genetics are beginning to be apparent even among ordinary people, race is becoming more and more identified with the general problem of democracy and subject to all the pressures of the democratic ideal, and more and more of us are experiencing the discovery that in the people of other races there are other lives to learn about and to learn from. The idea of race is beginning to decline before the facts of biology, of politics, and of human nature.

It is at the point of their decline, it seems, that the dominating ideas and forces of history come to be recognized and studied, when already, perhaps, some new ideas are beginning to take the place of the old. At any rate, so far as the subject of race is concerned, the volume of popular literature and serious study grows greater and greater.

• 8 •

Race in the Modern World

The Failure of Racial Knowledge

Ed Howe said he knew all about women, said he once visited a place where young men were trained to be doctors and watched the students cut one up.

For a long time now we have been photographing, measuring, and cutting up Negroes, Caucasians, and Mongolians and to some of us, as to Ed Howe, the knowledge gained has been sufficient. Our scientists have given us the facts. Hankins shows us that race is only a highly variable statistical concept,[1] while Barzun dismisses it as a mere superstition.[2] Benedict and Weltfish argue with sweet reasonableness that all men are really brothers under the skin,[3] and Huxley and Haddon explain that there really is no such thing as race and that we ought to substitute such terms as *ethnic group* or *sub-species.*[4]

But the people remain impervious to all these scientific facts. Huxley and Haddon may be willing to give up race but ordinary men and women will not do so, and it is in the minds of ordinary men and women, not in the concepts of scientists, that the race problem exists. The recent reaffirmation of the doctrine of white supremacy by the legislature of the State of South Carolina is a fact in an order of facts not amenable to the methods of biology and physical anthropology. In this order of facts a scientific statement like that by Benedict and Weltfish is viewed as an attack, not as a clarification and a resolution of a problem. When their attractive and authentic little bulletin was labelled communist propaganda the Army withdrew its order for 50,000 copies. It

SOURCE *The Journal of Negro Education,* Summer Number, 1944, pp. 270–79.

must all be very puzzling to the scientists when the facts seem so clear.

On the other hand, ordinary common sense knowledge of race, that kind of knowledge held by ordinary men and women and which has been sufficient for all practical purposes in the past, is now inadequate too. Some old laws of nature are behaving unlawfully. In the South whites have always professed a thoroughgoing knowledge of Negro nature, and Europeans have claimed a complete understanding of colonial native minds. When, therefore, it is considered that the place in nature of each group is thoroughly ascertained beyond the shadow of doubt, it is nothing short of exasperating when the creatures refuse to stay in their proper places and persist in acting in unexpected and human ways. The members of the dominant races and of the imperialist states must understand how Balaam felt when his ass addressed him in his own language. The ass was not acting as a good ass should, but we have it on good authority that Balaam was disturbed. So also are the *Herrenvolk* disturbed when the subject races address their rulers in the language of the latter's own values. It is all so very confusing and disturbing when the facts are so clear. Why are not inferior peoples content to be inferior peoples and behave accordingly?

In spite of all claims to the contrary, the common sense knowledge of race has never been complete. Just as men have long occupied themselves with speculation over the workings of the mind of woman, so also have the master classes puzzled at times over the strange and unpredictable mind of the peasant, the native, the Negro, or the Oriental. Although white Southerners have professed a thorough knowledge and understanding of the Negro they have, at the same time, acknowledged the existence in him of something inscrutable and mysterious. The novel thing about the present situation is that the Negro and other subordinate peoples seem to have gone completely berserk. They of the docile instinct are acting entirely out of character. They are rising up and running *amok* all around the world. It is as if our social world were experiencing an earthquake and the once stable foundations of racial certainty were shaking under our feet.

Our old presumptive knowledge of race is no longer sufficient, but that does not mean the matter is a dead issue. On the contrary, the subject of race is interesting and important over wider and wider circles around the world. It rivals business prosperity, the weather, and the war as topics of discussion. We may be uncertain about what race is but we know it is something about which we are ready to fight. It is an issue somewhat like that of the Monroe Doctrine.

There is a story about two American acquaintances who chanced to meet at the street corner. One said to the other, "Say, I hear you have been making derogatory remarks about the Monroe Doctrine. Now just let me tell you this, anyone who criticizes the Monroe Doctrine is not a good American. You ought to be ashamed of yourself."

The other said, "Why, I've never said anything against the Monroe Doctrine. I believe in the Monroe Doctrine. I would fight for the Monroe Doctrine. I would even give my life if necessary for the Monroe Doctrine. All I ever said about the Monroe Doctrine is that I don't really understand what it is."

We are not agreed as to what the Monroe Doctrine is, but we know it is something we have in reserve for which we will fight, something which can be counted upon to unite us. As Mead put it, "The only issue involved in the Monroe Doctrine is this, are you a patriot, are you a red-blooded American, or are you a mollycoddle?" [5]

Now the fundamental issue involved in race, as it concerns the rank and file of people, is very much the same. It is not a question of what race is but of what race does, of how the idea functions. Rightly or wrongly, for good or for ill, it is an issue which originated and is maintained to arouse the fighting spirit and for the sake of its effect in drawing men together. As Voegelin says, ". . . the race idea with its implications is not a body of knowledge organized in a systematic form, but a political idea in the technical sense of the word. A political idea does not attempt to describe social reality as it is, but it sets up symbols, be they single language units or more elaborate dogmas, which have the function of creating the image of a group as a unit." [6]

The absence among the people of a clearly formulated definition of race, far from weakening it, actually adds to the potency of the race idea. We can each assume that our individual view of the matter is also the view of every other right-thinking member of our group since we are not aware of any fixed and objective rule the conscious interpretation of which would put us at odds.

Whatever our individual assumptions about race are, we can feel that we have our group behind us, and we are united.

To say that race is principally an idea in the minds of men and only secondarily a biological fact does not mean that it can be dismissed as a mere superstition. Ideas are notoriously tough and unyielding. Certain ideas possess us "as evil spirits were once said to have entered into witches and possessed them and made them do their bidding. Under the spell of these ideas a madness seems to sweep over a people . . . " [7] The problem of our age is to get possession of our ideas. To achieve control we shall need more social knowledge than we now have and a more effective educational diffusion of it.

Race and Race Relations

The racial group which emerges from the measurements of anthropologists and the dissections of biologists is quite a different thing from the racial group which exists in the minds of its members. In different racially conscious groups the criterion of membership varies. It may be language, religion, temperament, or pigmentation, but whatever it is the race group is composed of those who regard themselves as belonging to it and who are so regarded by others.

The different ethnic stocks studied by anthropologists developed originally under conditions of regional segregation in adaptation to food, climate, water, and general habitat. Under circumstances of geographical isolation and relatively close in-breeding over long periods of time it was inevitable that groups of men physically distinct from each other in varying degree should result. But through the long ages of isolation "when providence set apart the nations" these physical differences were not realized by the people characterized by them and bore no special significance in their minds. Negroes in the middle of Africa did not know themselves to be Negroes, and white men in the middle of Europe did not know themselves as Caucasians. It was not until the nations of Europe began to expand, to invade and to conquer, not until the world began to shrink enough for men of strikingly diverse cultures and noticeably different physical appearance to come into close and continuous contact that the stage was set for the eventual emergence of race consciousness and race ideas.

What is called "race" must be understood, therefore, not in isolation, but in contact situations, and the focus for such an understanding must be upon race relations and not upon race differences. The alleged differences, it would seem, are an incident of the relations and can be understood only by understanding the circumstances under which the relations originally were established and the circumstances under which they subsequently developed. The areas around the world where race relations are more or less problematic and more or less involved in the existing political and social arrangements bear no necessary relation to the original race homelands. However, the different systems of racial relationships, with their accompanying codes, attitudes, and expressions, are in a sense also geographical expressions. Race relations are bound up with the general culture of a society, and culture is a local and regional phenomenon. Each system of racial relationships must be understood, therefore, in the setting of its own habitat.

We have a fairly large and growing literature dealing with problems in a number of race relations "regions," but the systematic use of the materials for the comparative study of race relations has scarcely begun.

Society as a Group of Groups

Sumner's conception of society as a "group of groups" affords a useful and illuminating point of view for the organization and analysis of interracial as well as other types of societies. In the following paragraphs quoted from *Folkways* Sumner states his conception in connection with primitive society but it is no less useful when applied to modern or civilized society. He says:

The conception of "primitive society" which we ought to form is that of small groups scattered over a territory. . . . A group of groups may have some relation to each other (kin, neighborhood, alliance, connubium and commercium) which draws them together and differentiates them from others. Thus a differentiation arises between ourselves, the we-group, or in-group, and everybody else, or the others-groups, out-groups. The insiders in a we-group are in a relation of peace, order, law, government, and industry, to each other. Their relation to all outsiders, or others-groups, is one of war and plunder, except so far as agreements have modified it. . . .

The relation of comradeship and peace in the we-group and that of hostility and war toward others-groups are correlative to each other. The exigencies of war with outsiders are what make peace inside, lest internal discord should weaken the we-group for war. These exigencies also make government and law in the in-group, in order to prevent quarrels and enforce discipline. Thus war and peace have reacted on each other and developed each other, one within the group, the other in the intergroup relation. The closer the neighbors, and the stronger they are, the intenser is the warfare, and then the intenser is the internal organization and discipline of each. Sentiments are produced to correspond. Loyalty to the group, sacrifice for it, hatred and contempt for outsiders, brotherhood within, warlikeness without—all grow together, common products of the same situation.[8]

A society is a group within which smaller groups are in a continuous state of interaction. Thus there is not one but many societies and the concept "society" becomes a highly relative one varying from a group of neighboring families on up to a group of nations. The condition of competition, conflict and rivalry between the groups of which a society is composed tends to increase the solidarity of each "in" or we-group. It is this conflict which turns an aggregation of individuals into a group whose members are conscious of membership in it. "We" expresses this consciousness but in the course of a single conversation a modern man may use "we" in several different societal contexts. Thus in "we Smiths" the "others" obviously are other families and the society is a group of families, whereas in "we Negroes" the others are other race groups and the society is a group of racial groups. What is not so clear is the source of the ideas which bring about the realignment of individuals into new and different "we" groups as time passes. Race is one of these relatively new alignments.

Because each group is bound to be more controlled and guided by its own experiences than by the experiences of other people it either becomes more or less ethnocentric or it ceases to be a group. The disposition to evaluate the strange in terms of the known converts the realization of difference into a moral judgment. We judge ourselves by our best traits and others by their worst, and our best traits include practically all the traits we have; virtue is defined by the qualities we attribute to ourselves. Thus Houston Stewart Chamberlain speaks of "a certain noble striving for property" which he finds among the Aryans, while among the Jews this same tendency is referred to as "the most

despicable usury." [9] Ethnocentrism is rooted in the division between friend and foe but it transforms this division into one
between good and bad.

To Sumner "primitive society" is composed of "small groups
scattered over a territory." It is a territorial society, but the member groups are not intermixed upon the territory. There is a sort
of "no man's land" between them so that the cultural distinctiveness of each is obvious. Ethnocentrism therefore needs no great
transcendental myth, for spatial distance is sufficient to protect
the exclusiveness of the tribe or clan. But when conquest, immigration, and trade intermix men of different complexion and
culture on soil which all may claim as a common social if not legal
inheritance there is a tendency to seek or to create some principle for maintaining social distance. When society becomes a con-
geries of groups and the members of one group cannot put physical distance between themselves and the others, a principle like
language, religion, nationality, or race may be employed to effect
separation.

With the intermixing of groups upon the same soil comes the
state, and states lie alongside each other with no "no man's land"
between. Boundaries become sharp and sensitive lines of demar-
cation as relations of trade and war effect a new and larger intergroup or society. Such a society was Europe where the idea
of nationality was evolved to serve as a basis for state rivalries
and for claims to territories and populations lying within other
states. The idea of nationality is closely related to the idea of
race.

The series of changes which began in the period of the Great
Discoveries and which led to, and followed, the Industrial Revolution resulted in an ever widening circle of political and economic relations. This series of changes might be described as a
revolution in distance since it greatly increased control over a
larger part of the physical world by making the resources of
every part more available to other parts. One of the first effects
of the revolution in distance was the transformation of the Atlantic into an inland sea. The Atlantic became an area of interaction,
an interaction which continually changed the character of all the
peoples on both sides of it and tended to give them a common
European culture. To this new and larger society Ramsay

Traquair has given the name the Commonwealth of the Atlantic.[10]

The expansion of Europe and the opening up of overseas areas for trade and settlement involved a change whereby native and non-European peoples, many of them at any rate, gradually became integral parts of the white man's economic order. This was less true of North America where the Indian was pushed aside. He was culturally distinct and highly "visible," but his group has never become an integral member of the Atlantic group of groups. Hence the attitude toward him has settled down into one of relative indifference. It is significant that he has posed no serious race problem. Rather it was in connection with the incorporation of the Negro into this society that racial ideas became useful. The idea of race developed as a working element in colonial areas as a means of effecting control over the Negro's labor and of fixing him in a permanent caste position.

For a long time certain hermit nations like Japan continued to remain outside the family of nations. They possessed little or no national or racial consciousness since they were not concerned about their status in a society of which they were not members. But advances in cheaper and faster means of transportation and communication continued to reduce the size of the planet and to bring all the peoples living on it closer together. Their very differences made them useful to one another and customers of one another. When Japan, for example, began to trade with the rest of the world her people began to expand out over the Pacific. The Pacific became a commonwealth of nations as the Atlantic had become earlier. It was in Hawaii, in California, in Australia, and in Malaya that Japanese became conscious of the low place assigned their country by the other nationals. People who have known defeat and that "sickening sense of inferiority" are the people who discover their souls, and so it is too with nations. When the Japanese became group conscious and involved themselves in a struggle to improve their status their membership in the family of nations became a fact.

The Great Society, as Graham Wallas calls it, has become a fact too. The struggle for status between races and nations has become world-wide; the subject peoples are struggling to be free and the sovereign states are struggling to maintain or to raise their prestige. It is significant that in their fight for places in the sun the two Axis partners, Germany in Europe and Japan in Asia, should both base their claims upon the principle of race. But they are not employing the principle in exactly the same way.

The Idea of Race

The race idea has grown from a fusion and synthesis of elements present in the thought of ancient society and subsequently added to by religious and philosophical movements down to the modern period.[11] It is only in the modern period that men have attributed such an inner significance to external physical differences as to make race a pivotal human grouping and a basis of group ethnocentrism. To study the religious and philosophical elements in the genesis and growth of the race idea, as Voegelin has done, is important, but it seems even more important to understand the specific situations in which it is generated or into which it falls. For ideas have their natural habitats, and a living idea must be observed on the soil where it works in behalf of a way of life.

Our knowledge is not sufficient to give satisfactory accounts of the various intergroup situations where the idea of race functions but some of them may be suggested.

In the first place there is the master-servant or employer-employee situation, particularly in plantation societies. The plantation provides an almost ideal race-making situation. It requires a uniform type of unskilled labor fitted to routine tasks outside the immediate family of the planter. The situation is one in which men ordinarily do not voluntarily offer themselves and so the planter takes advantage of opportunities to hold whatever labor he is able to get and to keep it in its place. The conditions under which the crop must be produced are highly isolating and this fact, together with the need to hold labor the year around, turns the plantation into a little feudal domain as well as a farm. The crop is produced for a distant market but the purpose of the activities of the workers is not immediately apparent to them. They do not directly experience the discipline which the requirements of the market impose; they are conscious only of the close and continuous supervision and control of the planter.

It is significant that in all or practically all plantation societies racial ideas enter powerfully into the economic and political arrangements. It was the plantation which created in Virginia and in the South the social conditions under which racial ideas were propagated and circulated. On the sugar plantations in Formosa it appears that the Japanese overlords and the Chinese and native workers have been differentiated into superior and inferior "races." In Queensland, Australia, Italians and Greeks imported as Caucasians under the white Australia policy after the repatriation of Kanaka sugar cane workers almost immediately fell into a racial category. Australians of English descent spoke of the "olive peril."

War is another situation favorable to the race idea. Burke's statement that a whole nation cannot be indicted is often quoted but apparently unless it is indicted war against it is impossible. French writers and orators referred to the first World War as *une guerre des espéces,* not a war between peoples since the Germans were not really human.[12] A similar view of the Germans and the Japanese is present in England and America at the present time. As a part of the process of the indictment of the German people for the crimes committed in the name of racism there is a certain similarity to the racism which is indicted.

Other possible race-making situations include those where religious proselytes encounter stubborn natures unwilling to yield to the true faith [13] and those involving competition between labor groups where the idea of race is used to eliminate competitors or reduce their competition. Under appropriate circumstances it may be possible, too, for a labor and socialist movement to endow the bourgeoise of popular Marxism with a racial character.

In different situations and under different circumstances it may be possible for the race idea to assume different shapes and to take different directions and to have different consequences, but essentially it always involves the imputation of traits and characters to the members of the other group which are regarded as biologically inheritable and immutable. These traits and characters contrast with those of ourselves in ways that are favorable to us. We look for some sign or mark, such as skin color, in order to categorize and identify the others and upon which we can pin our beliefs. Race thinking is therefore essentially biological thinking and the race idea is essentially a body idea.

"Body experiences," says Voegelin, "are basic human experiences and every symbol which can use them as a material starting point can be sure of a strong emotional hold over its believers." [14]

Race thinking simply carries to its logical extreme the popular assumption that not merely physical but social traits are inherited, an assumption which begins with the lively interest we have in tracing family resemblances in our children. Because we can see individuals, whereas we have to be trained to see the facts of culture, we are always prone to overemphasize biology at the expense of culture. It is almost a cultural fact that we explain cultural facts biologically.

In a period of change when our interests are threatened and our social position challenged we have an emotional need for some principle of stability and certainty like that which seems to be provided by biological inheritance. It should not be strange, therefore, that, in the societies where the idea of race has seemed to serve men's needs for an absolute, or a first cause, so well, an attack upon it is almost equivalent to an attack upon God Himself.

Finally, let it be noted that, whatever the circumstances of its origin, the race idea, like other ideas, has severed itself from these circumstances and has elevated itself beyond the local and regional situations in which it has operated. From a local and concrete idea it has become, or has tended to become, general and abstract. It has become a world-idea, "the myth of the twentieth century," which for a time threatened to reorganize the world and determine its political relations for a long time to come. The threat has not completely abated yet.

Race Conflict and Progress

The members of an interracial society are at once separated from each other and integrated into a common community. Each has to live in a common space or environment with the others so that "to live" necessarily means "to live with" the rest. The competition, rivalry, or prejudice between the groups which compose the society is not a denial of societal unity but rather an affirmation of it. Men do not compete or fight for ends which all do not prize. Competition and conflict therefore invariably go on within a circle of common values and interests, or values and interests held in common up to a point. This is why society is a "group of groups."

The fact that a group within a society is in conflict with other groups to whom it nevertheless is bound suggests why European immigrants in American cities so frequently settle down alongside their hereditary enemies.[15] It would seem that they have to stick together in order to stay apart, for the image which a group forms of itself is bound up with the way the other groups within the same society regard it. It follows that if a group wishes to maintain its values, its historical memories, and, in general, its conception of itself it has some need for the constant reminders provided by its enemies.

Common interests and common societal values are required to point up the issues for conflict, and the more the member groups of a society hold in common the intenser the conflict. It is well known that there is no fight like a family fight, not only because those who are presumed to love each other have the power to hurt each other most, but also because they share experiences from which it is impossible for each member to free himself. Great bitterness also is observed in religious sectarian conflict and in intra-trade union and political party fights. Feuds between mountain families inhabiting the same cove are particularly uncompromisable and long-lasting. Civil wars have the reputation of being bitterer than international wars. Anti-Semitism in Christian lands is surely connected with the fact that both Jew and Gentile have "prayed to the same God, preached more or less the same morals, feared the same evils, and hoped for the same heaven." Similarly Southern whites and Negroes have more interests in common with one another than either has with any group outside the South, but in the economy which they pursue together the competition and conflict between them are constant. On a larger scale whites and Negroes in the United States have more in common than either group has with any group outside.

Here is the paradox: it is precisely because the members of both groups profess belief in the ethics of the Sermon on the Mount, in the principles of the Declaration of Independence, and in the doctrines of trial by a jury of one's peers and no taxation without representation that there is racial prejudice and conflict. Without these common beliefs and ideals that could be no basis for making claims and there could be nothing to point up these claims into issues. Neither group can advance by asserting its own interests against the interest of the whole; each must state and argue its case in terms of the values accepted by all. Minority and subordinate groups fighting for democracy and justice and freedom for themselves find it necessary to wage the fight in behalf of all.

When we look beyond the borders of American society out to the competitions and rivalries of the nations and races composing the Great Society what we have to observe, to the extent we can subordinate our emotions to the facts, is something very similar. The nations are in that society because they have some measure of common interests and common values. Beyond that measure their interests and values are their own. But they each accuse others of breaking the peace, of restricting trade, and of destroying civilization. In the fight arising out of these accusations and counter-accusations in which we presently are engaged, the freedom for which we fight will have to be won, as Pearl Buck has somewhere said, not race by race, or nation by nation, but as a human essence.

The process is costly and not according to our heart's desire but it seems to be the way of progress. The conflicts go on between groups within a larger group of common interest and value but each group centers its attention upon the other and not upon the larger community which encloses both. The process of progress might be less costly as well as far more satisfying if we could somehow learn to keep the societal whole in the focus of attention; if we could find a way to transform race pride from the kind of ingrowing thing which it usually is into the kind which takes satisfaction from the contribution which race members have made and are making to the larger race of mankind. To find a way to do this, and to do it, is the great opportunity of education in modern society.

• 9 •

School Desegregation: Condition
and Status

On March 17, 1954, the Supreme Court of the United States reversed its ruling of sixty years standing and declared the segregated education of Negro children in the public schools of the country by reason of race alone to be unconstitutional. In 1896 the Court had sanctioned the separate education of the races under its famous "separate but equal" formula.

The unanimous shift of opinion among the members of the Court deeply shocked the white South. The new decision was widely characterized as a "sociological" one because it was made, apparently, not on grounds of legal and constitutional precedent, but because the Court doubted "that any child may be expected to succeed in life if he is denied the opportunity of an education. Such an education . . . is a right which must be available to all on equal terms."

The recent decision is a sociological one, however, in a much more accurate and fundamental sense for it made the American school somewhat less an agency of the parents of school children and somewhat more an instrument of the state than it had been before. By so doing the Court disrupted the traditional accommodation that had been established between legal status and social status in the relations between whites and Negroes in the Southern States.

The issue drawn by the decision of the Court is clearly and sharply that of social status uncomplicated by the presence of factors found in other intercultural and interracial situations

SOURCE Paper delivered at meeting of the Southern Sociological Society, Atlanta, Georgia April 13, 1957.

where educational problems also loom large. The issue in the South is not one involving the use of the schools to conserve or to promote any special or distinctive white or Negro culture since, unlike the situation in South Africa, neither group has any radically distinctive culture. Neither is it an issue involving education in this or that set of religious values as is the case in Canada's "two nations." It is not an issue involving this or that language as a medium of instruction such as trouble bilingual commonwealths like Belgium. Nor is it an issue involving different philosophies of education or different theories of educational method. The issue is centered solely on the right of the Negro child to sit and to be taught in the classrooms of the school alongside the children of other American citizens of whatever race or color.

A peripheral factor in race relations only a few generations ago, education today in almost every multi-racial society in the world has moved around to a position of central importance. In almost every such society education has become an integral aspect of the race problem and as such is changing the nature of race relations.[1] Everywhere, in various forms and under various names, one hears of segregation and desegregation in the schools of the land. The 1954 decision of the Supreme Court of the United States has had repercussions wherever there are problems of educating the children of heterogeneous populations, and this is almost everywhere. The decision has, for one thing, focussed public attention upon these problems and helped define them in terms of the status aspirations of the peoples involved.

In the Southern States there has been a presumption that the decision of the Court has precipitated a situation unprecedented and unparalleled. The present Southern experience is unique, however, only in the sense that every social experience is unique to a degree; beyond that, it is of a kind with similar experiences elsewhere. It is natural to the people of every society to suppose that their experience is more unique than it actually is. This fact suggests that the study of parallels to racial segregation and desegregation in the schools of the South in other times and places might prove very rewarding. Such study might serve to make clearer to us what really is essential and what incidental and accidental in movements of change in race relations generally as well as education in particular.

One such essential and fundamental principle illuminated by existing studies is to be found in the distinction between advancing the status of a people and improving the "condition" of a people. In an interracial situation the efforts of members of the lower race to gain an education are, of course, not made *sui generis*. They are both stimulated and limited by the fluctuating sentiment of the surrounding dominant populations in regard to the existing and prospective place of the lower race in the larger society. The race problem, and the problem of education insofar as it is an aspect of the race problem, revolves around a struggle for status among the races of the society who are at the same time involved in a biological and economic struggle for existence. These two "struggles" enter into the educational process, and into every other conscious program for inducing change, as efforts to advance status on the one hand and to improve condition on the other.

It may be argued, of course, that every improvement in condition involved at least some shift in status and every advance in status is signalized by some visible improvement in condition. This may be true, but the two are separate and distinct conceptions nevertheless. The "condition" of a people describes the material and moral circumstances under which they live, and these circumstances may be changed without a corresponding change in social station. A condition is, more or less, an environmental incident. A status, on the other hand, is a position in a system of statuses, a position in a society. It is organically bound to every other status in the system, a high status for one necessitating a low status for another with a change in status inevitably bringing about adjusting changes in every other status throughout the system.

The items of a given condition become important for status when they are defined not in terms of physical misery or well-being, but in terms of personal and social degradation or prestige. This happens when events bring about opportunities for inner and sensitive comparisons and contrasts which in turn generate self and group consciousness. There is a story of a young African who enrolled at the London School of Economics in the days when Harold Laski and others of his persuasion were lambasting capitalism and colonialism. After a term or two he was asked how he was getting on. "Very well," he answered, "I have learned what my grievances are." When men begin to learn what their grievances are their condition is on the way to becoming a status as well.

The distinction between condition and status becomes significant and useful in the analysis of developments in education when it is remembered that education is both an instrument of control in the hands of the dominant race and a means of emancipation for the people of the lower races. But it is not likely to be the same kind of education. In interracial societies the control of education is ordinarily vested in a racial oligarchy whose original purpose in yielding the privilege of education is to insure that the children of the laboring races will remain laborers. If education there must be let it be an education designed to make hewers of wood and drawers of water into better hewers of wood and drawers of water, that is, let it be an occupational education. Thus will their condition be improved. This is an education designed not only to take apparent racial differences into account, but to extend and to perpetuate them as well. It is an education intended to discipline the classes that occupy the lower levels of the racial division of labor; if it contributes anything to the culture of the nation this will be accidental.

It is obvious that education intended to improve the condition of a people must be segregated from the education of those whose condition requires no improvement, who, indeed, are themselves the improvers. Different classes of the dominant race are likely to have different ideas about what constitutes improving the condition of the lower race—in the South those whites of lower class who have been in direct economic competition with Negroes have rarely agreed with upper class whites concerning the improvement of Negroes—but the general idea of improving the condition of the lower race is not normally resisted by the prestige classes of the dominant race. On the contrary, it is a means of demonstrating their own high status and will be favored by them just so long as the members of the lower race do not get the idea that they have any right to improve their own condition. Then it becomes a matter of status and will be resisted by members of the dominant race generally. Booker Washington was well aware of this when he said in welcoming a conference of white Southern university presidents to Tuskegee in 1912: "We are trying to instil into the Negro mind that if education does not make the Negro humble, simple, and of service to the community, then it will not be encouraged." [2]

Barbara Ward, surveying the present world scene from the standpoint of race relations, points out that "the common denominator of the sense of equality, where it has appeared, has been education." [3] The education desired is the prestige education formerly reserved for the children of the racial oligarchy, an education in the sciences, the liberal arts, and in the professions. It is such an education in unsegregated institutions which will emancipate from the thralldom of caste and class and race.

In the transition to prestige education it might be observed that educational standards seem to suffer greatly. It becomes apparent that the achievement of the right to an education commensurate with one's status ambitions is a very different thing from achieving the education itself. The fight for the right to a prestige education may be a deeply moving and exhilarating personal and social experience, comparable to an experience in any crusade or social movement; the individual becomes at one with his fellows as he shares with them the values of a common ideal. But achieving the education itself is something else again for the long hard hours of work and study required may be dull and drab hours.

From the point of view of the dominant race the transition to prestige education does the same thing to the people of the lower races that it did to Kipling's Russian peasant. "Let it be clearly understood," Kipling said, "that the Russian is a delightful fellow till he tucks his shirt in." All people, even college students in America, begin to tuck their shirts in when they really begin to get an education. But then they become conceited, arrogant, and vain, and think themselves as good as their betters. More than this, their pretentions threaten to depreciate the status of the rest to the level of the upstarts. Around the turn of the century, long before desegregation had become a popular word, a white Southerner named Edgar Gardner Murphy disclosed the real reason for the white man's opposition to the prestige education of the Negro when he wrote:

Much of the instinctive protest against the advance of the negro race has been due to the fear that its development would contribute to its encroachment upon the white man's life. The leaning toward arbitrary processes has largely sprung from no direct hatred of the negro, but from the vague suspicion that unless burdened with peculiar disabilities his progress might oppose the progress of the stronger race. Many have thus antagonized his education merely because they have seen in it a peril to themselves. They have not cared, primarily, to keep any man in ignorance; they have not personally desired the hopelessness of any class; but they have distrusted the bestowal of any power upon this weaker group which might strengthen its capacity for access into the life and destiny of the stronger.[4]

When problems of education move around to the center of the race relations complex generally, attention focuses upon children rather than upon adults. During the period of the slavery controversy in America attention focused upon the adults of the lower race. Adults, however, do not excite such pathos as children, particularly in the societies of the West where the traditionally almost perfect image of injustice is the unhappy child. It is difficult to defend a system of education which sets out to create a feeling of inferiority in a child, and if the outcome of any conflict in this world of multiple conflict can be predicted with any degree of confidence it is that in any war against children the children in the long run are bound to win. It is unfortunate for the opponents of desegregation in the schools of the South and throughout the world that, as the situation is being defined, they are pitted against children.

It has never been entirely true that matters can be arranged just as men consciously and deliberately wish to arrange them —impersonal social forces will always figure largely in determining final pattern—but so far as the South is concerned it is inescapably true that responsibility today for an understanding if not an agreement in matters of education rests with individual men, white and black, to a greater degree than ever before. There is no question now of waiting until one race or the other is "ready." There is no longer any choice; now it is necessary to act together with as much wisdom and with "all deliberate speed," not just because the Supreme Court ordered this, but because the movement of events demand it. We sociologists remember that it was Cooley who told us that it is the business of an institution to help people make up their minds. The institutions many of us are connected with are very slow to function institutionally.

As the debates over educational segregation and desegregation proceed in the South and in other interracial societies around the world it may turn out that it is the society itself, and not just the children in the schools, which will receive the profoundest education.

• 10 •

The "Little Races"

I

Eugene Griessman of Auburn University and the contributors to this series are directing our attention to a significant body of social phenomena which, so far, in spite of a fair amount of literature, have been only slightly utilized in our continuing search for the nature and meaning of the social, the racial, and the simply human. They are asking us to pay more attention to the comparative study of race relations and of the significance of the "little races" of the earth in such study. For social science is possible only on the assumption that all societies are comparable, and the assumption of comparability leads finally to the problem of understanding human nature, the sociological absolute, that lies behind all cultures no matter how seemingly different they are from one another. What I think we must finally search for, if sociology is to be worthy of its name, is that property or those properties of mankind *qua* mankind, and not of people only as members of this or that race, class, nationality, or tribe. To this end, we require laboratories, situations, groups, or personalities where human behavior is best highlighted in its representative capacity. It may be suggested that it is the marginal or peripheral individuals and groups that play the part of a scientific lens through which the theoretical as well as the practical problems of race relations can best be analyzed and understood. By shifting our focus to peripheral groups, we may bring to light and make more observable the human factors involved in social relations generally. The systematic study of the "little races" may contribute much to the search.

SOURCE *American Anthropologist,* October 1972, pp. 1296–1306.

Varieties of mankind differentiated all over the world at a time when everything tended to isolate groups of men for long periods of time. Ever since, those who wish to promote a more civilized world have faced the very practical and difficult problem of overcoming the barriers to intergroup understanding thrown up by physical, social, and ideological distances. Perhaps the best way to break down the barriers erected by racial and cultural diversity and to lay bare the simply human is by better understanding how and why the barriers come to be erected in the first place. For the barriers are not just passive obstructions to communication; they actively constitute aggregates into the kind of peoples they are or become—tribes, nationalities, races, or what not. It has never been sufficient simply to belong to the human race; world economic processes and catholic religions seem themselves to give rise to the fragmentations among men they are meant to oppose. The centuries that gave rise to the ideals of world brotherhood and the Rights of Man are the same centuries that gave us sectarianism, nationalism, and racism. It is humanly imperative to seek refuge in some differentiated community, even a fictitious community if necessary, if men are to know who they are in relation to other men, to find comfort in the sentiment of belonging, and to experience some feeling of certainty and security. It is equally important to account for the social and human forces that generate the collective consciousness which operates to maintain the barriers that appear essential to the survival of the community. Human nature is forever at play originating, maintaining, terminating, and rearranging social groupings.

II

During the eras of global migrations, and particularly during the past two or three centuries, peoples identified and named as culturally or racially different met on the frontiers of the world, pushed each other around, intermixed, or exterminated one or the other. The more numerous or powerful streams pushed on to newer frontiers, there to begin again another stage of racial and cultural anarchy until some new social order could be established; but left behind in the wake of such movements were various sorts of little ethnic and cultural islands. All of Europe, and the frontier areas overseas where Europeans penetrated, contain many little enclaves of curious mixtures or communities where the people have resisted further mixing. Shifts in national boundaries have produced irredentism or left certain other groups such as the Wends in Germany, the Welsh in Britain, the Bretons in France, and the Basques in Spain stranded or relatively unincorporated in the larger society around them. There were and are mixed Teutonic and Slavic groups in Eastern Europe, and mixed Teutonic and Latin groups in Southern Europe. Racially mixed groups also may be found in Nova Scotia, New Brunswick, and the Gaspé peninsula in Canada. Elsewhere in the New World, physical descent and cultural assimilation sometimes part company to produce some interesting results; there are the French-speaking Germans of Louisiana (Deiler 1909:119–128) and the almost "pure" physical Negroes with an almost "pure" Indian culture of British Honduras (Taylor 1951). Many bi- and tri-racial communities are present in the West Indies, Central and South America, and in Africa, particularly in southern Africa.

It is apparent that racially mixed communities are to be found in probably every continental division of the earth. They are not be be considered, as so often they are considered in popular magazine and newspaper stories, as racial freaks or as merely quaint blendings of peoples. On the contrary, they may serve to lay bare the elementary processes of racial formation and meaning as race is sociologically understood and, given sufficient isolation and imbreeding, even biologically and anthropologically understood. At the present time when the social integers we commonly look at, and are most concerned about, are cities, nationalities, and large racial groups, we are in this series brought back, as ethnologists are always bringing us back (e.g., see Redfield 1955), to the consideration of small but whole communities more or less territorially isolated, continuing over time in their own system of incomplete but separate institutions, and yet embedded in a larger society. The study of the little races will be most useful if they are viewed and typed within a wide frame of reference alongside tribes, clans, sects, utopian or ideological communities, and various sorts of odd lot, leftover, and "lost" peoples.

Like the Japanese, the Russians, the Chinese, and the nationals of other countries, the people of the United States are preoccupied with "big" powers and "big" problems. We are preoccupied right now with the problem of the confrontation of massive racial groups in the United States, in Rhodesia, in the Republic of South Africa, and in many other areas around the world. Of course we should be concerned. But the literature on these racial confrontations is enormous and continues to grow to the point where many of us are overwhelmed by it all. There are so many factors and variables involved, that fundamental questions having to do with the nature of race and race relations are in danger of getting lost. This is not to deny the importance of the study of massive racial confrontations, for the idea of race as we know it today is essentially a mass phenomenon, but I do mean to suggest that the little races can teach us something about race not at once apparent when we confine our attention to the great races only.

A careful comparison of the little races and the big races, noting significant similarities and differences, should contribute to conceptual clarity. Josiah Royce was fond of speaking of "the fecundity of aggregations," by which he meant that when you put a lot of things or people together, something changes. When individuals are aggregated, some things are true of the individuals that are not true of the aggregation, and some things are true of the aggregation that are not true of the individuals, but how small or how large the aggregation is makes a considerable difference. Without presuming to develop here the comparison between little and big races exhaustively it may be suggested that a "great" race [1] can constitute a "people" with a full complement of institutions; the little race is organized around only one or more of the basic institutions, depending upon its size. One achieved a college which now is a university; others barely managed a school or a church. A Negro cannot possibly know personally every other Negro, nor can a White possibly know every other White man. But a member of several of the little races can personally know every other member of his community, may, in fact, be connected with them through ties of kinship. The members of the little race can, therefore, act together more easily and informally without the aid of printed newspapers; the school serves as a sort of local community newspaper. The members of the little race emphasize their common descent;

members of the larger groups emphasize their common race (Hudson 1970, especially Ch. 4). But this is in large measure the dilemma of the small group; it is imperfectly joined, in America and in southern Africa, to the White-Black omnipresence. Its members are a raceless people in a racial society.

III

I suppose human groups have always found a principle of some sort to support claims to a humanity superior to other groups around them, if only because "we" are here and "they" are there with some extent of no-man's land in between. A transcendental myth such as race appears to emerge as a divisive measure when we and they are intermixed on the same land. Probably almost every "we," no matter how innocently used, contains at least the germ of the idea of superiority and every "they" the germ of the idea of inferiority. We may at last know the others to be "criminal tribes," as in India (Gillin 1931, Chs. 4, 5), or "bad races," as in earlier France, that is, people who do not know what life is like without being an object of contempt (Michel 1847; McCloy 1955). They are "criminal" or "bad" merely by being members of an ethnic group other than our own; the very idea of race carries this moral implication, faintly or extravagantly.

During the past several centuries, a somewhat more sophisticated and "scientific" disposition to classify men into alleged biologically superior or inferior races has developed. This development has had particular appeal in situations where people of different complexions and physiognomies have come together on the same land, and especially where the rate of cultural assimilation has been so rapid as to leave physical appearance the principal basis of distinction. In such situations, the people classify themselves on this basis without serious regard to the measurements of physical anthropologists.

Always there is amalgamation as well as assimilation; miscegenation, or race mixture, is inevitable. As Charles Darwin in *The Descent of Man* put it years ago, "The races of man are not sufficiently distinct to inhabit the same country without fusion . . . In all ordinary cases, the male is so eager that he will accept any female" (1896:174,420). The sexes of different races mate no matter how great or how deep the antipathies between them;

the stern Calvinism of the Dutch in South Africa was not sufficient to prevent the sexual use of Bantu and Hottentot women.
The appearance of the mixed blood begins the process of
"muddying up" and rendering physical types less distinct and
more ambiguous than the parent stocks. His very appearance
raises questions and starts discussion as to who he is and how he
should be racially classified. The parent stocks have then to be
classified and accounted for also, and ideas about their mental,
moral, and physical characteristics are generated. In order to
clarify the questions and the answers recourse is had to such
"scientific," historical, ethnographic, and religious literature as
seems to justify and naturalize the answers best serving the needs
of the situation. The parent stocks may be regarded as racially
unmixed in spite of the fact that physical anthropologists have
demonstrated that there are no "pure" races; when today we
speak of mixed bloods, we are really referring to the relative
recency of the mixture of peoples popularly identified as racially
different.

Actually, there are Negro genes in Americans regarded by
themselves and by others as White, and Caucasian genes in those
who regard themselves and are regarded by others as Black.
There are Negro genes in Americans who regard themselves as
Indians and Indian genes in those who regard themselves as
Negro. There probably are more Indian genes in those who regard themselves as White and are regarded by others as White,
especially in our so-called "poor White" population, than is commonly supposed. These are the people who have few or no problems of racial identity.

But there are other highly self-conscious individuals of doubtful race in America and in other parts of the world who are
tagged and variously named. Sociologists and others, following
the lead of Robert E. Park (1929:64–77) and Everett Stonequist
have brought all these regional names and types together under
the general term, "marginal man" (Stonequist 1937:vii). The type
tends to disperse more or less individually throughout the general population. Often, however, detribalized or déraciné
Whites, Blacks, natives or mixed bloods establish and stabilize
themselves in little endogamous settlements set sparsely apart
from the parent stocks and seek, or are assigned by epithet, a
separate identity and name. These are the little races. Such

groups also occupy an uncertain and undefined identity in our midst, but they choose to live by themselves and for themselves on land which they and their ancestors may have occupied for two or three hundred years. They do not or cannot completely incorporate into the larger territorial unit nor identify with one or another of the larger and established races surrounding them. They are a "marginal people," but not necessarily an aggregation of marginal men. The individual member may be almost as completely adjusted to his fellows and to a way of life as any man. Individual marginal men and women have produced and published a fairly large number of autobiographical documents in which they tell what it means to be constantly thrown back upon one's self, to be continually compelled to answer questions that the ordinary man is not expected to answer, and to feel the conflict of divergent purposes. But no similar personal document produced by a member of any one of the little races has come to my attention, perhaps because within his own group the individual member has a recognized place and status. The community within which he lives may not be wholly sure of itself, but the individual member may be as completely self-assured as most men normally are. But not, perhaps, when he travels.

IV

Popular as well as scholarly writers who have written about the sort of communities described in this series have a variety of expressions to denominate them. They have been called "native aliens," "citizen aliens," the "differently born," "cultural or racial illegitimates," "racial dropouts," "racial hybrids," "racial islanders," "forgotten people," "racial miscreants," "indeterminate or misplaced people," "mestizos," "ambiguous people," "neither here nor there people," "racial isolates," "bi- or tri-racial mixtures," "marooned communities," "God's stepchildren," and "spurious people." [2] I prefer the term "little races" as more objective and neutral and as avoiding the popular judgments and values implicit in the attitudes of prejudice or pathos. The term is at once more inclusive and limiting. It may serve to throw the groups here under consideration more completely into the general field of race and race relations bringing to bear upon their study the large body of funded knowledge we now possess. At the same time, it should invite new questions and promote further research. It is not an expression of my own invention; it is said by Magnus Hirshfeld to have originated in the middle of the nineteenth century when scholars working under the influence of de Gobineau puzzled over the proper classification of "new specimens of mankind," as Herder called them, then coming to the attention of public and intellectual figures (Hirshfeld 1938: 120). Then, as now, they were peoples or races that did not seem to fit into accepted racial categories.

The people of the little races are to be found in situations where race is deemed so important that to be raceless is not to be able to take one's world or the place of one's people in the world for granted. Here some racial affiliation is imperative. Somewhere I read an account of the effort of the good ladies of a Midwestern town to take a complete religious census of the people of the community. Armed with a list of sects, denominations, and religious organizations arranged in alphabetical order, one of the women called at the home of a man who declared himself an atheist. The lady looked at her list and said, "You can't be an atheist; it's not on the list." When the man insisted, she asked about his father, "Well, he's an atheist too." She then inquired about his grandfather, who turned out of have been a Methodist. So she recorded the gentleman being questioned as a Methodist, a denomination which did appear on the list. It apparently was inconceivable that anyone should have no connection whatever with an approved religious organization.

In the southern part of the United States, in the Republic of South Africa, and elsewhere, some sort of connection with a traditional racial group is a sort of categorical imperative even if the census taker has to make an arbitrary assignment. But exiled communities prefer to establish themselves as a true race in their own right. Not to be on the racial list is not to be able to live freely, spontaneously, instinctively; it is not to have an eminent place in society and a view of life ready at birth. We see this in the plea of representatives of Buys' Bastaards, a South African community of racial orphans, to get on the list of respectables, before a government commission. They were asking for racial legitimation and for the citizenship rights recognized by such legitimation, and their petition is a moving illustration of the importance of racial accreditation in that country. "To see fine old fellows like Conraed Buys and Jafta Buys, the last of the best type of the older generation of this family, standing before the meeting bareheaded and with the intensity of feeling born of a lost cause and a lost people—for the Buys are a lost people—could not but move even the most callously indifferent to an understanding of the tragedy of this rapidly disappearing race of men and women" (Report of the Commission of Inquiry Regarding the Cape Coloured Population, 1937).

V

The aspiration is for membership in a "pure" race and not just in *a* race. The problem of purity in connection with sanitation, hygiene, food, and the taboos intended to insure stainlessness in these matters, has been investigated (Douglas 1966), and this kind of interest is, of course, relevant, but I am not aware of any systematic effort to inquire into all that is involved in claims to ethnic or group purity. In all the talk about "pure races," no one appears to objectively specify just what is meant. Nevertheless, the *idea* of ethnic purity is and has been a widespread social and historical fact and has had a tremendous impact upon social attitudes, social conduct, and even law. Presumably, a pure group or individual is one of standardized mixture; even a purebred dog or horse is of mixed ancestry, but at some point ideal criteria are introduced by man the master. No such rigid standardization has ever been deliberately achieved in human society. Yet I suggest that a society becomes a people of some sort when it develops a ideal of purity of some kind and undertakes to separate out all extraneous elements in order to free itself from moral defilement or guilt. It may be that a historical people must have a collective representation signifying purity to hold to, and that the kind of people they are, or conceive themselves to be, depends upon the nature of the symbol regarded as "pure" by the whole group. The symbol may be racial, linguistic, religious, or some other.

Concern with the matter of racial purity led to such writing as that produced by Count Arthur de Gobineau (1915) and Houston Stewart Chamberlain (1913) in Europe and by Madison Grant (1918) and Lothrop Stoddard (1922) in America. White Americans and White South Africans read these books and found the racial ideals they had for themselves amply confirmed by such high authorities. In the golden age of Spain, *limpieza de sangre* figured importantly in the Inquisition (Lea 1906–07, Ch. 4). During that period, the mere mention of the Jewish ancestry of a popular priest was enough to bring charges of poisonous libel followed by official censorship. Jewish purity was and is fundamentally a struggle to maintain the identity of Israel by asserting and protecting the distinctiveness of the Jews as a chosen people. So convinced were those Englishmen who settled early New England that they and they alone followed a pure and true faith that they called themselves Puritans. Caste purity is highly cherished in India; it may cost an upper caste Indian a lot of money to get pure and to stay pure. Other people such as the French, as well as those involved in nationalistic movements, are or have been greatly concerned with linguistic purity. The ideal of racial purity should therefore be considered as just one expression of purity ideals generally.

The point assumes some importance in the case of the little races. With great races around them regarding themselves as pure, and ostracizing in public opinion and in law those known to have violated the code through intermarriage, how can a demonstrably mixed community at least approximate an ideal of racial purity deemed necessary to social acceptance? It can point to some old and "good" and proud families who have refused further mixing, and many if not most of the mixed communities in eastern America seem to have done so. Or something like caste lines can be drawn within the community based upon an alleged degree of descent from the master race. According to Eugen Fischer the Rehoboth Bastaards of Southwest Africa ranked themselves into "European," "Hottentot," and "Intermediate" in that order (Fischer 1913). But much more interesting was an actual count of "pure" and "non-pure" members of the Buys community in South Africa in 1934. The enumerator found 218 "pure" Buys and sixty-three "non-pure" Buys in that year. Naturally there was a division of opinion among the Buys people as to who was legitimately Buys and who was not.

The retrogressive element of the tribe contend that anyone living on the Buys farm or a Buys man or woman by any sort of union is a Buys. The progressive element, however, takes the attitude that children of the Buys girls by a European, whether they are married to him or not, are members of the Buys tribe. They also contend that if a Buys male lawfully marries a native woman the offspring are not Buys [Report of the Commission, *op. cit.*].

The descent of the Buys, pure or nonpure, from the union of the first Conraed de Buys, a White Dutchman, and his numerous African and Hottentot wives can be fully documented, but at some point in their post-colonial history some of them at least became pure-blooded mongrels. Incidentally, so have Germans, Americans, Anglo-Saxons, Japanese, and all the other established races and nationalities of the world. What the little races are showing us here is that where the idea of race and racial status is virile, concern with in-group purification in order to protect against the misguided ways of the unconcerned apparently is universal in race as well as in group relations generally. It figures in the present desperate struggle for racial status in America and in other parts of the world.

VI

Closely related to the problem of purity and status is the issue of a proper name to go by. People who live completely in a homogeneous racial or cultural society are not usually called upon to choose a race to which to belong or to choose a name for their group. The problem of choice is the problem of the marginal man or group, not just of the intellectual or political leaders, but of the ordinary men and women as well. In the case of mixed blood individuals and communities, there seem to be three terminological situations. In the first situation, the father, who doesn't take off his hat when be begets offspring, a temporary sojourner who then moves on and doesn't write, leaves behind a progeny which is adopted into the mother's family or tribe. The children may be known to be part Polynesian and part sailor, but they tend to take on the name of the mother's people and identify with them.

In the second situation, the father recognizes and remains with his mixed blood offspring who take his name and seek to identify with his racial status. He may be one like the Dutch missionary Vanderkemp who married and had children by a native woman in early South Africa because he regarded this action as his Christian duty (Millin 1924). Or he might be a Scottish trader on the

American frontier or an outlaw such as Conraed de Buys the elder who escaped from the Cape in South Africa toward the north (Millin 1949). This rough and tough man probably referred to his children as "my bastards" and the children might very well have answered "We are Buys' bastards" to inquiring visitors since they had no idea of the disparaging meaning of this European word. Other groups designated as Bastards, or Bastaards in Dutch, by members and non-members alike, such as the Koranas, the Manaquas, the Bergenaars, the Dunns, and the Rehoboths, appeared along the South and Southwest African frontier. Unlike southern Africa, most American mixed communities did not take the name of the alleged founder.[3]

The third situation arrives when the mixed community becomes more status conscious and more sensitive to the derogatory connotation of the epithet applied to it as a name by the larger society. The community then seeks to change its name, or have it changed for it, in the hope that higher status may be achieved by synonym. Consciousness of wounding experiences and low esteem suffered as effects of a disparaging epithet leads to a search for a new name of dignity and respect, a search which involves a break with the naming power of the superordinate race and enhances the authority of the community to determinate for itself who belongs and who does not belong. Awareness of the derogatory implications of the old name and of the need for a new one may come more or less suddenly as suggested by an entry in the diary of the Rev. John Campbell, missionary, on August 6, 1813, during the course of his travels in South Africa. We read:

The people of this part, being a mixed race, went by the name of Bastards; but having represented to the principle persons the offensiveness of the word to an English or Dutch ear, they resolved to assume some other name. On consulting among themselves they found the majority were descended from a person of the name of Griqua, and they resolved hereafter to be called Griquaas. In the evening there was thunder but no rain [Campbell 1816:235].[4]

VII

Efforts to escape name prejudice have characterized many marginal individuals and groups in America, Africa, and elsewhere. The act of "passing," or "going for white," an effort on the part of individuals to avoid minority group classification, is and has been a commonplace occurrence. What is involved in "passing" is well stated by W. D. Jordan:

Passing would have been unnecessary if the mixed ancestry had been regarded as midway between black and white. It was the existence of a broad chasm which necessitated a sudden leap which passing represented . . . The success of the passing mechanism depended upon its operating in silence. Passing was a conspiracy of silence not only for the individual but for a biracial society which had drawn a rigid color line based on visibility [1962:189, 191–192].

The efforts of southern African mixed communities and their American counterparts to shake off such scurrilous names as "Bastards," "Jerry Brindles," "Red Bones," "Red Legs," "We-sorts," "Ramp Eaters," "Brass Ankles," "Buckheads," "Domi-neckers," "Yellow Hammers," or "No Papas" [5] is of an entirely different order of aspiration from that of "passing." Of course, individuals as individuals from mixed communities have moved out into the larger and anonymous world of cities and "passed," but when the collective community seeks through a name change or an old name emphasis a new image of itself while retaining group cohesion, something very different from "passing," as Jordan defines the process, is going on. Here it is not a "sudden leap . . . operating in silence." On the contrary; it may be well publicized. There is involved here a deliberate choice of an approved name with all the moral and behavioral consequences that the choice may entail. There may be, as there have been, appeals to legislation, to the courts, to the political process, and to public opinion. There may be demands for curriculum changes in the schools. It is an endeavor, not to pass, but to upgrade themselves by redefining a biological ancestry and achieving an acceptable social ancestry in order to account for the darker skin color, while at the same time avoiding the imputation of "inferior" race connections. The endeavor is witness to a dual struggle: for survival and enhancement of group pride on the one hand, and for acceptance by the larger society and its set of national values on the other. A few communities such as the Guineas and the Coe Ridgers may acknowledge the presence of Black blood but usually this is vigorously denied. Brewton Berry's informant put it this way:

"Tell you the truth, Mr. Berry," said one old fellow whose confidence had been won through long hours of chitchat, *"we don't known what the hell we is.* Some folks say we is Indians. Well, maybe so and maybe not. My old man used to say we was part Cherokee and part Irish. I dunno. *But we know we ain't niggers.* We know that." And he made his point emphatic by pounding his right fist into the palm of his left hand [Berry, 1963:32].

Apparently, the most frequent resort of the mixed communities in America is to emphasize the Indian component in the ancestry. This has been a long time precedent; Southern court records extending back to colonial days "reveal many efforts to prove that persons of doubtful ancestry were descendants of Indians and not Negroes" (Johnson 1929:43). The degree of Indian admixture as over against White and Black admixture is, of course, difficult if not impossible to establish, but it is certain that communities such as the Choctaw in Mississippi and several others in Virginia are predominantly Indian. For such groups, this is a matter of fact; for most of the others, the degree, if any, is a matter of opinion, but it is likely that most American mixed communities have at least *some* Indian blood.

Alternative explanations of the darker skin coloration of members of mixed communities, offered by them to counter the assumption of local Whites and Blacks that they are predominantly Negroid, have developed along with, or in place of, the Indian origin version. Origin myths involving claims to Portuguese and Moorish ancestry are especially widespread. A small group in Northampton county in North Carolina call themselves Portuguese, and have been registered on the election books as such, but complain that they are not accepted for what they are by local Whites and Negroes who call them "resentful names." In February, 1958, according to newspaper stories, a representative from the Portuguese embassy in Washington visited the settlement because, he said, there was a feeling of "great indignation" in Portugal over the alleged mistreatment of these people (Anonymous 1958). The embassy representative reported that he was "inclined to think" that there was some connection between Portugal and the North Carolina colony and intended to submit a "strong protest" to the U.S. State Department. No further information is available. A similar ancestral claim of the "Turks," the fighting gamecocks of Thomas Sumter's Revolutionary War band, has been investigated by Turkish nationals which resulted in mixed opinions. The "Moors" of Delaware are known to us chiefly through the writings of C. A. Weslanger (1943), and a small group known as "Free Moors" once existed in the Santee-Cooper area of lower South Carolina. In the "Deep Creek" section of Crawford and Taylor counties of Georgia formerly lived a group claiming Italian descent but known to local people as "poor Whites." A people formerly known as "Cubans," and now designated as Indians of Person County, live in that county in North Carolina and spill over into adjoining counties in Virginia. The Lumbees of Robeson and adjoining counties in North Carolina, formerly known as "Croatans," cherish the tradition of descent from Sir Walter Raleigh's lost colony, a tradition which not only gives them "White blood" but "superior White blood." The Creoles of southern Alabama claim to be of French descent and discount any Indian and Negro connections. Malayan, Greek, and Arab ancestral elements also are sometimes claimed.

VIII

What of the future of the little races? They came into existence when they were recognized and named; one community known to me is said to have achieved an identity and a name within the past thirty years. Perhaps others will in time achieve similar recognition. Still others will disappear, as some already have disappeared, when they can no longer isolate themselves from the larger society or as the larger society moves in upon them. American industry, no longer allowed to tap all the cheap labor it wants from other parts of the world, is mopping up available cultural and racial islanders within the boundaries of this country. Automobiles and the call of the city promote nation-wide mobility; little race ghettos are appearing in several cities. Highway construction is making inroads into community lands, perhaps the community's most important principle of ancestral order and continuity. Many of the little races have tenaciously persisted for generations on the same land, but they are not likely to persist there forever. Soldiers, White and Black, in Southern military posts, marry the attractive girls from the communities, while the local boys range far and wide looking for mates. The segregated school, built by and especially designed for the children of the mixed bloods and long the chief center of community life, is on the way out in response to court orders. "Our school," where questions regarding racial origin were not asked or recorded, is no longer "our school." The tri-racial mixtures in South Carolina are said to be making gains toward White status, whereas the Creole community of lower Alabama is said to accept the Negro component in its mixture as well as its Negro neighbors more readily. E. G. Malherbe writes from South Africa that "the Buys island is fast becoming a mere peninsula—culturally as well as genetically" (1971). Ethnologists appear to be running out of culturally uninfected tribes, and we may be running out of little races. Madison Grant (1918) worried about the "passing of the great race," but only a few of their own members appear to be worried about the passing of the little races. Now is the time to take a more systematic and comprehensive look at the sort of communities discussed by the contributors to this series. I have tried to suggest a frame of reference, and a series of propositions which could be turned into researchable questions, appropriate to a comprehensive inquiry.

The "Little Races" and Racial Theory

I regard the study of what I have elsewhere called the "little races," particularly in the South and in South Africa, as bearing most significantly upon the problem of race and race relations generally. It does not help a great deal if these communities are viewed merely as exotic groups in isolation from their neighbors and outside the context of social theory if for no other reason than that they help overcome the stereotyped images of too many of us that the boundaries of racial groups are fixed and clear-cut.

Out of the massive confrontation of whites and blacks in at least these two race relations regions of the world there have

SOURCE Paper delivered at meeting of the American Anthropological Association, New Orleans, December 2, 1973.

appeared third races struggling to be born. They are relatively recent biological and social hybrids occupying a position and playing a role intermediate between the original racial and cultural groups to which they are most nearly related.

In America they have in them, in varying proportions, the blood of the native Indian which ordinarily they prefer to elevate above the possibly more preponderate other ethnic components to the status of principal ancestor. In Latin America, Indians mixed with other ethnics, originally called *mestizos, ladinos, cholos,* etc., have tended to lose identity as Indians and to become Mexicans, Peruvians, or Bolivians.[1] In the United States, the "little races" have moved in the opposite direction; they have progressively emphasized the Indian connection. If the members of the mixed community in America resist identification as blacks, and if they are not accepted by whites, there is no alternative to the Indian claim, other than local and unacceptable origin myths, in a situation like that of the South where "belonging" not only to *a* race but to a major historical race is almost a cultural imperative. Belonging to a race, any race, is a necessary way of underwriting social arrangements in order to have a recognized place in them.

The marginal or in-between communities of mixed bloods have been territorially segregated, or have segregated themselves, in sanctuaries into which their members can retreat from their partial association with neighboring black and white groups whose members are highly prejudiced against them. In these sanctuaries they have built up functional social systems of their own around one or more institutions. Separated spatially they are, or come to be, separated qualitatively also. They and their neighbors recognize social and institutional as well as territorial boundaries. Individuals from the three ethnics frequently cross the boundaries, but the community itself continues to live on through many generations.

It is essential that we understand the "little race" in the context of a society, that is, as a group living inside a larger group. The marginality of the mixed communities have everywhere been defined for them by the acknowledged races living around them which in the course of time named them by epithet. The naming process contributed to the realization, the establishment, and the segregation of the mixed community and by so doing contributed also to the racial identification of the surrounding peoples; the "nowhere belongers" helped name and identify the rest of us who do belong somewhere. They served to strengthen the racial categories in which we have placed whites and blacks; they at least served to remind blacks that not all dark people can be grouped with them. Contrast or negative beliefs about them are needed by the numerically and politically dominant groups as they grope toward a positive conception of themselves. Out of such a dialectic races as well as other sorts of groups are born. Of course we are white or we are black but what are we whites or blacks against? Each "race" threatens each of the others and each feels the need of protection from each of the others. In a climate of race the mixed community of underdogs has to struggle to be a race also. Mixed-blood groups in the United States are backed up against the authenticity, not only of their color as in the case of whites and blacks, but principally against the tradition of the noble red man and this has to become the chief basis of their pride and of their survival. This is set against the stigma of former slavery in the case of the blacks and against the alleged avarice of the whites. Their dilemma originates in part in the tension between having an identity and remaining poor on ancestral lands or losing identity and moving out into the mainstream of American life.

The "little races" pose some very interesting and important theoretical considerations about which we may speculate. If we are disposed to suppose that the boundaries of racial groups are clear-cut we also tend to think of them as static entities. If now we are conscious of racial divisions in our society and throughout the world our disposition is to assume that we have always had such divisions. We read our present racial distinctions far back into the past. It was God who originally set the races apart in the act of creation. But, of course, social and biological races are a constant becoming. Universal miscegenation has always violated the boundaries of such groupings to create new groups some of which, as the idea of race settled upon men, tended to become new races. An immutable process goes on. As in some universal Virginia reel, individuals are continually dancing off in new directions, embracing new partners, with groups joining and conjoining, forming, transforming, reforming, deforming, alternatively becoming rigid and then flexible, only to dissolve and start all over again in the everlasting process of group-making. In the process new names and new group types appear, some now called races, but the underlying process itself, like the tides of the ocean, is ceaseless. At some point the members of new groups become conscious of membership and aware of a kinship with each other and an apartness from others. The we-they dichotomy in a common societal frame is necessary and inevitable in human affairs always and everywhere. Race, and the ideologies intended to account for it, is one of the relatively more recent expressions of this highly dynamic process. The "little races" afford a dramatic opportunity to study the particulars of this process near at hand.

Out of the welter of colonial settlers from Europe, often originally at odds with one another and strongly committed to various national loyalties, there developed at long last that race now known as white because that was the color of their skins and about all they had in common. Scores of men and women from different tribes from Africa, originally unable to understand even the speech of one another, came under the shared sameness of slavery to know themselves as Negroes or blacks because that skin color was about all they had in common. The native Indians did not even know they were Indians—they were members of this or that tribe—but eventually they came to know themselves as red Indians because this was what the others called them. But racial identification did not come overnight, and the self-conception of men as white and the self-conception of men as black have altered many times between 1619 and the present. Whites are not now the same kind of whites their fathers were and blacks are not now the same kind of black men as their fathers. There will be further identity changes as time passes. The "little races" may help us better understand race-making situations generally and the processes of racial formation and change in them.

With the formation of the "little races" there inevitably arose a number of origin myths accounting for the existence of each community. Critical historiography must deny or discount these stories even though they are essential to human needs for dignity and identity. We humanly need to know who we are and where we came from and even mythical answers are necessary and functional. But realistic speculation on the origin or origins of the little races in America require the reconstruction in imagination, with what facts we can come by, of what must have been the kind of situation in which the grouping of *déraciné* or rootless individuals might have come about. Along the colonial American frontier from Canada to Florida there were several little bands of settlers whose homelands were across the Atlantic. They lived precariously on the edge of a forested and moral wilderness which stretched into an unknown west, a wilderness where men might escape the rules of community and consort with whom they pleased in the common business of living and mutual protection.

We know from records of the time that, at least on the unruly Southeast frontier, there was an indiscriminate mingling of whites, Indians, and Negroes [2] and that for a time, in the 1780's, the marriage of white men and women to Indian men and women was favored.[3] In the back country marriage was unnecessary. Except for the Indians there was a decided sexual imbalance in favor of white and black males. When these men wanted women they had recourse to Indian women or none at all and all evidence indicated that they took full advantage of their opportunities.[4] It is to be expected that groups of divergent race and mixture would form, perhaps nucleated around settlement or "parchcorn" Indians. The Handbook of American Indians (Bulletin 30) spoke of such groups as "people who combine in themselves the blood of wasted native tribes, the early colonists or forest rovers, the runaway slaves or other negroes, and probably also of stray seamen of the Latin races from coastal vessels in the West Indian or Brazilian trade."

These little islands of nondescript people, later augmented by other and similar elements from time to time, living in or near swamps, hills or stradled across state boundary lines, formed in all probability the genesis of the communities we call "the little races." As white farm and slave plantation settlement moved in around them drawing unfavorable distinctions, as a racial ideology evolved in the larger society, and as close in-marriage and intermarriage among the outcastes became the only avenue of mating and procreation, the stage was set for the emergence of new groups of unstable racial identities.

Students of native societies in Africa, now reeling under the impact of widespread change and disorganization, remark often of detribalization and tribalization. We have the same phenomena in America although we do not often use these concepts. But consideration of the problem of the little races may serve to call attention to the corresponding problem of de-racialization and racialization. How are races made, dissolved, and recreated both biologically and sociologically? All peoples begin as a mix, but why and when does a mixed community itself come to propound sanctions against miscegenation? Under what circumstances does such a community come to regard itself, and to be regarded, as a new race? To what extent is the presence of a "little race" an index of the character of existing relations between the larger and acknowledged races around them? What is the role and function of buffer groups generally?

III

The South: A Morally Sensitive Society

Cabin in the cotton

• 11 •

Sociology and Sociological Research
in the South

A Time for Appraisal

We used to think of the South as a culturally passive area where people assumed that what had always been would always be. Unlike the urban North, where change initiated from within seems almost to have been the very life principle of the society itself, change in the feudal and agrarian South has appeared as something forced from without in the form of market fluctuations and northern carpetbaggers.[1] The South has seemed to live inside its people like an instinct. The Middle West, on the other hand, has appeared in the inhabitants of that area more like a habit. Time and new surroundings can break a habit, but an instinct is unbreakable and unchangeable.

The past and the future of sociology and of sociological research in the South is an appropriate theme for discussion at a time when the southern instinct is being discarded along with all the other alleged instincts. For this region, like other parts of the world, is seething with active and contradictory movement, and sociologists have long regarded social change as one of the cardinal problems of their science. Today the ordinary citizen and reader of newspapers can hardly escape reflection upon the meaning of the changes going on so rapidly around him, while sociologists are required by the very nature of their occupation to probe deeply for these meanings. Our study of the nature and meaning of social change will include, naturally, a consideration

SOURCE From Howard W. Odum and Katherine Jocher (eds.), *In Search of the Regional Balance in America*, University of North Carolina Press, 1945, pp. 114–123.

of the changes that have taken and are taking place in the science in which we have a professional interest. It is obvious that changes in society and changes in sociology are not unrelated. Sociological study in the South, like sociological study every- where else, has never proceeded in a vacuum. On the contrary, it has gone forward in close relationship to the movements of change in the community where sociologists live and carry on their work. We ourselves are part of the object of our study. It is true, of course, that the sociological fraternity extends far beyond the boundaries of region and State. Science has a world- wide character, and research in it is carried on through the infec- tions of enthusiasm and discussion over which no one group, race, or nation has a monopoly. Nevertheless, there are certain situa- tional imperatives in every society which have much to do with the generation, the transmission, and the increase of knowledge, and it is therefore well for us to try to understand southern sociology in its regional and institutional setting.

It seems obvious that if we could secure such an understanding we would be in a better position to aid in the reorientation of southern sociology for the tasks ahead. Just now when our whole outlook on the future seems to be undergoing change is a good time to face the east a little more exactly and to seek again the proper bearings and relations of sociology. A time when we seem to have reached a dividing point in the history of our civilization is a good time to do a little stock-taking and a good time to do a little soul-searching. It is a good time to ask ourselves some of the more elementary questions we ask our beginning students such as, What is knowledge? What kind of knowledge is scientific knowledge? What is sociological knowledge? What is research? What is the place of valuation in science and in scientific re- search? We would do well to clear our minds of some of our pet conceptions over which we now stand guard as though they were property rights and approach these questions and others like them with a certain primitive innocence.

But sociology has been determined and probably will continue to be determined, not so much by rules of logical necessity, as historically and on the basis of interest. Sociology has been deter- mined by what has been done and what is being done by men who call themselves sociologists. If sociology is what sociologists think about, talk about, and write about, then we have a good many sociologies, perhaps about as many sociologies as we have sociologists. Nevertheless, there is little doubt but that region and *Zeitgeist* have impressed themselves upon the sociological movement and have helped define its problems. Certainly this has been true of the South. "It is certainly no accident," Myrdal remarks, "that a 'regional approach' in social science has been stressed in the South." [2] Neither is it an accident that in the old Southern Sociological Congress the South possessed what probably was the first of the regional sociological societies. Like Catholic sociology and rural sociology, southern sociology has been deeply concerned to defend rather than to analyze a body of mores. For this reason Catholic sociology has remained entirely outside the American Sociological Society, rural sociology has been in and out, and southern sociology has been in but until now, perhaps, not entirely at home in it.

An effort to outline the historical relations of the South to sociology might with some profit and insight be organized around the three prepositions, *for, of,* and *in,* most often used to indicate the relation of objects to actions. I shall speak of sociology *for* the South as that sociology which, as a body of doctrine, has been used or is being used either to resist impending change or to promote social change. Sociology *of* the South is a sociology which has achieved and is achieving the meritorious result of advancing somewhat our understanding of the object studied but which is not itself thereby advanced. Sociology *in* the South is a sociology which, viewing the South as a kind of social laboratory, undertakes to exploit the rich experiences of southern life to advance our knowledge of human nature and the processes of social change generally.

Sociology for the South

When in 1854 George Fitzhugh published his *Sociology for the South* he had in mind, as did certain contemporaries of his, a sociology battling in behalf of a regional interest and a sectional sentiment. To understand what the argument was all about let us note how the South arose first as a *region,* or a part of a region, and then later as a *section.*

The South was originally differentiated as part of an economic region in an expanding world of commerce and production for

commerce after the sixteenth century. (Advances in communication and cheap water transportation turned the Atlantic into an
inland sea and gave the warmer lands in and surrounding the
Caribbean and Gulf of Mexico divisions of labor in the larger
community of western civilization as producers of agricultural
staples for the markets of Europe. The South, with outlets along
the Atlantic coast and the Gulf of Mexico, became the northern
part of the Gulf-Caribbean region. The agricultural resources of
this tropical or semi-tropical region were found to supplement
those of northern Europe, and the profitable market invited
large-scale development. Throughout the region the labor requirements of large-scale agriculture led to the displacement of
native populations by new populations imported from Europe
but more especially from Africa.) In the absence of a self-distributing labor market, agricultural entrepreneurs could secure
and hold labor only by means of slavery, and the slavery was
fastened upon the imported Negroes. The institution of the plantation arose in this region as a factory for producing the staples
and at the same time as a means of accommodating peoples of
diverse race and culture to each other. The region became a
natural habitat for the plantation, and the plantation in turn
defined and characterized the region.

The fact that, as a part of the United States, the South had its
North—had, in other words, political ties with a people who
seemed to stand about engaging in constant and irritating criticism of the southern way of life—led the people of the South to
that degree of conscious reflection and justification of their customs which lifted them to the level of mores.[3] Thus the South
became differentiated as a section through conflict with other
sections of the United States. Sectionalism was induced in the
South, Craven tells us, "by a drive launched first against her labor
system and then broadened into an attack against the character
of her people and their entire way of life."[4] North and South
came to form different conceptions of themselves but they were,
nevertheless, differentiated as counterparts of each other out of
the same dialectical process. Struggling within the limits of the
same *Lebensraum* the contest for ascendency in the Union was
for the way of life of each section a struggle for existence.[5] It was
George Fitzhugh who first made the remark, later to be repeated
by Lincoln, that the Nation could not continue to exist half slave
and half free.

Strong sectional feeling is without much doubt mainly responsible for the fact that the leading form of social scholarship in the South has long been in the field of history. In sectionalism as in nationalism it is the historian along with the orator and the poet who functions to define and express the hopes, the fears, and the cause of a people. The historians of the South have functioned, as historians everywhere have functioned, to create and preserve the values of their society. They have done this through the method of contrast, a method which has served to emphasize the differences between the South and other parts of the United States. It is not too much to say that, not only have they worked under the influence of sectional feeling, but they also have been prime movers in its creation.

Now if southern history has functioned to traditionalize the life of the South, sociology made its appearance in this area before the Civil War in an effort to naturalize and to rationalize that life. Only recently have we begun to realize the importance of the slavery controversy upon the beginnings of sociology in the United States. In 1849 George Frederick Holmes, a naturalized southerner originally from the plantation society of British Guiana, began to discuss the necessity for a "sociology" to oppose the liberalism of his day. Holmes was familiar with the writings of Auguste Comte, with whom he corresponded, and by 1852 was the foremost interpreter and critic of Comte in America. He was the doctrinal predecessor of Henry Hughes of Mississippi, called by Bernard the "first American sociologist," and of George Fitzhugh of Virginia.[6] There were important differences between these men, of course, but they all were united in a common effort to establish intellectual sanctions for slavery. In view of our present tendency to associate sociology with liberal doctrines it may come as a surprise to find the subject beginning its career in America as a vigorous and often extravagant defender of the vested interests. As a matter of fact, however, these early southern sociologists were thinking well within the Comtean solution of the problem of freedom versus order. They differed from Comte in segments of their thought, and Comte probably would not have approved the slavery which they were concerned to justify, but they shared in the essential conservatism of his views.[7]

It has been suggested that "the sense of belonging to a definitely ordered society may have been one reason why southerners were the first Americans to make much use of the word 'sociology'." [8] All these sociologists wrote in a spirit inspired by "the sense of belonging to a definitely ordered society," but it was Fitzhugh, the best known and the most influential of them, who felt most sensitively the threat of gathering forces opposed to the southern order. It was Fitzhugh who best stated the issues involved and who so addressed himself to them as to carry the controversy aggressively into the camp of the opposition. In doing so he defined sociology in such a way as to make of it not merely a doctrine supporting the southern position, but also a "science" directly at war with an enemy of its own, namely, political economy. "Political economy," Fitzhugh explained, "is the science of free society," *i.e.*, the science supporting laissez faire, free competition, and democracy. Fitzhugh opposed the teaching of political economy in southern universities and once spoke of the necessity of giving that "science" the *coup de grace.* Apparently the science being groomed to do this was sociology.[9]

Fitzhugh did not base his defense of slavery and of the southern order upon grounds of racial and biological superiority except incidentally, and in this respect he departed from other rationalizers of the slave order. Fitzhugh elevated the pro-slavery argument to the level of a "slavery principle," which in turn was raised to the level of a "conservative principle," which in its turn is finally the principle of control and subordination which he found running through all forms of human association—marriage, the family, the state. This more abstract principle *is* sociology.

It is not necessary to elaborate the particular use Fitzhugh made of his doctrine nor the particular form taken by the doctrine itself. Let it suffice for us to recognize that sociology in the hands of the sociologists of the Old South *was* a doctrine and as such was a part of the ideology of southern sectionalism. Doctrines are formulations and rationalizations of a faith evolved during the course of controversy and oriented toward political action. Once formulated there is a tendency to regard them as objective "principles" and to appeal to them as men appeal to a just God. It is satisfying to feel that we fight on the side of eternal principles and not merely that the principles are fighting for us. Doctrines are therefore very important in collective action and they deserve a high place in the study of society, but they never constitute a scientific explanation of society. We lose our competence to understand and to deal with them when we ourselves become doctrinaires.

Just how and when sociology in the South changed from a conservative to a liberal doctrine we do not know, but the change was under way shortly after the Civil War. In April, 1867, Miss Anna Gardner, a young northern woman who conducted a school for Negroes in Virginia, wrote a local white printer to ask him to make a donation of printed diplomas to the school. She had heard that Mr. Southall, the printer, was a "true friend" of the cause of Negro education. Mr. Southall replied that, while he was as deeply interested in the welfare of the Negro race as anyone, he was not willing to furnish the diplomas because he opposed the teaching of "sociology" to Negroes and he shared in the opinion of white citizens of the community that Miss Gardner was guilty of teaching social equality. Miss Gardner defended the teaching of "sociology" with the quotation, "Whatsoever ye would that men should do to you, do ye even so unto them." [10] Other and similar uses of the word indicate that sociology was being understood by southerners as a doctrine of a radically different sort scarcely fifteen years after Fitzhugh and others had employed it as a doctrine in defense of the slave order.

The tendency to interpret sociology as a liberal doctrine has continued down to the present time and the disposition to do so is perhaps stronger in the South than in any other part of the Nation. Or at least a glance through the topics listed in the annual census of research in progress issued by the Southern Sociological Society indicates that such an interpretation predominates. Whether speaking for the South, or to it, it appears that many of our sociologists are and have been more interested in their own preaching than in people. Now we have seen what doctrinal obsessions have done to corrupt the scientific spirit in such totalitarian countries as Germany, where the theory of relativity was held to be a Jewish attack on "Nordic physics," and in Russia where such statements as "we stand for the party in mathematics" and "we stand for Marxist-Leninist theory in surgery" appear in scientific journals. While spurning such "science" we need to become aware of the possibility of ethnocentrism in scientific circles in our own society, especially in the social sciences. Nordic physics is no more invalid as science than the Christian sociology sometimes offered in American college courses. Our decided preference as citizens for the values of democratic society should not blind us as scientists to the fact that science is not advanced by conversion from one set of doctrines to another. The climate of democracy is undoubtedly more favorable to a free system of science than totalitarian climates, but the pressure of democratic dogmas may in some respects be as inimical to science as the pressure of totalitarian dogmas. Our chronic debate over the question of values in sociology, a question which ought long ago to have been settled, is perhaps one expression of the influence of the pathos of democracy in social science. Another is our suspicion of theory as such and our insistence upon immediate and practical results from research.

Democratic doctrines have set up goals and assumptions which have been accepted as "facts" and "principles" in much the same way that other societies have accepted other goals and assumptions as "facts" or "principles." It may be suggested that much of what we are calling sociological research in the South consists of a documentation of "facts" for or against some system of values in connection with social problems. Such "research" exhibits the ideology of the liberal or conservative and results, consequently, in a low level of abstraction. The very word research is often used so loosely that it has come to mean almost anything.

Every science seems to have its sworn enemy. Astronomy has its astrology, chemistry its alchemy, and sociology—well, the enemy of sociology is cleverer; it calls itself sociology, too.

Sociology of the South

The sociology of the South is the sociology of one who, whether southerner or nonsoutherner, native or outsider, endeavors to maintain something of the detachment of the stranger as he looks at the South and examines it. For him the South together with its contents is a social object to be studied as he studies other social objects like a family or a city area. The genesis of the conception of the South as an object of sociological investigation perhaps dates back to observations made by travellers in this section from Europe and from the North.

In 1880 Horace E. Scudder noted that "the South is still a foreign land to the North." [11] It had long been such and to some extent continues to be. To the urban North the Far or Lower South became in time the Deep South inhabited by natives whose customs and superstitions must have seemed almost as strange as those of the natives of Deep Africa. It was a land remote, dark, deep, and mysterious. The reports of travellers who went into this region and lived to return made interesting reading for the cosmopolites of the North. Frederick Law Olmsted, among others, reported and analyzed the workings of southern society before the Civil War, and such men as Whitelaw Reid, Carl Schurz, Ray Stannard Baker, and others continued to visit and report on the state of the South after the War. Many of these men, if not most of them, were newspaper men and journalists and of course were not regarded, and did not regard themselves, as social scientists. But they did introduce something of the objectivity of the stranger into their observations which even for us today possess considerable insight and value. The transition from the use of the South as an object of muckraking by northern journalists to its use for anthropological field work by northern investigators has been made in recent years by John Dollard, Hortense Powdermaker, W. Lloyd Warner, and others. Their contributions to an understanding of the society of this section have been most important and are most welcome. Incidentally let it be noted here that the observations about the South of both northern journalists and social scientists have almost invariably focused upon the issue of race and race relations.

Sociology in the Old South had its origins outside educational institutions but its development in the post-bellum South has occurred through college and university channels.[12] Thus in the South, as elsewhere, the transmission and increase of sociological knowledge have fallen largely within the ambit of the academician. Now in the pursuit of knowledge much depends upon who is doing the pursuing, whether priest, teacher, or man of leisure. We are not well prepared to say just how sociology has been shaped by the kind of institution which has monopolized it, but it is reasonably certain that the influence has been great. The nature and degree of that influence upon southern sociology might better be understood if we investigated it in connection with the special history and role of southern higher education, and such an investigation might prove very revealing. We might, for one thing, better appreciate the significant differences in the sociologies taught and studied in agricultural and land grant colleges, denominational colleges, State universities, and white and Negro institutions.

When sociology entered the curriculum of colleges and universities it became subject to the laws of academic inheritance. A professor, like everyone else, likes to express his individuality by differing from his colleagues about this or that, but all in all professors are a rather tradition-bound group and have great respect for university and subject precedents. Like well brought up children they do not like to depart too far from their training, and in some academic fields the lines of training lead far back into the past. Our professors were trained by their professors who in turn were trained by other professors.

We are just beginning to get a generation of sociologists in the South who were trained in southern institutions. Their teachers in these institutions were trained in European and northern universities. This northern trained generation of teachers of sociology in southern institutions studied and carried out graduate research under some of sociology's great architects and system builders. These men were such inspiring teachers and such wise counselors that their students became loyal and devoted disciples. When their students came to the South or returned to the South they turned the methods and points of view of their mentors in the direction of a sounder and more rewarding study of southern society than this society had ever before received.[13] They have advanced the sociology of the South and things southern to the status of a respectable body of knowledge and for this the rest of us will ever be indebted to them.

But the fact seems to be that in the process of passing sociology along from one generation to another some of us have inherited a conception of sociology as a dialectic to be advanced by criticism of the concepts of the various "schools." Preoccupations with such logicisms may make us very sharp and brilliant but it lands us in a vicious circle from which there is no escape. The consequence is a sort of sociological scholasticism. Immersed in such scholasticism we can discuss almost any of the problems of sociology without once looking to see what concretely we have in the problem. We refer rather to what the authors of textbooks, i.e., the authorities, have said about it.

Another result, apparently, of academic inheritance is the fact that much of the procedure of sociological research in the South as elsewhere falls in the domain of custom, and too often the methods used are only survivals of older ones or blind imitations of the methods of others. This seems particularly true of statistics, a procedure so "objective" as to have a minimum use for the facts of experience. Professor R. E. Park has illuminated us upon the subject of rote learning.[14] We need also to consider the subject of rote teaching but of more immediate interest to us is the matter of rote research. Rote research is manifest by the extent to which we flounder around in the rituals and mysteries of methodology, that mouth-filling word we sociologists love so well. It appears that many of us become so much concerned with methodology that the thing to be studied comes to seem unimportant. Perhaps we have committed to memory the steps to be taken in "correct" scientific procedure. We have defined the problem and ascertained the sources of data. We have formulated a hypothesis and we have read the literature. We have consulted the statistician and he has told us just what questions we must ask in the questionnaire in order to treat the returns statistically. And finally we have decided whom to interview and we think we had better collect some cases. The only trouble is we are not particularly interested in the matter we have decided to study.

Speaking of a disposition to follow too closely the procedures of the masters rather than their spirit of inquiry, Dr. W. I. Thomas wrote in a letter, "You will remember that the chemist Ostwald followed the careers of all his students and that in his *Grosse Männer* he said that all his students who attended his lectures regularly and were attentive failed to amount to anything while all those who neglected the lectures became distinguished. My aversion to the formal attention to methodology is just here—that it is not only unfruitful but it tends to a fixation of habits and sterility."[15] One of the almost inevitable consequences of inheritance of any kind is a tendency toward formalism, and to combat this in the field of sociology it is necessary for us to wage continuous battle against rote teaching and rote research.

The obsession with fact gathering as an end in itself, an obsession which places some of us at the opposite extreme from the scholastics, is perhaps a result of the cult of formal objectivity.

The fact gatherer proceeds under the assumption that the facts need only be gathered and allowed "to speak for themselves." His conclusions are his opinions concerning what the facts say. Perhaps the investigations of the fact gatherer are really in the nature of surveys. They are not ordinarily related to hypotheses and there is a minimum utilization of available theory. Ordinarily the facts are gathered and organized under common sense concepts. Many if not most of these investigations are carried out to aid in the formulation of policies or as instruments of reform. As such they are useful and effective. When reform is needed there is no gainsaying the value of a shovelful of facts to help it along. And there certainly is no quarrel with any sociologist who has a healthy respect for those compulsory experiences we call facts. Most of us would profit if we paid more attention to the facts and many of us would do well if we left our offices and campuses more often to get closer to the grass roots. But the mere fact gatherer is far from being a man of science. As John Dewey has said, "No amount of mere fact finding develops science nor the scientific attitude in either physics or social affairs. Facts merely amassed and piled up are dead; a burden which only adds to confusion. When ideas, hypotheses, begin the play upon facts, when they are methods for experimental use in action, then light dawns; then it becomes possible to discriminate significant from trivial facts, and relations begin to take the place of intellectual scraps."

It may be suggested that while the thing studied, that is, the South, is now somewhat better understood, the sociology of the South has not appreciably advanced the fundamental body of sociological theory. There has not yet come out of the South, I believe, a volume comparable to *Folkways, The Theory of the Leisure Class, Human Nature and the Social Order,* or *The Polish Peasant.* If the value of sociology or any other science is to be tested by the question, Does it yield a better understanding and control than can be had by common sense? and if the answer is yes, then the science in its existing state of theory is, of course, valuable. It follows, however, that advances in social theory are an indispensable desideratum for advances in understanding and control. Research and theory should react upon each other and develop each other. The point is that southern sociological research is obligated to advance our knowledge of the South but it also is under obligation to advance the science of sociology.

Shall southern sociologists continue to leave to sociologists in other parts of the world the formulation of newer viewpoints as a guide to research, or will they use the rich resources of southern experience to help advance the body of sociological theory themselves? Is it sufficient to mark out the South as historians mark it out, that is, as an area to be studied as an end in itself, for its own sake alone, or is it not also a part of our business to use the South as a field of observation for the study of human nature and society generally?

It has been charged that the South has been on the defensive so long that its people have lost the art of self-examination, and Lambert Davis asserted that "Southerners have made surprisingly few discoveries about the South chiefly because they assumed they already knew it." [16] Perhaps we have not made the discoveries about the South we ought to have made and perhaps our passion for self-discovery has not been commensurate with our opportunity. If so, it is a challenge to advance the sociology of the South. But the real question goes much deeper than this and becomes: Have southern sociologists made the discoveries about the nature of social organization and social processes we ought to have made and how great is our interest in utilizing the southern situation to make such discoveries? To the extent we are concerning ourselves with this fundamental question we have sociology in the South.

Sociology in the South

The sociology of the South at its extreme is the sociology of self-conscious intellectuals who minimize the facts of their own experience and the life experiences of the people in the community around them. It is the sociology of the career or office sociologist, the sociologist of the book. It is rather paradoxical that sociology, the science which, more than any other, is charged with the study and understanding of the simply human, should itself stand in need of humanizing. Sociology requires devotees who like people and who find people interesting, all kinds and conditions of people, people as they are, the good and the bad, the white and the black alike. To the sociologist in a special sort of way nothing human is alien.

Now the South is a land of sprawling diversity and great contrasts, and the people in it have combined and recombined to effect all sorts of relationships and types. Regardless of what its partisans or its enemies may think of this land, the South is full of the matter of sheer human interest. In the 1880's when American writers were discovering provincial types, dialects, and customs they found in the South, more than in any other section, the sort of literary material demanded. The human nature resources of the region were exploited so thoroughly that Professor Pattee called the period "The Era of Southern Themes and Writers." "Nowhere else," said he, exaggerating a bit perhaps, "were to be found such a variety of picturesque types of humanity: Negroes, crackers, creoles, mountaineers, moonshiners, and all those incongruous elements that had resulted from the great social upheaval of 1861–65. Behind it in an increasingly romantic perspective lay the old regime destroyed by the war; nearer was the war itself, most heroic of struggles; and still nearer was the tragedy of reconstruction with its carpetbagger, its freed slaves, and its Ku Klux terror. Nowhere in America, not even in California, had there been such richness of literary material." [17] The literary interest in the South, it might be added, is perhaps even stronger today than it was in the 1880's.

Not only are the materials for a great literature present in the South but also for a great sociological renaissance. Recently two southerners, Jonathan Daniels, white, and J. Saunders Redding, Negro, took to their automobiles and travelled around the South to see what was going on and to talk to hitchhikers, filling station operators, waitresses, farm laborers, TVA officials, miners, planters, textile workers, and State officials. [18] Readers who viewed the panorama of southern life through the eyes of these two writers could hardly have failed to be deeply impressed by the stirring human drama being enacted in this section of the nation. In another book, edited by W. T. Couch, entitled *These Are Our Lives,* these same types of people are permitted to speak up for themselves, and we were surprised to find that, in spite of the apparent drabness of their lives, they had interesting and human stories to tell. All around the South social experiments are going on, some planned and some just happening. The people are talking and asking questions, more concerned about the future than southern folk usually are thought of as being. In short, the South is a region where human nature and social processes can be observed and studied somewhat as a naturalist studies vital behavior in the field and where the student possesses some special advantages for observation. And when such an authority as Wesley Mitchell tells us that "the most urgent item of unfinished business is to increase our knowledge of human behavior," such study assumes greater significance than the mere expression of idle curiosity.

Not that there is anything wrong with having idle curiosity. Quite the contrary. Scientific research does not begin with data nor with method but with an individual who ardently wants to find out something, and who is not deterred by the difficulties he encounters in his search for the answer. Most people possess some native curiosity which is, however, dissipated when difficulties are encountered. But there are a few sociological Galileos and Pasteurs and Darwins whose appetite for knowledge is simply whetted by the difficulties and who drive ahead. They seek facts that are relevant to the questions that trouble them, construct hypotheses in imagination, and then test the hypotheses by pitting the facts against them. They become concerned with methodological problems after they have discovered an interest. They have questions to ask of the data and they devise their own methods for getting answers or choose intelligently from existing methods. There is no substitute in any kind of scientific research for the curious and inquiring mind. Much more important than the methods of science is the spirit of science, and this spirit, says Charles R. Stockard, "is a fleeting and tenuous affair. It never exists where time and routine are important. It disappears with an eight-hour day or a six-day week or a nine-month year. The atmosphere is inspiring only where all time belongs to the spirit of science." [19]

A genuine spirit of scientific research in sociology is certainly not absent in southern sociology. In at least two southern universities—at the University of North Carolina under Dr. Howard W. Odum and at Fisk University under Dr. Charles S. Johnson—it can be seen in action, and its results are distinguished throughout the whole sociological fraternity.

A few years ago I visited a meeting of Alpha Kappa Delta, at the University of North Carolina, and during the course of the program a member read a list of the studies being carried on by the students and faculty. The list was very interesting. The studies were concerned almost entirely with problems in southern, mostly North Carolina, counties, or with aspects of southern state or regional life and welfare. It happened that shortly before I had visited Fisk University and there attended a meeting held by Dr. Johnson and his graduate students. It was a sort of acquaintance meeting, and each student was asked to state the problem upon which he was working. These studies ranged the world; students were writing theses on aspects of society in Brazil, South Africa, the Philippines, and some of the islands of the Pacific and of the West Indies. The contrast between the character of the studies announced at these two meetings was striking, but at both institutions one felt the presence of enthusiasm and life. The important thing at each university was not the number of the students and faculty engaged in research, nor the nature of their projects, but the spirit of the place. Spirit is a hazy thing to describe but it is all-important, nevertheless, and when it is absent no amount of money available for research, no amount of personnel or distinguished talent, no amount of equipment and convenience will carry research very far or learn very much beyond mere formal knowledge about the world in which we live.

The impression gained of the work of the sociologists at the University of North Carolina is that they frankly are interested first and foremost in immediate social welfare and social control. Their view, apparently, is that the way to build up a knowledge of social facts in their significant relations is by the pragmatic device of entering upon a course of social planning and experimentation, that science does not precede but follows efforts at control. The University of North Carolina sociologists have concerned themselves particularly with the so-called Negro problem as the focal point in the complex of southern social problems, but they have taught us to see all our problems in their interrelations and in the context of southern life as a whole. They pursue investigations along this line under the rubric of regionalism.

The sociologists at Fisk University also have studied and are studying immediate aspects of southern life, but they seem to be much more interested in the comparative use of nonsouthern experience in the analysis of southern society. Their studies are not confined to southern horizons or to southern historical levels. They seek to wrench analysis clear of the particularistic assumptions of a single culture and to put the phenomena of southern life in a wider context of relationship and meaning. Especially are they concerned to make a contribution to the comparative study of race relations. It might be fair to say that the sociologists at the University of North Carolina are interested primarily in *conditions* while those at Fisk University are more interested in *processes.*

Men probing for solutions to the social problems of their day often end up by discovering society. They sometimes rise above place and time through the paradox of putting themselves more intensely into their place and time. At this point there is a tendency for interest in social problems to at least make room for an interest in sociological problems and for the pursuit of a kind of knowledge which does not promise to be immediately useful but without which rational control in the practical affairs of life may never be gained. This requires comparative study. The South as a unique historical society cannot be compared with anything, but regions and sections, not only in the United States but throughout the world, are subject to comparative study. So is the plantation, and so are race and race relations.

There is, of course, no reason why southern sociologists should not turn their attention to the study of any segment of social life in which they may be interested. Southern sociology would be the poorer if interest in the family, population, crime, et cetera, were not strongly represented here. But a review of the history of southern sociology suggests that the lines along which it may make its greatest contribution, not only to an understanding of the South and its problems, but to the progress of science generally already have been marked out for it. The relations between the races is the axis upon which southern life has turned for a hundred years or more. Southern sociology began with it, developed with it, and must continue with it. In the midst of wide diversity of economic interests and social backgrounds there still is just one South because of the Negro problem. More than anything else it has defined the section. More than anything else it has defined and influenced southern sociology. To be sure the race problem is no longer a sectional or even a national problem. It now is a world problem. This means that the scope of comparative study has been widened immeasurably and it also means that southern studies in race relations have value and meaning in an ever-widening circle of social science. It is in the field of race relations, perhaps, that southern sociologists have their finest opportunity to contribute to the science of sociology itself.

It is probable that the South will feel the impact of the changes to follow the present world war more acutely than any other region of the nation. As Southern sociology adjusts to these changes, and attempts to study and control them, it may undergo profound change itself.

• 12 •

The Planter in the Pattern of
Race Relations in the South

Without the planter there either would have been no race problem in the South or it would have assumed an altogether different form. Without its landed aristocracy the South might have turned out to be a society made up largely of poor whites and Indians. But in the actual course of southern civilization as it developed historically no other single factor in the situation had an importance equal to that of the planter and his work. There proceeded from his activities a process of social differentiation which not only established his own class but the lower white and Negro classes as well.

These various classes have competed and struggled within the limits of a common territorial, economic, and cultural order. Out of the interaction between them the idea of race arose and functioned as a social myth by means of which men established ties of affinity with each other and at the same time created social and spiritual distances which separated them from other men. But more particularly the history of the idea of race in America is bound up with the evolution of the status and the needs of the planter. It was primarily his need for labor and for authority over labor in a situation where men did not voluntarily offer themselves as laborers which led to the development of the idea of race as a principle of control. Slavery was merely one mechanism through which this principle was put into effect. Today, according to Monroe Work, "the legal attitudes of tenancy are on the basis of race." [1]

It is advantageous to look at any economic and political situa-

SOURCE *Social Forces*, December 1940, pp. 244–50.

tion from the point of view of those elements in it which take the initiative and which become the controlling forces. In the South the planter has been the active agent in the situation. Unlike certain other types of land barons of history he, like the modern industrialist, operates in a market economy for which his plant produces a commodity for sale. The market for which he produces is a world market, or at least a market remote in space and in time. It is necessary for the planter as a private entrepreneur to keep in mind the planting enterprise as a whole and to keep in view the market toward which it is oriented. This places upon him a concern which is likely to remain outside the view of the field laborers who do the actual work of planting, cultivating, and harvesting the crops. He stands between the market and the mass of workers who have little direct knowledge of the discipline which the requirements of the market impose. It becomes the problem of the planter, therefore, not only to secure and hold workers, but to organize their activities for a purpose not immediately apparent to them. Authority is requisite for the carrying out of this purpose, but authority must be founded upon some principle more or less implicitly accepted by all the members of the community. A continuous control is impossible which is not founded upon a body of ideas and beliefs common to all. In the South such a principle of control was supplied by the idea of race the validity of which, once established, was denied by none, not even by members of the subject race.

Relative to the total population of the South the planter class has never been large, but it is generally agreed that this class has exercised an influence entirely out of proportion to its numbers. In the ante-bellum South the status of the planter came to represent success, and men measured their progress up the ladder of achievement by the degree to which they approximated the rank of the great planters. Physicians, lawyers, merchants, and even ministers often deserted their professions when opportunities to become planters presented themselves. Everyone was familiar with the jingle:

> All I want in this creation
> Is a pretty little wife and a big plantation.

What Roland was to the youth of the Middle Ages, what the scholar is for Chinese and what the millionaire is for American youth today, that the planter was for the young men of the Old South. Exclusive attention upon the status of the planter tended to inhibit the development of other types. Once established, planting as a pattern of success not merely tended to persist but to become a regional way of thinking. The intoxication which accompanied the struggle for plantation estates affected those who had not as well as those who had. Even free Negroes before the Civil War and freed Negroes after the War assimilated the tradition and sometimes became planters.

The term "planter" itself has a long and interesting history. In Murray's *New English Dictionary* a number of uses of the term are given. Owing to the wide meaning assumed by the infinitive "to plant" and its extensive use by the people of medieval England, planter evolved in meaning from a word denoting one who placed plants in the soil that they might grow to one who established or founded anything as, for example, a religion or a colony. In the early days of American colonization, however, the term, along with "plantationer," "plantationite," and "plantator," was more likely to designate one who was planted or settled.

In the organization of the Virginia Company of London in 1606 two classes of members were distinguished. (1) "adventurers of the purse," or those who subscribed money toward a capital stock, and (2) "adventurers of the person," or "planters," who agreed to go in person to settle the new territory and who were expected by their industry or trade to contribute to the profits of the enterprise. The group of people migrating from England to Virginia was a "plantation" and the planter was simply an individual member of such a group. For his personal adventure the planter received stock in the company on a basis of equality with those who invested funds. He also was entitled to support from the Company for a period of five or seven years.

As the Company's settlement in Virginia moved away from its original purpose of trading with the natives and came to depend upon the development of the resources of the country the status of the planters declined and they became hirelings of the Company and tenants on the Company's land. But in 1619, when the Company made a division of lands among their "adventurers of the person," those who had arrived in the Colony before 1616 and who, as pioneers, had endured the greatest hardships, were each given 100 acres of land per share of stock. Of these, according to Wertenbaker, "a fair proportion became proprietors and were

regarded by later comers with especial esteem as 'ancient planters'." [2]

Here we have a hint as to the probable reason why the term
"planter," which originally meant simply one planted or settled,
came to gain prestige value as the title of the plantation aristocracy. There seems to be in human nature a general disposition
to accord distinction to first things. There is a disposition in every
group to remember and honor its pioneers. And from what we
know of pioneers generally the "ancient planter" must have possessed something of the pride, the inner dignity, and the strength
of a first settler. On every frontier there is an inevitable contrast
between the oldtimer and the greenhorn or tenderfoot, a contrast all to the advantage of the former.

In one of his most interesting essays Josiah Royce, who grew
up in the mining camps of California, made a significant observation of one of the factors in the origin of status in those communities. Out of the raw and extreme democracy of these camps there
emerged a semblance of an aristocracy composed of those who
got there first. The first to arrive acquired the most favorable sites
but above all they acquired an experience which the newcomers
did not possess.[3] This is something like the relation between the
generations—the newcomers have to sit at the feet of the old-
timers and learn.

It must have been similar in early Virginia. Those who pion-
eered at Jamestown gained experiences and rights which entitled them to respect and made them "ancient" planters in the
eyes of those who came later. For, of course, those who came
later, especially the indentured servants, crossed the ocean and
settled in Virginia under entirely different circumstances. These
later arrivals were immigrants, not planters, in the original sense
of that term. When the cultivation of tobacco began, the connection of "planter" with agriculture was easily made. When it became necessary to distinguish between the holder of indentured
servants and slaves and those free white colonists who did not
hold servants or slaves the term planter functioned to designate
the former and to meet the needs of ordinary conversation. In
short, "planter" came to designate, not simply a vocation, but a
status, a status to be achieved.[4]

By the time of the Revolution, the South had developed from
within a well-entrenched aristocracy. The status of planter had

not only been achieved by many but the status itself had advanced upward to new heights. Authority, prestige, wealth, leisure, all in high degree united in establishing that type of eighteenth century planter which was represented by such men as Madison, Middleton, Lee, and many others. However, the exploitative and wasteful methods of cultivation identified with the planter caused some plantation owners, including Washington, to prefer the title "farmer" since they counted themselves followers of the most progressive cultivators of England and Europe. But this preference did not last and with the westward expansion of cotton cultivation "planter" as a badge of status became more firmly established than ever. By 1850 the United States census, under the superintendency of J. D. B. DeBow, of Louisiana, was distinguishing between "planters" and "farmers."

The planter in America grew up during our first heroic age. The planter as hero was a sort of land and settlement outlaw. Sombart has somewhere remarked that it is exceedingly hard to distinguish the last pirate and the first entrepreneur as persons separate and distinct. Every adventurer in a foreign land is something of an outlaw since he is essentially an individualist making his way outside former group and cultural ties. At any rate, it is worth noting that the planter type began to take form in the West Indies and in eastern North and South America in the seventeenth century when buccaneering in the Caribbean and along the Atlantic coasts was on the wane. A little earlier piracy and privateering in these areas had reached extreme proportions and sea pirates made the staggering hauls for which they became famous. The ramifications of piracy were extensive and reached into the ranks of officialdom and business. But with the decline of the rich profits to be made from looting the gold-laden Spanish galleons, the prosperity of piracy took second place to that of plantation agriculture. In the West Indies there was almost an economic succession from piracy to planting. From cutting throats to flogging slaves was not a very big step.

It was in the midst of such a tradition of lawlessness that the tiny colonies in the New World were founded, and the "emancipating spaces" of the American environment contributed to its continuation. On new frontiers, as settlement pushed westward, the outlaw reappeared. Characters like Mason, Murrell, the Harpes robbed and murdered up and down the Natchez Trace and then gave way to other equally notorious outlaws operating further west. Yet the depredations of these men were only a matter of a higher degree. In the situation all life was predatory and many men were either outlaws or linked with the outlawry of others. Coates, who has written most interestingly of the lives of some of the most famous bandits of the Old Southwest, reminds us that the behavior of these characters was a concomitant of the behavior of the land pirates and settlers of the area in general. Such was the general pattern of life of the place and the period. The line between legality and illegality was a thin and vague one and men stepped from one side to the other as convenience and expediency dictated.[5]

The land pirate who also found ways and means of impressing others into his service as laborers had at least one great advantage over the other type—he could found a dynasty. The lawless planter came himself to represent the law to the ruder societies and individuals about him. Planters and members of the planter class established and enforced their own rules. Out of illegality thus came a new form of law, and eventually planters themselves became more or less bound by their own rules. Through their heirs and through the generations of planters a lawless society was transformed into an ordered and disciplined one.

John Smith and others described the early settlers of Virginia as a rough and contentious lot. Men of this stamp, and particularly those who had access to capital and were willing to use it adventurously, were the men who seized the opportunity of amassing wealth by the cultivation of tobacco. Wertenbaker has characterized the planters of seventeenth century Virginia as hard, crude, and grasping.[6] George W. Cable speaks of the early planters of Louisiana as having "an attitude of arrogant superiority over all restraint." They were "unrestrained, proud, intrepid, self-reliant, rudely voluptuous, of a high intellectual order, yet uneducated, unreasoning, impulsive, and inflammable."[7]

The business of planting is one characterized by the presence of operations demanding a uniform type of unskilled labor. Machine methods for such operations either do not exist or are uneconomic. The result has been since the days of early settlement an active demand for cheap agricultural labor. The demand was purely and simply a demand for labor, not, in its origin, a demand for indentured servants or for slaves. But because the demand did not meet with an adequate response it grew into a demand for slaves. It was a demand for labor in a situation where no one need voluntarily offer himself as a laborer to another since he might easily take up land and farm for himself. Under the circumstances the planter has had to resort to a succession of methods for obtaining, concentrating, and controlling labor adequate to meet his needs. Through a succession of incidents Negro slavery gradually displaced white servitude, a change which also involved a shift from class and religion to race as the fundamental principle of control. The line of distinction between Europeans and Africans was originally less effected by differences of skin color than by differences of religion. The original justification for Negro slavery was based upon these religious differences; the Negro was an infidel or a heathen. This justification was a continuation of the European tradition that unbelievers might rightfully be made slaves by Christian people. But the Old World Christians and non-Christians, e.g., Mohammedans, were not sharply distinguished by color differences, whereas in America and in South Africa religious differences coincided with differences in color so that different religious groups were uniformed, and so readily visible to each other.[8] In this situation it is apparent that color would easily become the more basic line of separation, especially since religious differences need not be, and were not, permanent differences.

There is the further fact that a justification which sanctioned initial enslavement and the slave trade, under the view that by enslavement the unbeliever would be brought into the true faith, presented difficulties when it came to be a question of continuing in slavery the converted slave. In the American colonies it was generally believed that the conversion of a Negro slave to Christianity entitled him to his freedom. Many planters, for this reason, refused to allow Christian ministers and missionaries to come near their plantations. In this dilemma it became necessary for colonial legislatures, beginning with the legislature of Maryland in 1664, formally to affirm the principle that baptism and conversion did not entail freedom.

It was then that the evolving idea of race began to function. The idea of race was generated out of the situation as a working element in that situation. It was no transcendental idea having an existence apart from the life experiences of men; it was instrumentally and pragmatically bound up with their needs and purposes as they sought to put them into effect in a concrete situation.

The idea grew that people possessing similar physical traits were innately and immutably "different" from those possessing other physical traits, almost different enough to constitute a separate species. However, it is not sufficient to say that whites came simply to regard Negroes as different; they came to regard them as opposite, like the sexes, and sometimes spoke of "the opposite race." As Copeland has pointed out, the idea of race in the South functioned as a "contrast conception." [9]

The general idea behind the planter's government of his slaves was that Negroes have to be treated differently from other Europeans; not because they are black, nor because they are slaves, but because they think differently from the white men. The idea of fundamental racial difference is normally reinforced in a situation such as that in which the planter found himself by the fact that the man who undertakes to administer a policy generally becomes aware of incalculable factors in the nature of those under him which he does not understand but which have to be reckoned with. The members of the master class do not ever really know those whom they are trying to control, and unexpected and subtle behavior appears as further proof that the members of the subordinate class are of a different order of men. The unknowable Negro has appeared when his mater or employer has had some program which ignored his own wishes and interests.

If the planter determined the activities of his dependents, his slaves, or his tenants, he also came to assume responsibility for what he considered to be their needs. Regarding the behavior of those under him as capricious and child-like it was inevitable that he should develop an attitude of paternalism. The Negro slave was doomed to a sort of perpetual childhood, a status which was not entirely destroyed by the Civil War. The planter's disposition was to treat all dependents, regardless of age, as children and do for them what they might as well have done for themselves under the assumption that they were more or less incapable of managing themselves. The plantation thus came to resemble the patriarchal family with authority and affection, subordination and personal responsibility existing side by side. The planter often boasted of what he did for his people and of his defense of them. He often regarded a wrong done to his slaves as an outrage to himself and championed their cause against others. A sense of magnanimity and *noblesse oblige* thus developed more or less directly out of the planter's original exuberation of strength and individuality.

Although the Civil War did not entirely destroy the antebellum planter class the power of this class was consideraby weakened. Many of these old planters who tried to carry on with "free niggers" in the post-War period failed in business and were forced to sell their properties. Many moved into the towns and cities and entered other occupations. It was noticeable that insurance companies operating in the South often selected planters and ex-Confederate generals as their agents. Many became real estate dealers. Some who had employed overseers found it necessary to supervise their own planting operations while other ex-planters themselves engaged as overseers.

By 1880 a new planter class, recruited from the ranks of doctors, lawyers, and especially merchants, was fast taking the place, so far as that was possible, of the older plantation gentry and their sons. The rôle of the new planter as master underwent considerable reduction after the Civil War but his rôle as landlord became a much more important one.

The Negro's place at the bottom of the social scale was in large part determined not only by his color and by his previous condition of slavery but by his landlessness. He had only his labor to offer and so, like the landless poor white, he became a tenant on the land of the planter. He was free to move away at the end of the year but only to become a tenant on the land of another planter.

The changes that have taken place in race relations in the South since the Civil War are in large measure correlated with changes that have taken place in land utilization and tenure. The poor white and the Negro are back together on the plantation as tenants under a common planter and landlord. And because there are degrees of tenancy ranging from the share-cropper at the bottom to the renter and part-owner at the top, race relations, so far as the planter and the Negro are concerned, differ somewhat with the status of the tenant. They become something else again when the Negro becomes a landowner and independent farmer. We may expect that future changes in race relations in the South will depend much upon changes that take place in the relations of the races to the land.

Although there is a tendency toward reconcentration of land ownership, a tendency which is halting the acquisition of land by Negroes, it is probable that the end of plantation life in the South is only a matter of time. At any rate, the status of the planter since the Civil War has declined considerably and continues to decline. The rise of the poor and middle class white man to political influence, the competition of new urban and industrial classes, and radical changes in market conditions have made it impossible for the new planter class to rise to the heights of a true aristocracy and the descendants of the old planter aristocracy are broken and scattered. There continues to exist, however, the aristocratic planter tradition of good breeding, quiet living, family honor, and high social standards. The South has arrived at a point where, in many communities, there exists an aristocratic tradition without any aristocrats.

• 13 •

The Natural History of Agricultural Labor in the South

I. "The Collapse of Cotton Tenancy"

Under the title *The Collapse of Cotton Tenancy* there was published in 1935 the result of a two-year investigation made at the University of North Carolina and Fisk University.[1] It is a very short book of less than a hundred pages, but it pictures the present plight of the South in language so clear and so convincing that it is bound to leave the ordinary American reader very much moved and decidedly disturbed. The present situation in the South is described as "our greatest social humiliation," and cotton tenancy is pictured as possibly even worse than slavery. It is easy to understand after reading this book why President Roosevelt recently called the South "the nation's Economic Problem Number One." The system of cotton tenancy, the authors suggest, is about to "collapse." There are vast impersonal forces operating to end or to transform it—forces connected with the credit system, the concentration of land under corporate ownership, soil exhaustion, competition of other fabrics, loss of world markets, and the mechanization of production.

As important as any of these factors, however, are those that have to do with dignity and status, or the lack of them. Various agencies, writers, and agitators are now giving the tenant farmer a self-recognizable account of his own experiences, an account which is leading him to ask questions about things which formerly he took for granted. With a good deal of help from both his friends and his enemies he is discovering not only his poverty

SOURCE In D. K. Jackson (ed.), *Essays in Honor of William K. Boyd*, Duke University Press, 1940, pp. 110–74.

but also his low status. There are opportunities in the present situation for him to make comparisons and contrasts; as a result, he is becoming conscious of his social nakedness. He is ashamed, and filled with a human and moral concern for covering himself.

If it is true that people are not oppressed until they know and feel it, then the great mass of Southern farm tenants have not been oppressed. They have had a great many personal complaints and grievances against planter and overseer but no general indignation against the system of tenancy. They have not characterized it as evil because they have not characterized it at all. Very few of them have reflected upon the existence of a system of tenancy. Born to the situation, they simply took it for granted. But now they are no longer taking it for granted. The spirit of protest is beginning to stir among them, a protest which fundamentally is against the low status connected with farm labor and with poverty.

In American society generally the supporting philosophy of the system of share-tenancy is beginning to decline and to assume a defensive position. The inconsistencies and contradictions in the system are being searched out and made known, and the tragic aspects of life in the situation are coming prominently to the fore. We are being led to feel that an essentially human quality is being outraged in the lowly sharecropper, and inevitably our indignation is aroused.

When the tragic aspects of a society come strikingly to the front, that society is breaking up. But more than this, what is breaking up the present order in the South—what perhaps breaks up any social order—is a conception of something different and better in the light of which the existing situation seems intolerable. This fact suggests an interesting parallel between the present discussion of share-tenancy and the discussion of slavery before the Civil War.

On ante-bellum plantations slavery was not an abstract problem of right and justice to be debated. One does not discuss the rightness and the wrongness of that which is regarded as a part of nature; one simply assumes it to be right. Slavery was a set of concrete and very commonplace relationships with individual Negroes like Henry and Tom for the very practical purpose of making a crop of cotton or tobacco. The ordinary planter, the overseer, the poor white, and even the slave did not often discuss it.[2] Discussion went on elsewhere—in the halls of Congress and in university and urban centers.

Now share-tenancy has been an established practice for at least seventy-five years, perhaps much longer. The plantation system of which it is a part has had a continuous history from the days of original settlement. Like slavery, share-tenancy survived because it worked, and it worked long enough to become an accepted and customary social arrangement.[3] In the rural areas of the South planters and tenants have been accustomed to discussing problems connected with the crops they grow, but not the system of social and economic relationships which surrounds the growing.

For forty years or more teachers and leaders like the late Dr. E. C. Branson and others have been studying and discussing the problem of farm-tenancy in the South. Again the discussion went on at the top, in university and urban centers. It did not reach the plantations.

What distinguishes present from past discussion of share-tenancy is the implication of the present discussion for action. In the minds of teachers, students, farm leaders, administrators, and politicians a program of action is taking form. If the discussion of slavery led to the Civil War and the overthrow of that system of labor, the present discussion of share-tenancy in the South threatens the plantation itself. A social movement with the small farm as a goal is in process of formation. *The Collapse of Cotton Tenancy* is a contribution to this movement.

Reflection upon the "collapse" of a system of society as vast and as complicated as that which rests upon share-tenancy, and speculation upon the consequences of the movement for an ideal something to take its place, invite a rearward look at the systems of agricultural labor control in the South which preceded tenancy. For tenancy is just the most recent of several systems. The plight of tenants does not arise from any inherited constitutional pathology; share tenants are not, as Mr. Mencken characterized them, "perambulating test tubes for the culture of hookworms." Neither is their condition owing, as our moralists either charge or assume, to wilful conspiracy on the part of planters living and dead. On the contrary, share-tenancy, like slavery before it, is the unintended result of the intentions of several generations of men. No one sought to make the situation just what it has become.

It is the purpose of this essay to review the history of agricultural labor in the South with attention to those of its features which illuminate the processes that established precedent, rules of practice, and customary patterns of action and outlook generally. We shall not deal with events but with processes of change in an effort to understand how the present agricultural labor situation has come to be what it is and to understand the situation that may prevail. Within the limitations of this purpose it is proposed to consider: the nature of the plantation institution and the universality of its baleful reputation; the sort of situation in which forced labor and the plantation arises; the planter as the active agent in the situation; the succession of labor systems historically connected with the Southern plantation—indentured servitude, slavery, and tenancy; with a briefer discussion of the relation between the planter's labor problems and the institutionalization of the plantation.

II. The Plantation Institution and its Reputation

However diversified plantation institutions in various parts of the world may be—and they present a wide variety of forms—they all have this characteristic in common, every one of them is an organization designed primarily to advance, express, and defend the interests of a planter or a planter class through the formal or political control of a subordinate class.

In this fact there is nothing unique about the plantation. Most economic institutions in our modern capitalistic order are also political institutions, that is, they, like the state, rest finally upon the authority principle. But the authority of the planter ordinarily operates in a situation which throws the connection between political means and economic ends into a certain relief.

In the first place, the planter's authority is exercised for the purpose of producing an agricultural staple for sale. Of all modes of land utilization, the raising of crops and livestock requires the most space. For large-scale agriculture the planter needs a relatively large land area. This means that the plantation, the area over which the planter's authority extends, is not merely a point but a territory and this means, in turn, that the plantation by nature isolates itself. The result is a community in which the planter possesses power not only over the laborer's job, but also over his home, his recreation, and his daily relations with others.

In the second place, capital and labor relations on the plantation are commonly at the same time race relations. Or, at least, the plantation type of relation tends to stereotype the confrontation of people of different race as one of capital and labor.[4] The laborer and the planter face each other as representatives of different racial or cultural groups. Relations between them are relations of subordination and superordination. The subordinate members of the plantation under the authority of the planter are commanded, regimented, and disciplined, not for conflict with rival plantations or with the state, but for the work of cultivating and harvesting the crop. Plantation agriculture may be described as military agriculture.

In the American tradition the plantation and the ranch are the two rural institutions which have been objects of considerable romantic interest. In the ranch tradition it is not the rancher but the cowboy, the laborer, who, mounted, wild and free, has captured our imagination. But there is little about the plantation laborer to invite emulation. The lot of the man who labors in the soil with his hands, and especially when he labors under the direction of another and to the profit of another, is not envied. We do not regard him as really free, even though the law may so define him. Like the serf he is in some measure bound to the land and a part of it.

The source of romantic interest in the plantation is not the laborer but the planter who, in the tradition, is master of a little kingdom which he rules in courtly splendor.[5] The feudal lord, who owns the land which others cultivate, tends always to approximate the role of the turbulent land baron in semi-, sometimes in full, revolt against the king or state. So did the Virginia planter challenge the authority of the King of England,[6] and so did the Southern planter rise in revolt against the government of the United States. The American people admired the hotheaded aristocrat, victorious or defeated.

Nevertheless, in spite of this romantic interest which centered around the planter, plantation societies in America and throughout the world generally have never borne the best of reputations. Conditions in the frontier areas where staple and luxury agricultural goods are produced contrast, or are alleged to contrast, with conditions in the older areas where these goods are marketed and consumed. The contrast is to the very great disadvantage of the plantation areas and hence the low, sometimes unsavory, reputations of these areas. At one time in English history the phrase "to the plantations" seems to have had something of the meaning which "to the galleys" had in Rome.[7]

Historically the expansion of Europe and the opening up of overseas areas for trade and settlement involved a change whereby the colored and so-called primitive peoples of the world gradually assumed positions analogous to those held by unskilled and unorganized workers in Europe and America. It was a change whereby native and non-European peoples, many of them at any rate, gradually became integral parts of the white man's economic order. But the very nature of the change brought about glaring contrasts between countries of advanced civilization and those colonial areas, including plantation areas, where colored labor was used most extensively.

In addition to the racial contrast there were sharp differences in living standards and in the remuneration of labor. But the contrast which chiefly accounted for the plantation's bad reputation was that between the free labor of Europe and the forced labor of the plantation areas in the colonies.[8]

"Plantation colonies have regularly been the seats of wholesale enslavement," says Keller, and adds that the abolition of slavery leads only to various substitutes and subterfuges.[9] In various parts of Africa, for example, hut and poll taxes have been imposed on natives in an effort to force them into the labor market. In the former German colonies in Africa natives were forcibly recruited for work out of their districts, and with cattle-owning, their sole means of independent livelihood, prohibited, they were forced to engage as plantation laborers. In Surinam laborers were forbidden to cultivate bananas, and existing banana trees were destroyed in order to compel them to earn subsistence on the plantations. These and similar schemes for coercing natives by striking at the food supply have been widely employed.

More extreme forms of coercion have been used in connection with the recruiting and transporting of laborers for plantation work. The African slave trade, which supplied New World plantations with labor for several centuries, is the best known and historically the most important instance. Not so well known is the practice of "blackbirding," formerly quite extensively employed in the Pacific area where kidnapped islanders were virtually sold into plantation slavery in Fiji and in Queensland. More recently the so-called "coolie trade" flourished in the Pacific and Indian ocean areas. Chinese and Indian coolies, contracting to work for white planters, had to agree to penal sanctions for the enforcement of their contracts.

The existence of forced labor in one form or another in the plantation society of the American South is, therefore, not exceptional. Southern experience corresponds with the experience of plantation areas generally. This fact suggests that, in spite of the reputation which the presence of such labor has given the South in the larger moral order of which it is a part, a reputation concerning which Southern people long have been sensitive, a proper explanation of compulsory labor will account for it not in terms of vice and virtue but in terms of an economic and social situation of a certain kind. This situation is described as one of "open resources."

III. The Labor Situation: Open and Closed Resources

When Tacitus, the Roman, went into the land of the Germans he was impressed with the abundance of waste and unappro priated land—*superest ager*. It was the "free" land of the Roman frontier. Perhaps, in the existing state of German culture, the resources of the country were being fully utilized, but to Tacitus, viewing the country through the eyes of one accustomed to Roman techniques and methods, it was an area of "open" resources, capable of far greater yields to sustain a far greater population.

In other words, in the language of Isaiah Bowman,

man himself . . . is a part of his own environment; his skill and knowledge are assets to him as definitely as that which nature provides in the raw. We cannot determine the capacity of a land from its physical aspects alone, its soil, its water supply, its temperature means and extremes, its forests, or the presence or absence of fisheries and the like. Greenland was one kind of country to the Vikings; it was another kind of country to the Eskimos; it would be still another kind of country to us. Its *capacity,* or potential, would vary widely in these three cases.[10]

It is probable that the resources of the New World, from the point of view of the aboriginal Indians, were being utilized about as completely as possible when this country came to be occupied by people with the experience of Europe behind them. But like Tacitus in Germany, the English in Virginia were greatly impressed by the great abundance of virgin land.[11]

Resources become open or closed, therefore, only in the relation between two cultures. We should bear this in mind as we read the following quotation from Nieboer, in which he defines his twin concepts *open* and *closed* resources, concepts arrived at from a study of the conditions under which slavery and other forms of forced labor typically arise.

The most important result of our investigation [he says] is the division . . . of all peoples of the earth into peoples with *open* and with *closed* *resources.* Among the former labour is the principal factor of production, and a man who does not possess anything but his own strength and skill, is able to provide for himself independently of any capitalist or landlord. There may be capital which enhances the productiveness of labour, and particularly fertile or favorably situated grounds the ownership of which gives great advantage; but a man can do without these advantages. Among peoples with closed resources it is otherwise. Here subsistence is dependent upon material resources of which there is only a limited supply, and which accordingly have all been appropriated. These resources can consist in capital, the supply of which is always limited; then those who own no capital are dependent on the capitalists. They can also consist in land. Such is the case when all land has been appropriated; then people destitute of land are dependent on the landowners.[12]

Where there is more land than there is labor to till it, where a profitable market for the products of the land exists, and where men of capital are competing with each other for labor, some form of forced labor is probable, especially if a class of people can be stamped and categorized for the purpose. Here two masters are running after one laborer, and the master who succeeds in getting him, will hold him if he can. Such a situation of open resources may lead, as it has led, to a "kennel economy of chattel slavery."

On the other hand, where men are driven to competing with each other for a place on the land or in a factory, wages may be reduced to a level lower than the cost of keeping them as slaves. Where two laborers are running after one master, the laborer who succeeds in catching him, will hold him if he can. There is, however, always the threat of the masterless and unemployed man. Such a situation of clased resources may lead, as it has led, to a "jungle economy of 'free' labor."

Indentured servitude, slavery, cropper-tenancy, and other forms of controlled labor, are devices for artificially altering the disproportion which unoccupied land bears to people. In this situation people rather than land is the factor which is subject to control, and social change operates to render people dependent upon a capitalist or landlord rather than directly upon the resources of the area. Labor unionism, on the other hand, is, in one of its functions, a device for altering the disproportion which surplus labor bears to land and capital.

In the American colonies with an abundance of free or cheap natural resources there was no reason for a man voluntarily to enter or remain long in the employ of another. On the frontier he had every opportunity to become an independent squatter or farmer. Forced labor in America was, therefore, mainly a defensive measure against the effects of the frontier on the labor market.

However, the assumption that the demand for labor is a corollary of abundant land is not always true in new settlements. There is a great difference in this respect between those colonial settlements that produce agricultural supplies for domestic consumption and those that emphasize the production of great staple crops, like tobacco or cotton—what the Germans call *Kolonialwaren*—intended primarily for foreign export.[13] Obviously the existence of the market relationship sets up a strong demand for labor; the condition of open resources leads to some form of compulsory labor.[14] The extent of the frontier area over which forced labor is profitable, and to a large extent necessary, is determined by the extent of the market relation.

Now the South has been, at least until the present economic depression, what Nieboer calls a country of open resources. In his *History of Virginia*, published in London in 1705, Beverly stated that the inhabitants of Virginia depended upon the liberality of nature "without endeavoring to improve its Gifts by Art or Industry. They spunge upon the Blessings of a warm Sun, and a fruitful Soil, and almost grutch the Pains of gathering the Bounties of the Earth." As late as 1925, J. Russell Smith could write of the South: "The working man in this region has two alternatives. He may work regularly, get wages and buy food, or he may work occasionally at the spasmodic labor of the farm and get an equal amount of food by going hunting, fishing or berrying—facts of profound influence in checking the development of manufacture." [15]

The cultivation and harvesting of the great agricultural staples of the South have been characterized by the presence of operations demanding a uniform type of unskilled labor. Machine methods for such operations either did not exist or were uneconomic. The result since the days of early settlement has been an active demand for cheap agricultural labor. This demand was purely and simply a demand for labor, not, in its origin, a demand for slaves. But because the demand did not meet with an adequate response, it grew into a demand for slaves.[16] Slavery, in turn, spread into the Southwest as the market for cotton and other staples expanded.

By the time of the Civil War economic changes in the Southeast had undoubtedly occurred which were in process of altering the relation between labor and cultivable land. But concerning the view that in 1860 slavery was being "strangled for lack of room to expand" Gray points out that in the South generally "the plantation system was not seriously limited by scarcity of land. It had utilized only a small fraction of the available land area. The most fertile and easily available soils may have been occupied, but there was a vast area remaining, a considerable part of which has been brought into cultivation since 1860. At the time of the Civil War railways were rapidly opening up new fertile areas to plantation agriculture. Far from being a decrepit institution tottering toward a decline for lack of abundant land, the economic motives for the continuance of slavery, from the standpoint of the employers, were never so strong as in the years just preceding the Civil War." [17]

The South continued to be, after the Civil War, a land of open resources with more land than there was labor to till it. In 1905 Alfred H. Stone wrote:

An adequate supply of labour is the first essential in the business of raising cotton. To secure it constitutes the most serious problem confronting the plantation management. Not for forty years has the supply equalled the demand in the alluvial section of Mississippi. Here the

Negro still has almost a monopoly of the field of manual labour, though at last his supremacy has been threatened by the white man. So great is the annual competition among planters for Negro labour that the latter is afforded opportunities for driving bargains superior to those possessed by any other class of agriculturists with which I have any acquaintance.[18]

It is not necessary to agree with Stone's opinion that Negro and white tenants have superior opportunities for driving bargains with the planters, since the result of their bargaining has been so pitifully small, in order to appreciate the importance of the fact that the economic and social situation originally responsible for slavery existed at least until comparatively recently. We have as much reason to relate share-tenancy to this situation as we have to relate slavery to it.

IV. The Planter as the Active Agent in the Situation

The capital that migrates to overseas frontiers is quite different from the capital that stays at home. In the modern period, capital invested abroad usually is exempt from the governmental restrictions that are imposed upon it at home. But aside from such arbitrary differences there seems to be a more fundamental difference. According to Alvin Johnson:

The [capital that stays at home] . . . , which we may denominate capital proper, is characterized by cautious calculation, by a preference for sure if small gains, to dazzling winnings. The other, which we may call speculative enterprise, is characterized by a readiness to take risks, a thirst for brilliant gains. . . .

Capital proper thrives best in a settled order of society, where the risks of loss are at a minimum. It accepts favors from government, to be sure, but politics is no part of its game; peace, and freedom from disturbing innovations, are its great desiderata. Speculative enterprise, on the other hand, thrives best in the midst of disorder. Its favorite field of operations is the fringe of change, economic or political. It delights in the realm where laws ought to be, but have not yet made their appearance. To control the course of legal evolution, to retard it or divert it, are its favorite devices for prolonging the period of rich gains. Politics, thus, is an essential part of the game of speculative enterprise.[19]

But, of course, it is not abstract "capital" which exhibits these characteristics; they are exhibited by individual men. Capital is an instrument of power in the hands of a man who may use it either cautiously or adventurously. In a frontier situation where men have no reverential feeling for the customs and obligations of the social order from whence they come, where life is crude, optimistic, pragmatic, and impatiently progressive, there are, in the words of Parrington, "the raw materials of a race of capitalistic buccaneers." It is in the period of settlement that the bitterest competition for property occurs. Men bring to the struggle every resource they can command—the strength of their bodies, their weapons, their skills, their cunning, and their capital. In the situation in which we here are interested the successful man becomes a planter. The planter in turn becomes an engine of change, and the plantation institution takes its form and function from him.[20]

The planter is to be regarded as a variant of that class of individuals who historically have possessed the land and put themselves at the head of political institutions based upon the exploitation of the land. In his case capital is the main source of strength and power. Without it he does not establish a plantation. He becomes a commander of men because of his command of capital.

This point has an important bearing on the controversy among historians over the question of the source of Virginia's planter aristocracy. One group, represented by Professor P. A. Bruce, argues that a fairly large number of members of England's noble families settled in Virginia, and that from these Cavaliers stemmed the First Families of Virginia.[21] Another group, led by Professor T. J. Wertenbaker, argues that Virginia's aristocracy arose from men of humble circumstance with the development of the country and with Negro slavery and that it was distinctively of Colonial origin.[22] Thus Professor Bruce says of Samuel Mathews that he "had married the daughter of Sir Thomas Hinton, the son-in-law of Sir Sebastian Harvey, one of the most distinguished Lord Mayors of London in those times." [23] Wertenbaker, on the other hand, calls Samuel Mathews "a man of plain extraction, although well connected by marriage." [24] Again Bruce emphasizes the fact that "Adam Thoroughgood . . . was a brother of Sir John Thoroughgood . . . who was attached to the Court." [25] Wertenbaker calls attention to the fact that Adam Thoroughgood "came to Virginia as a servant or apprentice." [26] Samuel Mathews and Adam Thoroughgood and many others like them became men of property and affairs in Virginia. They originally were poor men who, however, were advantageously connected with other men presumably of wealth in England. It is evident that, commoner, noble or near-noble, those able to establish themselves as planters were those able to command capital from some source. The essential requisite to planting in early Virginia was not social rank but capital.

When the profits from tobacco were discovered only such men as merchants and ship captains, and others having connections with wealthy Englishmen, could muster the capital necessary for the initial expense of establishing a planting enterprise. If the enterprise was a large one the initial outlay might amount to a considerable sum. In 1690 William Fitzhugh advised anyone planning to raise tobacco in Virginia to deposit £150 to £200 in the hands of a London merchant with which to buy lands in the colony, and an equal amount with some member of the Royal African Company for slaves.[27] Of those who were able to raise such sums, and who had at the same time the desire, the courage, and the ability to supervise their investments in Virginia, some were men of social rank in England but probably most were not.

Wertenbaker describes the merchant-planters of seventeenth-century Virginia as hard, crude, and grasping. Governor Nicholson called Robert Carter, whose arrogance earned him the title "King" Carter, a man of "extraordinary pride and ambition." Carter was probably the wealthiest Virginia planter of his day and in his attitude typical of the first generation of planters. A change took place in the personality of the planter with the complete establishment of his rank and the fixation of the habits that went with it.

During the eighteenth century he gradually lost that arrogance that had been so characteristic of him in the age of Nicholson and Spotswood. At the time of the Revolution are found no longer men that do not hesitate to trample under foot the rights of others as Curtis, Byrd, and Carter had done. Nothing could be more foreign to the nature of Washington or Jefferson than the haughtiness of the typical Virginia planter of an earlier period. But it was arrogance only that had been lost, not self-respect or dignity.[28]

The evolution of the planter into the well-bred aristocrat was achieved more completely in the older plantation areas of tobacco and rice than on the new cotton plantation frontier. Before the Civil War the cotton plantation had produced only one or two generations of planters—men whose virtues were not, for the most part, those of niceness but of resourcefulness and enterprise. The new domain of cotton, a domain far more extensive than that of tobacco, rice, or sugar, created many *nouveaux riches,* or "cotton snobs," as they were termed.

Whether rude or aristocratic in manner, and regardless of the crop which produced his wealth, the status of the planter represented success. With economic opportunity limited almost entirely to agriculture in contrast to the variety of occupational possibilities in the North, the South was almost completely a rural agrarian world. The plantation made it also a feudal world.[29] With no large urban groups in the South to contest their control, planters exercised an influence on the economic and political system and defined a standard of life for the people out of all proportion to their numbers. The ambition of the farmer class was always to emulate the planters. The plantations which prevailed outside the tidewater areas were likely to be small in size, but every master of a few blacks tended to regard himself as in a class with the planters. By 1850 the census was distinguishing between "planters" and "farmers."

The Civil War weakened, but by no means destroyed, the planter. He has remained one of the dominant forces in the Lower South, but new conditions have not allowed his leadership to remain unchallenged. Urbanization and industrialization have introduced new economic interests to compete with him for labor, markets, and political control. An unexpected competitor was the poor and middle-class white man who registered his protest in the Populist uprising of 1890. Since this revolt the planter has been a factor of diminishing importance in Southern politics.

Nevertheless, in all that is historically and essentially "Southern" the planter's position is and has been central. If the South has been an area of open resources, the capital and the purposes of the planter were as indispensable in making it so as the physical resources themselves. He was the active agent in bringing the resources of a portion of the New World into the markets of the Old. The problem of labor which this involved was not for him an abstract economic problem; it was the concrete and very practical problem of the man who has work to be done of getting workers to do it. As he solved this problem well or poorly, his plantation prospered or failed. It was a problem which he faced in the early days of American settlement and it is a problem which has remained to plague him down to the present time. The Southern planter and his fellows, from Colonial days to the present, have faced labor emergencies as they arose and each has sought the most expedient way to free himself from perplexing difficulties. Out of the interaction of the efforts of many men have come certain tendencies and trends which appear to be more important than the mere temporal sequence of events. These "social forces" give to particular events, to individuals who are pushed out in front, and to the recording laws and literature, a significance they would not otherwise possess.

V. From Apprenticeship to Indentured Servitude

The experimental stage in the development of American slavery, so far as the South is concerned, belongs to the history of Virginia. Share-tenancy belongs to the history of the South generally. The story begins with the English folkway of apprenticeship which paved the way for white indentured servitude in the colonies. Indentured servitude, in turn, was the historic base upon which Negro slavery was constructed. Share-tenancy established itself somewhat more rapidly than the preceding forms of controlled labor, owing to the decision of the Civil War, but it probably represents the working out of consequences that Emancipation interrupted and altered but did not prevent. It has been suggested that the slave was probably predestined to be what he has since very largely become, a peasant farmer.

Apprenticeship is a system of industrial education, generally for minors. In Elizabethan England custom and law bound the apprentice to a master for a period of service generally seven years in length. The master was one skilled in a craft, a trade, or a profession. He was given authority over the apprentice, with power of corporal punishment, to aid in imparting his skill. Customary guild regulations and previous enactments were codified in the Statute of Artificers in 1562, which put a premium upon agricultural apprenticeship. The statute required a written contract between master and apprentice, a contract binding both parties, but one which apparently operated to the special advantage of the master. Justices of the peace and officers of the towns were later empowered to bind out unemployed minors to masters under certain conditions. In this way apprenticeship became a part of the system of poor relief.[30] This was the status of apprenticeship at the time of the plantation of America.

The word *plantation* originally had reference to an organized and controlled migration. Plantation was a method of moving and settling labor, especially in overseas territory, where it was needed and where it might be profitable. World changes incident to the discovery of new lands and to the shift in the routes and commodities of trade brought about in England an agrarian revolution. The reorganization of manorial estates, in order to supply rising urban markets, resulted in the uprooting of thousands of people who filled the highways and crowded the towns and cities. England regarded itself as overpopulated, and for the first time the nation officially realized that it had a problem of the poor. The poor laws and vagrancy laws, which were enacted during the first half of the sixteenth century, sought to restore the lost social equilibrium by re-establishing geographical and social stability.

Now the thinning-out of the rural population of England and the plantation of newly discovered lands abroad with new populations were both parts of the same fundamental and necessary process of population redistribution in an evolving world-economy. England was assuming a central position in this enlarging world-community. Plantation was an expression of an expanding overseas trade, and especially of trade which required the production of goods in overseas territory by European enterprise and management. It therefore involved the migration of European capital and European management. But it was where native people could not be brought under control as laborers, at least in sufficient number, and where a labor migration from Europe had therefore to be organized that the real nature of plantation was revealed. It was essentially an industrial army of occupation.

It was this to the men of capital in England who invested in the plantation of America and stood to profit from the enterprise. To other interests in England, however, plantation was not only a migration of a certain kind but a social movement bound up with the problem of the poor and regarded, like the Poor Laws, as in part a solution of that problem. "A Plantation," wrote William Penn, "seems a fit place for those Ingenious Spirits that being low in the World, are much Clogg'd and oppress'd about a Livelyhood, for the means of subsisting being easie there, they may have time and opportunity to gratify their inclinations." [31] Many before Penn had written to the same effect.

Plantation originally was transplantation, and the capitalist sponsors of the enterprise resided in England. Upon the rise of the planter resident in Virginia, an independent but responsible agent for the employment of English capital, migration changed to emigration and immigration. With a demand for labor on the part of the colonies, and with an oversupply in England, emigration to the colonies was a natural consequence. But the mechanism through which the new migration took place had to be different from that employed in plantation proper. It was no longer by means of an individual of wealth or a company transplanting or "planting" people in a wilderness. It now became a problem of delivering a potential laborer in England to a potential employer in America. It was a problem of how to transport the laborer since transportation was expensive and ordinarily quite beyond his means. A modification of the system of apprenticeship proved to be the solution. The laborer in return for the cost of his transportation voluntarily bound himself, or involuntarily was bound, to work for a master in the colonies for a specified period of years. Variations of this practice developed in time, but it remained the basic pattern during the period of indentured servitude.

"Indentured servitude was thus the Colonial analogue of the agricultural apprenticeship provided by the Statute of Artificers," says Douglas, "and as such flourished chiefly in the great agricultural areas of the South." [32] But apprenticeship and indentured servitude, originally very similar, quickly developed some very important differences. In the first place, the apprentice was generally a minor, while the status of indentured servant came to be held, usually, by an adult man or woman. In the second place, indentured servitude soon lost the educational function which was the essential mark of apprenticeship. Tobacco as then cultivated in Virginia required a good deal of hard labor but demanded no special skill on the part of anyone. The planter as entrepreneur was likely to be the only member of the plantation able to envisage the whole market situation, a situation more or less outside the view of the servant, and in this capacity his function was indispensable. But as master his knowledge of the art of cultivating tobacco probably did not long remain much greater than that of the servant. Or certainly he did not need seven years to teach the servant all he knew. The word *master* ceased to mean a man who was master of his craft and came to mean a man who was master of others. The element of skill dropped out, but the element of authority and discipline remained and became, in fact, stronger as time went on. This change operated to degrade the status of the servant, and later on, of course, the slave, to a position much lower than that of the apprentice.[33]

These and other differences between apprenticeship and indentured servitude developed from the fact that the latter was to function in a social and economic situation entirely unlike that in which apprenticeship functioned. It was again a difference between a situation of open and a situation of closed resources. For indentured servitude in the colonies served the double function of a system of labor recruitment and control and a means of promoting immigration. In its latter function it served also, in theory at least, as a principle regulating the alienation and acquisition of land. Through the "headright" system planters were in part compensated by the community for the expense to which they were put in bringing over servants. Servants, in turn, in some of the colonies, were given grants of land upon completion of their terms of service.

As property classes developed in such a colony as that of Virginia, where insurrectionary plots on the part of servants were discovered, the increased exercise of authority on the part of the planter was demanded by the community.[34] The harsh vagrancy laws of England furnished precedents for the intervention of the public in the contractural relations between master and servant. Such public coercion, as distinguished from the enforcement of contracts, was supposedly in the interest of the public, but it also coincided with the interest of the planter. The vagrancy laws upon which public coercion was based were the legal sources of the harsher features of Colonial servitude and of slavery.[35]

From the planter's point of view indentured servitude had an essential disadvantage in that, having been paid in advance, the servant had little inducement to work hard or to perform his work with care. Judged by the uncomplimentary remarks so frequently made by planters, he was inclined to work about as little as he could. Under the circumstances, punishment for breach of contract or for offenses against the interest of the planter could hardly take the form of dismissal. Such an action on the part of the planter would have been equivalent to throwing the rabbit into the briar patch. Neither could punishment take the form of a fine in money since the servant had generally no means wherewith to remit a fine. Many of the incidents which further differentiated indentured servitude from apprenticeship and prepared the way for slavery developed from the resort to apparently necessary alternative forms of punishment. The alternative forms were of two general types: (1) corporal punishment and (2) the lengthening of the period of servitude.

The offenses which ordinarily required punishment were, in general, those which violated the planter's right to the full time and service of the servant under the terms of the indenture. Idleness was a common complaint, but running away was, perhaps, the most frequent offense. Even when the servant was recovered, the loss of time and the expense were serious to the planter. Offenses that partook more directly of infringements against the peace and order of the community, as well as against the interests of the planter, included robbery, rebellion, and crimes of violence.

In Virginia corporal punishment for these and other offenses was provided for in a law of 1619 which read, "If a servant wilfully neglect his master's commands he shall suffer bodily punishment." There was ample precedent for this in apprenticeship. Until 1662 the right of punishment was in the hands of the Assembly and the courts only, but undoubtedly it was exercised also by planters without legal right. Before the end of the seventeenth century corporal punishment had been extended to cover offenses against the dignity and status of the planter as well as offenses against his interests. Further control by the planter over the servant's person and liberty of action was granted after the discovery of a plot of servants in 1663. The great alarm led to the strict regulation of such liberties as leaving the plantation and assembling.

Punishment by means of extension of time had its beginnings in Virginia in 1619, when the first General Assembly ordered servitude for wages as a penalty for "idlers and renegades." This was to be service to the colony in public works and meant, of course, service in addition to the term of the contract. "In this," says Ballagh, "we have the germ of additions of time, a practice which later became the occasion of a very serious abuse of the servant's rights by the addition of terms altogether incommensurate with the offenses for which they were imposed." [36]

The offenses which made the servant liable to corporal punishment were also those which led to punishment by the addition of time. Often both punishments were inflicted. Offenses especially punishable by addition of time, however, seem to have been those involving relations between the sexes, e.g., marriage without the consent of the planter, fornication, and bearing bastard children. For these and other offenses "additions of time frequently amounted to as much as four or five years, or even seven years in some cases, and were often more than the original term of servitude." [37] Second and third offenses, of course, brought the addition of even more time so that we read of servants for twenty-five years, servants for forty years, and servants for life.

Not only were servants given additional time for offenses committed by them, but even when not guilty of offense they often were sold or held for periods longer than their indentures called for. A large number of suits for freedom came before the courts. With labor so greatly in demand the offenses were not all on the side of the servant.[38]

It is easy to see that slavery was on the way, but the displacement of servitude by slavery was also to involve the displacement of white labor by Negro labor on the plantations.

VI. From White Servitude to Negro Slavery

In the narrative of Master John Rolfe we are told that "about the last of August [1619] came in a Dutch man of Warre that sold us twenty negars." [39] In this sentence Rolfe noted the entrance into Virginia of a new group different in skin color, language, and religion. The members of this group did not voluntarily break the home ties of Africa and set out for a land of opportunity in America. Neither were they motivated by the land hunger which induced many a white servant to bind himself voluntarily to several years of hard labor. They were transported against their will. In America all Englishmen might hope to become "gentlemen" because all might hope with good chance of success to possess land, and in England the possession of land had carried that coveted status. But Negroes were not motivated by this particular tradition and purpose. They therefore were placed at a competitive disadvantage with white servants who shared in the European tradition of their masters.

Perhaps because John Rolfe used the word *sold* in his journal, and because Negro slaves later were sold, it has been assumed that complete slavery was introduced into Virginia in 1619. To be sure, white servants who waited until they had reached Virginia to find their masters frequently were sold to the planters by ship captains, but it was their time only which was sold, not their persons, in order to meet the cost of passage. Hence, as Russell says, "an inference that these twenty negroes were slaves, drawn from the fact that they were sold to the colony or to the planters would not be justified." [40] Mr. J. C. Ballagh in his *A History of Slavery in Virginia* was the first to call attention to the fact that Negroes were not originally introduced into the colony as slaves. His investigations seem to have established the proposition that "servitude . . . was the historic base upon which slavery, by the extension and addition of incidents, was constructed." [41]

In 1619 there was little in the mores of the English settlers in Virginia to countenance actual slavery. These Englishmen had had very little previous contact with Negroes and they had no traditional prejudice against them. The Negro was not a white man, and this difference must have been immediately felt, but there was no crystallized objection to him on the score of race. Antipathies based upon olfactory and hygienic objections, and prejudices based upon the fact that the black people were heathen, seem to have existed, but Negroes seem not to have been marked off as a distinct racial group. Indeed, between them and the white servants laboring at the same tasks on the plantations there existed for a while a spirit of camaraderie. Many masters held both the Negro and the white servant in equal contempt. [42]

In answer to the question which naturally would arise as to the status of the twenty Negroes before they were "sold" to the colony and to the planters, Ballagh says:

As the captives, not of warfare, but of piracy, they were under the protection of international law in maintaining their original status, and had they been citizens of a powerful civilized community they might have received it. They were, no doubt, slaves or captives of the Spanish, but no rights of ownership, even if just, could pass to the nation by whom they were made a prize of piracy. The masters of the Dutch and English privateers, therefore, had no rights of ownership which they could legally exercise or transfer over the negroes imported until rights were recognized by the law of England or of the Bermudas and Virginia. Until this recognition came, the negroes were persons of undetermined status to whom the privileges of the common law were not specifically extended.[43]

Negroes introduced into Virginia in 1619 and many years thereafter seem to have taken their places in the colony as indentured servants with all the rights and liberties of indentured servants. A census taken in 1624–25 enumerated twenty-three Negroes all listed as "servants." [44] Two Negroes, Anthony Johnson and Mary, his wife, both probably members of the original party of twenty, had not only served out their terms of servitude and become free, but a land patent of 1651 shows Johnson to have been the owner of 250 acres of land assigned to him in fee simple. In 1651 Richard Johnson came in either as a free Negro or as a servant. Only three years later he was given 100 acres of land for importing two other persons.[45]

Hence it appears that Negroes in early Virginia had taken their places as servants along with white servants, and upon completion of their terms of service they received the freedom dues to which servants were entitled. They themselves became landholders and masters of servants. It is even possible that for a time they held white servants, since a measure subsequently enacted forbade the holding of Christian, i.e., white, servants by Negro masters. In at least one instance white servants on a plantation worked under the direction of a Negro overseer.[46]

But Negro servants could not escape the operation of forces which, as we have seen, were forcing indentured servants generally into positions of more complete subordination. Not only did Negro servants not escape them, but because of the special disabilities under which they labored they were more easily victimized than were the white servants. In 1640 three servants of Hugh Gwyn, a white planter, two of them white and the third a Negro, ran away from the plantation of their master. Apprehended and brought back for trial, each received a flogging by order of the court. In addition, the two white servants were given an extra year of servitude, but "the third, being a negro . . . shall serve his said master or his assigns for the term of his natural life." [47] "Being a negro" was beginning to have its effect.

It is interesting to note, however, that Negro as well as white masters took advantage of Negro servants. Of course, there were only a few Negroes who were masters of servants, but these few responded to the situation very much as did the white masters. One especially interesting illustration of this is the case of Anthony Johnson, to whom reference already has been made. Johnson was the defendant in a suit brought against him by another Negro, John Casor, for his freedom. From the court records of Northampton County, Russell presents the following facts regarding the case:

According to the records made of the case, John Casor set up the claim in 1653 "Yt hee came unto Virginia for seaven or eight years of Indenture, yt hee had demanded his freedom of Anth. Johnson his Mayster; & further sd yt hee had kept him his serv[an]t seaven years longer than hee should or ought." Casor appealed to Captain Samuel Goldsmith to see that he was accorded his rights. Goldsmith demanded of Johnson the servant negro's indenture, and was told by Johnson that the latter had never seen any indenture, and "yt hee had ye Negro for his life." Casor stood firmly by his assertion that when he came in he had an indenture, and Messrs. Robert and George Parker confirmed his declaration, saying that "they knewe that ye sd Negro had an Indenture in one Mr. [Sandys] hand, on ye other side of ye Baye &. . . . if the sd Anth. Johnson did not let ye negro go free the said negro Jno. Casor would recover most of his Cows from him ye sd Johnson" in compensation for service rendered which was not due. Whereupon Anthony Johnson "was in a great feare" and his "sonne in Law, his wife, & his own two sonnes persuaded the old negro Anth. Johnson to let the sd. Jno. Casor free."

The case would be interesting enough and very instructive if it had ended here, but the sequel is more interesting still. Upon more mature deliberation Anthony Johnson determined to made complaint in court "against Mr. Robert Parker that hee detayneth one Jno. Casor a negro the plaintiff's Serv[an]t under pretense yt the sd Jno. Casor is a freeman." His complaint was received, and the court "seriously considering & weighing ye premises," rendered the following verdict, than which there are none stranger on record: "The court . . . doe fynd that ye sd Mr. Robert Parker most unrightly keepeth ye sd Negro John Casor from his r[igh]t Mayster Anthony Johnson & . . . Be it therefore ye

Judgment of ye court & ordered that ye sd Jno. Casor negro shall forthwith return into ye service of his sd Mayster Anthony Johnson and that the sd Mr. Robert Parker make payment of all charges in the suite and execution." [48]

A Negro master is successful in his suit against a white master and wins the right to hold his Negro servant for life! "Thus was rendered," Charles Johnson comments on this case, "in strange and fateful irony, the first legal decision involving the right to the perpetual services of a Negro. The decision was obviously not made on racial grounds, as the chance position and relationship of the litigants in the suit well establishes." [49]

For about fifteen years before the passage of the first acts of the Virginia slave code, Negro servants were being recorded as servants for life. Such servants "are call'd Slaves," said Beverly, "in respect of the time of their Servitude, because it is for Life." [50] They were servants against whom the usual punishments by addition of time could not hold. Slavery was therefore fast becoming established in custom, and it was only a question of time before it would receive the sanction of law.

In the decade 1660–70 various statutes were enacted affording this sanction and effecting the legal transition from servitude to slavery. In 1661 an act to punish "English running away with negroes" who were "incapable of making satisfaction by addition of time" was passed. Servitude for life, however, was not yet actual slavery, but with it came a problem, the practical solution of which was the final step in the transition to that condition. This was the problem of the status of the offspring of servants who were "incapable of making satisfaction by addition of time" because they were servants for life. "It was evident," says Ballagh, "that parents under an obligation of life service could make no valid provision for the support of their offspring, and that a just title to the service of the child might rest on the master's maintenance." [51]

Where both parents were servants for life the question of the disposition of the legitimate offspring was no very great problem since there was no difficulty in defining the status of the offspring. But illegitimacy and miscegenation had complicated the matter enough to require the formal establishment of some "principle of heredity." Illegitimacy without miscegenation was difficult enough since the instability and change of frontier life made the determination of parenthood on the male side more uncertain than is the case in stable communities. Notwithstanding the rule of English common law that the child should follow the condition of the father the opposite principle that the condition of the mother determined the status of the offspring was adopted in Virginia and in all the other colonies except Maryland. This was in keeping with the idea prevailing at the time and expressed in the saying that "Motherhood is a matter of fact, but fatherhood is a matter of opinion."

Miscegenation complicated the matter further by raising the question of the definition of a Negro. Where both parents were known to be Negroes there was no doubt as to the classification of the offspring. But there were serious doubts as to the position of mixed-bloods, and many, if not most, of the illegitimate children of female Negro servants for life were mulattoes. Peter Fontaine may have exaggerated when he said that the country swarmed with mulatto bastards, but undoubtedly there were many.[52]

The problem of interracial sexual contacts and illegitimacy was one of the most stubborn to confront the colony. Although the white planter class was not free from such contacts, the greatest amount of irregularity in the first century of settlement seems to have developed between white and Negro servants. These probably began shortly after the introduction of the first Negroes, for in 1630 the court entered an order of punishment for the offense. From this time on the assembly, the courts, and the church wrestled with the problem without success. It was one of a series of legislative acts dealing with the problem which became the means of finally and legally establishing complete slavery in Virginia. The act of 1662 reads as follows: "Whereas some doubts have arisen whether children got by any Englishman upon a negro woman should be slave or free, be it therefore enacted and declared by this present grand assembly, that all children borne in this country shall be held bond or free only according to the condition of the mother."[53]

The "principle of heredity" laid down in this act "was wholly foreign at that time to the condition of servitude, and broadly differentiated it from the system which resulted."[54] The term *slave* was used without definition of any kind, for the act was not intended to create a race of slaves but to settle a question which had arisen in the operation of a custom and to prevent sexual irregularities and race mixture. "Notwithstanding its effect it is clear that the purpose of the act of 1662 was primarily punitory." [55] Hereditary slavery grew directly out of the problem of the mulatto.

Negro slavery was thus a response to a situation whereby the planter got laborers to cultivate his tobacco and the Negro got someone who was responsible for his sustenance as a minimum consideration. It was the sort of labor desirable for tobacco-growing under frontier conditions. It involved certain relative advantages over white servitude since the tasks to which the Negro was put involved mainly routine manual labor and little use of machinery, tools, and techniques outside the culture of natives of Africa.[56] Negro slavery assured the planter a more or less long-time and stable supply of labor.

In addition to dependability it was necessary, also, that labor for the production of agricultural staples on the Southern frontier be movable. In the absence of cheap fertilizers, planters found it necessary after a few years of cultivation of particular tracts of land to move to virgin fertile soil. This is one reason why primogeniture and entail failed to secure a foothold in the transmission of landed estates through inheritance. The incidents through which indentured servitude and slavery developed were those which had survival value for a type of controlled labor highly mobile in character. American slavery reproduced, or tended to reproduce, the personal rights and obligations of European feudalism and serfdom but with the laborer's right to a secure place on the land left out. It was the personal and legal attachment to a master, wherever he might go, rather than to a lord as landlord, that characterized American slavery.[57]

Behind all these formal and legal facts in the development of American slavery were others of a more intangible sort. These were the facts of human nature, the sort of facts which, once grasped, makes any historical situation intelligible because it can then be measured against contemporary experiences and observations. The economic and legal systems in which men live are of great consequence to their actions, but these systems do not determine human relations entirely. The same human nature is present in any and every social system, and occasionally through the pages of history one gets a glimpse of it as something that illuminates and makes intelligible a situation whether one approves of that situation or not.

On the side of human nature the relations which took shape under the influence of daily contact and which eventuated in slavery, grew out of a community of interest in the production of a crop on an isolated plantation, and it would be difficult to exaggerate the extent of this isolation. In the wilderness of the forested Southern frontier master and man were subject to the law announced by Candide at the close of his unfortunate wanderings—they had to cultivate a garden together. Men of very different race and culture were associated together to make a living in accordance with the purposes of the planter and with the means at hand. Men who have to act together in any sort of capacity and for whatever purpose come to know what to expect of each other, and it would have been very strange indeed if between master and man a considerable degree of mutual confidence had not been established. Under the circumstances the relationship between them became, in all probability, a very comfortable one for both. It was something like a family relation; the master felt more secure and had a sense of added dignity and power because he had the permanent support and assistance of his man, particularly in trying times. In early Virginia the idea of a slave was, as we have seen, that of a servant for life, and slavery was, for the most part, a domestic relationship. It is necessary here to return to the subject of indentured servitude in order to see how the forces of human nature operated to effect the transition to slavery.

The servant, male or female, white or Negro, was usually a familyless individual living in close relation to the family of the master.[58] It is a natural thing for a familyless man and especially a familyless woman to attach himself or herself to a family to which they render service and from the members of which they receive support and affection.[59] Where the planter, his sons, and his servants worked together in the fields there could evolve very naturally a relationship which, when taken advantage of, might easily be made permanent.

The servant was an adult when he came to Virginia and began to serve out an indenture for perhaps five years or more. Five years of servitude in the isolation of the rural plantation would naturally build up habits of work and dependence and attitudes of subordination which would be well established when the day of freedom came. If for some delinquency the period of service is extended for perhaps five years longer, he would find it even more difficult suddenly to terminate old associations and go out on his own. Perhaps he is no longer a young man when his term of service is over, and advancing years have rendered him even more dependent upon the master and his family. It is easy to see why many such servants would rather remain and continue to perform accustomed work for an accustomed master than to go elsewhere.

The relationships of indentured servitude must undoubtedly have lent themselves to the building up of a state of moral insolvency among servants, a state of mind which would involve a tendency toward a dependence upon the master for protection and maintenance with a consequent surrender of responsibility for themselves. This human attitude is easily understood. Perhaps such an attitude induces many men to go into the army where one is assured of food, shelter, and clothing, and where someone else does the worrying. It is not unlike the religious attitude of surrender. In such circumstances what is demanded of the servant, the soldier, and the faithful is not merely service but loyalty.[60]

Thus the master and servant relationship, embedded as it was in attitude and custom, and reinforced by the economic demand for labor, tended to lengthen itself into additional years without necessarily calling in the power of the law to achieve that end. In the case of Negro servants, and especially Negro female servants, where it might be expected that social dependence would be stronger, the lengthening of the relationship into slavery followed without difficulty. Such relationships made possible new plantation settlements on the frontier in a manner analogous to that of any pioneer family settling in the forest, making a clearing, and planting a crop. The forest might seem to invite escape, but few think of escaping, for few brood over their fate and the fact of bondage is not ordinarily reflected upon.[61]

Slavery and the forms of discipline that went with it thus grew up in Virginia as a set of customary relations to meet the needs and exigencies of an agricultural situation of a certain kind. But it grew up, as we have seen, within the traditional and legal system of contract labor as it was known in England at the time.

Apprenticeship and indentured servitude were legally sanctioned and enforced means of regulating labor. Two incidents of
indentured servitude, corporal punishment and addition to the
time of service, proved to be highly important in the evolution
of slavery as a domestic relation. Still another incident in the legal
evolution of indentured servitude which was transmitted to slavery and which promoted an opposite and harsher set of relations
was that of the alienation of the servant or slave by sale or will.

One of the earliest legal questions in connection with indentured servitude to arise in Virginia concerned the right of the
master to assign his servant's contract. The courts recognized this
right whether the servant gave his consent or not.[62] The result
was more and more a disposition in the law to regard the servant
and the slave as chattel property.

The problem which this presents in understanding the history
of American slavery is the fundamental and ancient one of social
form and social content, the problem of determining just how
the formal and legal and conventional develop out of the simply
natural. In the transmission of a habit or custom from one people
to another, or from one generation to another, some of the meaning falls out and the practice inevitably undergoes some change.
Under certain conditions of change, form and content tend to
fall apart. Now with respect to slavery as it developed in Virginia,
the individual who bought, inherited, or hired the slave as property would, of course, rarely maintain the original content of
personal and shared experiences in which the slavery was embedded. On the plantations slavery develped as a domestic relation, but in the slave trade it tended to become an abstraction
divested of all its human association, restraints, and inhibitions.
In this latter form it was recognized in the law and maintained
by public authority. Hence in the slave trade the most ruthless
aspects of the system came to the fore, where, indeed, "ruthless-
ness was the law." Even the intimate relations of the slave family
could not withstand the separating effects of the slave trade.[63]

Upon this legal foundation for slavery the planter gained
greater control over his labor by investing a part of his capital
in its ownership. The status of planter was never defined with
any exactness before the Civil War, but a planter was generally
understood to mean one who owned slaves and employed them
in farming operations. The man who had the capital to invest in

labor and who thus kept that labor in his own hands and out of the hands of others and at the same time prevented it from following its own interests, was able to rise above his fellows. With property in slaves explicitly recognized by the law, slavery became more completely a capitalistic and industrial system and in this form was carried by the westward march of cotton cultivation into the Southwest. The slave trade, foreign and domestic, helped distribute labor where it was needed over the whole Southern region.

But with settlement, the planter and his slaves began again to develop a sense of community. Settlement set in operation the forces of communication and assimilation which partly restored to slavery as it actually existed on the scattered plantations of the South something of its original patriarchal and domestic character, a character much less harsh than a study of the laws of the slave states would lead one to believe.[64]

VII. From Slavery to Share-Tenancy

The impersonalization of slavery incident to the slave trade and other economic changes that took place in the South prior to the Civil War was "entirely analogous" to changes that took place in employer-employee relations in the industrial system of the North during the same period. Channing has called attention to the fact that the conflict which led to the Civil War and Emancipation was part of a general American labor movement reacting against impersonalization.[65]

The Civil War did not, contrary to an opinion often encountered outside the South, destroy the plantation system, but it did profoundly alter the legal status of one of its elements, labor. Share-tenancy proved to be one consequence of this alteration.

With respect to another element in the plantation system, land, the Civil War and Emancipation stopped short of any revolutionary change. Important changes took place within the legal system of landownership, but no important changes took place in the system itself. Legal slavery was abolished, but the large landed estate, the physical basis of controlled labor, remained—a fact which alone necessarily insured a high degree of continuity with the past.[66] A confiscation act passed by Congress in 1862, a militant agitation in Congress by Sumner and Stevens later, a strong demand for land among the freedmen and a general expectation that lands would be given them were threats which, fortunately for the planters, passed away without practical effect. Only in the coastal regions of South Carolina and Georgia were Negroes able to a slight extent to hold on to lands occupied during the Civil War.

Nevertheless, although the plantation as an institution remained intact, the post-bellum period witnessed the rise of a new planter class. Many ante-bellum period planters who tried to carry on with "free niggers" in the post-war period failed in business and were forced to sell their properties. To some extent a small farmer group, composed of both whites and Negroes, acquired the subdivided lands of some of the old estates by purchase, but more often, perhaps, they were sold as units and acquired by such classes of men as doctors, lawyers, and especially rising merchants. Men from these classes also acquired small farms and consolidated them into plantation estates. By 1880 a new planter class was fast taking the place, so far as that was possible, of the older plantation gentry and their sons.

More than we perhaps realize, the Civil War and Reconstruction had the effect of restoring frontier conditions in the South. The region had undergone a severe jolt in social and economic relations. Society had loosened up, and the barriers that had existed to prevent the free movement between the classes were at least lowered. Once again on this frontier appeared the pushing and aggressive individual scheming to acquire land and more land and to gain some sort of a control over other men. He was restricted in his operations by the laws enacted to secure the freedom of the former slaves, but he discovered means of circumventing these laws and even of transforming them into opportunities for himself. Many plantation owners of today can trace the origin of their position to the period of change, of failure, and of opportunity after the Civil War.

After the war the role of the planter as master underwent considerable reduction, but his role as landlord became a much more important one. Planter and laborer in the course of time assumed new relationships to each other based upon the relations of each to the land. Land began to enter into social relationships and social organization in a new and different manner. In Southern rural society the land came to be a mass of holdings and tenures of one kind or another that spread like a net over almost all property and held almost every individual in its meshes. A society came into existence which not merely rested upon the land and used the land but whose ways of life were part of the land. Furthermore, the system of land tenure came to be bound up with rank and status and with the exercise of political authority to an extent that was not true before. Land entered into and became a part of the concrete content of expectations and obligations, rights and duties, in the relations between planters and laborers. In short, land began to *function* in new and different ways in the determination of Southern social organization.

A farm tenant is one who lives on and cultivates the land of another. In the South tenants ordinarily are divided into three main classes: *renters,* or those who rent the land for a fixed amount; *share-tenants,* or those who have some capital of their own and who divide with the landlord the cash crops they raise in some agreed-upon ratio; and *share-croppers,* or those who furnish nothing but their labor and who divide with the landlord the cash crops they raise in such a ratio that they receive a smaller portion than share-tenants.

The first class of tenants, the renters, are not properly to be regarded as members of the plantation since they are not subject to the supervision of a planter. The outstanding characteristic which distinguishes share-tenancy and share-cropping from ordinary tenant farming in the rest of the United States is the fact that such tenants are subject to the supervision of the landlord. The actual degree of supervision exercised may vary from cases where it is so complete that the planter dictates almost every detail to other cases where tenants are largely left to their own devices. However, in the latter cases the planter's potential power may at almost any time go into action.

In actual practice the planter deals with his share-tenants about as he does with his share-croppers; he is likely to make little or no distinction between them in the practical affairs of operating a plantation. The courts, however, tend to follow the opinion of the Supreme Court of the State of Georgia, delivered in 1872, in distinguishing the cropper as one receiving a contingent wage in the form of a share of the crop from the share-tenant who is a small capitalist paying rent.[67] In many respects croppers do not differ from hired farm laborers and are not tenants at all, but since they occupy definitely defined tracts of land under an agreement with the planter like tenants proper they should be considered as part of the system of tenancy.[68]

Measured in terms of the number of tenants, the system which replaced slavery after the war has since grown rapidly in extent and in importance. In 1880, when census data on the subject first became available, 36.2 per cent of the farms of the South were operated by tenants. By 1920 the percentage had mounted to 49.6, and in 1930 it was 55.5.[69] In some sections of the South, particularly in the Cotton Belt, the percentage of tenant-operated farms reached over 75. Over a third of all tenants are croppers, and over a half of all Negro tenants are in this lowest category.[70]

Especially significant in Southern farm tenancy are the figures on the racial distribution of tenants as given in the 1930 census report. In the thirteen Southern States the total number of white croppers amounted to 380,356. The number of Negro croppers was slightly larger, 392,217. On the other hand, the white share-tenants proper in the same year numbered 684,228 against the much smaller figure of 303,888 for Negro share-tenants. Dr. Rupert Vance estimated that the total number of individuals in these tenant families of both classes are approximately five and a half million whites and slightly over three million Negroes. Between 1920 and 1930 white tenants increased by about 200,000 families while Negro tenants decreased by about 2,000 families.[71] It is evident from these facts that the problem of share-tenancy in the South is not one concerning the Negro only. It is even more important as a problem of native white families.

In the census and in statistical tables, facts pertaining to the Negro and to the white populations of the South are set off from each other in sharply separate columns. On the map, however, the dividing line, if it exists, is not nearly so hard and fast. Although there are black belts and white belts, although some areas are almost entirely white and others almost entirely black, over most of the rural South whites and Negroes live together on the land as neighbors. Farms owned or operated by whites lie alongside farms owned or operated by Negroes.

The plantation system is responsible for the fundamental fact that whites and blacks are highly intermixed over the countryside. The post-bellum plantation has grouped white and black tenants together in one geographic, economic, and political unit.

On the plantation white and Negro tenants recognize the authority of the same landlord and planter, frequently engage in joint tasks, and meet each other on Saturday afternoons at the commissary to get the next week's rations. Houses occupied one year by Negro tenants may be occupied the next by white tenants. Within the society of the same plantation members of the two races are thus in constant and continuous interaction, cooperation, competition, and conflict. The plantation has become a group of farms.

The interracial character of the present agricultural labor population of the South suggests that the succession of stages which led up to the plantation as a Negro labor institution before the Civil War has been reversed in the post-war period. The Southern plantation began in Virginia, as we have seen, with white labor.[72] Then came a transition period when white and Negro servants worked side by side for the same planter and master. The classic stage was the period when its laborers were almost entirely of the Negro race. This stage, which lasted for a hundred and fifty years, was the golden age of the Southern plantation, about which centers a large literature of reminiscence and romance. As plantation labor became predominantly Negro, there was a corresponding segregation of poor whites in the more inaccessible and less fertile parts of the South. After the Civil War they began returning to the plantations in large numbers as tenant farmers. So far as the racial composition of labor is concerned the presence on the plantations of whites as common laborers marks a return to an earlier stage, but the process of change is in the opposite direction.

The two races have come together again on the plantation through the mechanism of the system of share-tenancy. The historical origins of this system in the South are not well understood. One account supports the popular assumption that the system originated in the Reconstruction period when much trial and error experimentation demonstrated the practical advantages of a contingent wage plan over other forms of remuneration and control. Developed in connection with the problem of dealing with Negro labor just recently emancipated from slavery, share-tenancy later was extended to include poor white labor. From the point of view of this account Monroe Work writes: "Until recently, the problem of tenancy in the South was generally thought of in terms of the Negro. The fact was ignored that a system of tenancy based upon share-cropping and devised for Negroes had been extended to include white tenants." Hence, according to Work, "the legal attitudes toward tenancy are on the basis of race." [73]

Marjorie Mendenhall, on the other hand, finds inadequate the theory that share-tenancy grew out of the freeing of the slaves.[74] Using the process of agricultural decline in South Carolina after the eighteen-twenties to illustrate the general pattern that gave rise to tenancy in the South, Mendenhall finds that tenancy of a share-cropping type had appeared among white people long before the Civil War and that it was a result of an extractive, exploitative type of agriculture. It appeared first in regions other than those of the great plantations and followed "in the wake of soil erosion and exhaustion and the emigration of a large portion of the population." In a period of falling prices these changes greatly intensified the competitive situation. Some men of good hard sense adopted progressive farming measures and profited accordingly. They became great planters.[75] Outside the areas where their plantations dominated, however—"in the areas of less advanced planting and of subsistence farming"—planters and farmers in large numbers were reduced to lower social levels. In these areas, also, at least two decades before the Civil War, the white squatter and the white tenant appeared. The squatter and the tenant inhabited the interstitial areas between the plantations or the poorer land on the fringes of the plantations. In a situation where status for white men depended upon some degree of landownership they were landless. But in the social scale tenants were regarded as a grade above squatters who, according to Mendenhall, were the "poor whites" proper, that is, whites "who lived to a large extent by hunting and fishing and who were hardly a part of the agricultural population."

According to this account, therefore, share-tenancy in the South had an origin even more ignoble and degraded than most of us had supposed. It did not originate in an upward change of status for Negroes after the war; it originated in a downward change of status for whites long before the war. Not only was it bad enough in itself, but at the time of its development it was symptomatic of an ineffective and decadent system of agriculture and of society. And it was a system which spread rapidly throughout the South when the sanction of law was withdrawn from slavery.

It follows from Mendenhall's account of the historical origin of share-tenancy that her conclusion as to the nature of its spread after the Civil War would be just the reverse of Work's conclusion. It was a system not originally devised for Negroes and later extended to include whites but a system originating among whites and later extended to include Negroes.

Given the conditions that came after the Civil War, with Negro labor deprived of direction or unreceptive to it, and reduced in efficiency by something like a third, with capital reduced approximately to a tenth of its pre-war proportions, with declining cotton prices but an apparently inexhaustible demand, with a new emigration of planters (this time from occupation to occupation), and with an increase in fertilizers which shortened the growing season and gave a spurt of productiveness to worn-out lands—it was almost inevitable that the tenant system should spread among whites and appear among the Negro freedmen as well.[76]

Whether Negroes were the original share-tenants or not, the process whereby their condition of slavery was transformed into that of tenancy of this type is interesting and enlightening. We have some knowledge of this process. It began, of course, with a habit of mind accustomed to subordination and discipline. Under the conditions of his slavery, freedom to the slave would be, probably, what freedom finally is to everyone, the freedom move.[77] From contemporary records it is abundantly clear that to wander freely from one plantation to another, and from one town and city to another, came to be regarded by the freedman as the supreme test of his freedom.[78] If he did not invent, he at least popularized the excursion.[79]

One effect of freedom on the relations between whites and Negroes is well stated by Park:

When the Negro moved off the plantation upon which he was reared he severed the personal relations which bound him to his master's people. It was just at this point that the two races began to lose touch with each other. From this time on the relations of the black man and the white, which in slavery had been direct and personal, became every year, as the old associations were broken, more and more indirect and secondary. There lingers still the disposition on the part of the white man to treat every Negro familiarly, and the disposition on the part of every Negro to treat every white man respectfully. But these are habits which are gradually disappearing. The breaking down of the instincts and habits of servitude, and the acquisition, by the masses of the Negro people, of the instincts and habits of freedom have proceeded slowly but steadily.[80]

The share-tenant, Negro or white, even today is accustomed to move frequently from one plantation to another. In fact, the high annual turnover in the plantation's labor force is one of the most characteristic features of tenancy in the South.[81] It probably is very near the truth to say that this characteristic of Southern share-tenancy is in part, at least, a survival of a conception of freedom as liberty to move. The act of moving from one plantation to another may be and frequently is for the tenant who has some real or fancied grievance against the owner of the plantation a way of registering his protest. Common in the idiom of the plantation South are such phrases as "hit the big road," "hit the grit," "light a shuck," or more briefly, "light out." Many are the versions of the story of the tenant whose possessions were so few that he had only to "call the dog, spit in the fire, and git" in order to join the tragic game of "fruit basket turn over" played by thousands in late December and early January of every year.

There seems to be a general conviction among planters in the South that migratory tendencies characterize Negroes more than whites. About forty years ago Alfred H. Stone, a Mississippi planter, undertook an "experiment" on his plantation which had for its purpose the creation of a stable Negro peasantry. It was not a philanthropic experiment but one intended to secure for the plantation a lower labor turnover by offering a selected number of families especially favorable terms. "The problem before us," said Stone, "was to place in the hands of these people the means of acquiring something for themselves, and then, in every instance of deficient individual initiative, by proper supervision make them acquire it." [82] Through five years of effort to make the tenants reach a condition approaching independence "these families in turn demonstrated the fact of their independence by severing relations with us almost as promptly as we put them on their feet." [83]

Stone probably expresses the attitude of most planters when he confessed his inability to understand why a tenant, especially a Negro tenant, will move when he is prospering and remain when he is not. Most of us are disposed to regard as innate that which actually is acquired culturally and to suppose that those whose behavior differs from our own must have some sort of an instinct we do not have. Thus Stone concludes that Negroes "are a restless people. . . . They have been wanderers since emancipation gave free play to native instinct." [84] However, similar behavior on the part of white tenants, and other evidence, make it far more plausible to assume that frequent movement is part of the culture pattern of share-tenancy, that it is in the folkways, and that for Negroes at least it is part of the tradition of freedom.

Another direct effect of Emancipation was the moving away from the individual to the family as the labor unit. The rise of the family as the labor unit within the structure of the plantation involved a fundamental reorganization of the institution.

The Negro family has never been a very strong social group, particularly before the Civil War.[85] Severed from the African family system to be reformed under the difficult conditions of slavery and the slave trade in America, the family group was usually a very loose organization of mother, father, and children. The father was no more the breadwinner than the mother, and neither could be forced to assume any more responsibility for the children than the planter who owned all of them.[86]

Although the slave family was not a very strong institution, the production of children was a highly important matter. The deliberate breeding of slaves has often been charged, but whether this was true or not, it is certain that when the foreign slave trade was closed there was a great increase in the demand for "home-grown" slave labor. From the standpoint of the planter, the second generation presented a special problem of control, and we have seen how very important were the children of laborers, especially children of mixed blood, in the evolution of slavery in Virginia. Slavery defined in advance the status of the offspring of laborers and put them directly under the control of the planter along with their parents.

It has always been the disposition of the Southern planter to treat all dependents, regardless of age, as children and to do certain things for them that they might just as well do for themselves under the assumption that they are more or less incapable of managing themselves. This is the attitude of paternalism. Especially was the slave doomed to a sort of perpetual childhood, a fact which was as true of slave parents as it was of their offspring. The slave parents were the tamed and domesticated members of the plantation. The rearing of slave children was not so much a matter of incorporating them into a family life with their parents as it was a matter of disciplining them for a life as working members of the plantation itself.[87]

Now if freedom meant freedom to move, it also meant liberty for the freedman to pattern his behavior, as far as circumstances would permit, upon the model of those whose behavior he had always regarded as most free, i.e., members of the planter class. To be free was to acquire the dignity and to imitate the conduct, so far as he could, of his former master. His master, if typical, had been the head of a family, and his wife did not labor in the fields. Evidence shows that the significance of this fact was not lost upon the freedman. For a while after Emancipation contemporary accounts record the scarcity of Negro domestic help and the unwillingness of Negro women to work in the kitchens and fields of their former masters. Although this standard of family life could not long be maintained, since economic pressure soon forced their return to work, the Negro family did move to a somewhat higher plane of integration and solidarity.

In this connection let us look at certain changes that took place on the plantation of David C. Barrow, a Middle Georgia planter. They were typical of changes that were taking place on plantations all over the South except, perhaps, in the cane sugar-growing areas. Barrow operated his plantation before, during, and after the Civil War. In an article published in 1881 his son presented two maps of the plantation, one for 1860, just before the Civil War, and the second for 1881, about fifteen years after the close of the war.[88] In 1860 the slaves lived behind the Big House in the quarters.[89] By 1881 they had scattered in family groups over the plantation. Each family group under the supervision of the planter cultivated a definite tract of land. In the South generally the decentralization of the plantation, that is, the breakup of the quarters and the appearance of solitary cabins, was noticed by travelers as early as 1870.[90] (See accompanying maps.)

In his article Barrow described the process whereby the change took place on his father's plantation. It was a gradual one, he said, beginning with the division of the labor force into two squads, each under the control of a foreman. This plan differed from the labor-gang principle employed during slavery only in the fact that a spirit of rivalry between the two squads was encouraged, and there was no overseer. For several years this produced good results until even the liberal control of the foreman grew irksome. Each man wanted to be his own "boss" and to farm for himself. As a result, the squads were divided into still smaller squads, each working for a part of the crop. But this way was not satisfactory either to the planter or to the laborers, and so the final step of dividing up the plantation into tracts—one for each family—was taken.

The first trouble in the way of dividing up the plantation into farms was to provide the new-made tenants with mules. Up to this time their contracts had been such that they plowed with mules belonging to Mr. Barrow, and very few had bought mules of their own. This trouble was met by selling them mules on credit, and though the experiment looked risky at the time, the mules were paid for in almost every case. After this, the location of the houses caused considerable inconvenience, and so it was determined to scatter them. When the hands all worked together, it was desirable to have all of the houses in some central location, but after the division into farms, some of them had to walk more than a mile to reach their work; then, too, they began to "want more elbow-room," and so, one by one, they moved their houses on to their farms.[91]

The rural Negro family had become a tenant family. If the Negro tenant farmer was not in the midst of his own acres, he was in the midst of something which helped to satisfy his conception of what a man's estate ought to be. He had his family about him and he very often had property in a mule. The possession of this humble animal meant that the family had begun to acquire property and with property some greater measure of family self-respect and solidarity. In the course of time many share-tenants even acquired some equity in the plantation tract which they cultivated. When and where this event has happened, the Southern plantation has been dissolved into a number of independently owned and operated small farms. But this final step has thus far been the exception and not the rule except in a few localities.

At any rate, the plantation which the visitor in the South sees today, is generally an estate, a group of little farms, cultivated on shares. Dilapidated cabins are sprinkled over the estate, one to each tract or farm, all seeming to reach toward the Big House for protection and yet demanding independence. The austerely

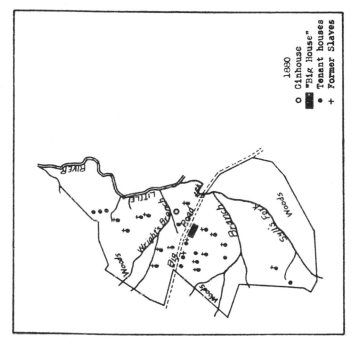

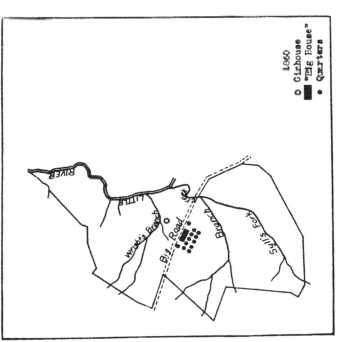

The geography of a plantation under slavery and freedom

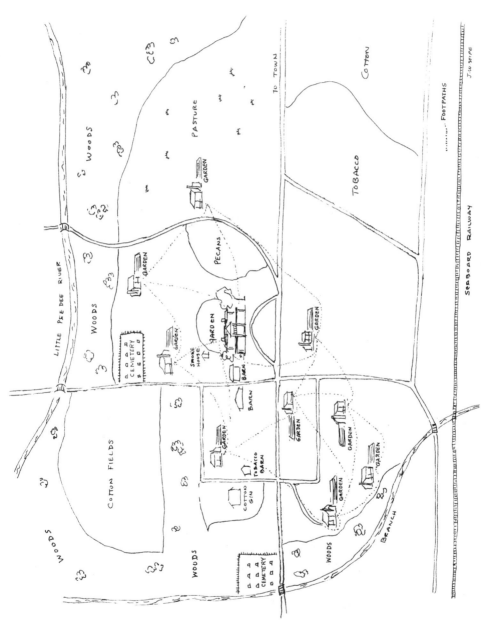

The geography of a recent Southern plantation

dignified but somewhat bowed-down Big House arises out of this society of tenant farms and centers it. This general and typical spacial pattern of the present-day Southern plantation, a spacial pattern quite different from that of slavery, represents at the same time the pattern of economic, political, and social relations involved in the share-tenant system.

The change from the individual to the family as the labor unit did not eliminate or even, in all probability, reduce woman and child labor—Southern tenant families live too close to the margin of subsistence for that—but it did shift the nature of the control over such labor, especially child labor. Child labor, enforced by parents rather than directly by the planter, helps to solve the problem of cheap labor supply and control. The unusually large amount of rural child labor in the South,[92] as compared with other sections of the United States, is bound up not only with the particular cultivation requirements of such staples as cotton and tobacco, but probably even more with the plantation method of producing those staples. Rural child labor in the South since the Civil War has been essentially a part of the system of share-tenancy. It is probable that under share-tenancy there is relatively more child labor than there was under slavery.

The understanding of child labor and share-tenancy generally, however, requires an understanding of the mechanism of control involved in the system. In slavery this mechanism rested, as we have seen, upon a personal and domestic relation between master and slave reinforced by legal sanctions which recognized the slave as the property of the master. The master had the right of corporal punishment, and the state assisted by policing plantation areas in the planter's interests. When the legal supports of slavery were withdrawn, the feudal and personal working relationships for the most part remained. This explains why Booker Washington said that the Negro "is more accustomed to work for persons than for wages."[93]

After Emancipation the economy of the situation was such that there was land to be tilled but no money, or very little money, to pay out in wages to laborers. Compensation for work had to be wholly or partly in produce and services. In addition, experiments with cash wages proved very unsatisfactory, from the point of view of the planter, because of the risks involved. Under a wage system the freedmen had no stake in the crop, and wages for the work of a few weeks or even days enabled them to live for a while without work. It was impossible for the planter to operate a plantation on such a basis especially when the season for making a crop was a long one and cash returns came in only once during the year. Hence it was necessary to employ a system in which laborers shared in the risks of the undertaking, which would hold them to steady labor, and in which the payment of wages in the form of a share of the crop was deferred until the crop was marketed or at least harvested.

Feudal principles of land tenure and individual relations seem always to resist the impersonal attitudes involved in a money economy. The improvidence of an agricultural working class which has never learned the value of money is often the basis of various devices, legal and extralegal, to get and hold labor. It is no accident that the period following Emancipation witnessed the rise of innumerable country stores all over the old plantation South [94] and of commissaries on individual plantations. The commissary and the store profited by charging excessive prices and usurious rates of interest. It cannot be denied that peonage, or forced servitude for debt,[95] has often been employed by planters as a means of holding tenants on their plantations from year to year. But share-tenancy is primarily tenancy for the duration of the crop. By postponing full settlement until the crop has been marketed or at least gathered, share-tenancy gives the planter control over tenants during the year, but a period of release comes toward the close of the year when they generally are free to renew arrangements with the planter or make other arrangements with another planter. The high annual turnover of tenants on the plantations argues against any very extensive amount of peonage in the South. White tenants would not accept peonage as easily as Negro tenants, and white tenancy has been increasing.

Although peonage has been present in the South since the Civil War, it is not now and never has been the primary basis of the planter's authority and control. Many factors operate to lodge power over tenants in the hands of the planter, but the essential mechanism of control is to be found in his relation to the nutrition process.[96] Food and other supplies are made available to the tenant directly or indirectly through the medium of the planter. The least important use of the commissary is to get the tenant in debt. Its chief function is to furnish food during the crop production period. For this "furnishing," as the practice is called in the South, the planter is paid out of the tenant's share of the crop when it has been harvested and marketed. Thus the planter has his hands on the throttle of the food supply, and it is in his power to turn it on or off.[97] And he does not hesitate to turn it off if in his opinion the tenant or wage-hand is not performing work expected of him even if the laborer's credit has not been overreached. This dependence upon the planter for food, although it has been present in all forms of plantation control which the South has known, has moved around to a position of central importance in the system of share-tenancy. Here is a mechanism of control applicable to white tenants as well as to Negro tenants. Slavery involved a principle of control which came to be based upon race, a principle which operated to exclude white labor, but the different principle of control involved in share-tenancy has enabled the white man to return to the plantation as a common laborer.

Because the plantation tends to specialize in one or more crops, such as cotton and tobacco, the raising of food crops is more or less excluded. The members of the plantation are dependent upon food which has to be imported from the outside. Incidentally, this fact operates to the advantage of the planter so far as the exercise of control is concerned. Diversification and the growing of his own foodstuffs by the tenant might lessen the planter's control over his labor.[98]

In the business of running a plantation the feeding of tenants and the feeding of livestock may be figured together on the same level and on the same terms. Vance quotes the following from the report of a plantation manager in the Mississippi Delta area:

All planters within the district are greatly concerned as to how they will go through the winter, take care of their livestock and labor, until such time as furnishing is started again in February. Every planter that we know is very much concerned with feeding his stock and tenants at a minimum cost, not only throughout the winter but throughout the entire growing period of next year's crop. We know of one concern who has a schedule by which he [*sic*] believes he can take care of his livestock for 15¢ a day and his tenants for $4.50 per month per head. If any planter in the Delta is interested in securing this formula, we shall be glad to send it to him upon request.[99]

Prices charged for commissary food and rates of interest for credit may be and usually are extremely high, but even when the planter does not profit, he continues directly or indirectly to supply food and credit to his tenants. The requirements of tenants usually are such that he must supply them whether he wants to or not. But aside from business motives and aside from the economics of the situation, the food-distribution process in plantation society functions as a means of maintaining an equilibrium in the social and moral relationships between the planter and his tenants.

On the part of the planter there may be nothing more than a "concern," to repeat the word used in the quotation above, to care for his tenants as well as for the dumb farm animals that also serve him, but the concern is there, and, in the case of the tenants, it is commonly more than a mere concern. In spite of many exceptions it usually is a feeling of real responsibility. For although the planter may pursue a certain conventional ideal of refinement and maintain a certain attitude of aloofness from the manners and tastes of the laboring population of tenant farmers, he is, nevertheless, an integral part of the society of his own plantation. He cannot avoid the claims of those dependent upon him, and he ordinarily assumes that the government of his tenants is not only his privilege but also his duty. The primal law of reciprocity determines that a planter who enjoys certain rights of authority and property thereby incurs certain duties, and that a tenant who performs his work comes to possess certain rights.

The feudal relations and attitudes that still exist on Southern plantations seem to rest largely on the fact that food on the estate is not ordinarily regarded as a mere commodity to be bought and sold, but as something which in return for work performed the planter is bound to supply and the tenant has a right to expect.[100] In spite of the fact that the planter charges these advances against the crop, the tenant is disposed to regard them in the nature of compensation for work done during the week. A form of compensation more personal and special than money, such as food, is better suited to the maintenance of customary and feudal relationships.[101] Even money when it is given out, as at Christmas time, tends to fall within this pattern.[102]

The discussion of share-tenancy up to this point has centered upon the economic, political, and social factors that co-operated to build it up out of the ruins of slavery. And now it is this system which is about to "collapse." Other economic, political, and social factors now are co-operating to destroy it, or, at least, to alter it fundamentally.

The market relationship without has much to do with the nature and form of the planter's control within the institution of the plantation, and the market relationships of all the great agricultural staples of the South are undergoing profound change. The principal factors that enter into the determination of these relationships are all those discussed by the authors of *The Collapse of Cotton Tenancy*—the credit system, the concentration of land under corporate ownership, soil exhaustion, competition of other fabrics, such as rayon, loss of world markets, and the mechanization of production.

Changes in these factors involved in the market relationships of the South's great agricultural staples are changing the competitive position of the regions of the South in the world economy. Great geographical shifts in the agriculture of the world are impending, if not actually taking place. Where they are taking place they are attended by severe stresses and strains. Every area engaged in producing the various forms of commercial agriculture in the United States is affected, but because plantation agriculture by reason of its very nature involves an especially large amount of human labor the changes in the South are being felt with unusual severity. The various efforts to control production and the increasing use of farm machinery along with other factors have brought the South in line with the rest of the United States as an area of closed resources. Probably for the first time in its history the South has the problem of the displaced farm laborer. There are now more farm laborers than there is farm work, and the situation seems to be getting worse.

Share-tenancy, like slavery before it, developed in response to a situation of open resources and has been maintained because it has continued to be a working adjustment to such a situation. If the South continues to have an army of surplus agricultural workers, the plantation system, if it survives, may abandon share-tenancy for some other form of labor control. It is not at all unthinkable, however, that if share-tenancy goes, the plantation system will go with it, since it is not merely share-tenancy which is threatened by present conditions but the power of the planter to exercise authority and control over any system of labor; for the plantation, as was pointed out earlier, is not merely an economic institution, nor merely an agricultural organization to grow cotton, tobacco, or sugar cane. It also is a political institution, that is to say, an institution based upon the authority principle. Its history is one of changing forms of control, but whatever the form of control, so long as the planter maintains his authority, the plantation is maintained. The plantation's career is ended not only by losing its market but also by losing its ability to govern.

Regardless of the form it takes, control is effective so long as the economic interdependence of the members of the plantation is "paralleled by a system or network of personal contacts, and the economic situation is handled through ideas and sentiments common to all the members." [103] Control begins to break down when economic interdependence is not accompanied by a co-ordination of personal attitudes. Unrest and dissatisfaction arise with the appearance of alternatives, with division of laborers, and with opportunities for, and experiences with, a different and contrasting way of life.

This may be illustrated by reference to a study made of the Eastern Piedmont region of Georgia by Professor R. P. Brooks and published in 1911. For about fifteen years before the study was published, some very important changes had been taking place in the counties of this black belt, changes involving a loss in the Negro population and an increase in the white population as a result of the immigration of a large number of mountain families. Brooks included in his article the following very revealing letter from a white citizen of Oglethorpe County:

The differences between the races here in Oglethorpe are growing more intense and troublesome. A few years ago in Oglethorpe the negro was the laborer and the white men were "bosses," generally, and workers, incidentally. That has all changed now, and the two races are coming into close competition as renters and day laborers. The negro has almost gone out of certain sections of our county, whites have filled in and are doing the work. . . . In the last few years some of our largest farms have been almost depopulated by the negroes' scattering to cities; and the counties above us, having increased in whites until they began to be crowded, and lands in those counties having gone up, these people, hearing of cheap lands in Oglethorpe, came down in great numbers and began to hire to our people. Those that were able began to buy land, so that land which was ten dollars per acre is now twenty-five and thirty dollars. Some of these people are very satisfactory and make good citizens. Others from the mountains, never having worked very much, do not want to be confined very closely and do not exactly fit in the cotton fields, which demand much work. I am still holding many negro families, but at some loss last year and this, by reason of the fact that they are getting out of my control and influence. They do nothing but make a crop, and I have to furnish all their supplies and costly mules, which they abuse in spite of all my caution. The day of cheap labor is over, and even if it could be had it is unreliable and unmanageable. It seems that the larger farmers of Oglethorpe will be compelled in self-defense to sell their lands, because the lawful per cent on the price the lands will bring will be far more profitable than what the farmer can get from renters and croppers.[104]

Note in this quotation how several things seem to go together and to react upon each other to effect social change—population changes, loss of a common ideology, loss of control, and the reduction in the size of land and operating units.

The changes that are taking place in agricultural labor relations in the present South have an interesting historical parallel in the changes that took place during the Reconstruction period. Both then and now the Federal government intervened in the local economy—in different ways, to be sure, but with similar consequences. During Reconstruction, says Tabeau, the planter all too commonly "no longer felt morally obliged to care for his laborers. Many a planter, going to live in town, lost intimate contact with his plantation and workers.[105] The physical well-being of the Negroes was no longer one of his chief concerns."[106] Most planters, however, probably felt a moral obligation to care for the dependents among their former slaves and deeply resented an order of the Freedmen's Bureau requiring individual planters in those states where the state itself made no provision for negro dependents to provide support.

. . . the order of the Bureau implied that they must provide for them whether they liked or not, and this stirred many planters to indignation. *The Southern Cultivator,* in July, 1865, commenting upon the order, stated that "The Law which freed the negro, at the same time freed the master. At the same moment, and for both parties, all obligations springing out of the relations of master and slave, except those of kindness, ceased mutually to exist. If any officer can make the master support the old and infirm slave, he can also make the slave continue under and support the old and infirm master." This attitude was based upon the fact that all parts of the plantation economy were necessary to sustain it. The withdrawal of the effective workers left no means for the support of the dependent ones.[107]

Like the activities of the Freedmen's Bureau and other agencies of the Federal government during the period of Reconstruction, the administration of relief and crop production control by Federal agencies during the last few years has greatly disturbed the principle of reciprocity implicit in the system of share-tenancy. Planters have had mixed feelings concerning these government activities of the past few years. On the one hand, they represent a threat to their control.[108] The planter fears, and from his point of view, quite rightly, that they are "spoiling" his tenants.[109] On the other hand, the activities of the Federal government may be welcomed as an opportunity to be relieved of obligations. When tenants can fall back on government relief, the way is open for planters who are in financial difficulties to evict and to dispossess without being too much troubled by the old feeling of responsibility.

As the cost of producing the old plantation staples mounts, the planter steadily loses his economic function and, also, tends either to lose control over his tenants or to exert what control he has to exploit them ruthlessly. At the same time there is evidence that many tenants are learning to keep themselves permanently indebted to the planter and thereby adding to the security of their tenure.[110] Indebtedness now, in many cases, might work to the advantage of the tenant.

With the number of jobs in agriculture shrinking and many tenants being turned into migratory workers and wage hands, there has been a disruption of the equilibrium of feudal reciprocity. The partial disintegration of the system of ideas and sentiments common to all has tended to raise questions concerning an economic system which makes some men's opportunity to work dependent upon what appears to resentful tenants to be the arbitrary will of other men. The feeling of grievance against the planter class which is slowly arising and finding expression in the tenant class is based upon the feeling that planters are evading the obligations of reciprocal service. The frequent charge, often true no doubt, that tenants are dispossessed or turned into day laborers by planters in order to avoid sharing government crop control benefit checks is used to give support to this feeling. Whether this growing belief is soundly based or not is another question; its existence is the important fact for the future.

VIII. The Labor Problem and the Plantation Institution

The South is that part of the United States where the planter has most powerfully impressed himself upon the form of society. The planter has faced many problems, but a review of his history from the days of original settlement down to the present impresses one with the fact that his chief problem always has been that of securing and controlling labor, year around labor for work in a rural and agricultural situation. The history of the South has very largely turned on the efforts that have been made to solve this problem.

A fuller appreciation of the significance of this fact may be gained by contrasting the planter with the squatter and the homesteader of the Middle West. Their frontier activities resembled each other in many respects. In the American West it was originally the policy of the Federal government to sell the land rather than grant it. But the settler who had won his land from the forest and the Indian regarded it as his "possession" and rejected the claims of one who had merely purchased from the government. In the face of this policy "not land itself, but the right to settle it became the sacred thing, an inalienable right to be defended even against the government." [111]

In the pioneering days of the Middle West every settler came to possess some land, legally or illegally, but relatively few possessed or needed more than was necessary for a small farm. Because there was plenty of land, labor could be employed only by the offer of high wages, but additional labor, outside that supplied by the homesteader and his family, was not ordinarily required. At that time the Middle West had little to contribute to world commerce, and the homesteader, unlike the planter, was not included in the society based upon the world market. When finally the wheat fields of the region were opened, the labor problem was solved by the invention of the harvester by Cyrus McCormick.

As compared with the squatter and the homesteader, the planter operated in a situation where the land was immediately utilized to produce a crop for sale. He occupied a more strategic position with reference to the market. In such a situation the mere right to settle the land was not enough. Labor, far more than land, was, in the absence of machine methods, the great need. The squatter occupied the land, and made his claim to a right to settle upon it a primary issue in the history of the Middle West. The planter asserted a right to press into his service in some form the labor of individuals outside the membership of his own family. The outcome was that he established himself as the master of a body politic independent of, and even contrary to, orthodox methods of conferring authority upon individuals.

What is the relation between what has always been the South's most difficult problem, the problem of agricultural labor, and what has always been the South's most distinctive and basic institution, the plantation? An answer to this question is suggested by something Dr. Everett C. Hughes, a student of institutions generally, has written concerning the nature of an institution. "Institutions," he says, "are just those social forms which grow up where men collectively face problems which are never completely settled" [112]—or perhaps not settled until the social situation in which the problem and the institution developed has given place to some other sort of situation. At any rate, institutions develop in connection with problems which are inherited as "perennially unfinished business" by several generations of men.

The suggestion that the Southern plantation arose to deal with a labor problem which was capable of no complete and satisfactory solution, but which had to be faced, is in line with the facts of Southern history. In the situation the labor problem was responsible for the plantation; the plantation was not responsible for the labor problem. Or, to put the matter in another way, the Southern plantation represents the institutionalization of the South's problem of agricultural labor.

Regardless of its evil reputation on the one hand and its romantic tradition on the other, the plantation has been a stabilizing influence in the relations between the races and the classes in the South. The important fact for this part of the nation, indeed for the nation itself, is that the situation which gave it birth and nourished it for several hundred years is passing away. The agricultural labor problem of the South is entering a new and radically different phase, and because of the historical connection between that problem and the institution of the plantation it is reasonable to expect profound changes in the plantation itself. Under the circumstances the South is forced to consider its future, and any consideration of the future raises the question of what is to take the place of the plantation system. It is well to inventory and to assess the region's resources, material and moral, but a plan to guide and to control the life that may prevail in the future of this section will have to be formulated in the light of the forces that have shaped its institutions in the past and in accordance with the changes that now are going on.

• 14 •

Purpose and Tradition in Southern
Rural Society: A Point of View
for Research

The rural peoples of the United States and of the world have in common the negative fact that they do not live in cities, but there the similarity between them ends. In a country as diverse as our country is, it is difficult to account for our assumption of rural homogeneity. Perhaps it developed as a consequence of our preoccupation with the rural-urban contrast, a preoccupation which has robbed rural sociology of much of the human interest which rightfully belongs to the study of so varied and colorful a subject matter. It was the rise of the city that gave point and content to the concept "rural" as a contrast conception and perhaps induced the illusion of rural homogeneity. We have explored this contrast to our profit but the further progress of rural sociology would seem to call for more comparative study of rural societies themselves.

Most rural societies rest upon an agricultural economy of some sort. Yet a common dependence upon agriculture, and even upon the same crops, leaves rural life far from standardized. The same plant crops go through practically the same processes of maturation wherever they are grown, but the social traditions which surround the growing may and do vary widely from society to society. On the other hand, similar traditions may characterize an agricultural society and an industrial society or a mining society.[1] But whatever the existing traditional patterns are they plead for themselves and resist change.[2] They must be isolated and brought under some measure of control, however, if the

SOURCE *Social Forces*, March 1947, pp. 270–80.

social and economic problems which are rooted in them are to be brought under control. It is not enough to relegate the observation of traditional patterns to a footnote as something merely quaint and interesting while we discourse on the agricultural problems of how to grow more and better cotton and tobacco and cows. Not only must we become more sensitively aware of the presence of cultural and traditional factors operating in social situations but we must consider and constantly reconsider better methods for screening out these factors and subjecting them to analysis. We must know what they are, how they originated, and how they developed before we can map out very effective programs for their control and change. To this end it seems important that rural sociologists apply themselves more emphatically than they have heretofore to the historical analysis and comparative study of rural societies.

These reflections are occasioned by the recent reading of a symposium volume edited by Ralph Wood and entitled *The Pennsylvania Germans.*[3] To one reared in the plantation South the contrasts pointed up by the various chapters are very enlightening. Kollmorgen's chapter on "The Pennsylvania German Farmer" is especially interesting to a Southerner. Indirectly it teaches almost as much about the plantation South as it does directly about the rural society of the Germans in Lancaster County, Pennsylvania.

The Germans who settled in Pennsylvania before the Revolution were members of a homogeneous cultural group. They were isolated from their neighbors by the barrier of language but religious affiliation was and remains the best index of separateness. Traditional Pennsylvania German agriculture was based upon the family farm intensively cultivated and highly diversified. In this system of society, livelihood was the principal norm of effort and planning; profits had only a secondary standing. The Pennsylvania German farmer "looked upon his calling as a preferred way of life and not primarily as a commercial occupation."[4] He operated his farm and his family affairs on a cash basis; it was said of him that he was "afraid of debt." All the members of his family, even his wife and daughters, had field work and farm chores to perform. Occasionally he might use the son or daughter of another German farmer when additional help was needed but this was not regarded as a violation of the saying, "The Germans do their own work." He enforced a strict family discipline but he generally succeeded in keeping his sons on the farm. He was concerned to secure enough land to provide them with farms and to conserve the land for their future use. He objected to farming practices that enriched the father but impoverished the sons.

The Pennsylvania German farmer could not conceive of a farm without numerous cattle but his attitude toward cattle was very different from that of the commercial rancher in the West or of the indifferent planter in the South. His cattle were part of an agricultural program which also included the growing of clover and the rotation of crops. For extra-family labor the farmer relied upon his horses. So far as energy was concerned, what slave manpower was to the ante-bellum southern plantation, horsepower was to the Pennsylvania German farm. The Pennsylvania German farmer was also quick to adopt labor-saving machinery.

Now horses and machines have to be cared for but they do not require government. The behavior of animals and machinery is, in general, expressed in a pattern which is predictable. Moreover, animals and machines do not sulk or talk back. They do not go on strike or riot. The human problems of the Pennsylvania German farmer were those of the head of a family. They were not ordinarily those of an employer of labor or of a lord of a manor. This little fact, insignificant or obvious as it may seem, is extremely important when it comes to understanding traditional plantation agriculture and how it differs from the agriculture of such a society as that of the Pennsylvania Germans. The planter might like to pursue a policy which would take account of the worker as simply a work animal or a machine but no matter how lowly the status of the worker as a slave or a sharecropper he does not cease to conceive of himself as a person and to act as a person. If the worker's wishes and interests are to be subordinated to the purposes of the institution of which he is a part he must be governed after a pattern not ordinarily applied to the members of a family.

Of course, the plantation is an economic institution. It tends to specialize in the production of a staple like cotton, tobacco, or sugar cane in the South, or coffee, rubber, or tea in other parts of the world. It produces to sell and not to consume, and the market for its staple is generally a world-market. But the economic factors in the definition of the plantation are only half the factors; equally important are the political factors of authority and control. In fact, these latter are the factors that best serve to distinguish the plantation from other types of rural land institutions. It is the presence of an authoritarian tradition which constitutes the plantation into something more than just a large farm. The history of the plantation is not just a history of the production of cotton, tobacco, sugar or rubber. It is even more a history of the changing forms of control over extra-family labor in the production of these staples, a fact which is just as significant in the present unrest and revolt in the Middle East of Asia as it was during the period of our own slavery controversy.

Like the state, the plantation is based upon the authority principle and within it the planter possesses power, not only over the laborer's job, but also over his home, his recreation, and his daily relations with others. There are, or have been, plantations with constitutions, laws, courts, jails, policemen, and even monetary systems of their own. At one time in the history of the South the planter possessed the power of life and death over the members of his plantation. Like the lords of European manors he possessed and exercised immunities from the laws of the state to which lesser men were strictly subordinated.[5]

The authority of the planter over his plantation is exercised, like the authority of the sovereign of the state is exercised, to preserve order and protect the peace. Disorder is against the interest of the planter just as it is against the interest of the sovereign of the state. But to limit our conception of the planter's authority to this rather negative and passive function would be totally inadequate. The planter is no mere lord of a *grundherr-schaft*. His authority is no mere restraining authority. Rather is it a positive and a daily inducement to action permeating all aspects of the plantation's life. It may help a little to describe plantation agriculture as military agriculture. The planter is not just the chief laborer in the field. He is no mere pace setter for the labor of others. He plans an agricultural campaign which his lieutenants and his workers carry out. He rides around on horseback or in his automobile inspecting and seeing that his orders are executed. Fanny Kemble and many others since her day have noted the planter's "habitual tone of command."

Of course the planter must know how to grow cotton or tobacco or sugar cane. He must know how to select his seed, when to plant, how to cultivate, when to apply fertilizer, when and how to harvest. But the requisite skills of the planter go beyond those of farmers generally. Not only good judgment but authority is exercised in the selection of seed and of planting, cultivating, fertilizing, and harvesting. Authority is woven into the fabric of the entire plantation pattern. The planter is disposed to look upon other men, not as ends, but as means to his own purposes. A planter, speaking of another planter, said to me, "Do you know how that man made his money? He made it with broken-down mules and nigger children." "A good overseer to manage mules and niggers," was the way ante-bellum planters sometimes advertised, and in the present South it is sometimes said in admiration of a certain type of white man, "He sure knows how to work niggers."

Just as insuperable difficulties are sometimes precipitated by floods or drought so may insuperable difficulties be occasioned by alterations in the pattern of authority relationships. After the Civil War many planters gave up and moved to town because, as they said, it was impossible to work "free niggers." Today it is much the same. Planters are experiencing serious production and marketing difficulties but their most difficult problems are connected with the fact that the customary controls over labor are breaking down. They know how to produce more cotton and tobacco and sugar cane per acre than ever before but the old common sense knowledge of race and class upon which they based their control over Negro and poor white sharecroppers is failing. In the face of these new and perplexing problems of labor relationships planters feel confused and frustrated. Their careers as planters are ended not only when they lose their land resources or the market for their staples but also when they lose their ability to govern.

Paralleling the disposition of the southern planter to look upon men of another race and class as means to his own purposes is his disposition to look upon the land as a resource to be cashed in. In 1937, Arthur Raper published a paper on "Gullies and What They Mean." [6] Of the nation's 150,000,000 acres of eroded land more than three-fifths are in the South. The gullied lands of this region of the United States, Dr. Raper pointed out, are the consequence of clean-culture cash crops, the unbalance between urban and rural economy, the exploitation of the Negro and the poor whites, and the plantation system. "If the traditional policy of southern agriculture is continued," Raper concluded, "the soil will be further depleted, the gullies will grow longer and deeper and wider, the Old South will continue to wash away." [7]

Gullies and eroded lands "are physical facts with social backgrounds and consequences." [8] Land killing is not only a fact but a tradition. Like the pattern of authority it is part of the plantation tradition in the South. What are these "social backgrounds and consequences"? What is the source of this tradition? There are several answers in the literature but it will be sufficient to examine two of them. One point of view which concludes that climate bears the chief responsibility was brought to explicit and formal statement by the sociologist Albert Galloway Keller many years ago.[9] The other finds the answer in the nature of the English cultural heritage and is represented in the writings of the historian, Richard Shryock.

In the well-known first chapter of his book on colonization Keller finds that all colonies may be classified into one of two fundamental types: the farm type and the plantation type. The determining factor in the development of each type of colony, according to Keller, is climate. Colonies in the temperate zone climates develop into farm colonies characterized by local diversified self-sufficiency, intensive cultivation, and the conservation of soil and other natural resources. The unit of social organization is the family and the population is fairly well divided between the two sexes. Its democratic and homogeneous society is based upon free labor.

In the tropical plantation colony, on the other hand, there is a marked tendency to specialize in an agricultural staple which ranks as a luxury good in the mother country. Cultivation is extensive and exploitative. Plantation agriculture is a "ruthless and wasteful one, not only of soil but of men. It is what the Germans graphically denominate Rabbau." [10] The colonists are predominately males, and the racial unit is the individual and not the family. Since "vital conditions do not permit the accomplishment of plantation labors at the hands of an unacclimatized race," laborers must be imported from other tropical regions if the natives cannot be coerced. These traits characterize plantation societies wherever they have been established and regardless of the nationality of the planters.

Keller apparently regards the plantation and all the traits that characterize plantation society as an inevitable and necessary consequence of the effort of Europeans to settle in and adjust to a tropical or semi-tropical situation. I have elsewhere [11] subjected this theory to critical examination and rejected it on four counts: it does not account for the existence of several historical plantation societies in areas of temperate climate; it does not account for small farm societies in areas of tropical climate; it does not account for the great and significant differences between plantation societies; and it does not account for the transition from plantation to farm, or *vice versa,* in particular areas while the climate remains stable.

American historians since Turner have tended to emphasize the creative experience of the frontier in American historical development. One student of southern history who has gone beyond description to explanation is Richard Shryock whose writings mark at least a partial return to the pre-Turner emphasis upon the cultural heritage from Old Europe. Shryock has been especially interested in the comparative study of British and German heritages in southern agriculture.[12] The differences are significant:

While the English settlers were girdling the trees or at best leaving the stumps in the fields, the Germans pulled everything out by the roots. While the English scratched their loose soils lightly, only to watch them erode with every heavy rain, the Germans ploughed their heavy lands deeply and held them intact. While the tidewater Virginians let their stock roam at will and actually claimed that to house cattle would ruin them, the Germans built their barns even before their houses were up—occasionally combining the two in the old Teutonic manner.

Instead of cultivating tobacco to the exclusion or serious limitation of other crops, the Germans rotated a varied series.[13]

After noting that other historians had described the English settlers in early Virginia as "obsessed by a desire for gold" and as possessing a "boundless faith in get-rich-quick possibilities" Shryock adds:

Here in Virginia were certainly a people lacking in agricultural tradition and quite naturally seeking the quickest way out of their difficulties. . . . One would not expect a people so motivated to "dig in" by intensive and varied cultivation—that way was long and hard. It required, moreover, certain knowledge and skills. One would not expect a people so handicapped to survive, unless they *could* find a money crop and that right soon. Tobacco alone assured immediate profits—or, at least, promised the most profit—and so tobacco must be grown regardless of the consequences. They could hardly foresee, in full, the destruction of soils, the mounting debts, the rural isolation, and the racial difficulties that were to follow.[14]

It was different with the Germans:

They were accustomed to and expected the hardest kind of labor. Coming to America to escape both religious and political persecution they were seeking a way of life rather than quick returns. Although their ideals were at times as materialistic as anything the Virginians desired, it was a different kind of materialism that was involved. While the latter set their eyes on profits, with the comfort and social position these would bring, the Germans dreamed rather of bigger and better barns. In a word, while the Virginians exhibited in America the ambitious economy of capitalism and exploitation, the Germans maintained the older semi-feudal economy of conservation.[15]

Again, "the Germans displayed an inveterate desire to do their own work and a corresponding disinclination to use negro slaves." [16] The English, on the other hand, were directly responsible for the southern race problem since the use of Negro slave labor was in line with their purposes.

The differences between the British settlers and the German settlers in America seem to have originated in differences in national heritage; ". . . It is difficult to find in the minor geographical differences" between the areas in the South where each group settled "an adequate explanation of the wide divergence of their agricultural and social systems." [17] "There is certainly considerable evidence," Shryock concludes, "that this divergence was due in part to the contrast in the motives, traditions, and skills of the two types of colonists." [18]

It appears that the same agricultural contrasts which Keller attributes to difference in the climates of the areas settled by Europeans, regardless of the national origins of the settlers, Shryock is inclined to attribute to difference in the national cultural heritage of the settlers. If the conclusion implicit in Shryock's studies is that the difference arises from the British character as formed in and by the total British culture in contrast to the German character as formed in and by the total German culture then it, too, like Keller's climatic theory, must be rejected. This conclusion would approach the assumption of the existence of something like a national instinct or temperament as the primary causal factor in the very different histories of many British and German agricultural settlements. I do not believe that such a conclusion would be entirely fair to Shryock but his writings on the subject, valuable as far as they go, might easily lead themselves to this interpretation because they do not go far enough. When the comparative method is employed investigation must continue until all the relevant cases are inspected, and not all the relevant cases have been inspected. The English in New England, for example, certainly built a rural society much closer to that of the Germans in Pennsylvania than to that of the English in Virginia. And the Germans in their former colonies in Togoland, East Africa (Tanganyika), Southwest Africa, and New Guinea behaved in a manner much nearer the English in Virginia than they did to the Germans in Pennsylvania and in various places in the South.[19]

It is not enough to break down the expansion of Europe into the national divisions that took part in the settlement of overseas areas. It is of course true that the competition between Portugal, Spain, France, Holland, England, and later Germany led to important differences between these states in settlement policy and consequence, but it also is true that national rivalry was not the only complicating factor. Within the various colonizing nations there existed the rivalry of different elements variously motivated. Commercial interests in competition with each other were also in opposition to organized philanthropic, educational, governmental, and religious forces which in their turn were often at cross purpose with each other. We cannot treat any migrating and colonial group *en bloc* from the standpoint of national heritage. The British planters in the New World had, in all probability, more in common with the French and Portuguese planters than they had with British missionaries and British Puritans.

When the comparative consideration of migration and settlement is carried far enough it appears that national culture as a whole is not sufficiently elementary to account for variations in colonial development. Of more tangible importance in the actual course of settlement were the differences in motives that mobilized factions within national groups into various action patterns, and in the colonizing activities of the nations of Europe these

different motives of special interest groups have worked themselves out into a variety of patterns. For what fundamentally
distinguishes human groups from each other is not so much the
stuff of which their yesterdays were made as the motives that
shape the present behavior of their members and the purposes
that fashion their goals. Motives are the social forces of history.

Migrating groups variously motivated present themselves in
a wide range of styles but in general they seem to fall into two
broad types. In the first place, there are those whose members,
possessing a sense of difference from others in political or religious faith, seek to withdraw and to segregate themselves from
the world. Such migrations as the Pilgrims who went to New
England, the Germans who went to Pennsylvania, and the Mor-
mons who went to Utah, represent cultural migrations. Members
of religious groups, trying to determine what the proper ends of
life are, look for secluded spots where they can get possession of
their own souls and direct their own lives within some scheme
or system of beliefs. They migrate and settle as a community and
they are concerned to maintain their institutions, including their
agricultural practices, intact. They tend to reproduce, so far as
circumstances allow, the folk agriculture of the lands from
whence they came.

In the second place, there are those whose members seem
possessed with a "will to power" and who move out into the
world with a sense of expansion and conquest. They conceive of
themselves as extending the frontiers of the world and of advancing their own status in it. They are adventurers, soldiers of fortune, traders, missionaries, planters, and administrators. The special purposes of these men may differ widely,[20] and with vastly
different consequences, but they all operate on the fringe of
change, "somewhere east of Suez," and they seek to adapt that
change to their own interests.

Those who came to the tidewater of colonial Virginia fell into
this latter class of settlers. They came from England, but the
motives which dominated the particular segment of the English
population which they represented did not originate in England.
The history of their purpose is far older than England. Just where
and when the motive of trade and production for trade originated need not concern us here. The story of its development,
however, would have to include the long episode of the trading

factory, an institution which went back to the Hanseatic League, the Italian *fondaco,* and beyond that to the Phoenician trading colony. The trading factory represents the original pattern of relations between overseas peoples of unequal economic development. Consequently the enterprising peoples have to maintain the trading terminus at each end. When the English, along with the Portuguese, the French, and the Dutch, adopted the pattern of the trading factory from the Italian and the Hanseatic merchants, they were, as were their predecessors, more concerned with trading facilities and the establishment of fortified harbors and stations than with command over the territory of the peoples with whom they traded. In the Orient, where the pattern of the trading factory took form, this simple commercial policy became a territorial policy when the factories of the English came into competition with those of other European nationals. But a territorial policy in the Orient did not require any wholesale migration of Englishmen to make it effective. The production of goods remained in the hands of natives. It was sufficient for the Europeans if the natives under their own rajas and sultans brought down the produce of spices, textiles, and tin to the factories in the seaports to be shipped to Europe and sold at extravagant prices.

It seems probable that the English establishment at Jamestown was founded on the model of the trading factory. Like the heads of English factories in India and elsewhere the head of the establishment at Jamestown was given the title of "president." The common store or magazine found in the factories of the Orient, the Levant, and the Baltic was reproduced at Jamestown. Again, those sent to early Jamestown by the Virginia Company were evidently not selected with reference to their fitness as farmers.[21] But the New World situation turned out to be an entirely different kind of situation from that in which the trading factory had functioned successfully. There were no towns or cities in which to locate. The native population was not familiar with the practice of trade and, save for a few minor commodities, did not produce the goods required and were not disposed to do so. Under the circumstances the trading factory evolved into the industrial plantation.

The plantation became an organization for the accommodation of men of diverse class and race to each other in the production of an agricultural staple. But it did much more than define the pattern of race relations. It embodied an agricultural tradition, a tradition of exploitative farming. Tradition, however, is not something disembodied. Its operation in the various segments of our population is revealed in the different ways in which the members of those segments define situations and act these definitions out. The detailed analysis of the present and historical South from this point of view would, I am sure, throw a great deal of light upon southern culture. What follows is a bare outline of the role of the planter class, the poor white class, and the Negro class when seen in relation to the plantation tradition.

The motive of the trader or factor, modified by experience, became the motive of the planter, and the agricultural traditions which accumulated in the South originated in this modification. The life-organization of the planter was formed by his purpose and his ambition. The land passed into his hands as part of the new industrial purpose and he undertook to produce for the market an agricultural commodity which was entirely outside the traditional and folk agriculture of England. In Virginia this was tobacco. He might just as readily have planted opium poppies had there been any profit in them. The Indian was no longer looked upon as a customer but as a potential laborer. But the Indian was as worthless as a laborer as he was as a customer or independent producer and it became obvious that Virginia and the South would have to be settled by a new population willing to work or capable of being forced to work. Accordingly, an industrial army of occupation was moved into the area consisting first of white indentured servants and later of Negro slaves. Thus there grew up around the activities of the planter on the southern frontier a kind of camp agriculture which came to be known as plantation agriculture.

The purpose of the planter required the subordination of land and labor alike to the production of the crop. Land was tamed, not domesticated. One English traveller observed that "every planter considers himself only a temporary occupant on the plantation on which he is settled. He therefore goes on from year to year 'racking it out', making it yield as much cotton and corn as he can without considering the future. He is always ready to sell out and travel further west." [22] Similarly, labor, white or Negro, was regarded mainly as instrumental to the end of staple crop production.

The purpose of the planter was incorporated into the structure of the plantation, but the purpose of the institution as a whole did not thereby become the purpose of all its members. By some the pattern of waste and the exploitation of natural resources were adopted and transmitted to later generations but with the incentive to profit in wealth and status from that exploitation left out. Here is where the southern poor whites and Negroes enter the story. Almost universal in the descriptive literature on the poor whites is the emphasis upon the "void of pointless leisure" in which their lives are lived. What happened to the strong purpose which motivated their ancestors to come to America?

The act of quitting a familiar life in England and Europe for a strange and perilous one in America in an age when travel and communication were slow and difficult must have been motivated by deeply-set purposes and a great determination to realize them. It would be difficult to overemphasize the strength of purpose on the part of men who voluntarily sailed from England to the wilderness of the New World frontier. It was so with those planted on these shores by the Virginia Company and who became the "ancient planters," and it was just as true of those who came later as indentured servants pledged to work five or seven years for a master in return for the cost of their passage. Some of these servants, possessed of some capital or with access to the capital of English investors, served out their time and became planters, but the opportunity to realize their intentions never came to most of them. In the competition for the status of planter relatively few were successful. The greater number failed and became the social ancestors of the present day "poor whites." Professor Abernethy suggests that the Scotch-Irish and German Protestants who flowed down the Valley of Virginia from Pennsylvania contributed mostly to the yeomanry of the South, whereas those who drifted west from the seaboard became the landless poor, the squatters and poor whites.[23]

Those whites who were unable to maintain purpose, and who therefore lost it, were at a competitive disadvantage with those whites who could and did maintain it. They were subsequently defined as a class by their Negro slave competitors. Both John Fiske [24] and T. J. Wertenbaker [25] noticed that the appearance of Negro laborers in Virginia also marked the appearance of a class of mean whites. They had lived and worked as servants alongside Negro servants and slaves on the estates of the planters, but gradually they had been edged off the plantations and subjected to a process of natural segregation as they drifted together, inter-married, and locked themselves off from the plantation world. There was even some cultural reversion toward the level of the Indians. The isolation in which they were confined was not only spatial but temporal; it has extended itself to successive genera-tions. In isolation other traditions were generated but the pattern of wasteful exploitation minus the motive of cumulative gain has persisted through the years more or less independently of the rest of the community.

The southern poor white is something more and at the same time something less than a white man who is poor. Just the way the words "po' white" are spoken by Negroes and by middle and even upper class whites in the South conveys a conception of him as belonging to a special category. He is to be rather sharply distinguished from the mountain white in the South in at least three ways: (1) he is in direct economic competition with Negroes; (2) he is not typically a landowner; and (3) he does not live in a folk society. Landless, for the most part, in a society where the ownership of land has been a badge of status and with only his labor to sell, he has exaggerated the color of his skin as a symbol of his connection with the dominant white class. Inse-cure in his status he has felt impelled to press his claim for racial superiority upon others.

Mountain whites are generally poor but, unlike the poor whites, they possess and maintain a tradition of inherent superi-ority of stock which goes beyond mere pride of color.[26] They picture themselves, and are pictured in stories and accounts con-cerning them, as capable of great cultural training and develop-ment. Once given a chance, their superior stock tells and they quickly go up in the world. This seems to be one of their cardinal beliefs. Poor whites, on the other hand, are inordinately proud of being white men, but have no outstanding pride of ancestry. They have lost consciousness of whatever fortune their ancestors may have had and are not greatly concerned to increase their stock of material to say nothing of spiritual goods. If this state-ment is not entirely true it at least expresses a widely held belief about them. As Broadus Mitchell has pointed out, very little has been said in depreciation of the mentality, the morals, or the ethics of Negroes that has not also been said about poor whites of the South by their own blood cousins.

The mountain white has lived in a folk society so organized

that there are always interesting things for its members to do. Their society has produced folk products and it possesses folk institutions. New experience comes as an incident of folk activity. The poor white, on the contrary, does not live in a robust society with his fellows, a society having its own stock of values and spiritual resources that satisfy. Periodically he has to go out looking for new experiences or "thrills." The mountain white identifies himself with his society and accepts its culture as a heritage of which he is proud. He derives strength as an individual from his consciousness of membership in it. Those around him are not only his neighbors but his kin. The lot of the poor white is different. His condition is expressed in the saying, "once a sharecropper always a sharecropper." In the plantation areas of the South the poor whites are rootless people with only weak kinship claims to soften their economic situation and without sufficient permanence of residence to build up neighborhood bonds. They move restlessly from farm to farm, from plantation to plantation, and from county to county.

Upper class whites of the South have been acccustomed to account for the laziness and inertia of the poor white as the marks of a biologically degenerate people. When they speculated about him in print they have sometimes made him the descendant of the scum of England, i.e., the indentured servants. Like the traits of Negroes, his traits have been regarded as the constitutional endowments of an entirely different kind of people. If post-Civil War Southerners centered their humor about the Negro "the great body of Southern antebellum humor centered about the poor white." [27] It was said of him that he was born lazy and had a relapse. He wouldn't drink coffee for breakfast because it was liable to keep him awake all morning.

Another popular explanation of the poor white substitutes poor health for bad biological inheritance. In 1902 Dr. C. W. Stiles announced the discovery of hookworm among the poorer masses of the South and suggested that the parasite probably accounted for the chronic fatigue which seemed especially to characterize the poor whites. Poor whites were not inherently lazy; their energy was being consumed by hookworms. The New York *Sun* headlined the discovery "Germ of Laziness Found?" after which hookworm became, to many Southerners, just a polite northern word for laziness. But it also became to Walter Hines Page, to the young men connected with the Rockefeller Sanitary Commission for the Eradication of Hookworm Disease, and to many others who took up the cause, the chief factor in the low state of civilization among the rural white masses of the South.

Stiles and his colleagues undertook to demonstrate that the "dirt-eating" and the chronic fatigue so widespread in the rural South were not themselves diseases, but symptoms of another disease, hookworm. The devoted efforts of these men and their successors to eliminate or at least reduce the incidence of hookworm in this region richly deserve all the praise and honor we have given them, but the probability remains that hookworm is itself symptomatic of an even more basic condition. This is, not inherent laziness, but a tradition of improvidence, moral degeneracy, lack of ambition, and indifference to profitable labor. It is a tradition traceable to social and economic factors in the poor white's connections with the rest of the community. What is missing is a sense of purpose or a clear-cut conception of the meaning of his existence. His state of aimlessness, of purposelessness, and of footlooseness expresses itself not merely in laziness and general inefficiency but also in demoralizing habits, crime, insanity, and disease.

It is not contended that the poor whites of the present South are necessarily the blood descendants of the original body of whites edged off the plantations into the sand hills and pine barrens. Individual poor whites have moved up and out of their class and the class has recruited some of its members from planter and yeoman whites who have moved down. Not much is known about the biological make-up of the original poor whites, and genealogies of contemporary poor whites would, in all probability, prove very little. But there is a poor white tradition and the overwhelming probability is that anyone brought up in it will remain a poor white regardless of the composition of the genes that made him. The poor whites are the social inheritors of that segment of the original colonial population of whites that lost purpose and momentum. They have come to a dead stop, and they cannot get started again without some aid from outside their own ranks. They cannot get started again without some filling of the social emptiness or void in which their individual members exist.

The story of the Negro is very different. As Booker T. Washington was fond of saying, he is the only one of our citizens whose ancestors came to these shores by special invitation. In contrast to the marked strength of purpose animating the original white settlers from Europe, the dominating will that brought the Negro here was not his own. We are accustomed to attribute the difference between the progress of whites and Negroes in America to differences in race and culture, but it is entirely reasonable to suppose that, had there been no original differences in race and culture, the sheer presence of purpose in one group and its absence in the other would in time have accounted for at least a part of the difference in progress made by whites as compared to the Negroes. Added to this original difference in purpose was one hundred and fifty years of slavery which effectively blocked the acquisition by Negroes of the American tradition of achievement and material progress.

It was inevitable that the habits of slavery and of subordination would continue to dispose Negroes after Emancipation to live and to shape their behavior by the pressure of contingencies alone. It was inevitable, too, and very human, that freedom should be defined in terms opposed to the forced labor of slavery. As Park says:

> The freeman was not able at once to enter into the spirit and tradition of a free competitive and industrial society. He had no conception, for example, of the secret terror that haunts the free laborer; the fear, namely, of losing his job and of being out of work. On the contrary, his first conception of freedom was that of a condition in which he would be permanently out of work. So far, therefore, from being possessed by that mania for owning things which is the characteristic, as the communists tell us, of a capitalistic society, his first impulse and aim were to get as deeply in debt as possible.[28]

In time, however, the greater measure of competition which freedom introduced into the life conditions of Negroes has forced more and more of them to seek work for which others, including whites, also were seeking. In 1904 William Garrott Brown called attention to the rise of white competition against the Negro. "The white man whom the Negro has to fear," he said, "is no longer the man who would force him to work. It is the man who would take his work away from him. The danger, the immediate menace, is from rivalry rather than oppression." [29] Now the almost revolutionary result of this competition is a profoundly changing attitude on the part of Negroes towards jobs and job opportunities. Negroes are more critically evaluating the jobs they have and are aspiring to jobs they have not had. The developing vocational consciousness among them means that many more Negroes than formerly are thinking less of jobs for the day only and more of careers. More and more Negroes are seeking to link up their lives with some continuous work promising honorable achievement. Numerous Negroes individually, and not just a few leaders of the race, are beginning to take stock of themselves against the future. Careers mean education and training. Hence the quickening interest on the part of Negroes, not only in the right to an education, but in the content of the educational process itself. The first of our non-English-speaking immigrants are the last to catch up with, and begin assimilating, the conception that America is something unfinished, and that all may contribute to its ultimate realization.

The contrast between poor whites and Negroes must not, of course, be exaggerated. The masses of southern Negroes, like the masses of southern whites, are impoverished both materially and spiritually. The great majority of Negroes face, in addition to problems purely racial, the same problems which confront the under-privileged white people of the South. But the general conclusion is, in my opinion, inescapable: the poor whites somewhere along the line suffered a failure of nerve and lost purpose; Negroes, on the contrary, came without purpose but are gaining it. The Negro is today mobilizing behind what is for him a great cause, the cause of interracial democracy. The poor white has no cause except the negative one of maintaining a precarious hold upon his position as a white man. Both Negroes and poor whites in the plantation areas of the South are caught in the same economic and social system so that the effort of one to rise invariably involves the other, but of the two the Negroes are in some respects the better off.

The improvement of seed, of livestock, and of farm machinery in the field of southern agriculture should and will continue but such improvements will not of themselves prevent what is left of the southern soil from washing away. They may, in fact, be used, as machine improvements have been used, to intensify the mining of the land and thus speed up the process of erosion. Legislative and administrative changes may be required but such changes alone will not solve our human problems. The standards of rural health in the South are scandalously low and must be raised but the total elimination of hookworm and malaria will not automatically restore incentive and ambition to the classes deficient in these qualities.

I have tried to interpret in terms of purpose and tradition some of the social problems of the South with its planter, poor white, and Negro components. My thesis is that the plantation has been important, not only in the establishment of the pattern of race relations, but also in the creation of an agricultural tradition which has taken a somewhat different course in the various segments of the southern population. It is a tradition which should be isolated and thoroughly analyzed. This is a task for anthropologists and sociologists. The task of transforming or modifying tradition is one for education and if education cannot do the job required in the South then perhaps nothing can. And education cannot do the job as our schools are at present organized and directed. Not much can be expected from the uninspired and routine type of education now being dispensed in the rural schools of the South. How can the formal educational process be used to alter the subtle yet powerful force of tradition as it is handed down informally in the family and in the community?

Education resides in the process of cultural transmission but where there is a poverty of purpose and the people aren't doing anything how can education be made meaningful and vital? There is some reason to believe that education by itself cannot be relied upon to effect fundamental changes in the masses of people except under conditions of collective feeling. It is no accident that the major transformations of history originated in mass movements. From what source can we get a mass movement capable of putting some fire into the bellies of the poorer whites and Negroes of the South? How can these people be moved to feel and believe that the South is a land with a future as well as a land with a past? How can such a movement be steered away from totalitarian controls and directed toward the fulfillment of the democratic ideal? Where can we get the educational statesmen capable of organizing our schools to make the fight of their lives against the tradition of exploitation on the one hand and the tradition of complacency on the other? How shall we fashion the lever and, once fashioned, where shall we rest it?

• 15 •

The South and the Second Emancipation

I

The South is a history in search of a country. In the middle of the nineteenth century various interests and values incubated in this history sought to structure themselves into a separate country, but the effort failed and left the South, as the 1949 edition of the *Encyclopaedia Britannica* tersely defined it, "a large area of the United States which presents certain distinctive characteristics." Within the frame of the United States the people of each region intuitively have defined the boundaries and characteristics of their own and of every other region. The South, then, is that part of the nation regarded as the South by non-Southerners and Southerners alike, and that popular assignment refers not merely to geographic location but to broad cultural distinctiveness as well. In the moral geography of the United States the South has been the most sensitive area. Today, in a shrinking world with nations in a position to look over into the backyards of each other and ever ready to pass judgment, this area, like South Africa, Germany, and others, has become one of the most morally sensitive areas of the world, an exasperated subject of prolonged criticism from the outside. The setting in which there is a public that appears to hiss the actors in the Southern scene is changing from the nation to that of the world, but white Southerners, like white South Africans, continue to deny the right of the rest of the world to reprimand and to pass judgment. Nevertheless, in the struggle to accommodate itself to changes and to judgments from without, the South has

SOURCE In Allan Sindler (ed.), *Change in the Contemporary South,* Duke University Press, 1963, pp. 93–118.

changed and will continue to change from within. In a special sense the South is a product of change and of reaction to change throughout its history. Its basic constitution has been determined by the way it has dealt with the problem of change in the past, and the changes it faces now and in the future may involve nothing less than a revolution in its fundamental institutional structure.

II

Perhaps the central problem of every society is that of preserving enough consistency to maintain a relatively stable organization on the one hand while coping with inevitable changes on the other. How much change can a society admit and yet remain the same society? This is the ancient and universal problem of preserving a balance between order and change, and it has occupied the thought of many generations of philosophers. The ideal solution, of course, is orderly change, and this is what modern constitutional government aims to achieve. But when the members of a society cannot agree on what the goals of change are, or even upon the desirability of change at all, and this usually is the case, the ideal of orderly change can only be approximated. Almost always and everywhere the social process is punctuated by disorderly episodes of one kind or another, but, orderly or disorderly, change is inevitable in all social life. It is, as John Dewey has somewhere put it, "the primary social fact as surely as motion is the primary physical fact."

Things lying inert and seemingly changeless tend to escape notice. Change induces attention, observation, concern, reflection, and study; it is at least one source of social awareness of diversity leading to conflict, particularly when individuals and groups change at different tempos. Hence something is learned about the nature of things and about ourselves in the course of efforts to effect, prevent, or minimize change. Often efforts to block change unwittingly help bring about subsequent changes more drastic than otherwise might have been the case. In this sense the true radicals may, in the perspective of the history of a society, be the conservatives.

Social change is, of course, not the same thing as the mere

passage of time. Nor is it just the accumulation of culture and of the artifacts of culture. It is something more than social circulation as in the elimination and replacement of group personnel, and it is something more than social succession as represented in the procession of the generations. In social change just what is it that changes? The central fact in social change appears to be alteration in the individual or group positions of the members of a society, that is, status change. An established social order is one in which there is an established status system; in the absence of such a system there is only a frontier.

Status is a broad term for the position of a person or group in a hierarchy of persons or groups. Like the struggle for existence, which operates in a biological and economic context, the struggle for higher status, which operates in a social and moral context, is, apparently, universal and eternal. "From this struggle," said Robert E. Park, "no philosophy of life has yet discovered a refuge."

It is important to distinguish status from the "condition" of an individual or group. "Condition" is more or less an environmental accident; the term describes the material and moral circumstances and standards under which individuals live, changes in which may occur without a corresponding change in social station. A status, on the other hand, is a position in a system of statuses, a position in a society. We speak of improving a condition but we speak of advancing a status. A status is organically bound up with every other status in the system. There could be no one to experience that "sickening sense of inferiority" if there were no others around to display the satisfactions and advantages of higher position. The items of a given condition become important for status when they are defined, not so much in terms of physical misery or comfort, but mainly in terms of personal or social degradation or prestige. This happens when events and an enlarging community bring about opportunities for sensitive inner comparisons and contrasts which in turn generate self and group consciousness. It happens when one becomes aware of what one's grievances or special privileges are in a world of those people whose estimate of one's self and of one's group seems important.

This is why the revision of the status system of a society will have repercussions throughout the entire social order. Any such revision *is* social change even though the causes of such change need not be social in their origins.

III

What, now, is the source of the popular commitment to race in social relations? If we abandon all the many good reasons that have been advanced and face the real reason, white Southerners and a great many white Americans generally would have to acknowledge that it stems from uncompromising status considerations, such as those having to do with interdining and intermarriage. It is important for the Best People of any society to know where to draw the line, and "racism," says Ruth Benedict, "is essentially a pretentious way of saying that 'I' belong to the Best People." Where the status of Best People entails some mark of obvious, permanent, and transmissible distincition, such as skin color, a distinction open to all born with the right complexion, it is possible to assert the claim of aristocratic status without benefit of education, wealth, family, or even good manners.

Southern society knows the discriminating force of education, family, fortune, office, religion, and other usual features of class in its status system, but cutting across all these features and distinguishing this society from most others is the long-time presence in it of an inherited status principle based upon race. The South, in a very special sense, is that part of the nation which is race-bound: race is the chief axis around which Southern life and thought has revolved for at least a hundred and fifty years. This region, as Jonathan Daniels put it, is two races, a racial moiety, with one race automatically assigned a superior status and the other just as automatically assigned an inferior one. This is true in spite of the fact, or perhaps because of it, that the two races have interdigitated, like the lacing of the fingers of the two hands, so that the lives of whites and of Negroes have played into the lives of each other. It is because the two groups have been so thoroughly intermixed in the same territory, because physical distance between them has been so insignificant a factor, that the ideology of race has been generated to effect a wide social distance. The believed-in differences between them pertain to little or nothing that is biologically or psychologically in one race that is not in the other, but rather to the social and historical situation in which both exist; only the intervention of the Other establishes the identity of individuals of different complexion as white or as Negro. Race functions as a contrast conception.

We have to understand the establishment of this kind of a status system in the South as a reaction to the problem of social change as this problem was presented in its early history. The changes presently going on amount to a veritable status revolution which is shaking the South to its very foundations, that is, in its social structure.

IV

At this point it may be useful to distinguish between change *in* race relations and change *and* race relations. A number of anthropologists and sociologists since W. H. R. Rivers have made us aware of the difference between those more formal and material aspects of a culture which change more or less easily and readily and those aspects which persist or offer considerable resistance to change. These institutional and persisting relationships constitute the social structure. In the social structure of most if not all societies, sex, age, and blood attributes and relationships get codified and legitimated. Insofar as such attributes and relationships are transmitted by educational institutions and sanctioned by religious institutions these, too, must be regarded as part of the structure. The more or less superficial changes which occur in the superstructure may have relatively little effect on the structural foundations of the society itself. All this is analogous to the different types of changes which physiologists observe in a developing organism. The point may be illustrated by the acculturation which, in the course of American history, fairly quickly erased the external signs of costume, mannerisms, and dialect that originally distinguished the members of one immigrant group from another, as well as from old-line Americans. But the resulting apparent homogeneity often obscured deeper differences of outlook and attitude which existed and probably continue to exist between them.

It is apparent that many changes have occurred in both our white and Negro populations, and in the relationships between them, during the past hundred years or more. But how deeply into the structure of Southern society do such changes go? Basic in the structure of a society are its institutions and its family and kinship relationships. Individuals in Southern society are born into a world of new artifacts and circumstances, but they continue to identify their membership in this society with a structure that they have been reared to believe is everlasting. They continue to regard themselves and to be regarded by others as Southerners. The institutional and kinship system of the South today may be described in almost precisely the same terms employed a century ago. Institutions then and now are divided along racial lines. Kinship as a network of communication and personal bonds divides itself now—as it did then—at the color line, notwithstanding an extensive amount of miscegenation which has occurred outside marriage. These elements of the social structure are regarded as of much more than temporary significance—factors of constancy and continuity are involved in them. One reading the journal of a Southern planter or matron of an earlier period often is impressed with the sense of certainty, the assurance, that the order of society in which they enjoyed high prestige would last forever. Today this sense of assurance is being deeply shaken, but it is likely that many, if not most, white Southerners feel that when the tumult of mass race demonstrations has passed, as similar threats have passed before, the basic tenets of their way of life will remain the same.

An integral part of the social structure of the South is and has been its status system, one predicated upon the complete acceptance of the idea of race. No idea has ever yet separated the strata of a society more completely, nor with a greater assumption of finality, than has that of race. In its most extreme expression the idea leads people who face each other across a status line to see the others as members of a different species. The idea contains the notion that race is something primary, something that goes back into a far past and will continue into a far future. How did the idea arise and establish itself in the structure of Southern society? The answer requires an examination of the connection between change *and* race relations.

V

The evidence indicates that blacks in Virginia and in the South were not originally identified as racially different from the European settlers, but as religiously different. They were "Moors" or at least non-Christians. However, this conception, inherited from the religious wars of Europe and used to justify the slave trade, broke down with the problem of maintaining Negroes in a state of slavery on the plantations. The religious rationalization implied emancipation upon conversion until colonial legislatures, following the example of the Maryland assembly in 1664, "altered the religious sanction for slavery and based its validity frankly upon race." [1] To be sure, the alteration had been building up in custom before it was formalized in the law. It was, nevertheless, a drastic alteration since it shifted social stratification from the English contractual and class arrangement to a biological heredity principle, a principle at once, in the case of the black man, highly visible, durable, predictable, and economically and socially meaningful. The asserted correspondence between color and slave status served to shunt the black man back into his racial place as he tried to imitate whites and climb higher in the social scale.

The racial principle was to take deepest root in what possibly was the most democratic part of the American frontier, the Southern frontier, an area productive of the leadership and doctrines of Jefferson and Jackson.[2] All along its course westward from North to South the American frontier developed practical working arrangements in which every man regarded himself and was regarded by others as being as good as any other man, that is, until the man of strange feature came along. The frontier had its own peculiar prejudices in that it demanded some kind of uniformity of outlook and appearance. Within such wide limits the stranger on the frontier easily fraternized with others and learned to compete and to co-operate with them. But the man of strange feature and color could not, in the nature of the case, conform to such requirements. The democratic code broke at the color line. Men who ardently believed in liberty became the masters of slaves.

In a feudal and military order assumptions of superiority and inferiority appear not to require elaborate ideological justifications. Concerning the virtual enslavement of native "kanaka" labor on the plantations of New Guinea by the Germans prior to World War I, Stephen W. Reed notes the absence among the Germans of assertions about high moral purpose on the one hand and justifications of exploitation on the other. Apparently the

Germans felt no need to rationalize the subordination of native labor in racial terms. In the South it became an article of faith to be proclaimed at every opportunity that the Negro was a racial inferior, but in German New Guinea such a profession about the natives would have sounded like an assent to the alphabet. Reed goes on to say that the white and democratic Australians who took over the plantations from the Germans in World War I, and who recruited and controlled labor in much the same manner, could not be indifferent to the contradictions in their own culture and behavior. They came to rationalize their relations with the natives in terms of race.[3]

A parallel with developments in the American South would seem to be obvious. The suggestion is strong that the Negro was established here as a separate race, not in spite of our democracy, but actually because of it. If democratic values for whites were to be retained it seemed necessary to introduce another component, that of race. If the white Southerner was to subordinate the Negro in slavery and at the same time maintain his democratic and Christian dogmas, it was necessary to deny the Negro the attributes of a human being. The idea of race thus permitted whites to affirm their belief in the freedom and equality of all men, even as they excluded Negroes from the scope of that belief, by persuading whites that Negroes were not really people. At the same time the idea of race induced in many Negroes an acceptance of his own and his race's inferiority. It is perhaps because Negroes in America have been excluded from the circle of conventional white Christian values and democratic rights that they have become among the most uncompromising supporters of these values and rights. They cannot demand these values and rights for themselves without demanding them for all. In a larger sense it appears to be true that the struggle of the lower classes generally to rise is the source of the theory of democracy. The men who are struggling to rise are the men who define and maintain it.

VI

It has been suggested that the intense democracy of the Southern frontier broke at the color line. We need now to examine some further aspects of the role of color and other physical markings in connection with social change and with the processes of acculturation which resulted in the making of Americans and the distinctions which they created among themselves. It seems reasonable to argue that it was the black man from Africa who became the original American. Certainly the tribal Indian who met the white settlers at the boat was not an American either in his own eyes or in the eyes of the newcomers. He was not even an Indian in his own view of himself. He was a tribesman bearing the name of a tribe, the only name for himself and for his fellows he knew. Only much later did he accept the white man's view of himself as an Indian, and this was when he identified with other tribesmen in a common opposition to the whites who were taking over the country. Much more time was to pass before he left the reservation, became detribalized, and came to regard himself as an American citizen. But for the most part he and his fellows continued to be regarded as native aliens.

The cultures of the white colonists from Europe, and especially England, underwent change as they adapted to a new environment and to a new social order, but the language they spoke, the religion they professed, the spirit of the laws and constitutions they adopted, the marriage, family, and kinship system they took for granted—all these features of their cultures they transplanted with little significant change from their European homelands. They infused a new spirit into their culture and institutions, to be sure, but the newness was largely a matter of degree.

The man almost totally transformed in the American environment, the man to whom the transplanted European culture and institutions were completely new, was the black man brought to these shores from Africa. Some authorities say he came almost culturally naked, but whether this is true or not it is certain that, as compared with those who came from Europe, the African cultural heritage was relatively small. In America he became a new man to a far greater extent than the white man.[4] He was a tribesman in Africa, but he did not remain for long a tribesman in America. Many if not most of the Negroes originally brought to the West Indies and to America were tribally designated and sold as such, but practically all tribal distinctions were lost in the second generation. As a slave on the plantations of the South he rapidly, even if imperfectly, took over a European language as a *lingua franca* not merely to understand the commands of his master, but even more importantly to understand his fellow blacks who came from linguistic backgrounds in Africa different from his own. In later generations this European language became a *lingua madre* as children were born into such slave family life as existed. Uprooted from an old way of life and thrown into the company of other detribalized strangers, he became a member of a new and greater tribe as represented by the Christian church.

The Negro was introduced into Virginia in 1619 before any white settlers had arrived in New England, before the Dutch came to New Amsterdam, the Germans to Pennsylvania, the Scotch-Irish to the back country of the Carolinas, the Swedes to New Jersey, or the French Huguenots to Charleston. From 1619 until the very eve of the Civil War he was brought to this country by the thousands, antedating most of the Irish and the Scotch, and all the Italians, the Norwegians, and the Poles. Today the Negro is an Old American, and many of his race could qualify for membership in the Colonial Dames or the Sons and Daughters of the American Revolution if only the records had been kept and the rules of these organizations allowed it.

In Africa he was never a Negro and he is not there a Negro today. Modern American newspapers and magazines now reporting the activities of the "Negroes" of Africa use this word in order to make the news intelligible in terms of our vocabulary, but the word as it pertains to Africans is entirely misleading. In Africa the black man still is a tribesman, albeit a tribesman in the process of becoming a Ghanian, a Nigerian, or some other kind of nationalist. Only in America is the black man a Negro, and he became so by reason of peculiarly American conditions and experiences. In America vis-à-vis the whites practically all persons with a black ancestor came to think of themselves as Negroes and were in turn regarded by whites as Negroes. But the American culture, which he so thoroughly acquired and which he has expanded perhaps more than any other single ethnic in our population, is the most distinctive thing about him. The statement by George Burton Adams is not overly exaggerated: "With most marvelous certainty, when we consider the conditions, the negro in the South could be trusted to perpetuate our political ideas and institutions, if our republic fell, as surely as the Gaul did his adopted institutions." [5] Kelly Miller, one of the most perceptive of Negro spokesmen of an earlier generation, said that one of the greatest injustices suffered by the black man in America was that he was not permitted to be patriotic, not permitted to feel at home in the only country and culture he knew. Up to now nothing has perhaps been more difficult than to interest him in tribal Africa.

VII

As cultural differences between Europeans and Negroes in the colonies receded, alleged racial differences advanced. Both race and counter-race would appear to be incidents of acculturation and assimilation. There is no marked emphasis upon race when ethnics are culturally recognizably different; the idea seems to come to the fore when members of the lower-status community begin to acquire the manners, the tastes, the costume, the speech, and the religion of the upper-status community. In his study of relations between the Spanish-speaking Ladinos and the Indian language-speaking groups of Guatemala, John Gillin has called attention to a separating status line almost as great as anything we know in the South between whites and Negroes.[6] In this situation, however, there has been no need to resort to racial ideas since individuals are readily identified as Ladino or Indian on the basis of speech, dress, and other cultural criteria.

The situation in the South developed very differently. As acculturation progressively stripped away cultural differences there was practically nothing of distinctiveness left to the Negroes but a black skin, a flat nose, large lips, and woolly hair. There was danger of Negro absorption into the European community and consequently of a breakdown of the exclusiveness of this community. It was expedient to seize upon those differences which acculturation could not erase, differences fixed in an inherited physical form, and to make the most of them. Making the most of them led to the assertion of race. Skin color, in particular, was to become a significant symbol of status difference. It was easy to impute to individuals of different color moral and social characteristics such as laziness, improvidence, immorality, stupidity, doglike fidelity, and criminal tendency. These alleged behavioral characteristics also were believed to be biologically inherited, and what is in the biological nature of a people is there to stay, the business of God alone since He put it there. Such ideas in the past have given us "the eternal feminine" and "the Jewish character," as well as "the black soul." Many of us may regret these ideas, and we may have enormous sympathy for such people because of the handicaps with which they must live. There appeared to be nothing, however, that anyone could do about it. From such ideas come the themes of human tragedy, of the struggle of man, not against other men but against fate, and, of course, fate is bound to win.

It is most comforting for the man of high station to feel that his lot in life is in accord with the will of God. It is agreeable to believe that some immutable principle sustains the status quo unless, of course, one happens to be near the bottom of the order. Ordinarily, the man of high station will agree with Aristotle, who, considering the matter from the point of view of an Athenian aristocrat, laid it down that changes in an established order should be as few and as slight as possible. Conservatives in general tend to deprecate change since it impugns the security of that to which they have given their allegiance and which guards their status. Liberals in general are at least more charitable toward change, especially when they are members of a class that is dissatisfied and motivated to remove barriers that obstruct their interests. In various situations the issues may be differently defined and the opposed parties may be differently labeled, but it may well be true that the basic cleavage in every society is the one between conservatives and liberals in their varying degrees. The racial situation is no different in kind; with reference to certain issues it tends to divide conservatives and liberals at the color line. Race prejudice, Robert Park remarked, "is merely an elementary expression of conservatism."

It is not true, of course, that all men instinctively fear and oppose change. Most men are always ready to enter into such new relationships as appear to them to involve a rise in their relative status or to be necessary to maintain existing status. They expect thereby to gain by change and they welcome it, especially when they are acutely conscious of the gap between their own status and that of those immediately above them. The narrower the status gap becomes the more sensitive are men to the differences that remain. The gains American Negroes have recently made can be expected to promote more, not less, dissatisfaction on their part.

Other men are just as quick to reject new relationships that appear to involve a loss of status. When circumstances force them lower on the scale in any way they are deeply hurt in the most sensitive aspect of their lives, their conception of themselves. They try desperately to hang on to the self-image they enjoyed at the highest point of the history of their class. They will respond, as white Southerners for some time have been doing, by an overemphasis upon the past, an orientation that tends to close the channels of interracial communication at just the times and points where communication is most needed. Incidentally, it would appear that in our more systematic investigations we have paid considerably more attention to the status-advancing aspirations of groups suffering from an oppression psychosis than to the consequences for personality and social organization of individuals and groups declining in status. (The opposite assertion might be made of themes popular among Southern novelists and playwrights.) Yet it may be just this fact that, in our day, is converting the race problem in the South from a Negro into a white problem. One is, to be sure, born a "white" man, but one has to wage continuous battle to remain a white man. When the Southern white loses some part of the social estate which his white skin has in the past automatically given him, he at the same time loses some part of his identity. He ceases by so much to know exactly who he is, and it is not at all surprising that he does not willingly surrender himself in the partial loss of his sense of self. Most of us today, white and black alike, might well consider that no effort in behalf of the black man that is not matched by a real sympathy for, and understanding of, the white man can really be socially constructive.

VIII

There is no true interracial society until and unless the idea of race enters the social structure and becomes a part of the society's "way of life" or "civilization," or *"pietas."* The idea may be of only local or provincial application but its adherents regard it as a universal. Always it appears to be the disposition of those who oppose change to appeal to something beyond experience, since experience is ever in a state of flux, in order to find stability and peace. The concept of God, "the rock of ages," has often been adopted as the solution to this problem, but lesser principles also have been found useful. It was not by accident that it was the aristocratic philosopher Plato who discovered the perfect and unchanging concept of the concept and who rooted concepts in the original nature of man. The principle of the divine right of kings supported the view of absolute and eternal monarchy until the execution of Charles I showed that circumstances could both make and unmake kings. God made the climate what it is, and climate requires the labor of people especially qualified for work on tropical plantations while other men not so qualified can repose on their verandas. We recognize, as firm and fixed, the ground beneath our feet—until there is an earthquake.

The very human need for some principle of certainty in a world of flux has led to an unending search for some sort of spiritual or cultural anchor without which we cannot hold on to what we have and to what we are or think we are. We have to understand our deep emotional investment in race in this context. It is one of the ideas thrown up in the more recent history of mankind and passed along from generation to generation because it has worked, and worked more or less satisfactorily until now, to stabilize the social hierarchies of whole social orders. When we look under the heading "race" in the *Oxford Dictionary*, we notice quite a large number of meanings historically associated with this word. Should we reflect upon these various meanings and uses of the word with the hope of uncovering some common denominator, we would in all likelihood conclude that each in its own way and with respect to its own reference implies the idea of something built in or entrenched, something permanent and immutable. The English language, and perhaps other languages as well, is rich in the variety of words expressing this idea, words such as inherent, constitutional, ingrained, inborn, intrinsic, incarnate, and many others. The idea of race is like a condition that was written into the lease at the time of creation governing relations among the men who are allowed to inhabit the earth. It came into the South, as in certain other interracial societies, to do duty as an absolute, as a symbol more effective and lasting than language or religion to insure the continued economic, political, and social security of the classes of highest status. To be sure, it has to be shared with landless and impecunious whites, but this was not a complete disadvantage since these whites functioned as a buffer class to absorb the shocks of race conflict. The poor whites of the South, because they are white men, served the cause of the Confederacy in behalf of economic interests they did not share. Statements documenting the proposition that the idea of race in the South has functioned in the manner indicated might be quoted almost without end. Let this quotation from the speech of a contemporary Southern Senator suffice: "By this bill [FEPC] there is an attempt to change something that God made. We did not make it. God made my face white and some other face yellow and some other face black. I did not do it. Congress cannot change that state of affairs." [7]

IX

A comparison between the roles and experiences of the Negro and the immigrant in American life may shed more light upon the difference between change *in* race relations and change *and* race relations. In 1930 Negroes and foreign-born in the United States were approximately equal in numbers, but, of course, Negroes now far outnumber the foreign-born as these two groups are identified and counted in the census. Technically, we all are descendants of immigrants, unless we are Indians, but we have come to use the word "immigrant" in a special way since the American Revolution and particularly since the coming of the Irish during and after the 1840's. Until about 1890 the influx from northern and western Europe predominated; after that date the tide turned increasingly toward newcomers from southern and eastern Europe. It was then that America began to be conscious of an "immigrant problem" and of the difficulties of assimilating alien peoples to what were deemed to be the values and standards of American life. There are a large number of autobiographies by immigrants, and even at this late date when the problem of the immigrant, if the Puerto Rican be excepted, no longer agitates us, these books constitute an instructive body of literature that vividly describes the personal and subjective aspects of "Americanization."

These are not, however, the aspects that concern us here. Nor can we detail the many and important differences between the experiences of various immigrant groups. Rather, we want to see if there is some pattern in the process of change in each immigrant group that may throw some light upon the prospective course of the Negro in American civilization.

Perhaps the first thing to be noticed is that in no case from first to last did the national elites of Europe break home ties and depart for America. On the contrary, to take the case of Sweden, the aristocracy considered the country to which their laborers were migrating to be a "paradise of scoundrels, cheats, and rascals." [8] The recurrent waves of mass immigration consisted, in the main, of the poor and the depressed strata of Europe. It began when such strata had to be "planted" in early Virginia by men of capital who remained in England, and it continued with the white indentured servant class for a century or more later. Then came Welsh, French Huguenots, Scotch-Irish, Austrians, Croats, Czechs, Hungarians, Greeks, Italians, and Jews to fill the territorial and economic vacancies at the bottom of American society, and thereby to facilitate the rise of the immigrant groups which preceded them.[9] Lord Bryce in *The American Common-wealth* explained the relatively high status of the skilled worker in America by the fact that "all unskilled labourers are comparatively recent immigrants."

On the whole, the members of each migrating group were desperately poor, but perhaps no migrations were ever more strongly motivated. Nothing else could account for the willingness to pull up stakes in a loved homeland, travel across a large and dangerous ocean in steerage accommodations, and then endeavor to take root again in a strange land among people of even stranger customs. Reporting what he had heard on a ship bringing a number of elderly Italians to America, a journalist wrote:

And the word that turned up most frequently in their conversation was "America." In colloquial Italian, "America" has come to mean something more than a geographical place. It is, by extension, any deposit of hopes, any tabernacle where all things too big, too difficult, too far beyond one's grasp take shape and become true—so true that all one needs in order to touch them is a ship that will take one there. "America" is, again, something one finds or makes, a stepping stone, a rung in the ladder that allows one to climb a little higher—not, of course, in the country called America but back home. "America" also means the treasure one finds when "America" (the rung in the ladder) is steadily under one's feet. Inevitably, the question that the old people asked one another, over and over, was "Is America America?" [10]

That America was to people such as these Italians a land of opportunity is no mere literary expression. In truth it was a land of hope and promise, and the immigrants of each wave and each group set out to make the promise come true. They identified with the country—their children even more so—and they came to say "we Americans" along with other Americans here long before them. But in their case it was a "we" of aspiration used in the same sense that the first white "Americans" had used the expression, as if they were saying "we are the people who are helping to build a better land for ourselves and for our children." The reference was to the future.

But as members of each group moved up the status ladder and acquired land, skill, or a place of residence outside the city ghettos in which they first had settled, as each group differentiated middle and upper classes within itself and produced successful men, they began to say "we Americans" in a somewhat different sense. Looking back at the past and considering the distance they had traveled and the degree of success and recognition they had won, they were more disposed to say, in effect, "We are the people who have made America what it is." [11] They now were concerned to establish societies called the Sons and Daughters of Something or Other intended to preserve and to glorify the record of these achievements and perhaps to object to the admission of any more lower-class immigrants.

Wave after wave of immigrants were destined to start at the very bottom with their eyes upon the hills. Very often they became the servants or the employees of the preceding group, but they were confident that hard work would win for themselves and their children an honorable place in the new land. To them this ideal conception of a country with a future was America.

The story of hopeful immigrants and successful self-made men of foreign birth or descent leap-frogging over each other was to be repeated many times as American history moved on. Both the relatively successful who had some status advantage to defend and the lowly beginners who hoped to rise had a kind of vested interest in preserving the essential social and institutional structure of the nation, since outside of it the positions they occupied or hoped to occupy would have been meaningless. Thus the changes sought by the immigrants posed, in general, no great threat to that structure. On the contrary, they supported it. To be sure, there did develop among old-line Americans, particularly in the North, a cult of Anglo-Saxonism provoked by the coming of large numbers of Catholics, Jews, and Latins from eastern and southern Europe, a cult which found some common ground with the racism of the South, but the chief effect of this concern was the final restriction of all immigration after World War I.

From the story of the immigrant we learn something of the true meaning of America and of Americanism. We began learning it in the social settlements that were established in the slums of our great cities of the North and that were intended to help solve the immigrant problem by teaching the newcomers the ideals of Americanism. These ideals were presumed by the teachers to have been derived from our history, and so the emphasis in this teaching was upon American achievement. But the immigrants did not agree with the assumption that almost everything valuable in American life had been handed down from the Teutons in the German forests, from the English, or from the pioneers on the American frontier. They insisted on the recognition of their own cultural contributions. The settlement-house experiments wound up with the immigrant students teaching the teachers that America means aspiration, especially to the immigrants who still lived in slums. These new Americans were not interested in looking back over American history, although over their shoulders they might hear the men of the past saying, "We were concerned to build a great cathedral but we had to leave it unfinished. It is for you to build on." It was an unfinished cathedral to which each new group of different culture might add a stone.

From the immigrants we learned this: the real America is something more than the America of the Daughters of the American Revolution. America is a nation of many histories and peoples, with relatively little by way of a common past. For this reason in times of national emergency this country cannot effectively appeal, as can England or France, to a common past in order to mobilize its people of many origins. It becomes necessary to appeal to a common hope, to a common aspiration, to a common future. Our literary historians have come to call this "the American Dream"—the conception that the future is ours to create.

In our very mobile population the differences between peoples upon which economic and symbiotic relations originally were based have been continually disappearing as peoples of low estate have been encouraged and even driven to struggle upward and to bring about occupational successions. While, on the one hand, this process has been accelerated by our "100 per cent American" policy and ideal, the same process on the other hand has supplied motives for the development of doctrines to prevent upward occupational movement from happening. As has been shown, such doctrines have been most effective in the case of the black man, but they also have operated against the Puerto Rican, the Mexican, and certain other minorities. The black man had not wanted to come to America, and after he came here he had no reason for wanting to remain here. He came because he was compelled to come, and he remained here without motive or purpose of his own. His life here, and the lives of his children, served the purpose of someone else. His conception of America was neither that of aspiration nor that of achievement. One neither looks back upon slavery in terms of achievement nor looks forward to sharecropping in terms of aspiration. There were exceptions, of course. Even before the Civil War free Negroes, many of whom were mulattoes, were establishing themselves as a class apart both in the South and in the North. But the black masses remained on the plantations of the South where their fathers before had lived and worked out their lives. They were American Negroes but not Negro Americans.

During the Civil War Negro slaves were freed by presidential proclamation. Their descendants have since learned from bitter experience that real emancipation is never achieved by proclamation. In the long run people have to emancipate themselves; and white people, too, at least some of them, have learned or are learning that freedom is never really handed over to another people by the simple device of issuing a proclamation. Real freedom is never within the prerogative of one people to give another. Members of the master race have at the same time morally to emancipate themselves, and it may be that Negroes cannot effectively gain their freedom until whites have freed themselves from race-bound self-conceptions. It is just now, one hundred years after Lincoln's proclamation, that both Negroes and whites in the South, and throughout the nation generally, are at last beginning to free themselves in some large and significant way from both the slavery and the mastership of the past. This does not involve just one more form of racial adjustment; it involves nothing less than the threatened penetration of the social structure itself.

Behavioristically described, freedom is freedom to move and to get about. After 1865 the Negro freedmen of the South manifested their freedom by moving from one plantation to another, and from the plantations to the villages, towns, and cities of the South and then later to the cities of the North. This greater liberty to move about is doubtless what the freedmen meant when they spoke of the "looseness" of freedom. But many of them moved through the gates of isolated rural plantations only to enter the gates of the segregated ghettos of the cities of both the South and the North.

If emancipation involves freedom to move it also involves freedom to appear. As slaves Negroes were hidden away on the private estates of the planters and as migrants to the cities they were concealed behind the walls of ghetto slums. Slavery consists not only in being deprived of freedom to move but also in being denied a public and visible existence. The changes we now are witnessing describe a process of Negroes rising into public sight from their previous obscurity in city ghettoes. They are putting in an appearance in the theaters, on the streets, on the highways, on the trains and buses, in the voting booths, and in the schools and colleges. They are everywhere, in places where before they rarely ventured. They are conspicuous, they are out in the public, they are being noticed. They are, in short, being emancipated a second time.

We are living in an age of worldwide emancipations. All sorts and conditions of people—women, children, teenagers, sectarians, workers, natives, colonials, peasants—are being emancipated from real or fancied states of oppression all over the world. Again we hear much talk of the "natural" rights of man, a kind of talk which tells more about situations of change than it does about what natural rights are, but all these people seeking more freedom agree on at least one natural and inalienable right in common and that is, the right to complain about their lack of rights. They are complaining so effectively that the holders of traditional status powers are recognizing rights of some sort on the part of those surging up from below and demanding them.

The second emancipation of the Negro, the American phase of this world-wide status struggle, is more fundamental and, for the future, far more important than the first one. Its present manifestations—such as freedom rides, restaurant picketing, school and university desegregation, and other events which command the headlines—may be mere surface manifestations of a more profound change taking place in the *ethos* of the Negro and an earnest of changes taking place or about to take place in the basic structure of Southern society. The first emancipation gave Negroes freedom to move around and to choose their own employers, but it widened racial distances and made Southern institutions much more racially exclusive. Legal slavery disappeared with the first emancipation, but the idea of race, which in part originated as a rationalization of slavery, became an end-value in itself and went even deeper into the structure of Southern society than before.

A social order based upon slavery or race will, of course, be especially sensitive to behavior and language which touches these nerves and which consequently will be deemed subversive. The Japanese have a term, *kiken shiso,* which is translated as "dangerous thought." In old Japan a man might be thrown into prison if suspected of dangerous thought or if he merely had read an outlawed book or had a knowing smile on his face.[12] Dangerous thoughts are thoughts regarded as dangerous to entertain even for a moment. They threaten, not just political authority or economic interests, but the fundamental social order itself. Since the Civil War dangerous thought in the South has turned, more than upon anything else, upon the issue of race. In 1903 Professor John A. Bassett, Professor of History at Trinity College, now Duke University, gave it as his opinion that Robert E. Lee and Booker T. Washington were the two greatest men produced in the South in a hundred years. To outsiders it seemed a harmless enough remark but to Southerners the linking of the name of Lee with the name of a Negro was an expression of dangerous thought, a sacrilege, and there were widespread demands for Bassett's expulsion from the state. Against this background it is easily understandable why the Supreme Court school desegregation decision opened to public view ideas long defined in the South as dangerous and subversive. It is understandable why Americans and especially Southerners who entertain dangerous thought about such things as racial equality should so often be regarded by other Southerners as Communists.[13] One step short of this is the disposition of Southern newspapers to label such people as "sociologists" and to refer to the 1954 decision of the

Supreme Court as a "sociological" decision. Since the social sciences raise for objective consideration questions which people ordinarily feel are already settled in the mores, much of the thought of social science in all its branches presents itself to the people as at least near-dangerous thought.

X

Yet no matter how deep into the social structure the idea of race might penetrate, the South was not permitted to become a separate nation completely free to control its domestic affairs and keep out all dangerous thought. The presence of the North made it impossible for relations between the races to avoid critical evaluation from some source, even from within the South itself. Impersonal forces of change, in addition, brought such pressures upon Southern society as to force something to give. Reaction to change brought the idea of race into existence as part of the Southern "way of life" in the first place; reaction to change is dramatically altering that way of life and the idea of race implicit in it today. These modern changes include the collapse of an obsolete cotton culture, geographic shifts in agriculture, the mechanization of agriculture, the movement away from share-cropping and the trend toward wage labor in agricultural enterprises, the development of competing areas in other parts of the world, overpopulation, urbanization, industrialization, the migration of both white and Negroes northward and westward, the foreign policy requirements of the State Department, the cold war with the Soviet Union, and many other developments. All these cannot be discussed in detail, but attention may be directed to a few of the more significant domestic changes now in process.

There now are more Negroes living outside the South than in it. The South, however, remains that part of the United States where rural Negroes are distributed; Northern and Western Negroes are concentrated in the large cities. The old adage that "city air makes free" continues to operate in behalf of Negroes in Northern and Southern urban areas as it has done historically in behalf of other disadvantaged groups. In the cities, especially in the North and West, Negroes have taken their place alongside the foreign-born whites and their children as a sort of belated immigrant group. The descendants of old-line black Americans have taken up where the white immigrants left off in 1924. In the manner of the newly arrived European immigrants, the contemporary Negro is saying "we Americans" in the same spirit of aspiration and with the same orientation toward the future. Largely because of the Negro, America continues to be what the steerage immigrants first taught us it was, an unfinished cathedral. The Negroes of our time intend to add more than one stone to the building.

There may, however, be an important difference between the aspiring white immigrant American and the aspiring Negro immigrant American. The former was drawn from a traditional European peasantry which declined to continue as such in America and which produced a pride of achievement when it developed middle and upper classes. Among Negroes, on the other hand, the "we" of aspiration appears first in the middle and upper classes and especially in the lower middle class, the class just one notch ahead of the ambitionless lower class. These Negroes are the ones who feel most acutely the need to affirm a distinction and some sense of equality with whites. They are the yeast of Negro society determined to move into a preferred position. Race makes the difference, and in America advance in class status does not erase it. So long as there is a color line there is still much that Negroes have to aspire to, satisfactions that the children of white immigrants have long since achieved.

Until the relatively recent past there was little by way of a Negro middle class in America. Some semblance of such a class made its appearance before the Civil War and the first emancipation added a few small landowners in the rural areas and a few small merchants and artisans in the villages and towns of the South. It was the ghettos of the large cities of the South and even more those of the North that made possible a rapid and extensive enlargement of this class, especially after about 1890. The statement that there is a large and growing Negro middle class in America will hardly be challenged by any competent student, but perhaps many whites, especially in the South, would be astonished to learn that all Negroes are not lower class by nature. A black middle class appears to be rising in parts of Africa; there are blacks in Brazil, but perhaps no middle class as such, since race and class are practically identical ideas there; and over most of the West Indies what would be a Negro middle class in America has become a separate "colored" group no longer locally identified as Negro. Certainly the development of a substantial Negro middle class differentiates the black population of America from Negroid populations in other parts of the world, and constitutes a critical factor in changes in race relations here. A Negro middle class has been taking form, almost entirely outside the awareness of whites, in segregated urban ghettoes. Indeed, it might be said that middle-class Negroes generally are those who have least contact with whites and who, consequently, are the most segregated. No matter how much modern Negro leaders may inveigh against these segregated areas, it is reasonable to suppose that in them were incubated and protected the occupations and institutions that trained large numbers of Negroes in middle-class skills and values.

The Negro middle class formed in urban black belts is now in the process of trying to break out of these areas by bidding for the respect and deference of the surrounding white world. With each success the Negro middle class becomes stronger. Every middle class anywhere seems to arise, where there was not one before, when a segment of the depressed population begins to refuse to play the role assigned to it by the traditional status system. When, inevitably, they meet resistance from sources in the traditional order, they are led to define the barriers as "discrimination." In the course of such encounters between those who would maintain or expand traditional status barriers and those who would set them aside and substitute other status standards, a middle class is born. The process is similar in the evolution of middle classes generally. In England, for example, as R. H. Grotton describes it, merchants and professionals pushing their way upward constituted themselves into a class between the aristocratic stratum on the one hand and the stratum of menial workers on the other. They encountered resistance from below as well as from above.[14]

In America the process of Negro middle-class formation has resulted in some degree of change in the conception, in both Negro and white society, of who a Negro is. Increasing awareness of the existence of a Negro middle class seems to have confused the lines of traditional racial identification just as the appearance of the mixed-blood, the mulatto, did in colonial America. The traditional dominant white race tries to strengthen the laws and customs against the upstarts but the latter counter by disciplining themselves in new rules of behavior appropriate to their new conception of themselves. A consequence of such discipline is the

development of traits and attitudes that are thought to characterize people of middle-class standing anywhere, that is, an emphasis on virtue, respectability, and individual worth, and an intense
effort to instill such values into the ambitions of their children.
Observers have often noted a kind of puritanism among middle-
class Negroes and a concern for precision in speech. It appears
as overprecision to white observers; Will Rogers once remarked
of Negroes at Tuskegee Institute that they spoke such good English he could hardly understand them.

Incidental to urbanization and the emergence of an aspiring
Negro middle class have come formal organizations designed to
clarify objectives, to mobilize effort among Negroes and their
white sympathizers, and to develop plans for action, e.g., the
National Association for the Advancement of Colored People.
They are countered by organizations like the White Citizens
Councils. The first emancipation in the last century was the result
of efforts on behalf of an enslaved people by organizations
formed and led by whites in the North. The second emancipation
in this century is the goal of organizations spearheaded by
Negroes themselves. They have launched into the general complex society of America a series of organizations that interact
with other organizations—industrial, labor, religious, political,
regional, and social—in ways that have produced interlockings,
conflicts, compromises, and accommodations that have measurably transformed the racial struggle into a more impersonal and
indirect affair. The shift away from the study of race relations in
direct and personal terms to their study in terms of mass organizational interaction is registered in the writings of such students
as Herbert Blumer, Joseph Lohman, and Dietrich Reitzes. The
course of future study of change and race relations in the United
States is likely to proceed further in this direction, and from it
we may expect to get a more realistic understanding of the racial
shape of things to come.

XI

But despite the obvious impact of these powerful new forces
on race relations, there remains the question of how deeply into
the fundamental structure of Southern society they can and will
go. Few white Southerners of intelligence, good will, and moder-
ation will deny that the problems presented the South by the

status advance of the Negro count as practically nothing compared with the problems that would be presented by his failure to advance both in status and in material culture. They are inclined to put their faith in education and in gradual economic advance. These programs can shift the color line somewhat nearer the democratic ideal without, however, erasing that line. The structural foundations of the color line may undergo comparatively little change. When we consider the question of structural change in other societies in the long perspective of history it would appear that gradual educational and cultural changes have had relatively little to do with it. The major transformations of historical societies have had their setting in periods of intense collective excitement, such as war, revolution, and migration. It may be that societies are more often and more fundamentally changed by mass action than by individual action. We may now be involved in a sort of slow-burning racial revolution in America, but unless the movement reaches a stage of more violent upheaval than we anticipate, it is likely that the idea of race and the deeper social structure that supports it will be with us for a very long time to come. Few white Americans are prepared to act, and to train their children to act, as if no such structure existed.

The Negro will continue to be, as he has always been, a symbol of change. We can expect him consciously to become more and more a protagonist of change. We will do well to support the conviction he inherited from the steerage immigrants that America stands for the future, and all of us can join him in helping the South take a more positive hand in the making of its own future as a part of America, a future of democracy and good will as well as of material progress.

There is in the conduct of race relations in the South much to repent, but there is no point in a people repenting its virtues as well as its sins. And certainly there is no point in repenting that which was brought about by the impersonal forces of the past. Whites can and should repent when they use their position of racial ascendency for unworthy purposes, or fail to use it for worthy ones. Insofar as they can, by taking thought, they should deliberately enter into and help to guide toward worthy ends and the changes that the future will have in store for us.

• 16 •

The South in Old and New Contexts

In this age of global thinking it is important that we try to understand our corner of the world, the South, in a frame much larger
than we are accustomed to employ. It is no longer sufficient to
study the South in terms of its own unique history; that way
arouses sentiment but yields very little knowledge. Nor is it sufficient to study it within the context of the United States only. The
South is part of a world organization which is not exactly a machine but which runs and shakes like a machine, and the South
is being shaken along with the rest of it. The units now in competition are entire regions and continents as well as local corpora-
tions and populations, and the laws and administrative regulations of the state are obstacles, such as mountains and seas once
were, that are being crossed in the widening competition for
goods and markets. The very competitions and conflicts between
the peoples of the world have, in a sense, as Hans Kohn has
pointed out,[1] given an impetus to the unification of mankind, so
that for the first time we live in a world community and a great
society which are coextensive with the inhabited globe. The
South is a differentiated part of this demographic, economic,
political, and moral order that extends far beyond the immediate
area within which its own historic values and ideals are held and
shared.

The South is a unit of territory and humanity which can be
viewed as a sociological unit or object, and to look at it as such
is probably what we mean by being objective. It is an object
because we point to it and talk about it as such. To be sure, it

SOURCE In John C. McKinney and Edgar T. Thompson (eds.), *The South in
Continuity and Change*, Duke University Press, 1965, pp. 451–80.

is an object not always easy to bound. The problem of identifying and separating it from other territorial areas or objects poses serious questions when it comes to making definite statements and to comparing statements different students and data-collecting agencies make about it. We sorely need some agreed-upon conception if only so that all can be sure they are talking about the same thing. As readers will note, no such consensus has been established among the score of contributors to this book. There is the further complication that the South as an object is, like every object, a somewhat different thing when placed in different relational and historical contexts. It is the purpose of this chapter to suggest what the thing we call the South has been and is in the various contexts in which it has existed. It is hoped that from this perspective the various chapters in this book, each the work of different authors, will find a place in a frame which may help integrate them into a more systematic whole.

I

The South is first of all a physical habitat which sustains a population. For all practical purposes the geography of the world as men have known it through historical time has been its most immutable element. Throughout this time the South is geographically where it has always been and physically what it has always been. There has always been an Appalachian-Ozark core bordered by piedmont areas to the east, south, and west. Beyond this the clay soils gave way, as they do now, to loamish and sandy soils to the very edge of the Atlantic Ocean, the Gulf of Mexico, and the Mississippi River. The present fairly heavy rainfall, the relatively mild winters, and the long growing season were facts about the geography and climate of the South long before the first Europeans ever saw this country. The same rivers, then as now, ran down from the same mountains to the same seas. The distribution of the South's mineral, land, climatic, and other resources will remain constant but, of course, the nature and extent of the exploitation of these resources are subject to change.

All the changes—past, present, and future—discussed in this book, and many not discussed, have taken place and will take place against the background of the physical geography of the

South. Geography separated this area by large water bodies from Europe and South America. Geography attached it to the southeastern part of the North American continent, but geography failed to separate it by any effective natural barrier from areas to the north and west of it. In the opinion of many southerners this was a mistake on the part of the Creator. Geography does not favor secession.

Because geography does not argue, because it simply is, because it presents us with that which stays, it is necessary for people cither to move away or come to terms with it. When he was Director of the Tennessee Valley Authority, David Lillienthal said of the Tennessee River, "A river has no politics." Perhaps most, if not all, so-called national and regional historical policies, such as the Monroe Doctrine of the United States, Russia's persistent effort to get to the sea, and the southern and South African determination to maintain white supremacy, have continued in one form or another under the vicissitudes of even opposing régimes and ideologies because many successive generations have to make substantially the same adjustment to the permanent elements of the physical environment. There have been, to be sure, many and important changes in southern society from colonial days to the present, but the changes are not beyond recognition. The abiding earth is the most elementary principle of certainty and social continuity.

In geographic nature there is, of course, no North, South, East, or West. In their various cultures, men themselves structure space in terms of their experiences with nature and in terms of their relations with neighboring people of other cultures. They do so because some principle of spatial orientation is clearly needed if people are to know where they are in the world and in which direction they are moving.

South, of course, is a point on the compass—a direction. In the most abstract and therefore the most universal cultural formulation imposed upon the dimensions of the world, the world of the compass, the cardinal directions exhibit two polar antitheses —east-west and north-south. The contrast between the lands of the rising sun and the evening lands, between Orient and Occident, have in the past suggested such cultural dichotomies as family and market place, tradition and progress, sacred and secu-

lar, immobility and mobility, continuity and change, and old
countries and frontiers. The movement from east to west historically has symbolized a graduated change from a higher to a lower
degree of cultural development.

In the northern hemisphere, the hemisphere of world history,
the contrasts between the lands of the north and the lands of the
south have in the past suggested such contrasting ideas as cold
climates and hot climates, cold-blooded and hot-blooded peoples,
peoples of active energy and peoples of passive leisure, commer-
cial-industrial economies and agricultural economies, and urban
societies and rural societies. The movement from north to south
or from south to north historically has symbolized contacts between one people and another so abrupt that they tend to be
thought of as peoples of different stock or race. It is significant
that the various climatic theories of society, from Aristotle to
Huntington, are closely associated with the various racial theories of society. Along with race, climate has long been used to
"explain" the South. In principle the North-South contrast is
mainly geographic, but in reality it is in good part charged with
ideas deeply held in the beliefs of the peoples concerned. Americans will recognize them as a mixture of fact and lore long accepted by the people of this country as they contemplate the
differences between northerners and southerners,[2] but actually
they tend to obtain over the whole of the northern hemisphere.
In the southern hemisphere the north-south conceptualizations
tend to be reversed.

South also is a place, and as such becomes "the South." To be
south is necessarily to be south of *something* which is, of course,
north or "the North." The south is often the more southernly part
of an area bearing the same name such as South Dakota, South
Carolina, South Africa, or South America. The assumption here
has to do with an area thought to be sufficiently homogeneous
geographically or historically to warrant a common name, but
also sufficiently different to require separate designations. England has its north and south and so has France, Germany, Italy,
India, and probably every other country. Perhaps because of the
large size of the United States and the intensity and scale of the
conflict between its two major historic areas eventuating in
bloody war, the southern part of this country became known as
"the South" in a special sort of way. To southerners themselves

it is "South for sure," and no funny business such as "Southeast" or "Southwest" will do; it must be the South, the sunny South, the magnolia South, or nothing.

II

If, for all practical purposes, the South has always been located between the same latitudes and longitudes, a location which gives a certain indigenous and persistent quality to its society, it also has been subject, as every other area on earth has been subject, to periodic shifts in its position in the world community. Every area occupies a space complementary to every other area, and these complementary relations, or positions, are constantly changing. The world is shrinking, we are accustomed to saying, but a much more important fact is that it does not shrink evenly, and new alignments between its parts followed by new stresses and strains between them are continually developing. New routes of trade, new sources of raw materials, new modes of co-operation, and new political adjustments and compromises have to be worked out. This uneven shrinkage of the world is brought about principally by advances in the time and cost of transportation and communication

It may be suggested that the area we now call "the South" was originally not south at all. It was north although it never became "the North." This area was originally differentiated as part of an economic region in an expanding world of commerce and production for commerce after the sixteenth century. Relatively cheap water transportation transformed the Atlantic Ocean into an inland sea, no larger than the Mediterranean once was, and gave the warmer lands in and surrounding the Caribbean and Gulf of Mexico territorial divisions of labor in the larger community of Western civilization as producers of agricultural staples for the markets of Europe. "The South," with outlets along the Atlantic coast and later the Gulf of Mexico,[3] became the northern part of a Caribbean-Gulf economic region which over the period from colonial days until now has included eastern Mexico, Middle America, northern and northeastern South America, and the islands of the West Indies.[4]

The cultivation of tobacco in this northern subregion was the first settled and specialized industry of any kind in mainland

America, and for decades the South's cotton was the most important American product—measured both in terms of the number of people engaged in its production and in the value of the export. Until well into the present century, cotton was relied on to settle our balance of foreign trade and to conserve the gold of our domestic commerce. The dependent positions of the southern areas specializing in these and other staples provided an American market which contributed most significantly to calling into existence supporting industries and areas in other parts of the nation such as the wheat belt, the corn belt, and the cattle and meat belts. New England was culturally dependent upon Old England, but economically its manufacturing and shipping were dependent upon the southern market. From this point of view a good case might be made for the argument that southern commercial agriculture has been the central fact in the economic history of the United States.

The northern subregion of the Caribbean-Gulf plantation region also was an important influence in the economic history of Western civilization. The contrast between English settlements in this subregion and northern settlements seems to have been apparent somewhat earlier in England than in the settlements themselves. In England the northern settlements often were referred to as "our northern colonies," whereas the southern settlements were more frequently referred to as "our southern plantations." The agricultural economies of the southern plantations supplemented and complemented the economy of England, which therefore favored them against the more competitive economies of the northern colonies. It was in England, perhaps, that the distinction between the American North and the American South was initially made. But not for long.[5]

On the international scene it was cotton, the plantation staple which required much more extensive processing after production than rice, indigo, or tobacco, that did most to transcend colonies and states and knit almost the entire area into a single economic system. Its development and extension would have been entirely impossible without the parallel development of processing machinery which could not take place in the areas of production but which did take place in England. In England, cotton imports from the American South, pressing against existing technology, led to a series of inventions in the textile industry and to those far-reaching changes in English economy and society which we since have called the Industrial Revolution. The American answer to each invention in England which increased the demand for cotton was, save in the case of the cotton gin, an expansion of the cotton-growing area toward the southwestern frontier.[6] The expansion reached around the northern rim of the Gulf of Mexico and by the time of the Civil War included eastern Texas. We may speculate that without the South's cotton there would have been no Industrial Revolution and without the Industrial Revolution there would have been no South. The heartland of the South became that great extent of cotton-exporting territory in southern and southwestern North America scooped out as by a great bulldozer based and energized in England.

The plantation could expand no farther nor faster into the southwest than the necessity for maintaining market connections allowed. The area over which cotton could be grown in terms of soil and climate was larger than the area over which cotton had to be grown in terms of market and profits. Since no commodity enters the world market except by way of the oceans, and since the plantation is everywhere an institution which produces for distant markets, plantation societies of the world, the South among them, are characteristically grouped around the water's edge. Without the Gulf of Mexico the area now included in the Southwest would have been even more landlocked than the Old Northwest originally was and might very well have had a climate and a terrain much like that of New Mexico and Arizona today.

III

What kind of civilization is and has been southern civilization? Is the model manorial Europe, Old Testament Hebrew, the classic Greek state, or what? All these and other models have been employed, but the civilization of the South really has to be understood in terms of an institution that came most significantly upon the world after the sixteenth century, the plantation. The plantation has been the molecular unit, the very quintessence, of the South and of southernism. In a sense the plantation is the South writ small and the South is the plantation writ large. It has given this society its fundamental principle of order and of continuity, and in it generations of southerners have found their identity. If now there are vital changes taking place in this society as it moves further and faster into the United States and the world, it is in large part because the plantation is being mechanized, consolidated into other types of enterprise, broken down into small farms, converted into a dude and hunting estate, abandoned, or otherwise disappearing. But whatever new order of social life may be in process of replacing it we shall not be able to escape entirely its heritage. Whether we conform to this heritage or revolt against it, the plantation norm will continue to glorify or to stain the culture and the attitudes of the South's people. If it is not with a dead ante-bellum institution that we have to deal but with a living tradition, then its nature and development deserve a closer look.

The outcome of economic succession and population invasion which appear to follow shifts in the ecological position of areas, but which tend to be concealed in great masses of historical detail, is everywhere about the same. People of different race and culture find themselves occupying the same territory. In the absence of a self-distributing labor market in the South, and in a situation where there was more land than labor to till it, entrepreneurs turned planters could secure, hold, and move labor only by means of slavery, and the slavery was fastened upon the highly visible blacks who were imported cheaply from Africa and who were not motivated in the economic traditions of Western Europe. In addition to its industrial function the plantation arose in this area as a means of accommodating peoples of different race and culture to each other. Without it, two such different peoples as European whites and African blacks could not, in all probability, have lived together on the same soil.

If, as Walter Webb has demonstrated,[7] the civilization of the Great Plains was made by men who left the timber for the great open spaces of the West, the civilization of the South was produced by men who entered the seemingly everlasting forest that stretched westward. "It was not the Atlantic," John Peale Bishop remarks in one of his essays, "that separated Americans from the European tradition, but the woods of the Old West." [8] Beyond the line of English coastal plantations and towns moved a stream of Scotch, Scotch-Irish, Welsh, Germans, and Englishmen liberated from indentured servitude. Out there these diverse population elements squatted on the land and built a way of life based upon the small diversified farm with free family labor which brought them into conflict with the wealthier planters of the tidewater. It was a conflict characterized by mutual contempt and bitter words, a conflict between farm and plantation such as the conflict between North and South was later in part to be. In this context the plantation society considered itself and was considered East and not South. However, as plantation settlement moved inland as far as Texas, the stage was set for the line separating East and West to swing around on an axis provided by the boundary line between Maryland and Pennsylvania, the Mason and Dixon line.

As the South became the area below the Mason and Dixon line, it spawned a distinctive culture which came to characterize a very large territory. Whatever is distinctive about a culture appears to be an incident of isolation, and this was an area separated in high degree from the tides and currents of world thought in somewhat the same manner and degree in which South Africa has been isolated. It is interesting that the extreme northeastern part of the United States, New England, and the southern part of the country, Dixie, are the only parts which have achieved areal names other than points of the compass. The people of each of these areas have given allegiance to entities intermediate between the states on the one hand and the nation on the other to a degree apparently stronger than have the people of any other region of the United States. There are sound historical reasons for this similarity; both underwent periods of avoidance by non-English-speaking white immigrants. In New England, 25,000 English immigrants settled in the thirty-year period between 1620 and 1650, and for a hundred years afterwards immigration into the area was negligible. Practically all of the 1,000,000 people in New England at the time of the first census in 1790 were descendants of the Englishmen who arrived before 1650. This isolation and the almost complete freedom from admixture during this period produced a distinctive American type, the New England Yankee. The South, too, has been comparatively unaffected by the great variety of stocks which occupied the middle colonies and states. Of the more than 2,500,000 aliens arriving in the United States between 1820 and 1850, only about 300,000 came to reside in the South. Before and after the Civil

War the great tide of immigration from foreign countries swept around the plantation areas, thus avoiding competition with low-cost Negro labor. By so doing they helped define the northern and northwestern boundaries of the South and gave white southerners cause to boast of their "pure" Anglo-Saxon ancestry.

There was another and more local source of isolation in the development of southern culture. As farmers and planters moved farther into the Southwest, their farms and plantations appeared as small clearings widely separated from each other by the forest. In the South, as in other plantation areas in the world, tales of wild beasts and wild game hunting form a substantial part of the lore of settlement and planting. The forest into which the planters went and to which outlaws and restless individuals could escape marked the boundary of effective control by the central authority of the colony or state. Since the type of organization in which authority resides seems to depend, ultimately, upon the means and extent of communication, each settlement and particularly each plantation became in some considerable measure a state in itself. As a state or as a subdivision of the state, the plantation developed a monopoly of authority within a closed territory. Law was such compulsion as the planter, himself a sort of settlement outlaw and the strongest power of the moment, chose to enforce. Under the circumstances that old conception inherited from England to the effect that it is better for the law to be consistent than for the law to be just did not always apply. Southern law became somewhat like Chinese law, that is, implicated in a network of personal relations and differentially enforced upon individuals according to social standing.[9]

On the isolated plantation in the forest whatever was and is distinctive about the culture of the South took form. The institution was and to some extent continues to be characteristically one of those aggregations of persons which, like the family, exists in the fact that people are reckoned as belonging to each other. It was this "reckoning together" that made the plantation, again much like the family, a unit of collective expectation and obligation, where social relations are so primary and personal that people do not talk of rights and duties; this kind of talk is reserved for the more formal relationships of the city and the larger state. On the plantation, in general, persons descended from or appended to the same individual were reckoned together and their characteristics attributed to that one from whom they are descended or to whom they belonged or upon whose "place" they lived. This "reckoning together" of the past with the present and of the black with the white means that, not only were persons counted together, but were designated as "belonging" to the plantation, the planter and his family no less than his slaves or tenants, as though the plantation were another something existing apart from the very members who made it up. It became a structure living in the mind and in culture, and fashioning the personalities and outlooks of those who lived upon it. To understand this fact is to understand much that is otherwise puzzling about the culture of the Old South, the base line from which we have to understand the present South. In this context words that meant one thing in the North meant something at least slightly different in the South. It is likely that the word *slave* came to have somewhat different meanings North and South, and northerners and southerners debating the issue were not always talking about the same thing. As late as 1945 Ruth Landes, an anthropologist, could write:

> My own experience taught me that one must live a while in the South with Southerners, in order to learn the key words and what they mean. Thus, one hears a familiar vocabulary, but the timbre echoes differently. To sense the implications, one must follow the tones of the voice, gather the things that are left unsaid, hear the eloquent silences, note the special actions. In very truth, these words serve another style of living.[10]

No wonder it is easier to *feel* the differences between North and South than it is to conceive them intellectually or to state them formally. Perhaps it is much like the feeling we have for the differences between Orient and Occident or the feeling that the Romans and the Greeks must have had for the differences between their respective social worlds.

IV

The plantation was a small single-purpose enterprise which progressively mobilized several different layers of people upon the same territory and steadily got itself involved with others like it. Some amount of co-operation between individual despotisms for the solution of common problems such as transportation and marketing was necessary. Normally every institution survives by becoming part of a social system or by generating a social system around itself and controlling that system. The plantations of Brazil, numerous and important though they were, seem never to have centered an institutional system; an impression gained from the literature is that they never succeeded in subordinating the Catholic Church.[11] Hawaii developed a system of plantations but perhaps not a plantation system.

A plantation system did arise in the South, or, it might be better to say, the scattered plantations in this region systematized themselves into the South, for the plantation system and the South seem to have been almost synonymous expressions. Because here the interdependency between most or all institutions was centered and held together by the plantation it became a plantation system, that is to say, a plantation survival system. The plantation centered the system in the South because it developed in this region unchallenged by any other established institutional interest, economic, political, or religious.[12] In time it formed the family, white and black, in its own image and according to its own requirements. Its planters dominated the state and filled its offices. The state universities and military academies trained their sons to succeed them as another generation of planters. The church gave moral sanction to the principle of rank order among kinds of men. Originally there was no manufacturing industry to compete for its labor; when such industry did develop it retained the paternalistic principle of the plantation. The small farm sometimes got in the way, but yeoman farmers and even poor whites aspired to become planters themselves.

In the southern system, orthogenetic cities such as Charleston and New Orleans grew up as plantation capitals. In these capital cities what Redfield [13] calls "the little tradition" of the individual and isolated plantations, each varying a little from every other, was reshaped and articulated by poets, novelists, theologians, scholars, and editors into a "great tradition" generally accepted all over the South and which gave southerners their stock clichés, platitudes, and rationalizations. The individual plantations fed their experiences, beliefs, problems, and lore to the wise men and prophets of the capitals; these experiences and this lore came back in standardized form as ideology and conviction.

If the capital cities of the southern plantation system belonged to the planters, the heterogenetic cities of the present South belong to the merchants and manufacturers. Atlanta and Dallas, according to Winsborough, have taken the place of Charleston and New Orleans and chambers of commerce have taken the place of planters' associations.

V

The South became "the South" as a section, not, as we are distinquishing the words, as a region or subregion. It began as that part of the Caribbean-Gulf plantation region settled principally by whites of English origin as against the southern parts which were settled, in the main, by whites of Latin origin. English-speaking whites along coastal North America staged a common revolt against the mother country which was successful and which paved the way for a new nation. Consequently the northern part of the Caribbean-Gulf region became part of a political entity, the United States, to which other parts of the same region did not belong. It was to become a politically conscious section of the new nation in conflict with other sections. We have to understand the sectionally conscious South, as southerners themselves came to understand it, in terms of the enemies it acquired. Without a common enemy the loose aggregation of states along the South Atlantic and the Gulf of Mexico probably never would have become "the South" in anything more than a directional sense.

Political bipolarity is not unusual in the history of nations. A northern area of strength and prestige in China stood repeatedly against a southern area of lesser strength, and Upper and Lower Egypt were set off against each other at various times historically.[14] The fact that the South had its North as Carthage had its Rome, had, in other words, cultural and political ties with the people of another part of the same commonwealth with whom it was, nevertheless, in a state of tension and conflict, led the people of the South to that degree of conscious reflection upon, and justification of, their way of life as to generate a conception of themselves as a different people. To know who we are it is first necessary to know who we are not, and southerners came to know and to thank God they were not Yankees. The North was stereotyped, as England once was, as a nation of traders and peddlers, and southerners could, along with General Lee, refer to Americans opposing them as "those people." Thus it was that the people of the North and the people of the South came to form conceptions of themselves as different peoples but they were, of course, differentiated as counterparts of each other out of the same dialectical process. They do not and could not exist apart from each other. The South became that part of the nation regarded as the South by the people of the North and vice versa.

An order of society whose economy produced primarily for foreign markets and which consequently sought low tariffs, which was based upon unfree labor, and which pressed for *lebensraum* toward the west, inevitably aroused the opposition of economic competitors and ideological antagonists. Before about 1830 there was a great deal of such opposition in the western small farm areas within the South itself. This early opposition proposed change by way of reform. After about 1830 the opposition moved north and assumed a much more virulent and revolutionary character. Northern and southern newspapers began to take sides and to divide public opinion into two hostile camps. Revolutionary abolitionism in the North began with an attack upon the evils of slavery and the dark purposes of the slave power and later broadened out into a bitter and indiscriminate condemnation of the southern "way of life" generally. With John C. Calhoun, southerners moved from defense to attack on everything northern which became equally intemperate. Between 1830 and 1860 the North and the South engaged each other in a prolonged cold war, during which time the partisans of each side added to their cultures elaborate tissues of rationalizations and doctrines intended to naturalize and to sanction their own institutions. There is nothing exceptional about this process; it is the way the customs of every society enter the *mores* and come to be regarded as essential to societal survival. In a plantation society similar to that of the South, Brazil, this process did not occur, which fact probably accounts in considerable measure for the present differences between the two.

In the war that followed, southerners experienced what they fought for, the South, as northerners experienced what they fought for, the Union, "It was the war with the Yankee," says Cash, "which really created the concept of the South as something more than a matter of geography."

The armies had brought men together from the four quarters, molding them to a common purpose for four years, teaching them more and more to say and think the same things, giving them common memories—memories transcending all that had gone before and sealed with the great seal of pain and hunger and sweat. . . .

Local patriotism was far from being dead in them, but nobody remembered now that they had ever gone out to die merely for Virginia or Carolina or Georgia. In their years together, a hundred control phrases, struck from the eloquent lips of their captains in the smoke and heat of battle, had burned themselves into their brains—phrases which would ever after be to them as the sounding of trumpets and the rolling of drums, to set their blood to mounting, their muscles to tensing, their eyes to stinging, to call forth in them the highest loyalties and the most active responses. And of these phrases the great master key was in every case the adjective Southern.

Moreover, four years of fighting for the preservation of their world and their heritage, four years of measuring themselves against the Yankee in the intimate and searching contact of battle, had left these Southerners far more self-conscious than they had been before, far more aware of their differences and of the line which divided what was Southern from what was not. And upon that line all their intensified patriotism and love, all their high pride in the knowledge that they had fought a good fight and had yielded only to irresistible force, was concentrated, to issue in a determination, immensely more potent than in the past, to hold fast to their own, to maintain their divergencies, to remain what they had been and were [15]

The American Civil War, like the similar Boer War in South Africa, was one of the last of the romantic wars and one of the first of the modern wars. For the South it ended in defeat, and for the establishment of the southern tradition this is perhaps the most important fact of all. Had the South been victorious there probably would have been no South today at all. Secession in America, like *apartheid* in South Africa, is not a principle upon which a strong unity can be built. It was not simply divergent economic and cultural interests that made the South a nation within a nation. More than anything else, perhaps, it was a common emotion and a common loss that bound the people of the South together. Walter Ratheneau, speaking of Germany after World War I, remarked that only those nations which have known defeat have souls. It was the defeat of 1865 that gave the South something like a national soul and a conception of a past finer, in its own opinion, than its present. Both New England and the South have Golden Age traditions, but it has to be asserted that the tradition in the South seems much the stronger.[16] In this connection there comes to mind the volume contributed to by twelve nostalgic southerners three decades ago entitled *I'll Take My Stand,*[17] and the popular literature issued by the devoted ladies who belong to the United Daughters of the Confederacy.

In all the racial strife and turmoil of today perhaps the thing that rankles and embitters most is what appears to be the bland assumption on the part of the outlanders that the natives of the Deep South, like the natives of Deep Africa, are benighted and primitive enough to be urgently in need of conversion. Now if there is one thing certain about the inheritors of an old and proud tradition it is the fact that they strongly resist conversion as they resist any other assault upon their identity. Southerners experienced such an assault during the post-Civil War period when northern victory was felt to justify the imposition of the principles and the way of life for which the North had fought and won as well as a military peace treaty. As Sherman was about to march to the sea, the Reverend Lyman Abbot wrote, "We have not only to conquer the South, we have also to convert it." [18] So following the war it was inevitable that the South be "reconstructed," a northern effort which the people of this section never felt the need for and never really accepted. Along with northern armies of occupation and carpetbaggers came teachers and missionaries,[19] as along with federal marshals they are coming now and with very much the same southern reaction against them. Because of them, in part, the intersectional cold war continues, but whether southerners like it or not it is well to remember that in the kind of mutual watching and listening world in which we live today, the process of passing judgment over other people is inevitable and will continue. The missionaries may not do the South justice but they may do the South good. At any rate, Reconstruction, then as now, had for its principal object the transformation of racial attitudes.

VI

We are brought now to the Great Division, superseding all others, which runs like a thread through about all that has been said in this book and which everyone thinks of when the South is mentioned in ordinary conversation. No matter where or in what form questions of race arise anywhere in the United States and in much of the rest of the world, always in the background the South is there. It is by no means, of course, the only assortment of human oddities in the world. Relations between odd lot peoples, called minorities, and their hosts are implicated in the persistent problems of most if not all modern societies. Every such society must have problems peculiarly its own, or believed to be its own, with which it must live, if only because its problems distinguish it from all other societies. There are no problems like our problems, and a certain indignation is aroused in us when others dare compare their problems with our own. The long-time problem of the South, the one which does most to identify it, is its race problem. It is a problem now in process of changing its character, as it has changed its character several times before, and the change is an earnest of another orientation which the South is undergoing in the United States and in the world.

As race and race relations are commonly considered, the most general assumption is that from the very beginning there is race. But race has to be accounted for and not assumed as an original fact. Races are made in culture, not found in nature. We have only human aggregations to begin with, which, when welded together by crucial events of history, select out certain characteristics held or alleged to be held in common, and become "peoples" of a certain sort—nations, nationalities, religious communities, linguistic communities, folks, or races. These terms represent something more than mere categories; they are wholes or totalities large enough or old enough to be more or less self-contained and to have a self-perpetuating social system. A people is a socially or culturally defined emergent from a society and not just a demographic component of it. What kind of people a collectivity will become will be determined by the history and circumstances of the situation it is in and by the kind of other peoples with which it is in contact and interaction. A people, every people, is constantly changing its limits and its constitution; in no one form does it last forever if it lasts at all. Old peoples are constantly being replaced by new peoples.[20]

The plural society, that is, a group of peoples, is by its very nature localized in particular areas occupied by particular peoples who have particular relations with each other. It is found, for example, not in the relations between Christians and Moslems in general but in Lebanon, not in the relations between Jews and Gentiles in general but in Germany, not in the relations between whites and Negroes in general but in the South. Negroes are not Negroes in general but blacks under various names vis-à-vis other peoples in particular areas. Their names are not just the names of entities but of the relationships that each people has with other people in the same general area. No people can come to consciousness as a people against other people in general but only against particular other people in the context of a particular society. One does not know how to take the others into account in general; one knows or learns how to take the others into account in actual situations. Thus the events out of which a people come and the actions it is engaged in must be understood in terms of the particular concatenation of peoples of which it is a part at a given time and place and in a given situation.

Peoples now regarded as racial in character were not necessarily always so nor are they necessarily destined to remain so. In early Virginia, African blacks appear to have been regarded as religiously different, that is, as non-Christians sometimes called Moors. As the color of their skin merged with religious ideas about them, they were sometimes called blackamoors or tawnymoors. With the development of the slave trade and plantation slavery they came to be regarded as labor battalions in an industrial army of occupation. It was during the course of this development that the conception of whites and blacks as different races took form in the South.[21] Here it functioned first to naturalize and to rationalize slavery but with abolition it has turned into an end-value in itself, and was politically used to disenfranchise the Negro and to segregate him in separate areas and institutions.[22]

The Negroes of the United States now are a vastly different people from their African ancestors, not only because they have mixed their blood with Indians and whites, but principally because they now are realizing themselves in mass action. They now are speaking and acting for themselves through their own writers, politicians, and institutions. In her chapter, Burgess calls attention to the large and growing Negro middle class, a class which barely existed in 1860, in changing American Negroes into a different people with an entirely different conception of themselves. With the change in the Negro people, southern whites are becoming a new people also. It is very important in understanding recent white behavior in the South to realize that native whites born of native parents who in the past grandly or reluctantly made concessions of rights to the Negro minority now constitute a minority group themselves. They are seeking to convert old customs into "rights."

VII

The dominant white people of the South structured society upon the premise that Negro people are a subordinate group immutably confined to their condition. This assumption made the South, like the White Highlands of Kenya and the cities of South Africa, a "white man's country," a phrase which carries with it the unspoken corollary that it is not a black man's country even in areas where blacks outnumber whites. A white man's country would appear to be any part of the world where white men can live and breed and control its institutions.

In the South there were and are the institutions directly controlled by the white majority but which included or serviced members of both races. Foremost among these is the plantation, which intermixed whites and blacks on the land albeit in different stations within it. After the Civil War, white and Negro sharecroppers often worked the land side by side. Another common institution which became especially important in the postwar period was the country store, about which relatively little has been written. Because of the impersonal and symbiotic character of trade generally, the full force of the local community's population, white and Negro, focused upon it as upon no other institution. Consequently community life tended to center around it and southern villages and towns, especially in the plantation areas, developed from it and around it. The southern country store could effect the exchange of goods and services with a minimum amount of hard money, since for most of its people the South's economy was traditionally nonpecuniary and the times did not favor the possession of much money anyway. Indeed, there was a certain contempt for money and for the monied class; there were too many values and sentiments that "money can't buy," and that only a Yankee would think of trying to buy.[23] In addition to general merchandise the country store was often the post office, the funeral parlor, the railway depot, the newspaper, and sometimes the place where the fraternal orders, religious groups, and even school classes met. It was also a bank because it was about the only institution around possessing an iron safe. As the merchant became affluent and cashed in on his mortgages and crop liens he often became a planter, entering into or taking the place of the old planter class. Or he might become a banker and often did. As money and credit became a new basis for power and control, as banks and diversified businesses proliferated, as money and goods circulated as landed property could not, the South became more and more regionally as well as sectionally oriented toward the great financial and commercial centers of the North and became, in fact, a colonial province of the North. Finance, even more than politics, has made the United States one community and has, of course, drawn the South into a tighter integration with the rest of the nation. But the southern masses remain, perhaps, less pecuniary-minded than the generality of people in any other part of the nation. No one section of the country has a monopoly over improvidence (there are other words for it), but the people of the South have more than their share of it. Here it is not just a fact but a tradition.

Industrial institutions, particularly textile manufacturing, emerged in the post-Civil War period out of a social movement intended to solve the "poor white" problem of the South by affording new occupational opportunities to them. The poor whites were that class of whites said to have a lot of kinfolks but no ancestors, or hardly conscious of any. As the plantation economy had earlier almost completely eliminated all except Negro labor, the initial program of industry omitted almost all except white labor. In non-textile industry this pattern of ethnic segregation did not prevail, although the distinction between skilled and unskilled work generally held to the color line. As is true of colonial territories generally, some capital for the development of industrial institutions in the recent and present South originated in the great investment markets of England, but mainly it came from the North. Contrary to the general assumption that the industrialization of colonial areas is everywhere a major force in transforming race relations and in undermining the traditional order, southern industry, stemming from northern as well as southern capital and management, has until now accommodated itself to the plantation pattern and to the prevailing racial mores.[24] Nevertheless, these institutions, controlled as they are by finance capital centered outside the South, have been instrumental in launching southern society into the general complex economy of America and the world subject to all the varied forces playing upon that economy, and have helped transform the race problem into a more impersonal and indirect affair in which unionism and automation will progressively play an important part.

Between peoples, so long as they are separate peoples, there appears always to be some institutional segregation, voluntary or involuntary, complementary or parallel, enforced by law or enforced by custom. Segregation appears as a spatial and/or institutional division of labor, and of course carries with it some kind and degree of isolation. Some peoples have preferred their institutions segregated, others have protested against it, and at times and places peoples have changed their preference. It was when segregation became a matter of public policy as it did in the South after the 1880's, with the aim of consolidating old social differences between the races, that the stage was set for a change in preference on the part of Negroes leading to the present revolt. The present drive is for what is called an "open society," and it may be expected to change or eliminate certain old forms of segregation; but it may just as well institute new forms.

The present drive was launched against the maintenance of separate schools for the two major races, but it has broadened out into an assault on the principle of racial segregation generally. Southern whites have not strongly objected to education for Negroes so long as it was defined as a way of improving the "condition" of underlings, but they have strenuously objected to any form of status education which threatened "our schools." Now our school, our personal school, our almost private school, the school from which we get the news and gossip of the community, is being invaded, or threatened with invasion, by Negroes. It is shocking to realize that it no longer is our school but an impersonal institution of the state over which we no longer have complete control and in which classes have to begin on time because it has ceased to be a common community of family gossip. In the course of time, however, the desegregation and impersonalization of the schools may lead us to talk somewhat less about better white schools or even better Negro schools and somewhat more about just better schools.

Actually, southerners will have to do this because the problem of education in the South, as elsewhere, is itself changing with changes in the nation and in the world. In the stable agricultural society of the pre-twentieth century South, it was not really necessary that the generality of men have much formal education. Many men became great landholders and members of the legislature without any at all. Other men knew a little Latin and Greek and wore this kind of learning like medals on their chests. The real educational forces derived from the forces of production; men were and still are educated by what they are making and doing. The men who had to buy fertilizer, keep the commissary accounts of their tenants, and negotiate the selling of their cotton or tobacco had necessarily to pick up enough reading, writing, and arithmetic in order to get along.

The drive to educate the children of everybody does not stop with the public schools. It does not stop even with undergraduate education at the college level. In the South as elsewhere in the nation it presses on to higher quality education in the colleges and universities, not just college by college and university by university, but into a complex of colleges and universities qualified to meet the demands of modern science and research. We shall continue to call it education but actually the drive is for survival, societal survival.[25]

That which does most to sustain and continue a people is perhaps that which is most deeply rooted in its family values, and a people will not change from one form to another until these primary group values are assaulted and changed. If we wish to know why Brazil is less dominated by the idea of race, the answer probably will be found in the nature and values of Brazilian family life. It is difficult, in Brazil to draw a color line, because such a line would cut across families.[26] Family life in Brazil is not defined in racial terms; but this is precisely how it is defined in the South. White and Negro southerners do have kin across the color line but they are not publicly recognized, and we may not expect the fundamental social structure of southern society to change appreciably until and unless the family finally yields to desegregation.

"The Southern white woman and the Negro man," says Charles H. Fairbanks, are psychologically the focal points of the South's fear of desegregation." [27] It is at this point that American values represented by racial equality run head-on into values that represent sex equality. Everywhere, it seems, an approximate equality between the sexes is taken to be a requisite to what the world is coming to understand by "modern." In Moslem countries women are dropping the veil, and in India women are coming out of purdah. In Japan women are mingling more freely with men. These countries are becoming, as we say, "modern," and freer association between men and women is generally taken as sign and symbol of the fact. In regions where race relations are a problem, as in South Africa and the American South, the racial restrictions that have been placed upon and accepted by white women, and the racial restrictions that have been placed upon Negro men, may be of the same order of traditional phenomena resisting modernization and final emancipation. We have our own versions of purdah and the veil.

It is in the nature of institutions, once established, to resist change and uphold old ways of life. This is less true of industrial and financial institutions than it is of others, but as the world shifts and changes around them, all institutions at different tempos have to change also. In the South there are geographical shifts in agriculture and occupational changes in the racial division of labor as well as in the economy generally. All these changes are bound up with the replacement of the plantation system by a metropolitan system in which southern cities link up with each other as well as with the cities of the nation and of the world. It is by reason of its cities that the South is now experiencing its first general emancipation from its geographical locus. Even in the most isolated rural communities in the South, communities like Possum Trot, Alabama,[28] places where readjustments are made with most difficulty, changes are taking place which cumulatively build up into major changes in the life of the region and the nation. Radio, television, and electric lights are being introduced into the humblest tenant homes, and electric bills have to be paid regularly each month. Almost for the first time, these tenants are entering into the decision-making process along with farmers and planters as to how the land shall be used and how and when the products shall be marketed. Incidentally, our social scientists are not adequately taking these local changes into account; it appears that we know more now about the South at federal and state levels than we know at the grass-roots level.

• 17 •

God and the Southern Plantation System

I

I believe it was Uncle Remus who told the little boy who listened to his nightly stories that experience is what you get when you don't listen to your ma and pa. It also is what you get when you go outside other authorities such as books. There comes a time when the thoughts of probably every social scientist who is immersed in his subject take a personal turn; when he distinguishes between his life experience and his study experience and undertakes to determine what each has contributed to the other. This essay will attempt to put the facts of my own experiences and observations, widened and deepened by the literature, into a context which, for me, illuminates the nature and meaning of religion in the South.

I well remember the old Methodist church I rather reluctantly but regularly attended when I was growing up on a plantation in South Carolina. Founded by Bishop Francis Asbury long before the War Between the States, it still stands, though services no longer are held in it. One of the thousands of abandoned or dying rural churches in the United States it, like most of the others, fell before good roads and automobiles, but its general spirit and outlook were transplanted to the nearby town center. Southern town and even city churches generally might almost be described as transplanted rural institutions. The old church I knew was once a flourishing thing attended by the gentry and

SOURCE In Samuel J. Hill, Jr. (ed.), *Religion and the Solid South*, Abingdon Press, 1972, Ch. 3.

their hangers-on of the community who "in the hush of every Sunday morning had nothing else to do except wait for church." Before the war the slaves of the planters sat in the gallery. The dead of the gentry, once buried on individual plantations, later were laid to rest in the cemetery surrounding the church where their poorer relatives and even family pets also were buried. Some of the pets were black servants. The size and quality of the stone monuments marked the degree of affluence, or lack of it, of the ones buried beneath them, an index of the community's status hierarchy.

A succession of ministers lived with their families in the parsonage nearby. The minister was not the only one who chastised us for our sins, but it was he who was expected, licensed, and even paid to do so. It was difficult for him to be "one of the boys" but occasionally one came along who could unbend enough to be called "our kind of preacher." The annual revival during the cotton lay-by season marked the high point of the minister's efforts. Ill provided with public amusements, except for Saturday night brawls during this season of general idleness, the revival normally enjoyed great success. Periodically the minister sought through regular and special collections from the congregation to raise money for his own salary and to help support the denomination's missionaries abroad. The good men of the congregation, but more especially the devout women who formed masculine-approved missionary societies, generously supported this cause even though, before the War Between the States, it might be necessary to sell a slave or so in order to do so. Or so the scoffers sometimes unfeelingly said. The minister rarely if ever had anything to say about child labor, sharecropping, illiteracy, or race relations. I had known child laborers, sharecroppers, and illiterates, white and black, all my life but I did not know the condition of these people constituted social problems until I was well along in college. We heard much, however, about the evils of dancing, card-playing, and the consumption of alcoholic beverages. It was only after the relative loss of control over Negroes incident to their mass emancipation from slavery that the Methodists particularly became concerned about the dangers of strong drink.

The mood of the community generally was one of piety if we think of this word as involving the sharing and the orientation of experience. Piety has to do with personal support of that system of traditional values and sentiments appropriate to the requirements of a situation. It is, as Kenneth Burke epigrammatically puts it, "the sense of what properly goes with what." [1] In my case, and in the case of thousands of other Southerners, it was an experience which went well beyond my life upon the immediate plantation where I grew up and the church I attended. It was, in addition, an experience with a system of society, a plantation system, including all the institutions in that system. In it I was located and knew who I was supposed to be and what I was expected to do and to think. Of course, like many others, I took the system and the situation in which it operated for granted but now I propose to try to make sense of it, to "size up the situation," as we say.

Of course, my effort in this brief chapter will be incomplete, but it may serve to show the context in which the southern church and its religion should, I think, be understood.

II

Whether economic or cultural factors predominate in shaping the institutions of a given social order it is certain there is a strain toward consistency in the relations between them. The institutions of no society are transplanted without adaptation to another environment if they survive at all. Either the transplanted institutions transform the habitat, or the new habitat transforms them, or both are changed as they interact with each other. In any case, the result is the creation of a new and different "situation" which has to be analyzed in terms of the constituent interacting factors which produce and maintain it. I am concerned here with a certain constellation of factors and institutions, among them the church and the religion associated with it, which have defined the situation and which we have termed "the South."

I am considering the church and religion in the South as developing in response to a situational imperative apart from any judgment, good or bad, we may be tempted to pass upon it. Our conservatives or fundamentalists have pronounced religion in the South the best to be found anywhere [2] whereas our liberals or modernists have found it to be woefully inadequate and superstitious, but a rearward look suggests that the development of religion in the South, regardless of ethnic, denominational, or ecclesiastical differences, was and is the unintended result of the immediate intentions of many generations of men. No individual or group of individuals sought to make it what it finally became nor what it is becoming. It developed from situational factors and changes in these factors that lie at least in part outside human plan and purpose.[3]

Many observers of both liberal and conservative persuasion have commented upon the unique character of religious phenomena in the South. Kenneth Bailey has sketched this character and described the South at the turn of the twentieth century as "a land of piety and tradition" preoccupied "with individual repentance, a dogged insistence on Biblical inerrancy, a tendency toward overt expression of intense religious emotions: these legacies of frontier revivalism still held a primacy." [4] Of course, there were individual and local exceptions to the "almost single-minded emphasis upon individual regeneration," and of course peoples and areas outside the homogeneous South often exhibited very much the same emphasis, but the rise and spread of the social gospel with its compassion for depressed classes, its doctrinal unorthodoxy, its rational criticism, and its involvement in political movements looking to the elimination of social inequities was far more prevalent in the religious behavior of the heterogeneous and urban North and West.

Religion in the South began as an Old-World transplant, went through various modifying stages during the westward frontier expansion, and in the course of time acquired an institutional character implying constitution, stability, and tradition, and was reabsorbed with considerable modifications into preexisting ecclesiastical structures which, incident to the slavery controversy and the Civil War, separated from their northern counterparts. Belief-systems and institutional dogmas took deep root in an overwhelmingly rural society of planters, white and Negro peasants and squatters, and yeoman farmers. The cost of maintaining the more or less formal institutional structures was paid for by returns from various commercial staples such as cotton, tobacco, sugarcane, and lesser crops. The cost was returned in full measure by the moral support which the religious belief-system gave to the agricultural system at the center of which was the plantation.

Among the Protestant denominations various sorts of Baptists, the folk-church of the white South, seem to have become more "southern" than those of other denominations and the Quakers least so, but all these denominations were but minor variations from common points of cultural assumptions.[5] The tradition which they shared and supported raised an infallible Bible, and especially the King James Version of it, to the position which had been occupied by an infallible Pope leading cynics such as H. L. Mencken to characterize the South as the Bible Belt.[6] Even beneath the surface differences between those variations from white Protestantism represented by Catholicism, Judaism, and Negro Christianity there were and are common values, assumptions, and other intangibles which comprise that indefinable thing called the Southern Way of Life. Of course, there were important doctrinal and behavioral differences between Protestantism, Catholicism, and Judaism in the South as in other parts of the nation, and as the common southern culture underlying them developed and strengthened Southerners became more conscious of the differences that remained and more convinced that they were greater than actually was the case. There were ministerial and political politicians who clung to the differences and made a profession of advertising and manipulating them. Protestant hostility toward Judaism and Catholicism intensified, and suspicion grew among whites generally that Negro Christianity was spurious. But religious orthodoxy, a sort of fossilized piety, was at the core of southern cultural orthodoxy which, when challenged by scientific and theological advances, was consciously and defensively formulated, especially in white Protestantism, into what came to be called fundamentalism. Fundamentalism in the United States has had its greatest strength in the rural areas of the South.

III

But what is the South, the situation in which I propose that we try to understand its church and its religion? It is not simply the South of the census nor even of that geographical area which appears at the bottom of the map. I think we do not get at the nature or essence of the South by adding up the geographies and the histories of the political divisions which various authorities have called "southern states." The South is not a state, nor any one of the states, nor any combination of states. The history of North Carolina is not a chapter in the history of the South. The South is not recognized in the Constitution of the United States. Yet we have a name for it, and we talk about it as if it were an objective entity, as if it exists. At least on one occasion its people engaged in a collective enterprise when it waged war against a common enemy. As a result its members spoke of themselves as "we Southerners" set off in opposition to others referred to by General Lee as "those people." Yet when we have stripped away that which is common to all humanity, to the people of the Western world, to rural and agricultural people everywhere, to people who live in interracial situations, and to the people of the United States generally, what we have left, or some part of that we have left, is the South. But by that time the society is substantially rather thin amounting to little more than an abstraction or an idea. It was and is, however, an idea deemed significant because people both inside and outside the society chose to look at it significantly and to search for and to magnify differences both real and imagined. It was an idea originally laid down upon a territory whose boundaries were very indistinct. Today they are even more indistinct as the obvious uniformity of urban life steadily emancipates the South from its old territorial locus.

Significant or not there have been and are real differences between the South and the rest of the nation. In the context of the nation as a whole the South is stigmatized as an area of pervasive poverty especially since President Franklin Roosevelt characterized it as the nation's Economic Problem No. 1. More recently it has received widespread notice in connection with President Johnson's antipoverty program. After the War Between the States its political solidarity gained for the region the name of Solid South. Religious orthodoxy, poverty, and political conservatism are the three sets of factors which consistently appear together in each of the "Souths" of the world listed by Seymour Martin Lipset. Others mentioned are southern Italy, Quebec in Canada, the Scottish Highlands of Great Britain, western Norway in addition to the American South. It has been said that "every country has a South"—a social if not a geographical South. In these "relatively poor and economically less developed regions" citizens regularly vote conservative even when their own best interests would appear to dictate otherwise. The minds of the people, Lipset goes on to say, "are dominated by 'traditionalistic' values."

In these areas the social structure remains in some part the way it was before the age of capitalism and the free-market economy. The positions of rich and poor are defined as the natural order of things and are supported by personal, family, and local loyalties rather than viewed as a product of impersonal economic and social forces, subject to change through political action. At the same time the poor peasant or worker performs a role which has an obvious meaning and value, and he derives gratification from stable personal relationships and ceremonial activities embracing the whole community. Religious belief tends to be strong and to support the *status quo*.[7]

IV

The gross factors of economics, politics, and religion in the general situation as represented by these various "Souths" may show similarities, but when we come to probe their historical and social roots considerations more or less special to each have to be taken into account. Of particular importance in understanding the American South is the longtime presence in it of the plantation institution. The plantation was never present in the Scottish Highlands, but it does appear to have been the central fact in the determination and history of the American South. Let me outline some of its more salient features.

Since Columbus the New World has received or spawned a large number of movements, enterprises, and organizations most of which failed to catch on and subsequently died. The effort to transplant the English manor to Maryland and elsewhere failed, but an enterprise directed toward the exploitation of virtually free land to produce agricultural staples for the European market which took form in various parts of Latin America, the West Indies, and the American South succeeded, spread, and came to be called the plantation. In the American South this institution—which must be distinguished from settlements called by the same name in New England—came by 1860 to occupy favorable lands from Maryland to eastern Texas or wherever it could get its staples down to the ocean at low cost. From the West Indies it was transplanted to South Carolina and to Louisiana, but in Virginia and Maryland it began an independent development as profit from the cultivation of tobacco began to be realized.

The reduction of vast forests and the cultivation of land almost free for the taking in the American Southeast required a great output of labor, beyond the ability of European families such as there were, to supply. Recourse was first had to white indentured labor from Europe and later to Negro slaves from Africa. Thus what we have to observe getting under way in the very early days of this area are a number of small single-purpose enterprises each mobilizing a varying number of nondescript people to act together to clear away the trees and to produce a crop for which there promises to be a market and a profit. The single plantation is a loose collectivity somewhere out there on the moving frontier proximate to a navigable stream or river and later to a dirt road or railroad. Like every crescive institution anywhere, it begins with collective activity and a purpose which dominates the program of its leader or planter, but, as Everett Hughes has taught us, there is always some unfinished business.[8] From one generation to the next, there is always the problem of getting and controlling labor for ends outside the interests and wishes of those who are controlled. It was when these activities assumed a structure and became routine to the extent that plans for the future had to be made that the plantation as an institution can be said to have been accomplished. As it adapted its members to its own purpose and as people began to depend upon it, it became part of the accepted and natural order of things. Its head man, the planter, gained in practical economic and political importance as over against the ordinary trader and farmer, a fact sensed by himself and by the rest of the people. A family dynasty could be established as the son of the planter followed in the manner of the father. As a cross between farmers and knights, planters pursued a sort of military agriculture for which they thought it necessary to mold those who worked for them in the fields into good slaves or sharecroppers. The church and its religion fell into line to teach servants that they not only had to but should obey their masters. Thus the authority of the plantation came naturally to divide men into subordinates and superordinates as the institution moved along the southern frontier from Maryland to eastern Texas.

The plantation institution appeared in other parts of the New World but what is of major importance about the southern plantation is that it was the first frontier-created institution to take root and survive in this particular environment to overshadow those transplanted, however much modified, from abroad. In New England the transplanted church was to assume an unchallenged authority in relation to other institutions, which continued until the days of Channing and Emerson and even much later. In the South, however, the key role was to be played by a new institution not then known to Britain nor to any other part of continental North America. The plantation was not a transplanted English manor; it produced a specialized product to sell and not a variety of goods to be consumed locally. It established itself here before any other economic, political, administrative, educational, or religious institution became strong enough to flourish or even to survive. It was the mother factor in southern society, and this is why it is so important to understand its essential character and nature if we are to understand the system it built around itself.

V

Most Southerners have never physically lived within the bounds of a plantation estate, but I suggest that all properly designated as Southerners have lived within a "plantation system." There are and have been many other societies around the world in which the plantation isolate has been present, but in my reading of the literature I have not encountered any other society in which the expression "plantation system" has been so consistently and persistently used in both popular and academic circles as in the South. Hawaii has what might be called a system of plantations, but not, in the sense in which we understand the expression, a plantation system. In the South it is not an institution appearing on the periphery of another and older society as in Malaya and in the East Indies. On the contrary, it centered and formed whatever was distinctive about the South itself. In Brazil and elsewhere in Latin America the crown, the church, and the plantation seem to have competed for ultimate control of the social order.[9] In the South there was little else to contest its control. The king was far away and little concerned to claim and protect all his subjects. There was no powerful church with a traditionally recognized concern for souls.[10] About all that was left on this turbulent, disorderly southern frontier in the wilderness to interpose restraint in the relations between master and man was the ruth or aidôs of the master, those qualities of human nature which come into play when a man is almost totally free from any kind of institutional compulsion. Slaves were property, and a man can do what he will with his own unless inhibited by his own property interest or by some sentiment within himself.

But the lawless master and planter established law on his own plantation and increasingly engaged in various sorts of cooperation with neighboring despotisms as the frontier passed on and time brought common problems requiring common action. There was, for example, the problem of transporting and marketing the staple. Beyond the development of an economic order a moral order of mutual expectations and obligations, rights and duties, began to take form and to build themselves into a system of interrelated institutions the better to insure the institution's continuity and survival. The plantation system was in fact a plantation *survival* system intended to naturalize and legitimate the institution which stood at its center. Like the solar system with the sun at its center warming and holding its satellite planets in their several courses around it, the plantation came to center a system of attending and interacting institutions which it warmed and which in turn was warmed by them. The plantation system was not a series of disconnected institutions but an organism adapted to the situation in which people lived and carried on a common life. There were institutional forces of cohesion which bound them together and about which they later came to be conscious. They called this institutional complex the South.

In no kind of system, social or otherwise, can any single element be understood or be what it is apart from all the other elements or components of that system. The southern church and its religion was a part of the plantation system and so were other institutions such as the family, the school, the county and the state. Control of the system was exercised by consensus among a relatively small planter establishment.[11]

VI

The migration of Europeans and their settlement in that part of North America which became the South initially was predominantly masculine. As white women were imported and as the sexes evened out, white family life stabilized along income and class lines. Modeled after the European family it nevertheless underwent significant modifications as it adapted to frontier conditions. It underwent further modification as some men became *white* men vis-à-vis Indians and Negroes. It underwent further modification as some men became agricultural enterpreneurs, that is, planters, and masters not only of their white servants and black slaves but also of their families. From the beginning the planter families on their estates were highly isolated.[12] A planter in John Pendleton Kennedy's novel *Swallow Barn* voiced his opposition to a measure then before the legislature to improve the state's roads by declaring that "the home material of Virginia was never so good as when her roads were at their worst."

Ordinarily in the case of the small family farm the enterprise is bent toward the organization and requirements of the family, and this has been true in the South,[13] but in the case of the large estate the family ordinarily bends toward the organization and requirements of the enterprise. In Virginia the life of the planter family was geared to tobacco, in South Carolina and Mississippi to cotton; during the time of cultivation and harvesting wives and children took second place. But because there was no great amount of economic dependence upon other plantations producing the same staple in the same general area, such as has characterized neighboring small farms elsewhere, there was no extensive elaboration of local divisions of labor, and consequently there were few towns such as normally are required to integrate a variety of local economic activities. But perhaps for this very reason white families, and particularly planter families, characteristically were united by the interweaving by marriage and other social ties into extensive kinship clans whose members often held membership in the same church. A range of between perhaps a half to a dozen differently surnamed families constituted a local community familism whose members were almost as much at home in the homes of each other as they were in their own homes. Incidentally, southern kinship has never been systematically investigated.

A stable social order is stable because, for one important thing, its constituent families can be counted upon to conserve the old and the traditional. In the course of its development every new

movement looking toward the institutionalization of new purposes and goals finds itself in opposition to the tradition-bearing
family. The traditional family represents the *mores,* and the
emerging institution is always more or less at war with them. In
that process of "creative destruction" of which Joseph Schumpeter writes,[14] the family must be restructured to the point
where it supports, rather than opposes, the organization and aims
of the new institution. As a matter of fact, the "family" of the
slave members of the prewar southern plantation might almost
be said to have been the plantation itself somewhat in the sense
of the *familia rustica* in Roman society. The slave father was not
the principal breadwinner; it was rather the planter who was
looked to for material support as well as for discipline.[15] In the
course of time what Frazier called the "natural" family organized mainly around the Negro mother appeared.[16] Eventually
the plantation obtained its new members by birth within rather
than by recruitment from without. The plantation then came to
form part of the habits and customs of the family to be transmitted to succeeding generations especially by the mother.

VII

All social life is, of course, education, but not every society
provides that institutionalized form of communication and transmission which we call schools. The absence as well as the presence of formal education in schools in the social strata of a society
tells something about the way such institutions function in the
system. Those who labored in plantation fields were educated in
the process of becoming what they were and had to be, but it
was a bookless education without schools, the original and most
effective expression of vocational guidance. There probably is a
vocational aspect in the educational process of every society. In
plantation society it has been a very prominent aspect. In early
white indentured servitude, an outgrowth of English apprenticeship, there was a conscious vocational rationalization later expressed in the claim that the plantation itself was the proper
school for servants and slaves.

Perhaps men generally are more largely educated by what
they have to do to make a living than they are by their schools;
in stable, isolated societies there is relatively little need for formal

education. But when the society is becoming part of a larger world where there is change and movement, more formal education becomes necessary. For those whose business it was to plan and market the crop it was necessary to keep up with the market and to this end some amount of literacy was essential, but this was not necessarily obtained through formal schooling.[17] Before the War Between the States the percentage of literacy among slaveholders appeared much greater than among non-slaveholders.[18] A degree of literacy and education gained through informal as well as formal channels in order to make needed adjustments and decisions characterized Negro as well as white operators and landowners. This has continued to be the case.[19]

Well-to-do planters along the seaboard might employ tutors at home and then send their sons to European universities to acquire a certain amount of classical intellectual fodder beyond the practical requirements of plantation administration, but lesser members of this class in the interior patronized academies and agitated for state universities nearer them. The prestige colleges and universities of New England were private institutions, but in the South they became state universities established by planter members of the legislatures for their sons. Thus "college life became an important feature of the Old South," wrote H. C. Nixon, "especially of plantation society. . . . The slavocracy was more interested in higher education for the few than in effective secondary education for the many. . . . From the same background most of the colleges of the South have received a strong religious heritage, chiefly Protestant, and a respect for the form and organization of religion, though not necessarily for independent religious thought." [20] The church affiliated colleges of the South were much more democratically oriented than the state universities but they too operated under the shadow of the plantation. The need for military academies and colleges to support a racial hierarchy with its large strata of unfree agricultural workers at its base should be apparent.

VIII

Many of the patriotic county historians of the South described the county of which they wrote as one of "great plantations." Of course, there are counties in which plantations were or are not

physically present and which were characterized by their relative independency, such as "the independent republic of Horry"
County in South Carolina and "the free state of Jones" County
in Mississippi which, tradition says, seceded from Mississippi during the War Between the States. But the county as a primary
social as well as governmental unit in the South undoubtedly
developed as part of the plantation system. Local administrative
units originally called baronies in Maryland and elsewhere,
parishes in Louisiana and occasionally in Florida, hundreds,
shires, or cities in Virginia, eventually settled for the form if not
the name of county. River and road transportational development in relation to land acquisition and the marketing of the
staple in the tidewater South was the basis of the organization
of the county.[21] There might be something in the nature of formal subdivisions of the county such as the "beat" in Mississippi,
but in fact the county began as a sort of local organization of
plantations which were the actual subdivisions. The township as
a functional unit was a Reconstruction imposition.

The county, over much of the southern territory, became a
creature of tradition and stained itself indelibly upon the form
of society.[22] Often it was ruled by a coterie of county families
whose members left office only to be replaced by other members
of the clan.[23] They praised themselves for their unselfish devotion to public service. In the later plantation South, Indian enemies were supplanted by an inner enemy, the unfree laborers
of the estates against whom defense was even more imperative.
That social type, more or less peculiar to the system, the county
sheriff, continues his traditional role to this day as recent events
testify. Early county sheriffs as well as other officers of the law
often found it convenient to serve writs and warrants on Sundays
when it was easier to find delinquents attending parish churches.
Following the model of the ideal planter the sheriff and his depu-
ties often rode horseback to symbolize their connection with the
aristocracy. In 1711 Lancaster County, Virginia, ordered that
freedmen and laborers be prevented from keeping horses and
breeding mares and limited their ownership to persons who
owned or rented a certain amount of property.[24] The sheriff
could and did use "landlord" law and the organization of the
plantation after as well as before the War Between the States to
make arrests (occasionally the planter or overseer did this for

him) but he might well be careful not to make arrests during the cotton-picking season. He was likely to be well paid for his services, especially in the Black Belt counties. In "Imperial Bolivar" County, Mississippi, in the 1930s he had a net income of forty thousand dollars, ten times the salary of the governor of the state.[25]

That same establishment which the sheriff served could be confident that the courts could be relied upon to maintain its authority and protect its interests in both legal and extralegal ways.[26] Planter control of state government was not always so complete as was their control over county government in predominantly plantation areas, but it was strong enough to effect the seccession of eleven states by the middle of the last century. And it is not without significance that of the first twelve presidents of the United States eight were members of the planter class.

IX

In a developing social system where intermarriage within class and race limitations linked families at various points with other institutions in the larger society, giving the plantation points of reference with these other institutions, it was inevitable and even necessary that the church and whatever brand of doctrine it offered should find a place and a function. From diverse backgrounds and later organizational differentiations, Protestants and Catholics, as well as Jews articulated into the system and served it. The Protestant denominations were sharply competitive with each other, white denominations with each other and Negro denominations with each other, and all with the Catholic "enemy." Almost every minister and priest was a religious politician. They fought minor battles with each other, but planters, lesser farmers, poor whites, factors, ministers, priests, and laymen united in an acceptance of the legitimacy of the system and of the values it embodied. Even the old-time Negro preacher was an integral and useful part of the system, especially in the postwar period. Generally all supported it in the only way they could support it, if their churches hoped to survive, by seeking to transfer attention from the ills of this world to salvation in the next, by blessing the pious allegiance of ordinary people, by defining the "good man" whose superior achievement in reconciling religion and common practice singled him out for special praise, by urging obedience to the caesars of the day and patience in the face of poverty, trial, and tribulation. A faith was harnessed to canonize the system and to brand as atheistic any threat of change in it. That faith was inevitable and deterministic; denominational membership was, of course, optional. All church members were at the same time members of the community and as such were unable to compartmentalize their religious beliefs and practices from the interests and attitudes they held as members of other institutions.

Something special should be said about the Negro church and its religion in the system, but I have not found in the literature any significantly insightful or satisfying treatment of the subject although much has been written about it. So far as I know no fundamental point of view has informed this literature. But I suggest that if there is a line to be drawn, however lightly, between the ethos of various groups in the plantation South with regard to religious experience and orientation it will not be drawn between Protestant denominations or even between Protestant and Catholic but between white and black. The change-oriented black Protestantism and the continuity-oriented white Protestantism and Catholicism defined each other within the *same* system; the system supplied a basis for the kind of variation from it taken by its black segment. One has to look for this kind of variation not in the form or creed of Negro churches, but in its mood and spirit, in its philosophy of life generally. This is a difficult thing to get at and to state. I expect it has been there since the black man came in chains to these shores, but it is especially prominent today in black militancy.

Students of the black man in Africa have called attention to the role of the Christian missions there as an institution around which detribalized and lost natives often reestablished themselves into something like another tribe of Christian brothers and sisters. The missionaries had relatively little success among tightly organized tribal blacks. In America, where all imported blacks were, in the nature of the case, detribalized and disorganized, it is not surprising that the church, an "invisible institution" within the visibly white controlled and plantation connected church,[27] became for them the center of reorganization. It was in this institution that Negro slaves from diverse African tribal backgrounds began to find some meaning for their existence, and it was this institution that enlisted their deepest loyalties. Here a man might find and maintain a conception of himself as one of dignity and one which gave him a sense of individual worth.

Only four years after the coming of the first Negroes in 1619 there were black church members in the Jamestown settlement in Virginia,[28] but the separate "invisible church" took shape in the praise-house and the shout on individual seaboard plantations. Conversion to the religious forms of the white man spread under the influence of Baptist and Methodist preachers who presented Christianity to the blacks in a simple, emotional appeal which, combined with their own special life experience, developed into religious theater and came to characterize the folk-culture of Negroes generally. One interesting and important product of this culture was the spiritual and another was the folk-sermon which, so far as I know, was unique to the Negro Protestant South. James Weldon Johnson attempted to reproduce several of these sermons in verse.[29] Many of them, such as "The Valley of Dry Bones," were repeated and passed along like the spirituals with modifications from one community to another. They were not created *for* the people by the preacher; they were created *by* the people and belonged to the congregation to be delivered by the preacher on demand or by special invitation.

But perhaps precisely because of the appearance of the spiritual, the folk-sermon, the strong emphasis upon heaven rather than hell, and other manifestations of quaint differences from the usual white religious expression, the Negro church and its religion has been suspect by whites almost from the beginning. Christianity is the religion of the white man who has been embarrassed by its injunction to go out and preach the Gospel to the heathen of all the world. But were the heathen human and rational enough to accept it? The question arose in connection with the American Indian and the African Negro and has never really been satisfactorily settled. How can we whites, the guardians of pure Christianity, be sure that the conversion is genuine? We may not resort to the Inquisition as did the Spaniards with respect to the Jews and the Moors, but we have our doubts and freely express them in joke and ridicule.[30] Or we may champion the excellence of Negro Christianity with somewhat more fervor than is justified.

Attention is focused upon the differences between white and black religious behavior in both Protestantism and Catholicism when the truly significant thing is, perhaps, the remarkable extent to which the religion of the Negro in America has recapitulated the Christian cycle as it has turned many times before and continues, in the storefront churches of the cities, for example, to start all over again. For Christianity is *par excellence* the religion of the outcast and the defeated. In Rome it was taken up by the slaves, the slum-dwellers, and the poor who were especially blessed. The religion of the Negro in America developed under much the same conditions as primitive Christianity itself.[31] It came to segregate itself into an independent church among the free Negroes of northern cities before the War Between the States. After emancipation independent churches in the South absorbed the "invisible church" of plantation society and became the chief repositories of the traditions and aspirations of the black masses.

I think it is well-nigh impossible really to understand the development of the Negro church and its religion in the South as a counter to the white church and its religion without reference to the plantation and its system both before and after emancipation. The imagery and realities of the plantation lived on; God figured as a Great Planter in much the same way, perhaps, as he figured as a Great Lord in Britain from the time of the Roman missionaries onward. Allison Davis noted that "the analogy between the white landlord and the partriarchal Old Testament God was frequently used by rural ministers. . . . Following a prayer an officer in one church said that when each man came up for his reward in the after-life, he would receive just what he merited, adding, 'Ef you worked hard, you know you due yo' pay, but if you ain't, you know dere ain't no reward for you. Ain't no use goin' tuh de office unless you done made yo' crop.'"[32]

X

By 1830 the southern states had become, as John C. Calhoun noted, "an aggregate . . . of communities, not of individuals. Every plantation is a little community, . . . These small communities aggregated make the State in all." [33] Each plantation had its own notions of what was right and wrong; its own conception of the proper roles of its different characters; its own "little tradition," each varying a little from that of every other. A certain standardizing process was initiated when the student sons of planters gathered together, talked, and debated at the state colleges and universities, but probably much more important was the development of orthogenetic plantation capital cities [34] such as Williamsburg, Charleston, Savannah, Mobile, and New Orleans. Planters and people from the provinces generally went back and forth between these sacred cities and their local neighborhoods as in other great religious cultures men made periodic pilgrimages to Mecca, Lhasa, Rome, or some other holy city. In these cities the little traditions of individual plantations were reshaped and articulated by poets, novelists, theologians, ministers, scholars, and editors into a "great tradition" which came to be generally accepted all over the South and which gave Southerners their stock clichés, platitudes, and rationalizations. The tobacco, cotton, and sugar factors in these cities also made planters and farmers more aware of their common economic interests. The individual plantations fed their experiences, beliefs, problems, and lore to the wise men and the prophets of the capitals; these experiences and this lore came back in standardized form as ideology and conviction. The plantation system was achieving a culture for the South which was to differentiate it from other regions of the United States and perhaps of the world. While a social system is not always bound to a particular territory or geographical space, the fact that the plantation system was spatially defined did have a decisive influence upon its formation and maintenance. The plantation system and the South became almost synonymous expressions, the land of God corresponding to the land of his true worshipers.

A common culture arose in and from this system, but social scientists have defined culture in many different ways. Here it may be suggested that a culture is a system of conventional understandings general enough to influence everyone included within it. The number of people included within it may be small or large; the major cultures of the world include large numbers of people but with subcultural deviations. Millions of people have grown up within the culture or subculture of the South and have known no other, or very little of any other. Here an expression of the Christian religion has, perhaps more than any other force, operated to transform a heterogeneous aggregate into a homogeneous society binding together its segments and separate institutions and to build and preserve the morale of the people.[35] It has helped the system take over the children of all classes, keep them in their proper stations, enforce conformity to old custom, and preserve the order of power relations.

At the level of culture, life carries conviction and the deep assumption shared with all others in the community that the world will go on substantially in the same manner as it has so far, that what is accepted as valid up to now will continue to be valid. In the light of today's rapid change and uncertainty to read diaries and other documents written in the old Plantation South is almost to have one's breath taken away by the sense of certainty, the assurance that the then order of things would continue until the Day of Judgment. But this structure of shared assumptions tends to get lost in written rendition or even in verbalization. There was no doubt. All others will agree with us and with all that is personal to us and at our own valuation. One speaks with no reservations. To all orthodox statements there could be but one reply, "of course." In a culture so conceived the speech of the naïve one itself becomes behavior, in the elementary sense of that term, rather than explanation.

The culture of a society such as that of the Old South continuing into the New is to be found in the truths which are held to be self-evident, truths that hardly need to be examined and explained, truths held by a people innocent of their own character but sure of themselves. A poet might write of the ordinary people of the South, old and new, very much as Monk Gibbon wrote of French peasants:

> Those going home at dusk
>   Along the lane,
> After the day's warm work,
>   Do not complain.
>
> Were you to say to them,
>   "What does it mean?
> What is it all about,
>   This troubled dream?"

They would not understand,
    They'd go their way,
Or, if they spoke at all,
    They'd surely say:

"Dawn is the time to rise,
    Days are to earn
Bread and the midday rest,
    Dust to return;

"To be content, to pray,
    To hear songs sung
Or to make wayside love,
    If one is young.

"All from the good God comes,
    All then is good;
Sorrow is known to Him,
    And understood."

One who has questioned all,
    And was not wise,
Might be ashamed to meet
    Their quiet eyes.

All is so clear to them.
    All is so plain;
Those who go home at dusk,
    Along the lane.[36]

If naïveté be the subjective aspect of culture then we have in the endless number of stories and items which have appeared in newspapers, pamphlets, journals, and books for over two hundred years a vast literature exhibiting southern religiosity. The quickest way to get a few of these items would be to consult the Americana sections in each issue of *The American Mercury* during the days when editor H. L. Mencken was printing them in order to ridicule *Boobus Americanus* as he called us. It is not necessary to share his purpose to appreciate the cultural significance of this material. Here are a few of the items:

From Mississippi it was reported that "the Rev. William McCarty, now 96 years old, was called upon two weeks ago to preach at the funeral of a notorious sinner, a relative of Mrs. Levy Laird. The Reverend Mr. McCarty preached frankly on the sins of the deceased man and, instead of assuring the mourners that he was going to Heaven, boldly stated that he would go to a much hotter place. He exhorted the younger people to live righteously lest they go there too. The stuff that the Reverend Mr. McCarty was putting on her dead relative grew too hot for Mrs. Laird. She reached out and snatched at the preacher. When he ducked, she pursued him, and finally was successful in tearing most of his clothes, smashing his hat, and scratching him up so viciously that he had to see a physician. He had Mrs. Laird arrested. She was fined and sentenced to a term in the workhouse for disturbing public worship." [37]

The naïve person assumes that what he is naïve about, that is, what he takes for granted, is taken for granted by everyone else who is normal and sane. Thus from Tennessee: "A lot of bright-colored bathing suits, decks of cards and novels were missing from Madisonville homes today. They were burned in front of the Baptist church yesterday following a baptismal service in which thirty-five were baptised. The Reverend W. A. Carroll, who conducted a three-week revival, asked those in attendance to bring their bathing suits, cards and cheap novels. While 'I'll Never Turn Back' was being sung the Reverend Caroll set fire to them." [38]

It is not what United States Senator Cameron Morrison of North Carolina expressly says that is significant in the following but what, as one reads between the lines, he regards as obviously just about what any North Carolinian would expect of a man in public office: "I got to be Governor and lived in the executive mansion for four years, and while I was there God gave me a good, noble woman for my wife. She has some money. She, too, had seen much service and as a nurse had ministered to suffering humanity. We have retired to our farm and there she fights the devil through the Presbyterian church, and whatever money is left and I get hold of I use to fight the devil through the Democratic party. And I tell her they're about the same anyway." [39]

From Danville, Virginia, it was reported that "the Rev. McKendrie Long, who is conducting revivals here, warned tobacco chewers about their chances of salvation. They may all go to Heaven, he said, but 'they will have to go to Hell to expectorate, as the Lord does not allow spitting on the streets of gold.' " [40]

It is not so much what people say but what they are taking for granted when they say what they say that exhibits the culture of the society in which they live. The sensitive observer, especially one who ventures into the South from outside, today senses something different, maybe something special, something pervasive, something old and tenacious in the *pietas* of southern society. It is the Old South continuing on into the New.

XI

I have sought to probe the historical and cultural roots of the southern church and its religion the better to understand some of my own experiences and of many others like me. It appears that southern society, like societies generally, is of a piece, an entanglement of institutions of which the church was and is one of the most important. Along with the family, the school or college, and governmental units it was a satellite of the plantation institution and functioned effectively within the plantation system. The institution which centered the system utilized unfree or semifree labor and, to the extent it continues to linger on, its labor practices still are suspect. As an economic institution it depended upon a national and even international market for its staples, a market which underwent and continues to undergo change from time to time as supply, demand, competition, substitutes, fashion, and machine methods change or are introduced. Today we are seeing the plantation disappear or erode as cities grow and southern people, black and white, move into them, as sharecropping and tenancy are eliminated as slavery was before them, and as mechanization proceeds apace. Originally an institution of the frontier, the plantation was bound to change and at last disappear as the frontier moved on and new forces gathered in its wake. That it continued to function as the center of a system in one form or another for over two hundred years, surviving even a devastating civil war, is the remarkable fact, but even over this period of time it has not been a completely stable and unvarying center. It is as though in the solar system the sun dimmed or blacked out leaving its planet satellites to move out of their age-old orbits. The plantation no longer centers a system of satellite institutions; since the turn of the century and especially since World War I, each institution is moving out of old orbits into new directions. Kinship and family life, probably the most stable element in every social structure, are undergoing modification as land changes hands and migration turns cityward. The race of plantation laborers, formerly subordinated, is now winning its civil rights, and institutions, especially schools, are being racially integrated. The school is no longer "our school"; it belongs to the impersonal state. In an age of rapid transportation and communication local town and county governmental units find themselves in trouble, administratively and financially; planters have lost or are losing control to "courthouse gangs" and to poorer white and black voters and officeholders. The bell in the country church steeple may still be there; but all too often it no longer summons the families of the neighborhood to worship; the church may remain as merely a site for the annual homecoming of the widely scattered family and clan members. We may expect Protestant and Catholic church tribalism, white and black, to continue to offer congregational fellowship along social class and economic level of living lines and continue the struggle to conserve whatever principles of certainty the fathers found good. Even here, however, change is evident as new sects arise, as new class lines form, and as the urban church turns away from the doctrines and practices of its rural heritage. The southern church is at least altering its direction as the forces and vital needs that put it in the system in the first place are no longer functional.

One thinks of the prophetic line of W. B. Yeats, "Things fall apart; the centre cannot hold." Of course, the social as well as the geographical South is still here and will be here for a long time to come; there is always continuity as well as change. But, like a fortified city, its walls are down and its institutions stand exposed to criticism, rational and otherwise. Southern geocentrism will not want to admit it, but the plantation as the center of a social system developed no great civilization. It was a moral and intellectual failure. In time the South will get another system perhaps this time centered around its evolving constellation of cities and possibly just as full of piety and illusion as the old one, but which may bring its institutions into some greater degree of cohesion again. Some will call the movement toward a new and different system progress and be led to speak of another and newer New South promising a higher civilization while others will look back nostalgically to a lost Golden Age. The various expressions of the southern church and its religion will debate the problems presented by continuity versus change because it will be called upon to sustain and help integrate whatever system of society may be in store for us. It continues to be important to experience, to observe, to read the books and the daily newspapers, and to try to understand.

Notes

Introduction

1. Henri Baudet, *Paradise on Earth*, New Haven: Yale University Press, 1965, p. 58.

2. See Arthur S. Link (ed.), *Writing Southern History*, Baton Rouge: Louisiana State University Press, 1965.

3. F. Delaisi, *Les Deux Europes: Europe Industrielle et Europe Agricole*, Paris, 1929. Ch. X.

4. Walter Prescott Webb, *The Great Frontier*, Boston: Houghton Mifflin Co., 1952.

5. *Errand Into the Wilderness*, Cambridge, Mass.: The Belknap Press of the Harvard University Press, 1956, p. 101.

6. "An upper class is institutional in its very essence, since it is control of institutions that makes it an upper class, and men can hardly keep this control except as they put their heart into it." C. H. Cooley, *Social Organization*, New York: Charles Scribner's Sons, 1916. p. 140.

7. Edward P. Cheyney, "Some English Conditions Surrounding the Settlement of Virginia," *American Historical Review*, XXII (April, 1907), 507–528.

8. *The Voyages of the Cabots*, London: The Argonaut Press, 1929. Chs. VII–VIII. The French referred to such settlements as "habitations" and in some of their encyclopedias and dictionaries listed plantations "as they are called by the English." The Dutch spoke of "Volk-planting."

9. A. J. Toynbee, *A Study of History*, London: Oxford University Press, 1934–35. II, 465–466; William C. McLeod, *The American Indian Frontier*, New York: A. A. Knopf, 1928. p. 153.

10. Francis Bacon, *Essays*, London: Oxford University Press, H. Milford, 1940 edition. pp. 140–144. Planted woodlands or tree crops, such as rubber, are often known as plantations down to the present day. " . . . the plantation today is closer to certain forms of forestry than it is to grain crops or roots. One may think of it with advantage as intensive forestry conducted in regions of hitherto sparce population." C. R. Fay, "Plantation Economy," *The Economic Journal*, XLVI (December, 1936), 640–644.

11. Letter to John Locke in *South Carolina Historical Collections*, V (May 28, 1973), p. 423.

12. Alexander Brown, *The Genesis of the United States*, Boston: Houghton Mifflin and Company, 1897. 2 vols.

13. A. P. White, *The Colonizing Activities of the English Puritans*, New Haven: Yale University Press, 1914.

14. *Old Virginia and Her Neighbors*, Boston: Houghton Mifflin Co., 1898. I. Ch. V.

15. W. K. Hancock has classified frontiers according to the types of people leading the expansion: planters, traders, settlers, missionaries, etc. *Argument of Empire*, New York: Penguin Special, 1943. Ch. VII, "Moving Frontiers." The traders in certain English factories in India expanded into adjacent territory later called "presidencies." Such ex-territoriality in the East generally was intended to control the trade of an area against the competition of other nationals

rather than to organize and control production. Planters, on the contrary, looked to the control of production and of the labor required for production.

16. Frederick J. Teggart, *The Processes of History*, New Haven: Yale University Press, 1918. Ch. II. See also Franz Oppenheimer, *The State*, New York: Vanguard Press, 1914. *passim.*

17. An eighteenth century writer noted: "Every new discovery, every new plantation, every new branch of trade furnisheth some new thing, some rarity in nature, some specific in physic for the relief of a distempered world, which lay hid till navigation carried us to America." *Collection of Voyages and Travels from the Earl of Oxford*, Printed for Thomas Osborne, London, 1745–47. Introductory Discourse, p. 1.

18. "Those who raised tobacco and Indian corn are called planters, and those who cultivate small grain, farmers." Issac Weld, *Travels Through the States of North America*, London: John Stockdale, 1807, p. 156. After he shifted from tobacco to wheat on most of his acres, George Washington preferred to style himself a farmer. In a letter written in 1799 he stated ". . . I shall never turn Planter thereon." John C. Fitzpatrick (ed.), *Writings of George Washington*, Washington: U. S. Gov. Printing Office XXXVIII, 338. William Tatham, *Communications Concerning the Agriculture and Commerce of the United States of America*, London, 1800, p. 46, makes a similiar distinction.

19. "By this term we understand an agricultural process the continued production of which rests not on the biological nature of the plant but on the institutional atmosphere in which it is grown. The term may well be applied to annuals grown in one-crop regions where the opportunity to switch from the prevailing crop to alternate crops is entirely absent, or at least remote." E. W. Zimmerman, *World Resources and Industries*, New York: Harpers, 1951, p. 386. Cotton, too, was and is an annual but planned seasonally and from year to year and deeply ingrained in the habits and prospects of its cultivators as a perennial crop might be. See Rupert Vance, *Human Factors in Cotton Culture*, Chapel Hill: University of North Carolina Press, 1929. So deeply may the habit system attending an institutional perennial go that a shift to another crop might require cultivators from another ethnic background.

20. In the Records of the Virginia Company it is recorded, "The Collony being thus weake and the Treasury utterly exhaust, Itt pleased divers Lords, Knights, gentlement and Cittizens (greived to see this great Action fall to Nothinge) to take the matter a new in hand and at their private charges (joyninge themselves into societies) to set upp divers particularr Plantacions." *Records of the Virginia Company* (1906), I, 350.

21. L. D. Scisco, "The Plantation Type of Colony," *American Historical Review*, VIII (January, 1903), 260–270.

22. "Whether in the general or in the 'particular' . . . the vesting of jurisdiction was a feature; and this may explain the extension of the word *plantation*." U. B. Phillips, *Life and Labor in the Old South*, Boston: Little, Brown and Company, 1929, pp. 21–22.

23. "Most American farmers doubtless looked upon the hired man as normal and took him as a matter of course. But he was a highly specialized development; probably nothing like him ever existed before and may never exist again." T. N. Carver, *Readings in Rural Economics*, Boston: Ginn and Company, 1916. p. 547. The hired man was closely associated with the farm family, but never completely a member of it. He added to the burden of the farm wife and by his presence intruded on the privacy and freedom of the home. He thus prevented the farm family from qualifying as a primary group in the sense in which Ellsworth Faris conceived it. "The Primary Group: Essence and Acci-

dent," *The Nature of Human Nature*, New York: McGraw-Hill Book Company, Ch. IV. As an outsider the hired man served as a link with the larger number of human utilities of another class and color on the plantations further south who were formally much more remote from the proprietary family.

24. Newell L. Sims, *The Rural Community: Ancient and Modern*, New York: Charles Scribner's Sons, 1921, pp. 120–121.

25. The term "squatter" appeared first in Congressional Debates on February 14, 1806. *Annals of Congress*, 1805–1806, p. 409.

26. See Twelve Southerners, *I'll Take My Stand: The South and the Agrarian Tradition*, New York: Harper and Brothers, 1930.

27. It did so in colonial Brazil. See Gilberto Freyre, *The Masters and the Slaves*, New York: A. A. Knopf, 1946, p. xxxvi.

28. B. Malinowski, *Methods of Study of Culture Contact in Africa*. Memorandum XV, International Institute of African Languages and Cultures, 1938, p. xvii. *Analysis of B. Malinowski's Sociological Theories*, New York: Oxford University Press, 1949, pp. 11–13.

29. Lawrence Goodwin, *The South Central States*, Time-Life Library of the Americas. New York: Time, Inc., 1967. pp. 75–98; Joe Franz and Julian Choate, *The American Cowboy: Myth and Reality*, Norman, Oklahoma: Oklahoma University Press, 1951. Goodwin points out that more often than not the original cowboy of the Plains was an ex-Confederate soldier.

30. *The Great Plains*, Boston: Ginn and Company, 1931. p. 8.

31. "Alteration of the Argentine Pampa in the Colonial Period," Berkeley: University of California *Publications in Geography*, II (September 27, 1927), p. 317.

32. Carey McWilliams, *Factories in the Field*, Boston: Little, Brown and Company, 1939; P. S. Taylor and Tom Vasey, "Historical Background of California Farm Labor," *Rural Sociology*, I (September, 1936), 281–295.

33. See "The Planter as Expert in Matters of Race," State v. Asa Jacobs, 51 *North Carolina Reports* (1859), 282–286, in Edgar Thompson and Everett Hughes, *Race*, Glencoe, Ill.: The Free Press, 1958. pp. 517–519.

34. Ken Nakazawa, "Horse Bandits and Opium," *Forum*, LXXV (April, 1926), 576–581. Also Owen Lattimore, *Manchuria: Cradle of Conflict*, New York: The Macmillan Company, 1932. pp. 191–196.

35. Marvin Harris, *Patterns of Race in the Americas*, New York: Walker, 1964. p. 84.

36. Clive Day, *The Policy and Administration of the Dutch in Java*, New York: The Macmillan Company, 1904, *passim*.

37. J. H. Boeke, *The Evolution of the Netherlands Indies Economy*, New York: Netherlands and Netherlands Indies Council, Institute of Pacific Relations, 1946.

38. Robert Redfield, *The Primitive World and Its Transformation*, Ithaca, New York: Cornell University Press, 1953. p. 45.

39. "Haciendas and Plantations in Middle America and the Antilles," *Social and Economic Studies*, Mona, Jamaica: University College of the West Indies, VI (September, 1957), 380–412.

40. *Ibid.*, p. 380. See also Watt Stewart, *Chinese Bondage in Peru*, Durham, N.C.: Duke University Press, 1951.

41. Andrew W. Lind, *An Island Community: Ecological Succession in Hawaii*, Chicago: University of Chicago Press, 1938; Shannon McCune, "Sequence of Plantation Agriculture in Ceylon," *Economic Geography*, XXV (June, 1949), 226–235.

42. See William C. McLeod, *op. cit.*, p. 383 and *passim*.

43. Sidney Bradshaw Fay, "The Hohenzollern Household and Administration in the Sixteenth Century," *Smith College Studies in History*, II (October, 1916), 6–19.

44. The overseer on Southern plantations, and his counterpart elsewhere, was an index of the status "planter" of the owner; the owner was not assured of this status if he did not have an overseer. The overseer was something like a prime minister. His ministry might be of long or short duration for he served at the pleasure of the planter. Each ministry was an epoch; it was remembered for the events that occurred during it and thus was used to locate happenings in time. In the literature on the overseer, one of the best sources is J. S. Bassett, *The Southern Plantation Overseer as Revealed in His Letters.* Northampton: Smith College Publications, 1925. In a larger sense, the customs of the plantation system became the South's unwritten constitution.

45. *Slavery as an Industrial System*, The Hague: Martinus Nijhoff, 1910. *passim.*

46. Annie Weston Whitney, "American Negro Dialects," *The Independent*, LIII (August, 1901), 22–29.

1. Mines and Plantations and the Movements of Peoples

1. *North America*, p. 249.

2. *The Greek Commonwealth* (Oxford, 1922, 3d ed. rev.) p. 400.

3. *Ibid.*, p. 401.

4. The skeletal structure of the world community results from an interaction between the fixed distribution of mineral resources, especially iron, copper, and the mineral fuels (coal and petroleum), and the natural highways of cheap transportation such as oceans, seas, and lakes. The active agent in this interaction is man, and out of it are differentiated two types of cities—industrial and commercial. The extent of the interaction is, of course, modified by natural barriers such as climate and artificial barriers such as tariffs. Agriculture is not included in this "skeleton" even though historically it has often led in the spatial extension of division of labor and even though it furnishes the indispensable food resource. Nevertheless, in the present community, agriculture is timed to the exchange and the blast furnace, and if the organized community for any reason breaks down, agriculture more or less easily reverts to a self-sufficient state. On the other hand, agriculture today is something that is steadily being brought into an integrated relationship with the rest of the community, a relationship which assigns it space and classifies it into divisions of labor. For these reasons agriculture is conceived as being organized around the skeletal structure but is not itself a part of the skeleton.

5. *An Introduction to Economic Geography*, I, 269.

6. *Ibid.*, pp. 269–70.

7. *The Wanderings of Peoples*, p. 5.

8. Mueller, J. H., *The Automobile* (unpublished thesis in the University of Chicago library) p. 162. "The relation between 'route' and 'routine' is significant for the route represents a stereotyped movement from which the novel contacts are thereby excluded. The 'highway' does not carry this restrictive connotation."

9. Someone has said that the second voyage of Columbus was more important than the first since the second was concrete evidence that the network of European relations was being thrown across the Atlantic and staked there permanently.

10. The specialization of the mine cannot be commercially continued without other specializations in the community which its condition of dependence requires. It may be assumed, therefore, that the development and extension of mining operations is permitted and accompanied by an increasing division of labor in the community. Mining tends to force and speed up the knitting process. In the following quotation Kautsky states something of its rôle in the evolution of the community. "The mining and working of minerals, particularly metallic ores, is ill suited by its very nature for production for household use only. As soon as such industries attain even the smallest degree of development, they yield a great surplus beyond domestic needs; besides, they can attain a certain perfection only by regularly employing the labor of large bodies of workers, because the worker can in no other way acquire the necessary skill and experience, or make the necessary engineering structures profitable. Even in the Stone Age we already find great centers in which the manufacture of stone implements was carried on proficiently and on a large scale, being then distributed by barter from group to group or from clan to clan. These mineral products seem to have been the first commercial commodities. They probably are the very first to have been produced with the intention of serving for barter." *Foundations of Christianity* (New York, 1925), pp. 52–53.

11. "The correspondence of pig-iron production with manufacture, when both are adjusted for secular trend, is extraordinary. The correlation coefficient [1899–1919] is .97." E. E. Day, "An Index of the Physical Volume of Production," *Review of Economic Statistics*, 1920, p. 367.

12. The Firestone rubber plantation in Liberia is a case in point.

13. Herbert Hoover, *Foreign Combinations to Control Prices of Raw Materials*, United States Department of Commerce, Bureau of Foreign and Domestic Commerce, p. 8.

14. The acute need which England has long felt for timber gave rise, particularly after the Restoration, to a good deal of propaganda designed to stimulate arboriculture, "the art of forming plantations of trees." The classic work was produced by John Evelyn, the diarist, in 1662 entitled *Sylva: A Discourse of Minions*, in which he appealed to the landed gentry to relieve "the impolitic diminution of our timber." Partly as a result of this stimulation to tree-planting, and others which followed it, the term "plantation" in modern England and some of her colonies is applied to a forest of planted rather than indigenous trees.

15. McDougall, *Plant Ecology*, p. 209.

2. Comparative Education in Colonial Areas, with Special Reference to Plantation and Mission Frontiers

1. "There is little doubt that the plantation system is both absolutely and relatively more important in Mississippi than in any other state" (quoted from *Plantation Farming in the United States* [Census Bull. (1916)], p. 21.

2. These figures are taken from a little booklet entitled *School Money in Black and White*, published by the Julius Rosenwald Fund and prepared by a committee of which Fred McCuistion was chairman.

3. *Man and Culture* (New York: Thomas Y. Crowell Co., 1923), pp. 5–12.

4. Walter Wilbur, "Special Problems of the South," *Annals of the American Academy of Political and Social Science*, CLXXVI (November, 1934), 49–56.

5. Robert E. Park, "A Memorandum on Rote Learning," *American Journal of Sociology*, XLIII (July, 1937), 23–36.

6. Franz Oppenheimer, *The State* (New York: Vanguard Press, 1938).

7. See Konrad Bercovici, *Around the World in New York* (New York: Century Co., 1924).

8. Lucy G. Thurston, *Life and Times of Lucy Thurston* (Ann Arbor, Mich.: S. C. Andrews, 1882), pp. 125–31.

9. Andrew W. Lind, *An Island Community* (Chicago: University of Chicago Press, 1938), pp. 147, 149, 170, and 214.

10. A. G. Keller, *Colonization* (Boston: Ginn & Co., 1908), p. 286.

11. E. G. Bourne, *Spain in America, 1450–1580* (New York: Harper & Bros., 1904), pp. 305–6 (quoted in Keller, *op. cit.*, pp. 287–88).

12. Keller, *op. cit.*, p. 293.

13. *Ibid.*, p. 11; Lillian Knowles, *The Economic Development of the Overseas Empire* (London: G. Routledge & Sons, 1924), p. 219.

14. "Industrial Education for the Negro," in W. E. B. DuBois *et al.*, *The Negro Problem* (New York: James Pott & Co., 1903), p. 1.

15. Raymond L. Buell, *The Native Problem in Africa* (New York: Macmillan Co., 1928), I, 529.

16. The laws were enacted against the categorical Negro, but it appears to have been breached by whites in the case of individual Negroes whom they knew and toward whom they were personally sympathetic. In 1853 Mrs. Margaret Douglas encouraged her daughter to teach a class of Negro children in a room in her home in Norfolk. Mrs. Douglas was arrested and convicted by the court. In conducting her defense, Mrs. Douglas pointed out that an example had been set for her by the Sunday schools of the various churches of Norfolk. Concerning the case the *Petersburg [Va.] Daily Express* for November 30, 1853, observed: "It did not appear from the evidence of any of the gentlemen called upon by Mrs. Douglas, that they had actually seen negroes taught from books in any of the Sunday schools of the city, but the fact, as stated by them, that nearly all the negroes attending the Sunday schools could read, gave rise to a violent suspicion that many of the ladies and gentlemen of our city, moving in the highest circles of society, had been guilty of as flagrant a violation of the law as could be imputed to Mrs. Douglas and her daughter."

17. Quoted in Romanzo Adams, *The Education and Economic Outlook for the Boys of Hawaii: A Study in the Field of Race Relationships* (Honolulu: Institute of Pacific Relations, 1927), p. 15.

18. *Hawaiian Planters' Monthly*, I (1882), 187.

19. *Proceedings of the Hawaiian Sugar Planters' Association, 1925*, p. 13.

20. *Education in Malaya* (London, 1924), p. 15.

21. Quoted in H. A. Wyndham, *Native Education* (London: Oxford University Press, 1933), p. 46.

22. See, e.g., C. Y. Shepard, "Agricultural Labour in Trinidad," *Tropical Agriculture*, March, 1935, p. 63; and T. Walter Wallbank, "British Colonial Policy and Native Education in Kenya," *Journal of Negro Education*, October, 1938, p. 52.

23. Katherine Coman, *Economic Beginnings of the Far West* (New York: Macmillan Co., 1912), I, 150.

24. Keller, *op. cit.,* p. 154.

3. The Climatic Theory of the Plantation

1. Max Weber (*General Economic History,* tr. Frank H. Knight, New York, 1927, p. 80) and others classify these latifundia as "plantations," but I now have reservations about this classification.

2. "The sociological point of view makes its appearance in historical investigation as soon as the historian turns from the study of 'periods' to the study of institutions. The history of institutions, that is to say, the family, the church, economic institutions, political institutions, etc., leads inevitably to comparison, classification, the formation of class names or concepts, and eventually to the formulation of law. In the process, history becomes natural history, and natural history pases over into natural science. In short, history becomes sociology."—Robert E. Park and Ernest W. Burgess, *Introduction to the Science of Sociology,* 16 (Chicago, 1921).

3. Albert Galloway Keller, *Colonization; A Study of the Founding of New Societies,* 8 (Boston, 1908). To him colonization is a sort of special topic of the science of society; its study is "of that societal movement which commonly results in the formation of new societies in new environments" and therefore "to be ranged rather under the social sciences than under history in any moderate and reasonable understanding of the term."—*Ibid.,* x–xi. This statement illustrates the transition from history to sociology when a comparative study of an institution or a society is undertaken.

4. A. H. L. Hooren, *A Manual of the History of the Political System of Europe and Its Colonies,* translated from the fifth German edition, 336 (London, 1846); Wilhelm Roscher and Robert Jannasch, *Kolonien, Kolonialpolitik, und Auswanderung,* 23–32 (Leipzig, 1885); Paul Leroy-Beaulieu, *De la colonisation chez les peuples modernes,* 2:563–593 (Paris, 1902); Hugh Edward Egerton, *The Origin & Growth of the English Colonies and of Their System of Government,* 6 (Oxford, 1903); Benjamin Kidd, *The Control of the Tropics* (New York, 1898).

5. Keller, *Colonization,* 3–4 (Boston, 1908). This thesis is repeated and maintained in the revised edition of his *Societal Evolution,* 344–372 (New York, 1931).

6. Keller, *Colonization,* 10.

7. Mary Stoughton Locke, *Anti-Slavery in America,* 14 (Boston, 1901). See also Edward Channing, *The Narragansett Planters,* 105–123 (Baltimore, 1886); Matlack Price, "Narragansett Manors," *New England Magazine* (n.s.), 44:54–64 (March 1911); and William Davis Miller, "Narragansett Planters," American Antiquarian Society, *Proceedings* (n.s.), 43:49–115 (April 1933).

8. Carl J. Fuchs, "The Epochs of German Agrarian History and Agrarian Policy," p. 233–236, in Thomas Nixon Carver, ed., *Selected Readings in Rural Economics* (Boston, 1916).

9. A. Grenfell Price, "White Settlement in Saba Island, Dutch West Indies," *Geographical Review,* 24:42–60 (January 1934).

10. A. Grenfell Price, *White Settlers in the Tropics,* 122–135 (New York, 1939).

11. James G. Leyburn, "Frontier Society: A Study in the Growth of Culture," *Sociologus,* 9:177–178 (June 1933).

12. Vincent T. Harlow, *A History of Barbados, 1625–1685* (New York, 1926); Avery Craven, *Soil Exhaustion as a Factor in the Agricultural History of Virginia and Maryland, 1606–1860,* p. 160–161 (Urbana, Ill., 1925).

13. Nels August Bengtson and Willem Van Royen, *Fundamentals of Economic Geography,* 399 (New York, 1935).

14. Alfred Russell Wallace defined acclimatization as "the process of adaptation by which animals and plants are gradually rendered capable of surviving and flourishing in countries remote from their original habitats, or under meterological conditions different from those which they have usually to endure, and at first injurious to them."—*Encyclopedia Britannica,* ed. 11, 1:114.

15. Englishmen of the seventeenth and eighteenth centuries discussed the difficulties of acclimatization in Ireland. Thomas Pope Blount, *Essays on Several Subjects,* 65 (London, 1691); and Giles Jacob, *An Historical Account of the Lives and Writings of Our Most Considerable English Poets . . .,* 87 (London, 1720).

16. Kidd, *Control of the Tropics,* 54.

17. Ellsworth Huntington, *Civilization and Climate,* 41 (New Haven, 1915).

18. Madison Grant, *The Passing of the Great Race,* 41 (New York, 1921). He believed that whites in the South had deteriorated since the abolition of slavery for they had to plow their own fields and work in factories. See p. 42.

19. William Z. Ripley, "Acclimatization," *Popular Science Monthly,* 48:789–790 (April 1896).

20. For an early Southern expression of this belief, see the statement by John Tyler in the Virginia constitutional convention. Jonathan Elliot, *Debates,* 3:639 (ed. 2, Washington, 1836). For a similar Northern viewpoint, see the speech of Alexander Hamilton in the New York convention. *Ibid.,* 2:235–237.

21. Ulrich Bonnell Phillips, *Life and Labor in the Old South,* 3 (Boston, 1929).

22. Clarence Cason, *90° in the Shade* (Chapel Hill, N.C., 1935).

23. Thomas Cooper, *Lectures on the Elements of Political Economy,* 95 (Columbia, S.C., 1826).

24. Robert E. Park, "Human Migration and the Marginal Man," 64, in Ernest W. Burgess, ed., *Personality and the Social Group* (Chicago, 1929).

25. Earl Hanson, "Are the Tropics Unhealthy?" in *Harper's Magazine,* 167:563 (October 1933).

26. William E. Dodd, "The Plantation and Farm Systems in Southern Agriculture," in *The South in the Building of the Nation,* 5:74 (Richmond, Va., 1909).

27. Winthrop Moore Daniels, "The Slave Plantation in Retrospect," in *Atlantic Monthly,* 107:364 (March 1911).

4. The Plantation: The Physical Basis of Traditional Race Relations

1. John Dollard, *Caste and Class in a Southern Town* (New Haven, 1937), p. 412.

2. A special Census investigation made in 1910 and reported in 1916, the first

of its kind since the Civil War and not since repeated, reported that "the plantation as a unit for the general purposes of administration has not disappeared." For the purposes of this enumeration the plantation was defined as "a continuous tract of land of considerable area under the general supervision or control of a single individual or firm, all or a part of such tract being divided into at least five smaller tracts, which are leased to tenants." On the basis of this narrow definition a total of 39,073 tenant plantations were reported, not for the South as a whole, but for a restricted area comprising 325 counties in eleven Southern states (*Plantation Farming in the United States,* Washington, 1916).

3. J. C. Ballagh, *A History of Slavery in Virginia* (Baltimore, 1902), p. 44.

4. Alvin S. Johnson, "Capitalism of the Camp," *The New Republic,* VI, 237–239 (April 1, 1916).

5. "When Hakluyt wrote in 1584 his *Discourses of Western Planting* his theme was the project of American colonization; and when a settlement was planted at Jamestown, at Boston, or at Providence, as the case might be, it was called, regardless of the type, a plantation. This usage of the word in the sense of a colony ended only upon the rise of a new institution to which the original name was applied. The colonies at large came then to be known as provinces or dominions, while the sub colonies, the privately owned village estates which prevailed in the South, were alone called plantations. In the Creole colonies, however, these were known as *habitations*—dwelling places. This etymology of the name suggests the nature of the thing—an isolated place where people in somewhat peculiar groups settled and worked and had their being. The standard community comprised a white household in the midst of several or many negro families. The one was master, the many were slaves; the one was head, the many were members; the one was teacher, the many were pupils" (U. B. Phillips, *American Negro Slavery,* New York: D. Appleton and Co., 1918, p. 309).

6. H. J. Nieboer, *Slavery as an Industrial System* (The Hague, 1910), p. 418.

7. Isiah Bowman, *The Pioneer Fringe* (New York, 1931), p. 299.

8. Barnes says of the Boer farmer in South Africa that the only kind of relation he really understands is that of master and servant. "Of course one master may enter into relations with another master; but that kind of relation is terminable at will on either side. It is thus always avoidable, and in the last resort need not be reckoned with. But all unavoidable social relationships he instinctively seeks to interpret in terms of the master-servant relation" (Leonard Barnes, *Caliban in Africa,* London, Victor Gollancz, 1930, p. 21). These statements might also be made of the Southern planter, certainly of the ante-bellum Southern planter.

9. In one of his visits to the Southern states Sir Charles Lyell observed: "The condition of the negroes is the least enviable in such out-of-the-way and half-civilized districts, where there are many adventurers and uneducated settlers, who have little control over their passions, and who, when they oppress their slaves, are not checked by public opinion, as in more advanced communities" (*A Second Visit to the United States of America, 1845–1846,* New York, 1850, II, 181–182).

10. We may suppose that the planter's power of life and death developed in an isolated situation in very much the same way as did that of the Roman house-father who at one time had the recognized right to sell his children and even to inflict the death punishment upon them. His wife and adult sons and the latter's children were under his power. See Edward Westermarck, *The Origin and Development of the Moral Ideas* (London, 1912), I 428–429. The status of the family was very different then from what it now is, and the powers

which are now delegated to the larger community were then possessed by the head of the household. The *familia* included not only wife and children but also the slaves. If among the Southern Planter's slaves were some who were his own children, a parallel with the *potestas* of the Roman father would be closely approximated. For the *familia,* like the plantation, was itself a political institution and as such held the power of life and death over its members until this power was limited to the state during the reign of Hadrian.

11. *Lynchings and What They Mean: General Findings of the Southern Commission on the Study of Lynching* (Atlanta, 1931), pp. 30–31.

12. Marcus W. Jernegan, "Slavery and Conversion in the American Colonies," *American Historical Review,* XXI, 506 (April, 1916).

13. "After practicing folkways for an extended time, people acquire the conviction that they are indispensable to the welfare of society. They come to believe that their own ways are the only right ones, and that departure from them will involve calamity. It is with the addition of this welfare-element that folkways become mores" (W. G. Sumner and A. G. Keller, *The Science of Society,* New Haven, 1927, I, 33). Some of the implications of this are pointed out by Faris when he says that although the mores, like the folkways of a people, remain largely unformulated they are "more conscious and always in some degree emotional for the violation or threatened violation causes concern or resentment. The folkways, which are mere usages, exist in all societies alongside the mores, which are all but universal, but not quite so. It is possible to find isolated societies on small islands like the Andamans where hardly any folkways have risen to the conscious and emotional level of mores. This means that resentment at the violation of the folkways has not occurred because the violation has not sufficiently often taken place. . . . Thus even the mores seem to require a certain degree of interpenetration of groups to bring the folkways to the conscious level of morals" (Ellsworth Faris, "Social Evolution," in Shailer Mathews, ed., *Contributions of Science to Religion,* New York, D. Appleton and Co., 1924, p. 236).

14. In South Africa, too, and elsewhere practices based upon the idea of race entered the mores. In Brazil, apparently, they did not. In South Africa, the Dutch farmers on the land held Negro slaves while the English for the most part lived in the cities. "The Briton's presence makes the Dutch feel prisoners in their own country. They represent, in a sense, an embryonic group-mind struggling towards self-realization, and they hate to have strangers standing about, watching and commenting, from a standpoint of maddeningly aloof criticism, upon their antics" (Barnes, *op. cit.,* p. 50).

15. U. B. Phillips, *Plantation and Frontier, 1649–1863,* I, 94. In the series *Documentary History of American Industrial Society* (Cleveland, 1910).

16. "Racial Factors and Economic Forces in Land Tenure in the South," *Social Forces,* XV, 214 (Dec., 1936).

17. "In Mississippi there is justification for the old saying that only mules and black men can face the sun in July" (Clarence Cason, *90° in the Shade,* Chapel Hill, 1935, p. 5).

18. Quoted in Lyle Saxon, *Old Louisiana* (New York, 1929), p. 67.

19. Alfred H. Stone, *Studies in the American Race Problem* (New York, 1908), p. 144. The following statement by a South Carolina writer also bespeaks the planter attitude: "Of all the inscrutable peoples of the Eastern world, none is more secretive than the Negro, nor any so puzzling to the psychologist, for while it is easy to know that deceit lurks behind the mask of engaging frankness with which he seeks to disarm those who doubt him, the exact nature of the

deceit can seldom be discerned" (Gonzales, quoted in Reed Smith, *Gullah*, Columbia, S.C., 1926, footnote p. 12).

20. See George S. Schuyler, "Our White Folks," *The American Mercury*, XII, 387 (Dec., 1927).

21. These statements are drawn largely from Nieboer, *op. cit.*, p. 31.

22. John Spencer Bassett, *The Plantation Overseer as Revealed in His Letters* (Northampton, Mass., 1925), pp. 2, 3–4.

23. Robert Redfield, *Tepotzlan* (Chicago, 1930), p. 4.

24. Page Thacker, *Plantation Reminiscences* (1878), pp. 3, 10, 15, 20.

25. Lyle Saxon, *op. cit.*, pp. 308–309.

26. Francis P. Gaines, *The Southern Plantation* (New York, 1924), p. 212.

27. Quoted in C. E. Hedrick, *Social and Economic Aspects of Slavery in the Transmontane Prior to 1850* (Nashville, 1927), p. 83.

28. Guion Griffis Johnson, in T. J. Woofter, Jr., *Black Yeomanry* (New York, 1930), p. 22.

29. U. B. Phillips, "Plantations with Slave Labor and Free," *American Historical Review*, XXX, 743 (July, 1925).

30. Robert E. Park, "Racial Assimilation in Secondary Groups," *Publications of the American Sociological Society* (1913), VIII, 73.

31. David L. Cohn, *God Shakes Creation* (New York, 1935), p. 155. Du Bose Heyward in his *Mamba's Daughters* (Garden City, 1929), p. 14, shows how Mamba acquired "white folks" by insinuating herself into the good graces of an old but financially embarrassed Charleston family. She began by shining the shoes of the members of the family while they were away at church and thus forestalled ejection by setting up a claim on Mrs. Wentworth which the latter could not ignore. "Her position was now fairly secure. She had only to keep a favour ahead of her victim, leaving upon her the burden of an unrepaid obligation. The Wentworths had no money wherewith to compensate her, and so, in lieu thereof, she must be given food in the kitchen and the outworn and easily recognisable garments of her new mistress. To the neighbourhood, and even in her own eyes, this gave her the superficial colouration of a retainer of the aristocracy. Presently . . . she commenced to refer to the Wentworth household as 'my white folks.'" (Reprinted by permission of Doubleday, Doran and Co.)

32. Thacker, *op. cit.*, p. 16.

33. F. J. Teggart, *The Theory of History* (New Haven, 1925), pp. 189–190.

34. See Rupert B. Vance, *Human Factors in Cotton Culture* (Chapel Hill, 1929), chap. vi, "Around the Year with Cotton Growers."

35. Thacker, *op. cit.*, p. 11.

36. B. Malinowski, "Anthropology," *Encyclopaedia Britannica* (13th ed.), New Vols., I, 137.

37. "The Creole speech . . . is the speech of inferior beings and of a subordinate class whose superiors have never troubled nor desired to make them speak any language correctly" (J. Vendreyes, *Language: A Linguistic Introduction to History*, trans. Paul Radin, New York, 1925, p. 295).

38. Guy B. Johnson, in Woofter, *op. cit.*, p. 49.

39. Annie Weston Whitney, "Negro American Dialects," *The Independent*, LIII, 1929 (Aug. 22–29, 1901).

40. George Herbert Mead, "National-Mindedness and International-Mindedness," *International Journal of Ethics*, XXXIX, 395 (July, 1929).

41. Matthew G. Lewis, *Journal of a West India Proprietor* (London, 1834), pp. 62, 68–69.

42. P. Lestant Prudhomme, "A Record of the State of the Weather, the Daily News, and My Occupations and Amusements." About one sixth of this diary is printed in Lyle Saxon, *op. cit.,* pp. 170–229.

43. *Ibid.,* pp. 167–168. (Reprinted by permission of The Century Company.)

44. Bassett, *op. cit.,* pp. 86–87.

45. H. A. Miller, *Races, Nations and Classes* (Philadelphia, 1924), p. 149.

46. Beulah Amidon Ratliff, "Mississippi: Heart of Dixie," *The Nation,* CXIV, 588–589 (May 17, 1922).

47. T. S. Matthews, "In the Big City," *The New Republic,* LVI, 20 (Aug. 22, 1928).

48. ". . . all innovation is based on conformity, all heterodoxy on orthodoxy, all individuality on solidarity . . . the institution supplies a basis to the very individual who rebels against it" (C. H. Cooley, *Social Organization,* New York, 1909, p. 321).

49. See Eugene Gordon, "The Negro's Inhibitions," *The American Mercury* XIII, 159–165. (Feb., 1928), and Rudolph Fisher, "The South Lingers On," *Survey Graphic,* VI, 644–647 (March, 1925). The following letter from a Negro living in New York to a friend in the Southern Community where he formerly had lived illustrates the changes in personality and in attitude. "Dear Partner: . . . I am all fixed now and living well. I don't have to work hard. Don't have to mister every little boy comes along. I haven't heard a white man call a colored a nigger you know how—since I been here. I can ride in the street or steam car anywhere I can get a seat. I don't care to mix with white what I mean I am not crazy about being with white folks, but if I have to pay the same fare I have learn to want the same acomidation and if you are first in a place here shoping, you don't have to wait till all the white folk get thro trading yet amid all this I love the good old south and am praying that God may give every well wisher a chance to be a man regardless of his color . . ." (Charles S. Johnson, "Black Workers and the City," *Survey Graphic,* VI, 642, March, 1925).

6. Language and Race Relations

1. Friedrich Müller, *Lectures on the Science of Language* (New York: C. Scribner and Sons, 1868–1869), 2 vols.; *Three Lectures on the Science of Language* (Chicago: Open Court Publishing Company, 1899). Müller built on the work of Sir William Jones and Friedrich Schlegel. The link between language and race was even more directly asserted by Count Arthur de Gobineau in his famous *Essay on the Inequality of the Human Races* in a chapter entitled "Languages, being unequal among themselves, are completely linked to the relative merit of races." See Michael D. Biddiss, *Father of Racist Ideology,* New York: Weybright and Talley, 1970.

2. Thorstein Veblen, *Imperial Germany and the Industrial Revolution,* Introduction. Reprinted in Max Lerner (ed.), *The Portable Veblen* (New York: The Viking Press, 1948), p. 298.

3. Especially Dr. John E. Reinecke and his "Marginal Languages: A Sociological Survey of the Creole Languages and Trade Jargons," (Ph.D. dissertation, Yale University, 1937), and Dr. Hilda Hertz Golden and her "Language and the Social Situation: A Study in Race Relations" (Ph.D. dissertation, Duke University, 1950).

4. Dell Hymes (ed.), *Pidginization and Creolization of Languages*, Cambridge, [Eng.]: At the University Press, 1971.

5. I am adopting the term from Ernest Schultz, "Sklaven- und Dienersprachen," *Sociologus*, IX (December, 1933), 377–418.

6. Karl W. Deutsch, "Medieval Unity and Economic Conditions for an International Civilization," *Canadian Journal of Economics and Political Science*, X (February, 1944), 24. See also H. Kloss, "Sprachtabellem," *Vierteljahresschrift für Politik und Geschichte*, I, No. 2 (Berlin, 1929), 107–8.

7. John Dewey, *Democracy and Education* (New York: The Macmillan Company, 1920), p. 5.

8. In his review of Mead, George Herbert. *Mind, Self, and Society from the Standpoint of a Social Behaviorist*. Chicago: The University of Chicago Press, 1934, Professor Sidney Hook asked similar questions as follows: "Granted that the adjustive responses of the individual to his world acquire social dimensionality through the mechanism of language, how is language itself affected by other activities and institutions of social life? Is there any method by which the language process can be treated not only as the instrument of social communication but as the resultant effect of other social activities without raising futile and insoluble problems about the origin of language? To what extent can basic differences in linguistic structure be significantly correlated in social experience?" Sidney Hook, "A Philosophic Pathfinder," *The Nation*, CXL (February 13, 1935), 196.

9. Robert Ezra Park, "Human Nature and Collective Behavior," *American Journal of Sociology*, 32 (March, 1927), 735.

10. Grace DeLaguna, *Speech, Its Function and Development* (New Haven: Yale University Press, 1927), p. 19.

11. Bronislaw Malinowski, "The Problem of Meaning in Primitive Languages," in C. K. Ogdon and I. A. Richards, *The Meaning of Meaning* (New York: Harcourt, Brace and Company, 1923), pp. 472–74.

12. See C. Watts Cunningham, "On the Linguistic Meaning-Situation," *Philosophy and Phenomenological Research*, IV (December, 1943), 251–65.

13. Especially in Schultz, *op. cit.*

14. Carl Schurz, *The Reminiscences of Carl Schurz* (New York: The McClure Co., 1908), 11–12.

15. Henriqueta Chamberlain, *Where the Sabiá Sings: A Partial Autobiography* (New York: The Macmillan Company, 1947), pp. 2–3.

16. The we-language comes to be valued as a cultural possession or capital in which spiritual achievements are invested. It may become, as it often has become in European congregations transplanted to America, a sacred language. "It is known that immigrant churches have retained their native languages in church services for a considerable time after settlement in the United States, some longer than others. This is notably true of certain pietistic sects, such as the Mennonite groups, which continue after several generations in this country to conduct services in the German language. It is also true to a considerable extent of the various Lutheran churches—Norwegian, Swedish, Finnish, German, and Danish. Certain nationality groups of the Catholic faith, such as French, Bohemian, Polish, and German, have also continued some part of the service or prayers in their native tongues." Lowry Nelson, "Speaking of Tongues," *American Journal of Sociology*, LIV (November, 1948), 209–10.

17. W. F. Wertheim, "The Indo-European Problem in Indonesia," *Pacific Affairs*, XX (September, 1947), 21.

18. Maurice S. Evans, *Black and White in South East Africa: A Study in Sociology,* (London: Longmans, Green and Company, 1916), 51.

19. Mead, Margaret. "Talk-Boy," *Asia,* (XXXI), (March, 1931), pp. 150–151.

20. Robert E. Park, "The Nature of Race Relations," in Edgar T. Thompson (ed.), *Race Relations and the Race Problem* (Durham: Duke University Press, 1939), pp. 13–14.

21. Thomas D. Rambaut, "The Hudson's Bay Half-Breeds and Louis Reil's Rebellion," *Political Science Quarterly,* II (March, 1887), 139, 141; James G. Leyburn, *Frontier Folkways* (New Haven: Yale University Press, 1935), pp. 54.

22. P. H. J. Grierson, *The Silent Trade: A Contribution to the Early History of Human Intercourse* (Edinburgh, 1903).

23. Reinecke, *op. cit.*

24. In America, the speech of the post-Civil War immigrant from continental Europe was so little used outside his family that he had to drop it in order to find a place in a factory or in a shop. English was for him at first a commercial language. When he got a job it became a language of command. It is not surprising that among the first English words the immigrant learned were "job," "boss," "business," and "pay-day." "Naturalization of Tongues," *The Interpreter,* VII (April, 1928), 9–10.

25. See the *Encyclopedia Britannica* (11th ed.), VII, 509; J. Vendryes, *Language; A Linguistic Introduction to History* (New York: Alfred A. Knopf, 1925), p. 295; Reinecke, *op. cit.,* speaks of them as "plantation creole" dialects.

26. Frances Anne Kemble, *Journal of a Residence on a Georgia Plantation in 1838–1839* (New York: Harper & Brothers. 1863), p. 295.

27. Mrs. Overell relates the following incident on the New Guinea plantation when the country was governed by the Germans before World War I. "I tried giving my orders to the boys in vain—for they paid no attention. The Germans would repeat them in loud tone with excellent results. I heard one say: 'Sie ist doch viel zu höflich und bescheiden,' (She is too polite and modest) but it was not until I heard the German women speak to the natives that I realized my error. They did not *speak,* they yelled, they shouted, they roared, and the shuddering blacks flew to obey." Lillian Overell, *A Woman's Impressions of German New Guinea* (London: John Lane the Body Head, Ltd., 1924), p. 28.

Of the creole speech later in mandated New Guinea, Margaret Mead wrote: "After all, it is primarily a work-boy language, a language used between masters and the members of a 'lower race,' a language used between members of different tribes who view one another with suspicion and often with fear, a language used by the return work-boy to berate the young and scold his wife. Furthermore, those who used it first, in many cases, were sailors, adventurers, or even ex-convicts. Their own speech was not overnice, and the natives absorbed quickly all the Anglo-Saxon monosyllables which they now use with bland and touching innocence to visiting fine ladies." *op. cit.,* p. 150.

28. E. C. L. Adams, *Nigger to Nigger* (New York: C. Scribner's Sons, 1928), pp. 33–35; Ludwig Lewisohn, *Up Stream: An American Chronicle* (New York: Boni and Liveright, 1922).

29. George Herbert Mead, *Mind, Self and Society: From the standpoint of a social behaviorist.* (Chicago: The University of Chicago Press, 1934), *passim.*

30. Mead, *op. cit.,* p. 144.

31. English functioned as an interlanguage between Negro slaves originally of different speech in colonial America and this is one reason why Negroes in America acquired a minimum English so rapidly. See A. W. Reid, "The Speech

of Negroes in Colonial America," *Journal of Negro History*, XXIV (July, 1939), 247–58.

32. Stephen W. Reed, *The Making of Modern New Guinea* (Philadelphia: The American Philosophical Society, 1943), *passim*, especially Appendix I, "The Language Adjustment." Similar developments have occurred and are occurring in many other colonial areas of the world, e.g., the Belgian Congo. In his muckraking days, when he was Secretary of the Congo Reform Association, Dr. Park presented the background against which recent events in the Belgian Congo can be better understood. See his "A King in Business," *Everybody's*, XV (November, 1906), 624–33; "The Terrible Story of the Congo," *Everybody's*, XV (December, 1906), 763–72; and "Blood Money of the Congo," *Everybody's* XVI (January, 1907), 60–70.

7. The Idea of Race and the Race Problem

1. "Secret Sources of the Success of the Racist Ideology," *Review of Politics*, VII (January, 1945), 75.

2. *Histoire de France*, Paris, 1903. I, 50.

8. Race in the Modern World

1. Frank H. Hankins, *The Racial Basis of Civilization*. New York: A. A. Knopf, 1926.

2. J. Barzun, *Race: A Study in Modern Superstition*. New York: Harcourt Brace & Co., 1937.

3. Ruth Benedict and Gene Weltfish, *The Races of Mankind*. New York: Public Affairs Committee, 1943.

4. Julian Huxley and A. C. Haddon, *We Europeans*. New York: Harper and Bros., 1936.

5. George Herbert Mead, "National-Mindedness and International-Mindedness," *The International Journal of Ethics*, 39:398, July 1929.

6. Eric Voegelin, "The Growth of the Race Idea," *The Review of Politics*, 2:283–4, July 1940.

7. Max Lerner, *Ideas are Weapons*. New York: The Viking Press, 1939, p. 3.

8. William Graham Sumner, *Folkways*. Boston: Ginn and Co., 1906. Pp. 12–13.

9. Cited by Louis Wirth, "Race and Nationalism," *Introductory General Course in the Study of Contemporary Society, Selected Readings*. Chicago: University of Chicago Bookstore, 11th ed., 1941, Reading XXIV, p. 6.

10. "This community of Atlantic nations has as yet no name. Its essential unity has not yet been recognized sufficiently clearly for that and it has been torn by family quarrels. It is not an empire, for that suggests unity of rule as well as culture. We may perhaps call it a 'commonwealth,' the Commonwealth of the Atlantic—for the weal of each nation in it affects all the others." Ramsay Traquair, "The Commonwealth of the Atlantic," *The Atlantic Monthly*, 133: 606, May, 1924.

11. Eric Voegelin, *op. cit.*

12. During World War I Dr. Edgar Bérillon was authorized to lecture all over France on his discovery that the German race suffered from polychesia (excessive defecation) and bromidrosis (body odor). Also the German urine was found to contain 20 per cent non-uric nitrogen as against 15 percent for other races. Moreover, the large intestine of the German is about 9 feet longer than normal. Barzun, *op. cit.*, 239.

13. At one time in Spain the principle of *limpieza de sangre*, or purity of blood, was applied to those who embraced the true faith as opposed to obstinate heretics. Negroes in Spain were not as often contaminated by the obstinacy of previous religious convictions as Jews and Moors. Werner J. Cahnman, "The Mediterranean and Caribbean Regions—A Comparison in Race and Culture Contacts." *Social Forces*, 22:209, D 1943.

14. Voegelin, *op. cit.*, p. 316.

15. Konrad Bercovici, *Around the World in New York* (New York, 1924), pp. 14–21. Concerning the relationship of Jews in Chicago with their Polish neighbors Wirth says, "The two groups detest each other thoroughly, but they live side by side on the West Side, and even more generally on the Northwest Side. They have a profound feeling of disrespect and contempt for each other, bred by their contiguity and historical friction in the pale; but they trade with each other on Milwaukee Avenue and on Maxwell Street. . . . These two immigrant groups, having lived side by side in Poland and Galicia, are used to each other's business methods. They have accommodated themselves to one another, and this accommodation persists in America. . . . The members of the younger generation mingle in school and are members of the same gangs." Louis Wirth, *The Ghetto.* Chicago, The University of Chicago Press, 1928, p. 229.

9. School Desegregation: Condition and Status

1. See Robert E. Park, "The Nature of Race Relations," in Edgar T. Thompson (ed.), *Race Relations and the Race Problem.* Durham: Duke University Press, 1939. pp. 1–2.

2. C. Van Woodward, *The Strange Career of Jim Crow,* New York: Oxford University Press, 1955. p. 79.

3. "Race Relations as a World Issue," *The New York Times Magazine,* November 11, 1956. p. 12.

4. Edgar Gardner Murphy, *The Basis of Ascendency,* New York: Longman's Green, 1910, p. 51.

10. The Little Races

1. With a very different purpose in mind Madison Grant lamented the passing of a "great" race, the White race, which alone is capable of achieving civilization (Grant 1918).

2. "As yet . . . there is no sign of the emergence of a proper name to identify as a whole these mixed-blood groups, who are neither Whites, Indians, Negroes, or mulattoes, and for whom there is not even an acceptable classificatory designation in our language" (Dunlap and Weslanger 1947).

3. In America, "if the designation of eastern mixed-groups which perpetuate Indian tribal names be set aside and those of residual groups be examined, one finds that social pressure has forced the adoption of names to distinguish tri-racial groups from bi-racial groups on the one hand, and from Whites, Indians, and Negroes on the other hand. At first, family names were often generalized; then convenience dictated the use of more inclusive terms, which were imposed, as a rule, by the socially and economically dominant group. Such names were selected by catch-as-catch-can methods, with derisive impulses, color differences, physiological resemblances, and chance associations playing feature roles in the process. In the course of time, no doubt, some of the names . . . will be generalized to designate several related groups. This seems to have happened already in the case of the *Guineas* and *Melungeons,* and the development may be expected to continue" (Dunlap and Weslanger 1947:87).

4. For a more complete account of the Griquas, see Halford (1959).

5. Attention to the role of epithets in the naming process leads Everett and Helen Hughes to say, "Perhaps every group, even in an ideal society, where people get along well with one another, has need of a private epithet for the out-groupers, as well as a public name. The line between epithet and pet name is fine; there are affectionate epithets. To try to eliminate epithets completely is to institute a kind of thought control that may well drive thoughts and feelings to find other outlets . . . Far from denying naming and trying to use it as a defense of prejudice—because it shows the objects of prejudice are themselves prejudiced—we should recognize it and go further to find out to what extent people need epithets even about people they like. For it seems to be characteristically human behavior that people do not and perhaps cannot completely accept for all purposes other people's system of names but must have their own" (Hughes and Hughes 1952:144). Also interesting in this connection is Roback (1944).

References Cited (Chap. 10)

Anonymous
 1958 Durham, North Carolina, Morning Herald, March 1, p. 2.
Berry, Brewton
 1963 Almost White, New York: MacMillan
Campbell, John
 1816 Travels in South Africa Undertaken at the Request of the Missionary Society. Andover: Flagg and Gould.
Chamberlain, Houston Stewart
 1913 Foundations of the Nineteenth Century. New York: John Lane.
Darwin, Charles
 1896 The Descent of Man and Selection in Relation to Sex. New York: D. Appleton.
de Gobineau, Joseph Arthur
 1915 The Inequality of the Human Races. London: Heinemann.
Deiler, John Hanno
 1909 The German Coast of Louisiana. Philadelphia: Americana Germanica Press.

Douglas, Mary Tew
   1966 Purity and Danger: The Analysis of Concepts of Pollution and Taboo.
      New York: Praeger.
Dunlap, A. R., and C. A. Weslanger
   1947 Trends in the Naming of Tri-Racial Mixed-Blood Groups in the Eastern
      United States. American Speech 22:81–87.
Fischer, Eugen
   1913 Die Rehoboth Bastaards und das Bastardierungsproblem biem Mensc-
      hen. Jena: G. Fisher.
Gillin, John Lewis
   1931 Taming the Criminal. New York: MacMillan.
Grant, Madison
   1918 The Passing of a Great Race, or the Racial Basis of European History.
      New York: Charles Scribner's Sons.
Halford, Samuel James
   1950 The Griquas of Griqualand: A Historical Narrative of the Griqua People.
      Capetown, South Africa: Juta.
Hirshfeld, Magnus
   1938 Racism. London: Victor Gollancz.
Hudson, Charles M.
   1970 The Catawba Nation. University of Georgia Monographs, No. 18. Athens:
      University of Georgia Press.
Hughes, Everett, and Helen MacGill Hughes
   1952 Where Peoples Meet: Racial and Ethnic Frontiers. Glencoe, Illinois: The
      Free Press.
Johnson, J. H.
   1929 Documentary Evidence of Relations of Negroes and Indians. The Jour-
      nal of Negro History 14:21–43.
Jordan, Winthrop D.
   1962 American Chiaroscuro: The Status and Definition of Mulattoes in the
      British Colonies. William and Mary Quarterly 19:183–200.
Lea, Charles Henry
   1906–1907 A History of the Inquisition of Spain. Volume 2. New York: Macmil-
      lan.
Malherbe, E. G.
   1971 Personal letter to author. March 18.
McCloy, Shelby T.
   1955 The Cagots: A Despised People in France. The South Atlantic Quarterly
      54:44–55.
Michel, Francisque
   1847 Histoire des Races Maudites de la France et de l'Espagne. Paris:
      A. Franck.
Millin, Sarah Gertrude
   1924 God's Stepchildren. New York: Boni and Liveright.
   1949 King of the Bastards. New York: Harper and Brothers.
Park, Robert E.
   1929 Migration and the Marginal Man. In Personality and the Social Group.
      E. W. Burgess, Ed. Chicago: University of Chicago Press. pp 64–77.

Redfield, Robert
  1955 The Little Community: Viewpoints for the Study of a Human Whole.
    Chicago: University of Chicago Press.
Report on the Commission of Inquiry Regarding the Cape Coloured Population
  1937 Letter, Appendix 21. Pretoria: Union of South Africa, UG 54. pp. 287–
    288.
Roback, A. A.
  1944 A Dictionary of International Slurs. Cambridge, Massachusetts: Sci-Art
    Publishers.
Stoddard, Lothrop
  1922 The Rising Tide of Color Against White World-Supremacy. New York:
    Charles Scribner's Sons.
Stonequist, Everett V.
  1937 The Marginal Man: A Study in Personality and Culture Conflict. New
    York: Charles Scribner's Sons.
Taylor, Douglas
  1951 The Black Caribs of British Honduras. Viking Fund Publications in An-
    thropology, No. 17. New York: Wenner-Gren Foundation for Anthropologi-
    cal Research.
Weslanger, C. A.
  1943 Delaware's Forgotten Folk. Philadelphia: University of Pennsylvania
    Press.

The "Little Races" and Racial Theory

1. Charles Wagley, "Plantation America," in Vera Rubin (ed.), *Caribbean Studies: A Symposium*, Mona, Jamaica: University College of The West Indies, 1957. pp. 4–5.

2. Carter G. Woodson, "The Beginning of the Miscegenation of the Whites and the Blacks, "*Journal of Negro History*, iii (1918), 335–353; John Brickell, *Natural History of North Carolina*, Dublin, 1737, 272; Hugh Jones, *The Present State of Virginia*. London, 1724, 27; Andrew Burnaby, *Travels Through the Middle Settlements of North America*, London, 1798, 54.

3. Albert Beverage, *Life of John Marshall*, New York, 1919, I, 239–241.

4. Albert J. Pickett, *A History of Alabama, Georgia and Mississippi From the Earliest Period*, Charleston, South Carolina: Walker and James, 1851. 3rd. ed. *passim.*

11. Sociology and Sociological Research
in the South

1. During the course of his tour of the South in the 1850's Frederick Olmsted said of southerners: "They say this uneasiness—this passion for change— is a peculiarity of our diseased Northern nature. The Southern man finds Providence in all that is: Satan in all that might be" *A Journey in the Seaboard Slave States in the Years 1853–1854* (New York: G. P. Putnam's Sons, 1904), I, 2.

2. Gunnar Myrdal, _An American Dilemma,_ (New York: Harper, 1944), I, 70 footnote.

3. The old plantation society of Brazil, unlike the American plantation society, apparently did not experience criticism from other sections of Brazil nor to any considerable extent from the mother country of Portugal. This is one very important factor, among others, in the very different history of plantation Brazil.

4. A. O. Craven, _The Repressible Conflict, 1830–1861,_ (Baton Rouge: Louisiana State University Press, 1939), p. 27.

5. What the spokesmen of the Old South contended for was, as W. G. Brown put it, "not slavery alone, not cotton and rice and sugar-cane, not agriculture alone, but the whole social organism, the whole civilization. . . . The representatives of the planting interest must do more than stand on the defensive . . . they must rule." _The Lower South in American History_ (New York: The Macmillan Co., 1902), pp. 57–58.

6. Hughes published his _A Treatise on Sociology_ in 1854, the same year Fitzhugh brought out his _Sociology for the South._ See L. L. Bernard, "Henry Hughes, First American Sociologist," _Social Forces,_ XV (December 1936), 154–174; L. L. Bernard, "The Historic Pattern of Sociology in the South," _Social Forces,_ XVI (October 1937), 1–12; H. G. and Winnie Leach Duncan, "The Development of Sociology in the Old South," _American Journal of Sociology,_ XXXIX (March 1934), 649–656; Harvey Wish, "George Frederick Holmes and the Genesis of American Sociology," _American Journal of Sociology,_ XLVI (March 1941), 698–707; Harvey Wish, _George Fitzhugh, Propagandist of the Old South_ (Baton Rouge: Louisiana State University, 1943); L. L. and Jessie Bernard, _Origins of American Sociology_ (New York: Thomas Y. Crowell Co., 1943), Ch. XVI, "The Critical and Systematic Work of George Frederick Holmes in Social Science." An interesting attempt to put the social thought of the Old South in systematic order may be found in Julian S. Bach Jr., "The Social Thought of the Old South," _American Journal of Sociology,_ XLVI (September 1940), 179–190. Another early American sociologist was Stephen Pearl Andrews. Andrews, born in Massachusetts, became a wealthy slaveholder and lawyer in Mississippi, then returned to the North to become an abolitionist. See Harvey Wish, "Stephen Pearl Andrews, American Pioneer Sociologist," _Social Forces,_ XIX (May 1941), 477–482.

7. In a recent article Robert A Nisbet has shown us how sociology arose in France as a reaction against the excesses of the French Revolution and of the Revolution's attack upon the traditional French order of family and community. "The origins of sociology in France," Professor Nisbet says, "were characterized by a reversion, in certain respects, to ideas which had flourished during the medieval period. Comte's admiration for the Middle Ages was profound, and to no small degree this civilization served as an inspiration to this thinking." Nisbet, "The French Revolution and the Rise of Sociology in France," _American Journal of Sociology,_ LXIX (September 1943), 156–164.

8. Charles S. Sydnor, "The Southerner and the Laws," _The Journal of Southern History,_ VI (February 1940), 19.

9. Fitzhugh does not exactly say this but it seems to be assumed throughout his book and this is the interpretation placed upon his "sociology" by those who reviewed the book in contemporary periodicals. In the Preface to _Sociology for the South_ he apologized for using "the newly-coined word Sociology" but there seemed to be no other term adequate to describe the remedy for the ailments of Free Society. The word sociology was "not in use in slave countries," he said,

because "Slave Society, ancient and modern, has ever been in so happy a condition, so exempt from ailments, that no doctors have arisen to treat it of its complaints, or to propose remedies for their cure." In other words, slave society, already having sociology, had no conscious need to formulate it.

10. Walter Fleming, *Documentary History of Reconstruction* (Cleveland: The A. H. Clark Co., 1906–07), II, 183–184.

11. Fred Lewis Pattee, *American Literature Since 1870* (New York: The Century Co., 1916), pp. 264–65.

12. L. L. Bernard, "The Historic Pattern of Sociology in the South," *Social Forces*, XVI (October 1937), 10–12; also Bernard, "The Teaching of Sociology in Southern Colleges and Universities," *American Journal of Sociology*, XXIII (January 1918), 491–515.

13. One of the first of these was Dr. W. E. B. Du Bois who in 1896 went to Atlanta University and there undertook "what was perhaps the first real sociological research in the South." Guy B. Johnson, "Negro Race Movements and Leadership in the United States," *American Journal of Sociology* XLIII (July 1937), 65.

14. "A Memorandum on Rote Learning," *American Journal of Sociology*, XLIII (July 1937), 23–36.

15. Quoted in Louis Wirth, "Criteria and Objectives of Research in the Social Sciences," Conference of Representatives of University Social Science Research Organizations held at the Faculty Club, Cambridge, Mass., November 1937, p. 60.

16. In the *Saturday Review of Literature* XVIII (July 16, 1938), 5.

17. *Op. cit.*, pp. 295–96.

18. Jonathan Daniels, *A Southerner Discovers the South* (New York: Macmillan, 1938); J. Saunders Redding, *No Day of Triumph* (New York: Harper, 1942).

19. "The Spirit of the Laboratory," *Science*, LXXXV (April 9, 1937), 346.

12. The Planter in the Pattern of Race Relations in the South

1. Monroe Work, "Racial Factors and Economic Forces in Land Tenure in the South," *Social Forces*, 15, (December, 1936), p. 214.

2. T. J. Wertenbaker, *The Planters of Colonial Virginia* (Princeton, 1922), p. 73.

3. Josiah Royce, "Provincialism. Based upon a study of early conditions in California," *Putnam's* n.s., VII, 232–240.

4. In Virginia "there are certain particular designations to show calling which were applied generally without social discrimination. In one instance alone, perhaps, did such a designation carry a distinct inference of social importance without, however, nicely defining its degree; the word 'planter' probably at a later date conveyed such a meaning. Not long after the abolition of the Company, we find the term 'planter' applied to the lessees whose names appear in the grants of land belonging to the office of governor. The area contained in these grants was not extensive, and the lessees were men of no social consequence. Not many years later the term 'planter' was applied with great freedom, whether the patentee acquired title to a large tract or to a small; whether

he was a citizen of marked prominence in the colony, or possessed no prominence at all. But by 1675, we find in the ordinary conveyances, recorded in the county courts, an indifferent use by the same man, as applicable to himself, of the terms 'gentleman' and 'planter,' as if the two were practically interchangeable. At this time the estates, in many cases, spread over many thousand acres, and whilst all who owned and cultivated land of their own, whether great or small in area, were, in a strict sense, planters, the term may have come to have a subordinate social meaning as applicable to men of large estates, whose social position by forces of birth, as well as of worldly possessions, was among the foremost in the community. Or it may be, which seems on the whole more probable, the person drawing up one of these deeds designated himself there as 'gentleman' if he happened at the moment to think of his social rank, or as a 'planter' if he thought of his calling."—P. A. Bruce, *Social Life in Virginia in the Seventeenth Century* (Richmond, 1907), pp. 110–112.

5. Robert M. Coates, *The Outlaw Years* (New York, 1930).

6. T. J. Wertenbaker, *Patrician and Plebeian in Virginia* (Charlottesville, 1910), p. 57.

7. George W. Cable, "Who Are the Creoles?" *Century Magazine*, XXV (January, 1883), 395 (n.s., Vol. III).

8. See J. D. MacCrone, *Race Attitudes in South Africa* (London, 1937), p. 41.

9. Lewis C. Copeland, "The Negro as a Contrast Conception," in Edgar T. Thompson (ed.), *Race Relations and the Race Problem* (Durham, N.C., 1939), Ch. VI.

13. The Natural History of Agricultural Labor in the South

1. Charles S. Johnson, Edwin R. Embree, and W. W. Alexander, *The Collapse of Cotton Tenancy* (Chapel Hill, N.C., 1935).

2. See J. S. Bassett, *The Southern Plantation Overseer* (Northampton, Mass., 1925), pp. 86–87, and Lyle Saxon, *Old Louisiana* (New York, 1929), chap. xv.

3. Marjorie Mendenhall, "The Rise of Southern Tenancy," *Yale Review*, XXVII, 124–125 (Autumn, 1937).

4. Lord Olivier, *White Capital and Coloured Labour* (London, 1929), p. 50.

5. F. P. Gaines, *The Southern Plantation: A Study in the Development and the Accuracy of a Tradition* (New York, 1924).

6. "In all history barons have been famous for breaking away from their liege sovereigns and setting up for themselves, and to this extent the Virginia planters justified the title the romantic had given them" (Burton J. Hendrick, *The Lees of Virginia*, Boston, 1935, p. 80).

7. See W. H. S. Aubrey, " 'Sent to the Plantations,' " *Chamber's Journal*, LXXVIII, 812–816 (Dec. 2, 1901).

8. Apparently such distinct contrasts in the status of labor were not present, or, because of undeveloped communication, not so manifest, in the ancient world of Greece and Rome (R. H. Barrow, *Slavery in the Roman Empire*, London, 1928, pp. 20, 235–236). William Graham Sumner quotes Bücher as saying, "Not once, in all antiquity, does a serious thought about the abolition of slavery arise" (*Folkways*, Boston, 1906, p. 283). In the modern world, on the contrary, the contrast in the status of labor between different parts of the same

economic community was, perhaps, the most important factor in movements to abolish the slave trade and to emancipate slaves. In America abolitionism grew rapidly after about 1830 in the small farm and industrial areas of the North. The result of the crusade was to associate the small farm with American democratic mores and to make the plantation suspect.

9. A. G. Keller, *Colonization: A Study of the Founding of New Societies* (Boston, 1908), p. 11.

10. "Geography in the Creative Experiment," *Geographical Review*, XXVIII, (Jan., 1938). p. 11. E. W. Zimmerman expresses the same idea in emphasizing the relativity of the concept *resource* in his *World Resources and Industries* (New York, 1933), p. 3.

11. P. A. Bruce, *Economic History of Virginia in the Seventeenth Century* (New York, 1907), I, 74–75.

12. H. J. Nieboer, *Slavery as an Industrial System* (The Hague, 1910), p. 418. The concept *open resources* is closely related to the concepts *free land* and *frontier.* Free land has figured in the writings of economists, while the concept of the frontier gained currency among historians. Although not of popular or commonsense origin, the concept *open resources* has the scientific advantage of being more abstract and inclusive and suggests the relativity of the phenomena subsumed under it. It also points to its opposite concept *closed resources* Nieboer's work was carried out along the lines of hypotheses implicit or explicit in the works of such men as J. E. Cairnes, Max Weber, A. Loria, E. G. Wakefield, H. Merivale, Karl Marx, and others.

13. Failure to recognize this difference was one factor in the failure of Wakefield's plan of colonization in New Zealand, where a subsistence agriculture became the basis of settlement with no extensive demand for farm labor beyond that supplied by the settler and his family. Wakefield advocated a rational scheme to alter the proportion of land to people by establishing a restrictive price for land, that is, a price which would require immigrants to work for wages a few years before becoming landowners. See J. S. Marais, *The Colonization of New Zealand* (London, 1927), pp. 142–143.

14. Herman Merivale, *Lectures on Colonization and Colonies* (London, 1928), Lecture 9.

15. *Industrial and Commercial Geography* (New York, 1925), p. 381.

16. Arguments, such as those made by A. E. Parkins, *The South* (New York, 1938), pp. 230 ff., on the disadvantages of slave labor as compared with free labor are all beside the point. The alternative presented the Southern planter in the ante-bellum South was not slave labor or free labor, but slave labor or no labor at all.

17. L. C. Gray, "Economic Efficiency and the Competitive Advantages of Slavery Under the Plantation System," *Agricultural History*, IV, 43 (April, 1930).

18. A. H. Stone, *Studies in the American Race Problem* (New York, 1908), pp. 125–126.

19. Alvin Johnson, "The War—By an Economist," *Unpopular Review*, II, 420–421 (Oct.-Dec., 1914).

20. "For a century and a half the Spaniards, though they possessed the finest of the West Indian islands, had no plantations. Private enterprise is necessary to the successes of plantations; and the Spanish colonial system did not favour private enterprise. Cuba produced nothing of importance; nor was it until the vast trade of St. Domingo was destroyed in its terrible struggle for independence that the plantations of Cuba rose to supply its place. Even then, it was

long before a hundredth part of its surface was in a state of cultivation" (E. J. Payne, *History of European Colonies,* London, 1878, p. 72).

21. P. A. Bruce, *Social Life of Virginia in the Seventeenth Century* (Richmond, 1907), pp. 30–31, 79 ff., 83.

22. T. J. Wertenbaker, *Patrician and Plebeian in Virginia* (Charlottesville, 1910), pp. 1–3, 20 ff.

23. Bruce, *Social Life of Virginia in the Seventeenth Century,* p. 52.

24. Wertenbaker, *Patrician and Plebeian in Virginia,* p. 17.

25. Bruce, *Social Life of Virginia in the Seventeenth Century,* p. 52.

26. Wertenbaker, *Patrician and Plebeian in Virginia,* p. 17.

27. *Virginia Magazine of History and Biography,* III, 167 (Oct., 1895).

28. Wertenbaker, *op. cit.,* pp. 58–59.

29. In that world of approximately eight million whites in 1860 only 46,282 heads of families held twenty or more slaves (*Agriculture in the United States in 1860—U. S. Bureau of the Census,* II, 247). One thousand families in 1850 had an annual income of $50,000,000, whereas the remaining 666,000 families had only $60,000,000 a year (William E. Dodd, *The Cotton Kingdom,* New Haven, 1919, p. 24).

30. Paul H. Douglas, "American Apprenticeship and Industrial Education," *Columbia University Studies in History, Economics and Public Law* (1921), Vol. XCV, No. 2, pp. 25–27.

31. Albert Cook Myers (ed.), "Some Account of the Province of Pennsilvania, by William Penn, 1681," *Narratives of Early Pennsylvania, West New Jersey and Delaware, 1630–1707* (New York, 1912), p. 209.

32. Douglas, *op. cit.,* pp. 27–28.

33. It is easy to understand from the history of the word *master* in America why a substitute term was needed to describe a relationship with an employer or a teacher which did not reflect on the status of the apprentice or laborer. The substitute was found in the Dutch word *baas,* originally meaning the head of a household. The word was introduced by Dutch settlers in New York. Changed to *boss,* it became useful in America as *master* became an antonym of *slave.* The term, *boss,* according to the *New International Encyclopaedia,* "seems to have arisen from aversion to the word 'master' regarded as savoring too much of the relations between master and slave, and it has come largely into use among the American negroes since their emancipation." It is interesting to note that in the relations between Dutch and natives in South Africa the word *baas* seems to have had much the same history as the word *master* in America. In America today Communists are seeking to redefine the word *boss* to mean the equivalent of master of slaves.

34. In 1699 the Virginia House of Burgesses resolved that the arming and drilling of white servants would be unsafe because they "for the most part consist of the Worser Sort of the people of Europe . . . we have just reason to feare they may rise upon us" (H. R. McIlwaine, ed., *Journals of the House of Burgesses of Virginia, 1695–1702,* Richmond, 1913, p. 188).

35. L. C. Gray, *History of Agriculture in the Southern United States to 1860* (Washington, 1933), I, 342–343.

36. J. C. Ballagh, "White Servitude in the Colony of Virginia," *Johns Hopkins University Studies in History and Political Science,* 13th Ser. (Baltimore, 1913). Nos. 6–7, p. 45.

37. *Ibid.,* p. 58.

38. The First Assembly directed the severe punishment of any one who sought to allure a servant from the employment of his rightful master. This was

the first of a long series of laws enacted in the Southern colonies and states dealing with the problem of competition for labor between employers.

39. *Negar* or *nigger* do not appear to be corruptions of *Negro*. The Negro is a result of the compounding, under the conditions of life in America, of black people from probably a large number of African tribes into a group regarded as a racial unit by its own members as well as by whites. *Negro* is a mark of the developing race consciousness of this group. " 'Nigger' has been for generations a familiar phrase in our literature and life. In its most modern sense, it savors of contempt and obloquy. Vulgarly it is applied to all personages of dark complexion, however high in the social scale the race to which they belong may be. Probably there is no word in general use which is so widely accepted as of the nature of slang. And yet there are few names descriptive of a special type of people which have a more legitimate ancestry. 'Nigger' is really only the English form of the Portuguese *niger*—black. It was long in use before the more respectable 'negro' was commonly accepted. At all events, as far back as 1616 we find an East Indian Company's captain, in reporting to his superiors on a landing he made near the Cape, writing of the people as being 'mostly niggers.' Not very many years later—in the reign of Charles I—the word appears in official documents to designate slaves taken on the coast of Africa. In fine, it was the 'nigger' and not the negro who was first introduced to people in this country as the special victim of 'a most baleful traffic.' The very contempt into which the good old word has fallen is a proper measure of the degrading effect of 'man's inhumanity to man,' as illustrated in the slave system" (Arnold Wright, *The Romance of Colonisation*, New York, 1923, pp. 108–109).

40. J. H. Russell, "The Free Negro in Virginia, 1619–1865," *Johns Hopkins University Studies in History and Political Science*, 31st Ser. (Baltimore, 1913), No. 3, p. 22.

41. *A History of Slavery in Virginia* (Baltimore, 1902), pp. 31–32.

42. E. B. Reuter, *The Mulatto in the United States* (Boston, 1918), pp. 140–150, Jeffrey R. Brackett, *The Negro in Maryland* (Baltimore, 1889), pp. 33–34.

43. Ballagh, *A History of Slavery in Virginia*, pp. 28–29.

44. Russell, *op. cit.*, p. 23.

45. *Ibid.*, pp. 23–25.

46. *Ibid.*, p. 38.

47. *Ibid.*, pp. 29–30.

48. *Ibid.*, pp. 32–33.

49. W. D. Weatherford and C. S. Johnson, *Race Relations* (New York, 1934), p. 105.

50. Robert Beverly, *The History and Present State of Virginia* (London, 1705), Bk. IV, p. 35.

51. Ballagh, *A History of Slavery in Virginia*, pp. 38–39.

52. In Ann Maury, *Memoirs of a Hugenot Family* (New York, 1853), pp. 349–350.

53. W. W. Hening, *Statutes at Large of Virginia* (New York, 1823), II, 170.

54. Ballagh, *A History of Slavery in Virginia*, p. 38.

55. *Ibid.*, p. 44.

56. White servitude and Negro slavery were two competing systems of labor recruitment and control which grew up in Virginia and in the other American colonies together. In Virginia, Negro slavery won out over white servitude. In Pennsylvania, on the other hand, in a situation which favored small-scale farming and manufacturing, white servitude successfully competed with Negro slavery and tended to replace it. The trades especially required the skill and

discipline possessed by servants with the background of Europe behind them. Of the Pennsylvania situation Herrick says: "As one studies, even in outline, the history of slavery in Pennsylvania, he is impressed with the need for and the extent of white servitude as a substitute for slave labor. Had not white laborers under indenture been ready to hand, it would be more difficult to say how Pennsylvania would have stood on the question of slavery." The opposition to slavery "was in the nature of a demand for indentured and redemption servants that the labor needs of the colony might be supplied. . . . In her sentiment against Negro slavery, and in her labor history, Pennsylvania occupied a peculiar position, a position not to be easily explained without considering white servitude. The opposition of Pennsylvania to slavery as an institution was more than sentiment; the interest of the colony was in the direction of the use of this other form of labor. In all the antislavery discussion in America, Mason and Dixon's Line was a mark of separation of free from slave states, but Mason and Dixon's Line was the southern boundary of Pennsylvania. That the line of division between slavery and freedom was drawn south of Pennsylvania was due in no small measure to the substitute form of servile labor which was available in this state" (C. A. Herrick, *White Servitude in Pennsylvania*, Philadelphia, 1926, pp. 97, 99, 285).

57. U. B. Phillips, "The Economics of the Slave Trade, Foreign and Domestic," *The South in the Building of the Nation* (Richmond, 1909), V, 125.

58. "The estate of Mrs. Rowland Jones of York, in 1689, included among its items of property a mulatto man who had sixteen years to serve. Colonel John Walker was the owner of an African apprentice whose indenture was to remain in force for twenty-eight years. Among the laborers of Mr. George Light was a Negro who had come into Virginia a free man, and bound himself out for a period of five years" (Bruce, *Economic History of Virginia in the Seventeenth Century*, II, 52–53).

59. For example, Beth, the old servant in an English family in E. F. Benson's *Mother* (New York, 1925).

60. It is interesting to note in this connection that in Roman law freedmen might, on complaint of their patron, be re-enslaved on the ground of ingratitude (W. W. Buckland, *The Roman Law of Slavery*, Cambridge, England, 1908, pp. 422–424).

61. See the speech of Isaiah Montgomery, former slave of Joseph Davis, in the Mississippi Constitutional Convention of 1890 as reported in the New York *World* for Sept. 27, 1890, for a story illustrating this.

62. Ballagh, *White Servitude in the Colony of Virginia*, pp. 43–44, and Ballagh, *History of Slavery in Virginia*, p. 62. There was some protest against the practice both in England and in Virginia, but in the absence of means for arousing a strong public opinion the protest was not very effective. In the Hawaiian Islands, where a condition of contract labor existed from 1850 to 1900, both corporal punishment and addition of time were allowed. But public opinion registered itself against the sale and inheritance of contracts in no uncertain terms. These practices were not allowed by the courts. See John R. Commons and John B. Andrews, *Principles of Labor Legislation* (Rev. ed.; New York, 1916), pp. 42–43, and Katharine Coman, "The History of Contract Labor in the Hawaiian Islands," American Economic Association, *Publications*, 3d Ser. (Aug., 1903), Vol. IV, No. 3.

63. See the account of a slave auction in Frederic Bancroft, *Slave-Trading in the Old South* (Baltimore, 1931), pp. 109–110, for a good illustration of the formal, legal attitude in slavery.

64. In the West Indies, on the other hand, slavery in practice was probably something worse than the language of the law represented it to be.

65. Edward Channing, *A History of the United States* (New York, 1928), V, 120.

66. Social change is closely bound up with land tenure. Revolutionary institutional changes in a country are almost always accompanied by radical changes in the distribution of the land. The true revolutionary note is struck with the cry "all land to the peasants." Contrarily, an old social system is maintained to the extent that changes can be prevented in the existing system of landownership and tenure.

67. "There is an obvious distinction between a cropper and a tenant. One has a possession of the premises, exclusive of the landlord; the other has not; the one has a right for a fixed time; the other has only a right to go on the land to plant, work, and gather the crop. The possession of the land is with the owner as against the cropper. This is not so of the tenant. The case made in the record is not the case of a tenant. The owner of the land furnished the land and the supplies. The share of the cropper was to remain on the land and to be subject to the advances of the owner for supplies. The case of the cropper is rather a mode of paying wages than a tenacy. The title to the crop subject to the wages is in the owner of the land. We are of the opinion that no person can purchase or take a lien on the wages of the cropper, to-wit: his share of the crop until the bargain be completed, to-wit: until the advances of the planter to the cropper, for the supplies, have been paid for. A different rule might obtain, as to a tenant, the right of the landlord being only a lien. But the cropper's share of the crop is not his until he has complied with the bargain." See Appling *v.* Odum, 46 *Georgia Reports*, 583 (1872). Also Harrison *v.* Ricks, 71 *N. C.* 7 (1874); Almand *v.* Scott, 80 *Georgia* 95, 4 *S. E.* 892 (1888); Hammock *v.* Creekmore, 48 *Arkansas* 264, 3 *S. W.* 180 (1887).

68. For convenience I am using the term *tenancy* or *share-tenancy* to include share-tenancy proper and share-cropping except when the context indicates a more precise meaning.

69. Johnson, Embree, and Alexander, *op. cit.*, pp. 4–5.

70. *Ibid.*, p. 7.

71. *Ibid.*, pp. 4–5.

72. Of the seventeenth-century plantation of Richard Lee, Hendrick (*op. cit.*, p. 9) says: "The men and women bending over tobacco plants, the girls busy with milk pail and churn, the household servants hurrying about their tasks—all these were strangely unlike those immemorially associated with Virginia and the South. For all had skins as white as that of the master himself. Probably not a solitary negro ever appeared on Richard's farm."

73. "Racial Factors and Economic Forces in Land Tenure in the South," *Social Forces*, XV, 214 (Dec., 1936).

74. Mendenhall, *op. cit.*, XXVII, 110–129.

75. "We are familiar with the differentiation into planters and poor whites which came about in many sections where there were large, successfully managed plantations. But we are less familiar with the idea that the emergence of the great planters rested on something besides land monopoly and slave labor. Quite most important factor here was the improvement they made in the technique of production" (*ibid.*, XXVII, 119–120).

76. *Ibid.*, XXVII, 122.

77. Robert E. Park, "Racial Assimilation in Secondary Groups," *Publications of the American Sociological Society*, VIII, 75 (1913).

78. General O. O. Howard, Commissioner of the Freedman's Bureau, observed that they drifted "into nooks and corners like *débris* in sloughs and eddies; and were very soon to be found in varied ill conditioned masses, all the way from Maryland to Mexico, and the Gulf to the Ohio River" (*Autobiography*, New York, 1907, II, 164).

79. The following story by Booker T. Washington well expresses the meaning of freedom to the freedman: "I remember an acquaintance of mine telling me of an old colored man he had met somewhere in North Carolina, who had spent the greater part of his life in slavery. My friend, who had known the institution of slavery only through the medium of books, was anxious to find out just what the thing seemed like to a man who had lived in slavery most of his life. The old colored man said that he had had a good master, who was always kind and considerate; that the food he had to eat was always of the best quality and there was enough of it; he had nothing to complain of in regard to the clothing that was provided or the house that he lived in. He said both he and his family always had the best medical attention when they fell ill. To all appearances, as near as anyone could judge, the old man must have been a great deal better off in slavery than he was in freedom. Noticing these things, my friend became more inquisitive and wanted to know whether, after all, there was not a feeling deep down in his heart, that he would rather be back in slavery, with all the comforts that he had enjoyed there, than be free. The old man shrugged his shoulders, scratched his head, thought for a second, and then said: 'Boss, dere's a kind of looseness about dis y'ere freedom which I kinder enjoys'" (*The Story of the Negro*, New York, 1909, II, 34–35).

80. Park, *op. cit.*, VIII, 76.

81. That a propertyless laborer *could* move away from employment on one plantation with almost absolute assurance of getting work elsewhere is evidence that the South continued to be an area of open resources. There is evidence that the present transition to a situation of closed resources is curtailing greatly the annual migration of tenants from one plantation to another. See Fred C. Frey and T. Lynn Smith, "The Influence of the AAA Cotton Program upon the Tenant, Cropper, and Laborer," *Rural Sociology*, I, 504 (Dec., 1936).

82. Stone, *op. cit.*, pp. 127–128.

83. *Ibid.*, pp. 130–131.

84. *Ibid.*, p. 146. The statement is elaborated on pp. 145–146. Carlton H. Parker in his *The Casual Laborer and Other Essays* (New York, 1920) has used this "instinct" to explain casual and migratory laborers generally.

85. There were and are many outstanding exceptions to this statement, and the exceptions are becoming more and more numerous. See E. Franklin Frazier, *The Free Negro Family* (Nashville, Tenn., 1932).

86. Under the circumstances the mother emerged as the real head of the family because of her close biological ties with the children and her more constant association with them. Frazier has discussed "the tradition of female dominance with a corresponding maternal family pattern, which appears in its purest and most primitive form on the remnants of the old plantations of the South." See E. Franklin Frazier, "Traditions and Patterns of Negro Family Life in the United States," *Publications of the American Sociological Society*, XXVIII, 125–126 (1934).

87. On this point F. L. Olmsted observed: "Until the Negro is big enough for his labor to be plainly profitable to his master, he has no training to application or method, but only to idleness and carelessness. Before children arrive at a

working age, they hardly come under the notice of their owner. . . . The only whipping of slaves I have seen in Virginia has been of these wild, lazy children, as they are being broke into work. They cannot be depended upon a minute out of sight. You will see how difficult it would be, if it were attempted, to eradicate the indolent, careless, incogitant habits so formed in youth. But it is not systematically attempted, and the influences that continue to act upon a slave in the same direction, cultivating every quality at variance with industry, precision, forethought and providence, are innumerable" (*The Cotton Kingdom*, New York, 1861, p. 131).

88. David C. Barrow, Jr., "A Georgia Plantation," *Scribner's Monthly*, XXI, 830–836 (April, 1881).

89. The quarters on the ante-bellum Southern plantation, and on some estates in certain parts of the South even today, are typical of the pattern of plantation settlement everywhere. They are like the coolie "lines" on plantations in Malaya and Sumatra and the "camps" on plantations in Hawaii. The original pattern of plantation settlement is that of the camp, a word which implies the history and status of imported laborers who are dumped down on land which is not their own and where they live under supervision. In military language quarters are barracks—houses without privacy and intended primarily for individuals and not for families.

90. Edward King, *The Great South* (Hartford, 1875), pp. 273, 301; Robert Somers, *The Southern States Since the War* (New York, 1871), p. 120; Sir George Campbell, *White and Black* (London, 1879), p. 355. Sir Donald Mackenzie Wallace calls attention to the same changes on Russian estates when the authority of the landed proprietors was abolished in 1861. Every peasant "wished to be independent, and in a very short time nearly every able-bodied married peasant had a house of his own" (*Russia*, New York, 1877, p. 554).

91. Barrow, *op. cit.*, XXI, 832.

92. In 1936 more than three fourths of all farm labor in the United States was performed without wages by members of the farm operators' families. The heaviest concentration of unpaid female and child labor was in the Southern States ("Trends in Employment in Agriculture, 1903–1936," W.P.A. National Research Project. Released Dec. 18, 1938).

93. Quoted in A. L. Harris and S. D. Spero, "Negro Problem," *Encyclopaedia of the Social Sciences*, XI, 347.

94. The history of this part of the South since the Civil War might almost be written around the subject of the country store. The history of the Southern country store since 1865 is closely bound up with such matters as the redistribution of population, the rise of town life and with everything that went with town life—a new merchant-planter aristocracy, new forms of labor control, the rise of white democracy, new racial conflicts, new forms of racial accommodation, a public education and high-school movement, etc.

95. Peonage has been defined as a "status or condition of compulsory service based upon the indebtedness of the peon to the master." See Clyatt *v.* U.S., 197, U.S. 207, 25 Sup. Ct. 429 (1904). The basic fact is indebtedness, and this differentiates peonage from serfdom, its counterpart in a nonpecuniary society. Peonage utilizes a pecuniary system to hold nonpecuniary minded laborers on the land. On the other hand, in England through the medium of "quitrent" money became an emancipatory device. Both peonage and serfdom are characteristic of agricultural and rural societies. They do not exist in the city.

96. As Audrey I. Richards has shown in her *Hunger and Work in a Savage Tribe* (London, 1932), the nutrition process in human society cannot be consid-

ered from the biological aspect alone. Nor is it enough to extend its consideration to include economic factors. Because the compulsion to work by hunger
is always present or potential the nutrition process may become a part of the
mechanism of political control. "Legal constraint [to labor]," said the Reverend
Joseph Townsend in his argument against the English Poor Laws, "is attended
with too much trouble, violence, and noise . . . whereas hunger is not only a
peaceable, silent, unremitted pressure, but, as the most natural motive to industry and labor, it calls forth the most powerful exertions" (*A Dissertation on
the Poor Laws*, London, 1786, p. 14).

97. In this connection it is interesting to notice that, in the opinion of some
etymologists, certain English words denoting status originated around the production and the distribution of food. *Lord*, for example, in its primary sense
meant the head of a household in his relation to servants and dependents who
"eat his bread." As "loaf-ward," "Keeper and dispenser of bread," he was one
who had or obtained dominion over others and to whom service and obedience
were due. *Lady* has been explained as meaning originally one who kneaded
the bread and therefore one to whom obedience or feudal homage became due,
a mistress in relation to servants or slaves. In Scandinavian languages, "meat-
mother" is the designation applied by servants to their mistress. In certain of
the old Germanic languages which contributed to form the English language
the term for *servant* meant "bread-eater" and then one who is under obligation
to work for another.

98. Since the planter controls the food, he also controls the diet. On Southern
plantations the chief items in the diet are often described as the three
M's—meat (fat salt pork), meal, and molasses, foods that are relatively easily
preserved in the commissaries.

99. *Staple Cotton Review*, VIII, 5 (Nov., 1930); quoted in Rupert Vance, *Human Geography of the South* (Chapel Hill, N.C., 1932), p. 271.

100. See Richards, *op. cit.*, p. 31.

101. Prices for crops that are produced on the plantation for sale outside are
subject to wide fluctuations. On the other hand, compensation for goods and
services that originate on the plantation for consumption on the plantation, like
ditch-digging, laundrying, etc., vary little from time to time. Prices for such
goods and services tend to become customary, and any departure from a customary charge is cause for resentment. Goods and services that originate outside the plantation for consumption on the plantation, like food, medical service, etc., fluctuate in price but ordinarily pass to the tenant through the personal
medium of the planter and become a part of the system of feudal relationships.
On the books of the planter the price of these goods and services is charged
against the tenant, but, as the authors of *The Collapse of Cotton Tenancy* (p.
18) say, "The tenant does not know the money value of what he is receiving,
or, to be more exact, he does not know what he is being charged for it." They
might have added that in the nonpecuniary tradition of the plantation the
money price of what he receives seems to make very little difference if what
he receives is what he feels he has a right to expect.

102. On this point John Dollard, a Northern observer, says: "It seems almost
as if the Negroes regarded the money as a gift, quite overlooking that they have
to pay it back later. The planter who gives Christmas money would then fall
into the category of the generous parent; and the one who doesn't, into the role
of a niggardly person" (*Caste and Class in a Southern Town*, New Haven, 1937,
p. 403 n.).

103. Floyd N. House, *Industrial Morale* (Unpublished Ph.D. dissertation, University of Chicago, Aug., 1924), p. 33.

104. R. P. Brooks, "A Local Study of the Race Problem," *Political Science Quarterly*, XXVI, 202–203 (June, 1911).

105. More frequently, however, as was pointed out earlier, the roving freedman left the plantation of his former master.

106. C. W. Tabeau, *The Planter in the Lower South, 1865–1880* (Unpublished Ph.D. dissertation, State University of Iowa, June, 1933), pp. 95–96.

107. *Ibid.*, pp. 78–79.

108. ". . . in its program of rural rehabilitation in the South, the FERA was baffled by not a few cases in which landlords at the same time refused to advance money to their cash renters and also refused to waive the rent of these tenants in order to allow the benefits of direct federal relief. These landlords apparently preferred to hold the remnants of the old plantation system in their own hands; they did not relish 'outside interference' " (Clarence Cason, *90° in the Shade*, Chapel Hill, N.C., 1935, p. 36).

109. "There are other fears back of the landlord's attitude: the fear that the tenant will be removed from the influence of the landowner and learn that he is not entirely dependent on him; and the fear that the relief will raise the standard of living to the extent that bargaining on the old basis will be difficult" (Johnson, Embree, and Alexander, *op. cit.*, p. 59).

110. Frey and Smith, *op. cit.*, I, 503.

111. Everett C. Hughes, *The Chicago Real Estate Board: The Growth of an Institution* (Chicago, 1931), p. 13.

112. *Ibid.*, Preface.

14. Purpose and Tradition in Southern Rural Society: A Point of View for Research

1. During the course of his discussion of the characteristics of the Red River country in the South, J. Russell Smith remarked, "The organization of the plantation is much like that of a coal mine." *North America* (New York, 1925), p. 249.

2. Although the old-line tobacco farmer of North Carolina is the peer of tobacco farmers anywhere he is not finding it easy to adjust to the new methods required in the culture of Turkish tobacco. He is less successful in this field than farmers with no previous experience in growing tobacco. I am indebted to Mr. F. R. Darkis of Duke University for this information.

3. Princeton: Princeton University Press, 1942.

4. *Ibid.*, p. 33.

5. For an elaboration of the plantation as a political institution see the writer's "Population Expansion and the Plantation System," *American Journal of Sociology* XLI (1935), 314–326; "The Planter in the Pattern of Race Relations in the South," *Social Forces*, XIX, (1940), 244–252; "The Natural History of Agricultural Labor in the South," in D. K. Jackson (ed.), *American Studies in Honor of William Kenneth Boyd* (Durham, N.C., 1940); "Comparative Education in Colonial Areas, with Special Reference to Plantation and Mission Frontiers," *American Journal of Sociology*, XLVIII (1943), 82–93; and "The Plantation: the Physical Basis of Traditional Race Relations in the South," in Edgar T. Thompson (ed.), *Race Relations and the Race Problem* (Durham, N.C., 1939).

6. *Social Forces,* XVI (1937), 201–207.

7. *Ibid.,* p. 207.

8. *Ibid.,* p. 201.

9. *Colonization* (Boston, 1908). Keller repeated his thesis more recently in his *Societal Evolution* (rev. ed., New York, 1931), pp. 344–372.

10. *Colonization,* p. 11.

11. "The Climatic Theory of the Plantation," *Agricultural History,* XV (1941), 49–60.

12. See his "British versus German Traditions in Colonial Agriculture," *Mississippi Valley Historical Review* XXVI (1939), 39–54, and "Cultural Factors in the History of the South," *The Journal of Southern History,* V (1939), 333–346. Paralleling and supplementing Shryock's work are a number of articles on German "cultural islands" in the South by Walter Kollmorgen. These include "The German-Swiss in Franklin County, Tennessee," U. S. Dept. of Agriculture, May, 1940, and "The German Settlement in Cullman County, Alabama," U.S. Dept. of Agriculture, June, 1941.

13. "British versus German Traditions in Colonial Agriculture," *op. cit.,* p. 47.

14. *Ibid.,* p. 44.

15. *Ibid.,* pp. 46–47.

16. *Ibid.,* p. 49.

17. *Ibid.,* p. 54.

18. *Ibid.,* p. 54. Not only in Virginia and in the South, but wherever they settled in other parts of the world, Shryock contends, the British were seldom good agriculturalists. In addition, because of their control of the world's seaways and colonies, they tended to discourage settlement in the areas they monopolized by people of other nationality who were good agriculturalists. Contrarily, German settlers in other parts of the world, such as in Russia and in Roumania, stood out from their neighbors, as they did in America, as superior farmers. *Ibid.,* pp. 52–53.

19. Keller, *op. cit.,* chap. XIV.

20. The Natives have difficulty in distinguishing between these agents and their motives and tend to categorize all as Europeans.

21. See the evidence on this point presented by Shryock, "British versus German Traditions in Colonial Agriculture," *op. cit.,* pp. 42–44.

22. J. S. Buckingham, *The Slave States of America* (London, 1842), I, 258. That such statements were constantly being made by English observers from Robert Beverly in the early colonial period as well as by others through the post-Civil War period indicates that southern agriculture was no mere offshoot of English agriculture, no mere continuation of English farming traditions.

23. T. P. Abernethy, "Social and Political Control in the Old Southwest," *Mississippi Valley Historical Review* XVI (March, 1930), 534.

24. *Old Virginia and Her Neighbors* (Boston, 1898), II, 198.

25. *Patrician and Plebeian in Virginia* (Charlottesville, Virginia, 1910), p. 146.

26. See Charles Egbert Craddock's novels *The Prophet of the Great Smoky Mountains* (Boston, 1888), and *In the Tennessee Mountains* (Boston, 1884).

27. Jenette Tandy, *The Crackerbox Philosophers in American Humor and Satire* (New York, 1925), p. 66.

28. Robert E. Park in C. S. Johnson, *The Shadow of the Plantation* (Chicago, 1934), p. xxii.

29. William Garrott Brown, "The White Peril: the Immediate Danger of the Negro," *North American Review* CLXXIX (December, 1904), 839.

15. The South and the Second Emancipation

1. Marcus W. Jernegan, "Slavery and Conversion in the American Colonies," *American Historical Review*, XXI (April, 1916), 505.

2. For documentation of this proposition, see Charles Grier Sellers, "The Travail of Slavery," in Sellers, ed., *The Southerner as American* (Chapel Hill: University of North Carolina Press, 1960).

3. Stephen W. Reed, *The Making of Modern New Guinea* (Philadelphia: American Philosophical Society, 1942), pp. 245–246.

4. Crèvecoeur does not consider the case of the Negro in his famous essay, "What, Then, Is the American, This New Man?" See Arthur M. Schlesinger, *Paths to the Present* (New York: Macmillan Co., 1949), chap. i.

5. George Burton Adams, *Civilization during the Middle Ages* (Rev. ed.; New York: Charles Scribner's Sons, 1914), p. 30.

6. John Gillin, " 'Race' Relations without Conflict: A Guatemalan Town," *American Journal of Sociology*, LIII (March, 1948), 337–343.

7. *United States Congressional Record*, Seventy-ninth Congress, Second Session, XCII, Part 1 (Jan. 30, 1946), 563.

8. Hans Mattson, *Reminiscences: The Story of an Immigrant* (St. Paul: D. D. Merrill Co., 1891), p. 111.

9. See, for example, Maldwyn Jones, *American Immigration* (Chicago: University of Chicago Press, 1960); Marcus L. Hansen, *The Immigrant in American History* (Cambridge, Mass.: Harvard University Press, 1940); and Oscar Handlin, *The Uprooted* (Boston: Little Brown and Co., 1951).

10. Niccole Tucci, "The Underground Letters," *New Yorker*, XXVII (Aug. 4, 1951), 24.

11. Everett and Helen M. Hughes, *Where Peoples Meet* (Glencoe: Free Press, 1952), p. 140. Emerson distinguished between the Party of Memory and the Party of Hope.

12. John Paul Reed, *Kokutai* (Chicago: University of Chicago Libraries, 1940), chap. iii, "Dangerous Thoughts."

13. The South African Nationalist government has gone so far as legislatively to define such people as Communists. See Leo Kuper, *Passive Resistance in South Africa* (New Haven: Yale University Press, 1957), chap. ii, "Communism by Statute."

14. R. H. Grotton, *The British Middle Class* (London: G. Bell and Sons, Ltd., 1917).

16. The South in Old and New Contexts

1. "Education for the World," *Adult Education Journal*, VI (July, 1947), 129–133.

2. Thomas Jefferson was one of the first to give literary expression to our own contrasting North-South ideas in a letter to the Marquis de Chastellux in 1785. See John Richard Alden, *The First South* (Baton Rouge: Louisiana State University Press, 1961), p. 17.

3. "The South is the only region of the United States that fronts the sea on two sides, From Virginia to Key West it looks to Europe across the Atlantic; from Key West to Brownsville, it looks to Latin America. The South's shoreline

along the Atlantic is 1,099 miles; along the Gulf, 1,659 miles. It has a total shoreline of 2,758 miles. It has nearly four times the shoreline of the North, more than twice that of the Pacific coast, and nearly six hundred miles more seacost than the North and West combined." Walter Webb, "The South's Call to Greatness," *The Graduate Journal of the University of Texas.* III (1960), Supplement, 304.

4. This region, of course, extended to the southwest from the distant markets of Western Europe across the Atlantic Ocean. But it might be considered a segment of a frontier describing one of von Thünen's concentric circles which had its counterpart, where soil and climatic conditions were favorable, to the east of these centers. J. H. von Thünen, *Der Isolierte Staat in Beziehung auf Land wirtschaft und Nationalökonomie* (3 vols.; Berlin: Wiegandt, Hempel und Parey, 1875). Beyond the Elbe River in Germany there appeared large plantation-like estates producing for the same market centers. Rüstow suggests that the New World plantations actually formed the model for these eastern estates, but it is possible they developed independently in response to ecological and historical circumstances similar to those from which the New World plantations sprang. Alexander Rüstow, *Ortesbestimmung der Gergenwart* (Erlenbach-Zurich: Eugen Rentsch, 1950), pp. 62, 171–172.

5. Alden, *op. cit., passim.*

6. Thomas Ellison, *The Cotton Trade of Great Britain* (London: E. Wilson, 1886), p. 29; Harold Rugg, *Changing Civilization in the Modern World* (New York: Ginn and Co., 1930), p. 62; M. B. Hammond, *The Cotton Industry* (Ithaca, N. Y.: American Economic Association, 1897), Appendix I; L. C. A. Knowles, *The Industrial and Commercial Revolutions in Great Britain During the Nineteenth Century* (London: Routledge and Kegan Paul, 1926), p. 51; F. V. Emerson, "Geographical Influences in American Slavery," *American Geographic Society Bulletin,* XLIII (January-March, 1911), 13–26, 106–118, 170–181; U.S. Bureau of the Census, *Eleventh Census: 1890, Progress of the Nation, 1790–1890,* Part I, pp. xviii–xxviii.

7. Walter Webb, *The Great Plains* (Boston: Ginn and Co., 1931).

8. John Peale Bishop, *Collected Essays* (New York: Charles Scribner's Sons, 1948), p. 171.

9. In an Alabama county seat, according to a story remembered from the lectures of Robert E. Park, a sign at the entrance to the court house read: "No spitting—$100 fine for spitting." But all around was the evidence of vast expectoration. One morning an additional sign appeared which read: "If you don't stop this spitting we're going to enforce this law." For more on the history of the southern attitude toward law and its enforcement see Charles S. Sydnor, "The Southerner and the Laws," *Journal of Southern History,* VI (February, 1940), 3–23.

10. Ruth Landes, "A Northerner Views the South," *Social Forces,* XXIII (March, 1945), 376.

11. Stanley M. Elkins, *Slavery: A Problem in American Institutional Life* (Chicago: University of Chicago Press, 1959).

12. *Ibid.*

13. Robert Redfield and Milton B. Singer, "The Cultural Role of Cities," *Economic Development and Social Change,* III (October, 1954), 53–73.

14. J. H. Breasted, *A History of Egypt* (2nd ed.; New York: C. Scribner's Sons, 1912).

15. W. J. Cash, *The Mind of the South* (New York: A. A. Knopf, 1941), pp. 103–104.

16. See Francis P. Gaines, *The Southern Plantation: A Study in the Devel-*

opment and Accuracy of a Tradition (New York: Columbia University Press, 1924).

17. Twelve Southerners, *I'll Take My Stand: The South and the Agrarian Tradition* (New York: Harper and Brothers, 1930).

18. *New Englander*, XXIII (October, 1864), 701.

19. See, among other books on the Reconstruction period, Harry Lee Swint, *The Northern Teacher in the South, 1862–1870* (Nashville: Vanderbilt University Press, 1941).

20. Everett C. Hughes, "New Peoples," in Andrew W. Lind, *Race Relations in World Perspective* (Honolulu: University of Hawaii Press, 1955), Ch. V.

21. Edgar T. Thompson, "The Plantation as a Race-Making Situation," in Leonard Broom and Philip Selznick, *Sociology* (Evanston, Illinois: Row, Peterson and Company, 1955), pp. 506–507. Elsewhere I have tried to account more specifically for the rise and operation of various factors leading up to the definition of the relations between whites and blacks in the South as "race relations." "The South and the Second Emancipation," in Allan P. Sindler (ed.), *Change in the Contemporary South* (Durham: Duke University Press, 1963).

22. C. Vann Woodward, *The Strange Career of Jim Crow* (New York: Oxford University Press, 1955).

23. See W. F. Ogburn, "Southern Regional Folkways Regarding Money," *Social Forces*, XXI (March, 1943), 297–299.

24. Herbert Blumer, "Industrialisation and Race Relations," in Guy Hunter (ed.), *Industrialisation and Race Relations* (London: Oxford University Press, 1965).

25. Perhaps this is what Whitehead had in mind when he wrote: "In the conditions of modern life, the rule is absolute. The race which does not value trained intelligence is doomed. There will be no appeal from the judgment which will be pronounced on the uneducated." Alfred North Whitehead, *The Aims of Education and Other Essays* (New York: The Macmillan Company, 1929), pp. 22–23.

26. E. Franklin Frazier, "A Comparison Between Negro White Relations in Brazil and in the United States," *Transactions of the New York Academy of Sciences*, Series II, VI (May, 1944), 266.

27. *The Negro in American Society* (Tallahassee: Flordia State University Studies No. 28, 1958), p. 13.

28. H. C. Nixon, *Possum Trot* (Norman: University of Oklahoma Press, 1941). As local people are realigned into new and wider group relationships there is, among other things, a loss or a shift in group loyalties. "It is hard," Prof. Nixon says, "to be loyal to a highway, a rural route, or a bus line. It is hard to be loyal to a consolidated school which is located somewhere else."

17. God and the Southern Plantation System

1. Kenneth Burke, *Permanence and Change: An Anatomy of Purpose* (Indianapolis: Bobbs-Merrill, 1965), p. 74.

2. The opinion of the Reverend H. C. Morrison of Asbury College is representative. He doubted whether there was "another territory of like area beneath the sun, where there is a stronger, better faith in the Bible, where the Sabbath is better observed, where a larger per cent. of the people attend

church, where virtue in womanhood and honesty in manhood are more common and command a better premium" than in the South. Kenneth K. Bailey, *Southern White Protestantism in the Twentieth Century* (New York: Harper, 1964), p. 24.

3. Robert K. Merton, "The Unanticipated Consequences of Purposeful Social Action," *American Sociological Review* I (December, 1936), 894–904; William Graham Sumner, "Religion and the Mores," in *War and Other Essays* (New Haven: Yale University Press, 1919), chap. 5.

4. Bailey, *Southern White*, p. 24.

5. As late as 1935 Edwin McNeill Poteat, Jr., could write: "In spite of considerable ecclesiastical differences the theology of the South is the same in its broad essentials among all the religious groups. Whether one meets in a Quaker Meeting House in Guilford County, North Carolina, or in a Methodist Church in Savannah, or in St. Louis Cathedral in New Orleans, the basal religious philosophy is the same. Scratch any sectarian skin and the same orthodox blood flows. This is what accounts in a measure for the uniform dullness of most of the sectarian papers." In W. T. Couch, ed., *Culture in the South* (Chapel Hill: University of North Carolina Press, 1935), p. 261.

6. It is not enough to call the South the "Bible Belt" without emphasizing the kind of Bible it was and is. In a letter Everett Hughes points out that even the King James version was not the same Bible as the Bible of other parts of the United States. Elsewhere it was not always used in the same way as in the "Bible Belt."

In the Bible Belt, the Bible of the teacher of the men's Bible Class is frequently not the Bible of the minister's sermon.

7. Seymour Martin Lipset, *Political Man: The Social Basis of Politics* (Garden City: Doubleday Anchor Books, 1960), pp. 273–74.

8. Everett Hughes, *The Chicago Real Estate Board: The Growth of an Institution* (Chicago: University of Chicago Press, 1931), Preface.

9. Stanley M. Elkins, *Slavery: A Problem in American Institutional Life* (Chicago: University of Chicago Press, 1959), p. 81. But cf. T. Lynn Smith, *Brazil: People and Institutions* (Baton Rouge: Louisiana State University Press, 1954), *passim*.

10. Elkins, *Slavery*, 201–2; Winthrop D. Jordan speaks of the Anglican church in early Virginia as "an organizational monstrosity. . . . The Anglican Church was 'established' in the southern colonies, though the establishment was particularly shaky in North Carolina and Georgia. In Virginia the Church's position was relatively firm, but even there it could scarcely be termed a powerful institution; . . . the vestrymen were normally the leading planters of the parish. The established Anglican Church of Virginia . . . was in large measure dominated by slaveholders." *White Over Black* (Chapel Hill: University of North Carolina Press, 1968), pp. 206–7.

11. Wesley F. Craven, *Southern Colonies in the 17th Century, 1607–1689* (Baton Rouge: Louisiana State University Press, 1949), pp. 153, 159, 170–72, 274–78; Philip A. Bruce, *Institutional History of Virginia in the Seventeenth Century*, Vol. I (New York: Putnam, 1910), p. 468; George M. Brydon, *Virginia's Mother Church and the Political Conditions Under Which It Grew*, Vol. I (Richmond: Virginia Historical Society, 1947), pp. 94, 96, 232; Frank Lawrence Owsley, *Plain Folk of the Old South* (Baton Rouge: Louisiana State University Press, 1949), chap. 1; James McBride Dabbs, *Who Speaks for the South?* (New York: Funk and Wagnals, 1964), chap. 8.

12. Somers, speaking of Mississippi, said, "The farms and plantations, of which there are many, seem to have been picked out, far apart from one another, in

the recesses of the woods, without making any great impression on the natural wilderness of the country." Robert Somers, *The Southern States Since the War, 1870–1871* (New York: Macmillan, 1871), p. 240.

13. Owsley, *Plain Folk*, pp. 136–37.

14. Joseph Schumpeter, *Capitalism, Socialism, and Democracy* (New York: Harper, 1942), chap. 7.

15. See Edgar T. Thompson, "The Natural History of Agricultural Labor in the South," in *American Studies in Honor of W. K. Boyd*, D. K. Jackson, ed. (Durham, N.C.: Duke University Press, 1940), pp. 156–157.

16. E. Franklin Frazier, *The Negro Family in the United States* (Chicago: The University of Chicago Press, 1939), chaps. 2, 3.

17. See Edgar T. Thompson, "Comparative Education in Colonial Areas, with Special Reference to Plantation and Mission Frontiers," in *Education and the Cultural Process*, Charles S. Johnson, ed., reprinted from *The American Journal of Sociology*, XLVIII (May, 1943), 82–93.

18. See Blanche Henry Clark, *The Tennessee Yeoman, 1840–1860* (Nashville: Vanderbilt University Press, 1942), p. 16.

19. "There is a much greater tendency for Negroes to be able to read and write when they independently operate small farms, or if a family or so of them work for a single white family, than there is if they are grouped together in large numbers as wage hands, croppers, or share tenants on the plantations." T. Lynn Smith, *The Population of Louisiana*, Louisiana Bulletin no. 293 (Baton Rouge: Louisiana State University, 1937).

20. H. C. Nixon, "Colleges and Universities," in *Culture in the South*, W. T. Couch, ed. (Chapel Hill: University of North Carolina Press, 1935), p. 229.

21. Lewis W. Wilhern, "Local Institutions of Maryland," *Johns Hopkins University Studies in History and Political Science, 1885*, Vol. III, p. 65; Edward Ingle, "Local Institutions of Virginia," *ibid.*, pp. 45–46.

22. "Prior to 1851 the government of Maryland was in theory and practice a loose confederation of counties and cities similar in spirit to the national government under the Articles of Confederation." Chester Maxey, "The Political Integration of Metropolitan Communities," *National Municipal Review* XI (1922), 230. Several of the counties of this State are peninsulas which jut down into the Chesapeake Bay; the strong county solidarity of the State probably has this insular influence as its origin. Maryland virtually ratified the Federal constitution by counties. John V. L. McMahon, *An Historical View of the Government of Maryland* (Baltimore: 1831), p. 464.

23. "From 1670 to 1691 every official position in Henrico county [in Virginia] was filled by a member of the Randolph family or two other families. Four families got most of the military offices of the county. Similar conditions prevailed in all the older counties where certain families had been long enough to establish powerful and political connections." Arthur W. Calhoun, *A Social History of the American Family*, Vol. I (Cleveland: The Arthur H. Clark Co., 1917), p. 233.

24. Francis Joseph Tschan, "The Virginia Planter, 1700–1775." Ph.D. dissertation, University of Chicago, 1916, pp. 334–35. If the horse was the Cadillac of the plantation gentry, as has been said, he was also the Model T Ford of the Methodist circuit rider in the back country.

25. Arthur F. Raper, *The Tragedy of Lynching* (Chapel Hill: University of North Carolina Press, 1933), p. 104.

26. Joseph Rosenstein, "Government and Social Structure in a Deep South Community," Master's thesis, University of Chicago, 1941, p. 23; Charles S. Sydnor, *Gentlemen Freeholders: Political Practices in Washing-*

ton's Virginia (Chapel Hill: University of North Carolina Press, 1952), *passim.*

27. E. Franklin Frazier, *The Negro Church in America* (New York: Schocken Books, 1963), chap. 1.

28. E. B. Reuter, *The American Race Problems: A Study of the Negro,* rev. ed. (New York: Thomas Y. Crowell Company, 1938), p. 313.

29. *God's Trombones: Seven Negro Sermons in Verse* (New York: The Viking Press, 1927).

30. It is perhaps not unlike the separation of "European" and "non-European" Catholicism in Brazil. Cf. Donald Warren, Jr., "The Negro and Religion in Brazil," *Race,* VI (January, 1965), 99 ff.

31. Unlike their white masters who continued a core of fixed Christian tradition inherited from Europe, the black man in America took on a new creed, a new God, and especially a new Savior with the kind of fervor and seriousness that characterized the early Christians. *See God Struck Me Dead,* Social Science Source Documents, no. 2, Social Science Institute (Nashville: Fisk University, 1945). The note of militancy which perhaps has been present in American Negro Christianity since colonial days has recently been greatly accentuated. See Joseph R. Washington, Jr., *Black Religion* (Boston: Beacon Press, 1964); and James H. Cone, *Black Theology and Black Power* (New York: Seabury Press, 1969); Hart M. Nelsen, *et al.* eds., *The Black Church in America* (New York: Basic Books, 1971).

32. Allison Davis, "The Relation Between Color Caste and Economic Stratification in Two 'Black' Plantation Counties," Ph.D. dissertation, University of Chicago, 1942, p. 42.

33. Richard K. Crallé, ed., *The Works of John C. Calhoun,* Vol. III (New York: D. Appleton, 1851–1870), p. 180.

34. I am indebted to Robert Redfield and Milton B. Singer for the distinctions between the "little tradition" and the "great tradition" and between orthogenetic cities and heterogenetic cities. "The Cultural Role of Cities," *Economic Development and Cultural Change,* III (October, 1954), 53–73.

35. Paul Tillich argues that culture is the sort of order existing in a society which has a cult or a religion. It is the form or shape that religion takes. *Theology of Culture* (New York: Oxford University Press, 1968), chap. 4. *Systematic Theology,* Vol. III (Chicago: University of Chicago Press, 1963), p. 95.

36. Monk Gibbon, *For Daws to Peck At* (New York: Dodd, Mead and Co., n.d.), p. 41. By permission of Victor Gollancz, Ltd., London.

37. *American Mercury* XXVIII (January, 1933), 35.

38. *Ibid.,* XXVII (October, 1932), 163.

39. *Ibid.,* XXVI (May, 1932), 52.

40. *Ibid.,* XXVI (July, 1932), 313.

Bibliography

Abernethy, T. P. *From Frontier to Plantation in Tennessee.* University of North Carolina Press, 1932.

Adams, E. C. L. *Congaree Sketches: Scenes From Negro Life in the Swamps of the Congaree and Tales By Tad and Scip of Heaven and Hell With Other Miscellany.* University of North Carolina Press, 1927.

Adams, Samuel C., Jr. *The Changing Organization of a Rural Negro Community and Its Implications for Race Accommodation.* University of Chicago Library, Department of Photographic Reproduction, 1947. Positive Microfilm.

Adamson, Alan H. *Sugar Without Slaves: The Political Economy of British Guiana, 1838–1904.* Yale University Press, 1972.

Ainsworth, L. *The Confessions of a Planter in Malaya.* London: H. F. and L. Witherby, 1933.

Allen, George C. *Western Enterprise in Indonesia and Malaya; a Study in Economic Development.* London: George Allen and Unwin Ltd., 1957.

Allen, James S. *The Negro Question in the United States.* New York: International Publishers, 1936.

Anstey, Mrs. Vera. *The Trade of the Indian Ocean.* New York: Longmans, Green and Co., 1929.

Antrobus, H. *A History of the Assam Tea Company, 1839–1953.* Edinburgh: Private printing by T. and A. Constable, 1957.

Aubrey, W. H. S. "On Sending Prisoners to the Plantations," *Chamber's Journal* (December 2, 1901), 812–816.

Baasch, Ernst. *Holläendische Wirtschaftsgeschichte.* Jena: G. Fischer, 1927. [The Dutch East Indies]

Bacon, Francis, Viscount St. Albans. "Of Plantations," *Essays* (with an introduction by Geoffrey Grigson). London: Oxford University Press, H. Milford, 1940.

Ballagh, James C. *A History of Slavery in Virginia.* The Johns Hopkins Press, 1902.

Ballagh, James C. *White Servitude in the Colony of Virginia: A Study of Indentured Labor in the American Colonies.* The Johns Hopkins Press, 1895.

Barker, George M. *A Tea Planter's Life in Assam.* Calcutta: Thacker, Spink and Co., 1884.

Barnhart, John D. "Frontiersmen and Planters in the Formation of

Kentucky," *The Journal of Southern History* (February, 1941), 19–36.

Barrett, Ward. *The Sugar Hacienda of the Marqueses del Valle.* University of Minnesota Press, 1970.

Barrow, David C. "A Georgia Plantation," *Scribner's Monthly* (April, 1881), 830–836.

Bassett, John Spencer. "The Industrial Decay of Southern Planters," *South Atlantic Quarterly* (April, 1903), 107–113.

————. *Slavery and Servitude in the Colony of North Carolina.* The Johns Hopkins Press, 1896.

————. "Some Phases of Early Plantation Life in North Carolina," *The Trinity Archive* (December, 1892), 98–103.

————. *The Southern Plantation Overseer as Revealed in His Letters.* (Smith College Fiftieth Anniversary Publications, V. 5), Northampton, Massachusetts: Printed for Smith College, 1925.

Bauer, Peter. *The Rubber Industry: A Study in Competition and Monopoly,* Harvard University Press, 1948.

Baume, Frederick Ehrenfried. *Burnt Sugar.* Sidney: The New Century Press Ltd., 1938. [On the conflict between Italians and English in Queensland, Australia.]

Beals, Carleton. "The Black Belt of the Caribbean," *The American Mercury* (October, 1931), 129–138.

Beckford, George L. *Persistent Poverty; Underdevelopment in Plantation Economies of the Third World.* New York: The Oxford University Press, 1972.

————. *The West Indian Banana Industry.* Jamaica: University of the West Indies, 1967.

Benedict, Burton. *Mauritius; Problems of a Plural Society.* Published for the Institute of Race Relations, London: F. A. Praeger, 1965.

Binns, Sir Bernard O. *Plantations and Other Centrally Operated Estates.* Rome, Italy: Food Agriculture Organization of the United Nations, 1955.

Blixen, Karen. *Out of Africa* by Isak Dinesen (pseud.). Random House, 1938. [Kenya in East Africa]

Boeke, J. H. "Colonialism and Dualism." *Race Relations in World Perspective.* Ed. Andrew W. Lind. University of Hawaii Press, 1955. [The Dutch East Indies]

Boeke, J. H. *The Structure of Netherlands' Indian Economy.* New York: Institute of Pacific Relations, 1942.

Bonner, James C. "The Plantation Overseer and Southern Nationalism as Revealed in the Career of Garland D. Harmon," *Agricultural History* (January, 1945), 1–11.

Bradley, A. G. "The Ulster Plantation," *The Quarterly Review* (January, 1923), 27–39. [The Plantation of Ireland]

Brandfon, Robert L. *Cotton Kingdom of the New South: A History of the Yazoo Mississippi Delta from Reconstruction to the Twentieth Century.* Harvard University Press, 1967.

Brandt, Karl. "Fallacious Census Terminology and Its Consequences in Agriculture," *Social Research* (February, 1938), 19–36.

Bruchey, Stuart. *Cotton and the Growth of the American Economy, 1790–1860.* Harcourt, Brace, and World, Inc., 1967.

Bryce, LaPorte and Roy Simon. *Black Captivity: A Sociology of the Plantation Past.* Boston: Allyn-Bacon (forthcoming).

———. The Conceptualization of the American Slave Plantation, University of California at Los Angeles, Ph.D. dissertation, 1962.

———. "The Slave Plantation: Background to Present Conditions of Urban Blacks." *Race, Change and Urban Society.* Ed. Peter Orleans and William Russell Elis, Jr., Beverly Hills, Calif.: Sage Publications, 1971.

Buchanan, R. O. "A Note on Labour Requirements in Plantation Agriculture," *Geography* (1938), 156–164.

Burwell, Letitia M. *Plantation Reminiscences* by Page Thacker (pseud.). Owensboro, Kentucky, 1878.

Bush, Willard C. *Pahang.* The Macmillan Company, 1938. [Rubber Plantation in the Malay Peninsula]

Catterall, Mrs. Helen H. (Tunnicliff), Ed. *Judicial Cases Concerning American Slavery and the Negro.* Washington, D.C.: Carnegie Institution of Washington, 1937.

Channing, Edward. *The Narragansett Planters: A Study of Causes.* The Johns Hopkins Press, 1886.

Chesnut, Mary B. *A Diary From Dixie.* Houghton Mifflin Company, 1949.

Chirot, Daniel. *The Origins and Development of an Agrarian Crisis: The Social History of Wallachia, 1250–1917.* New York: East European Quarterly Press. Distributed by Columbia University Press (forthcoming).

Coene, R. de. "Agricultural Settlement Schemes in the Belgian Congo," *Tropical Agriculture* (1956), 1–12.

Commonwealth Economic Committee. *Plantation Crops,* Published since 1932.

Courtenay, Philip P. *Plantation Agriculture.* F. A. Praeger, 1965.

Craton, Michael and James Walvin. *A Jamaican Plantation; the History of Worthy Park, 1670–1970.* University of Toronto Press, 1970.

Cumper, G. E. "Labour Demand and Supply in the Jamaican Sugar Industry, 1840–1950," *Social and Economic Studies,* II, No. 4, Institute of Social and Economic Research, University College of the West Indies, Jamaica.

Cutter, Victor M. "Caribbean Tropics in Commercial Transition," *Economic Geography* (October, 1926), 494–508.

Dalton, Henry. *The History of British Guiana.* London: Longman, Brown, Green, and Longmans, 1855.

Das, Rajani K. *Plantation Labour in India.* Calcutta: R. Chatterjee, 1931.

Deerr, Nöel. *The History of Sugar.* London: Chapman and Hall Ltd., 1949–1950.

Diégues, Manuel Júnior. "Land Tenure and Use in the Brazilian Plantation System." *Plantation Systems of the New World.* Washington, D.C.: Social Science Monographs, 1959, 104–125. [A publication of the Pan-American Union]

Doar, David. *Rice and Rice Planting in the South Carolina Low Country.* The Charleston Museum, 1936.

Dowdey, Clifford. *The Great Plantation.* Rinehart and Company, 1957. [A Profile of Berkeley Hundred and Plantation in Early Virginia]

Dunlop, W. R. "Queensland and Jamaica: A Comparative Study in Geographical Economics," *Geographical Review* (October, 1926), 548–567.

Dunn, Richard S. *Sugar and Slaves; the Rise of the Planter Class in the English West Indies, 1624–1713.* The University of North Carolina Press, 1972.

Easterby, James H. *The South Carolina Rice Factor as Revealed in the Papers of Robert F. W. Allston.* University of Chicago Press, 1945.

Elkins, Stanley M. *Slavery: A Problem in American Institutional and Intellectual Life.* University of Chicago Press, 1969.

Elliot, Edwin A. "The Development of a Texas Cotton Plantation," *Southwestern Social Science Quarterly* (June, 1933), 1–14.

———. "An Economic Survey of a Texas Cotton Plantation as to Tenantry, Tenancy, and Management." Dissertation. University of Texas, 1930.

Erickson, Edgar L. "The Introduction of East Indian Coolies into the British West Indies," *The Journal of Modern History* (June, 1934), 127–146.

Everett, Frank E., Jr. *Brierfield: Plantation Home of Jefferson Davis.* University and College Press of Mississippi, 1973.

"Experiences of a Coffee Planter in Southern India," *Fraser's Magazine* (June, 1879), 703–708.

Farmer, B. H. "Peasant and Plantation in Ceylon," *Pacific Viewpoint* (March, 1963), 9–16.

Fay, C. R. "Plantation Economy: History of Indigo in India," *The Economic Journal* (December, 1936), 623–625.

Fithian, P. V. *Journal and Letters of Philip Vickers Fithian, 1773–1774: A Plantation Tutor of the Old Dominion.* Hunter D. Farish, Ed. Williamsburg, Va.: Colonial Williamsburg, Inc., 1943.

Flanders, Ralph B. *Plantation Slavery in Georgia.* University of North Carolina Press, 1933.

Fogel, Robert W., and Stanley Engerman. *Time on the Cross: The Economics of American Negro Slavery.* Little, Brown and Company, 1974, 2 vols.

Fontane, Theodor. *Der Stechlin Roman.* Berlin: S. Fischer, 1928. [Fiction. Life on the great estates of East Germany]

Forrest, D. M. *A Hundred Years of Ceylon Tea, 1867–1967.* London: Chato and Windus, 1967.

Foster, Phillips and Peter Creyke. *The Structure of Plantation Agriculture in Jamaica*. College Park: University of Maryland Agricultural Experiment Station, Misc. Publication 623, 1968.

Frank, Tenney. *An Economic History of Rome to the End of the Republic*. The Johns Hopkins Press, 1920.

Fraser, W. M. *The Recollections of a Tea Planter*. London: The Tea and Rubber Mail, 1935. [India]

Frazier, E. Franklin. *The Negro Family in the United States*. The University of Chicago Press, 1939. [Part I, "In the House of the Master."]

Freyre, G. *The Mansions and the Shanties*. Knopf, 1963. [Brazil]

———. *The Masters and the Slaves: A Study in the Development of Brazilian Civilization*. Knopf, 1946. [Brazil]

Fuchs, I. M. "Tucuman: A Transition from Primary to Cultural Landscape," *Geographical Review* (April, 1955), 267–268. [Argentina]

Furnivall, John S. *Colonial Policy and Practice; a Comparative Study of Burma and Netherlands India*. Issued in co operation with the International Secretariat, Institute of Public Relations. Cambridge, England: The University Press, 1948.

Gaines, F. P. *The Southern Plantation: A Study in the Development and Accuracy of a Tradition*. Columbia University Press, 1924. [The Southern Plantation in Literature]

Galloway, J. H. "The Last Years of Slavery on the Sugar Plantations of Northeastern Brazil," *Hispanic American Historical Review* (November, 1971), 586–605.

Geertz, C. *Agricultural Involution; the Process of Ecological Change in Indonesia*. University of California Press, 1963.

Genovese, Eugene D. "The Significance of the Slave Plantation for Southern Economic Development," *The Journal of Southern History* (November, 1962), 422–437.

———. *The World the Slaveholders Made: Two Essays in Interpretation*. Pantheon Books, 1969.

———. *Roll, Jordan, Roll: The World the Slaves Made*. New York: Pantheon Books, 1974.

Gray, Lewis C. *History of Agriculture in the Southern United States to 1860*. Washington, D.C.: The Carnegie Institution of Washington, 1933, 2 vols.

Greaves, Ida C. *Modern Production Among Backward Peoples*. London: Allen and Unwin, 1935.

———. "Plantations in World Economy," *Plantation Systems of the New World*. Paper and discussion summaries of the seminar held in San Juan, Puerto Rico, November 17–23, 1957. Washington, D.C.: Pan American Union, 1959.

Green, Fletcher M., Ed. *The Lides Go South . . . and West; the Record of a Planter Migration in 1835*. University of South Carolina Press, 1952.

Greenfield, Sidney M. "Slavery and the Plantation in the New World," *Journal of Inter-American Studies* (January, 1969), 44–57.

Gregor, Howard F. "The Changing Plantation," *Annals of the Association of American Geographers* (June, 1965), 221–238.

Guerra y Sanchez, Ramiro. *Sugar and Society in the Caribbean; an Economic History of Cuban Agriculture.* Yale University Press, 1964.

Hagelberg, G. B. *The Caribbean Sugar Industry: Constraints and Opportunities.* New Haven: Antilles Research Program, Yale University Occasional Papers No. 3, 1974.

Haggard, Phoebe. *The Master's Children.* London: John Lane, 1939. [Fiction, Brazil]

Hall, Gwendolyn M. *Social Control in Slave Plantation Societies.* The Johns Hopkins Press, 1971.

Handlin, Oscar and Mary F. Handlin. "Origins of the Southern Labor System," *The William and Mary Quarterly* (April, 1950), 199–222.

Harlow, Vincent T. *A History of Barbados, 1625–1685.* Oxford: The Clarendon Press, 1926.

Henry, Howell M. *The Police Control of the Slave in South Carolina.* Emory, Virginia, 1914.

Hertz, Hilda. "Language and the Social Situation: A Study in Race Relations." Ph.D. Dissertation, Duke University, 1950.

Heyward, Duncan C. *Seed From Madagascar.* University of North Carolina Press, 1937. [Rice]

Higginson, Francis. *New England's Plantation.* Massachusetts Historical Society, 1806.

Higman, B. W. "Sugar Plantations and Yeoman Farming in New South Wales," *Annals of the Association of American Geographers* (December, 1958), 697–719. [Australia]

Hoetink, Harmannus. *The Two Variants of Caribbean Race Relations: A Contribution to the Sociology of Segmented Societies.* Trans. M. Hooykaas. New York: The Oxford University Press, 1967.

Hofstader, Richard. "U. B. Phillips and the Plantation Legend," *Journal of Negro History* (April, 1944), 109–124.

Holley, William C., Ellen Winston, and T. J. Woofter, Jr. *The Plantation South, 1934–1937.* Freeport, New York: Books for Libraries Press, 1971.

Hopkins, James F. *A History of the Hemp Industry in Kentucky.* University of Kentucky Press, 1951.

Hutchinson, Harry W. *Village and Plantation Life in Northeastern Brazil.* University of Washington Press, 1957.

Iliffe, John. *Tanganyika Under German Rule, 1905–1912.* Cambridge University Press, 1969.

Jackson, James C. *Planters and Speculators; Chinese and European Agricultural Enterprise in Malaya, 1786–1921.* London: The Oxford University Press, 1968.

Jacob, Heinrich E. *Coffee; the Epic of a Commodity.* Viking Press, 1935.

Jayawardena, Chandra. *Conflict and Solidarity in a Guianese Plantation.* New York: The Humanities Press, 1963.

Johnson, Alvin S. "Capitalism of the Camp," *The New Republic* (April 1, 1916), 237–239. [The Mine]

Johnson, Charles S., E. R. Embree, and W. W. Alexander. *The Collapse of Cotton Tenancy.* University of North Carolina Press, 1935.

Johnson, Charles S. *Shadow of the Plantation.* University of Chicago Press, 1934.

Johnson, Guion G. *A Social History of the Sea Islands, With Special Reference to St. Helena Island, South Carolina.* University of North Carolina Press, 1930.

Jones, Katherine M. *The Plantation South.* The Bobbs Merrill Company, 1957.

Jones, William O. "Plantations." *International Encyclopedia of the Social Sciences,* 1968, XII, 154–159.

Jordan, Weymouth T. *Hugh Davis and His Alabama Plantation.* University of Alabama Press, 1948.

Kane, Harnett Thomas. *Plantation Parade; the Grand Manner in Louisiana.* W. Morrow and Company, 1945.

Keith, Robert G. "Encomienda, Hacienda and Corregimiento in Spanish America: A Structural Analysis," *Hispanic American Historical Review* (August, 1971), 431–446.

Keller, Albert Galloway. *Colonization; a Study of the Founding of New Societies.* Boston: Ginn and Company, 1908. [Plantation and Farm in Relation to Climate]

Kemble, Frances Anne. *Journal of a Residence on a Georgia Plantation in 1838–1839.* Harper and Brothers, 1863.

Kennedy, John P. *Swallow Barn, or, a Sojourn in the Old Dominion.* Harcourt, Brace and Company, 1929. [Fiction: Virginia. First published in 1832. Marked "the beginning of the literary tradition" of the plantation.]

Kepner, Charles D., Jr. *Social Aspects of the Banana Industry.* Columbia University Press, 1936.

———, Jr. and Jay Henry Soothill. *The Banana Empire; a Case Study of Economic Imperialism.* Vanguard Press, 1935.

Kloosterboer, W. *Involuntary Labour Since the Abolition of Slavery; a Survey of Compulsory Labour Throughout the World.* Leiden, Netherlands: E. J. Brill, 1960.

Langsford, E. L. and B. H. Thibodeaux. *Plantation Organization and Operation in the Yazoo-Mississippi Delta Area.* U.S. Department of Agriculture Technical Bulletin No. 682, 1939.

Lasker, Bruno. *Human Bondage in Southeast Asia.* University of North Carolina Press, 1950.

Leeds, Anthony. *Economic Cycles in Brazil: The Persistence of a Total Culture Pattern.* Columbia University Press, 1958.

Leigh, Frances B. *Ten Years on a Georgia Plantation Since the War.* London: R. Bentley and Son, 1883.

Leroy-Beaulieu, Paul. *De la Colonization chez les Peuples Modernes.*

Paris: Guillaumin et cie, 1886. [The plantation and other types of colonies]

Leyburn, James G. "Frontier Society: A Study in the Growth of Culture." *Sociologus; Zeitschrift für Völkerpsychologie und Soziologie,* IX (1933), 174–181.

Lier, Rudolf A. Jacob Von. *Frontier Society.* The Hague: Martinus Nijhoff, 1971. [Surinam]

Lind, Andrew W. *An Island Community; Ecological Succession in Hawaii.* University of Chicago Press, 1938.

———. "Occupation and Race on Certain Frontiers." *Race Relations in World Perspective.* Ed. Andrew W. Lind. University of Hawaii Press, 1955.

———. "Race Relations in New Guinea," *Current Affairs Bulletin* (June 30, 1969), 34–38.

Lockhart, James. "Encomienda and Hacienda; the Evolution of the Great Estate in the Spanish Indies," *Hispanic American Historical Review* (August, 1969), 411–429.

Lulofs, Madelon. *Coolie.* Trans. G. J. Renier and Irene Clephane. Viking Press, 1936. [Fiction. Southeast Asia]

———. *White Money; a Novel of the East Indies.* Trans. G. J. Renier and Irene Clephane. The Century Co., 1933. [Fiction, Southeast Asia]

McBride, George M. "Plantation," *Encyclopedia of the Social Sciences,* XI, 1937, 148–153.

McKenzie, R. D. "Race Invasion of Malaya," *Journal of Applied Sociology* (July–August, 1927), 525–540.

Macmillan, William M. *Warning From the West Indies; a Tract for the Empire.* London: Faber and Faber Ltd., 1936.

MacNair, J. C. H. "Old Indigo Plantations," *Edinburgh Review* (July, 1928), 164–171.

McWilliams, Carey. *Factories in the Field.* Archon Books, 1969. [Large-scale agriculture in California]

Manchester, Alan K. "The Rise of the Brazilian Aristocracy," *Hispanic American Historical Review* (May, 1931), 145–168.

Mangum, Charles S. *Legal Status of the Tenant Farmer in the Southeast.* University of North Carolina Press, 1952.

Mantero, F. *Portuguese Planters and British Humanitarians; the Case for S. Thomé.* Trans. Lieut.-Colonel J. A. Wyllie. Lisbon: Redacfão da Reforma, 1911.

May, Stacy and Galo Plaza. *The United Fruit Company in Latin America.* Washington, D.C.: National Planning Association, 1958.

Mayer, Adrian. *Indians in Fiji.* London: The Oxford University Press, 1963.

Maxwell, Constantia. "The Plantation in Ulster at the Beginning of James I's Reign," *The Sewanee Review* (April, 1923), 164–177.

Mendle, Jay R. "The Plantation Economy; an Essay in Definition," *Science and Society* (Spring, 1972), 49–62.

Metcalf, J. E. "The Decline of Plantation Agriculture in Indonesia," *Foreign Agriculture* (April, 1952), 74–76.

Mier, August and E. M. Rudwick. *From Plantation to Ghetto; an Interpretive History of American Negroes.* New York: Hill and Wang, 1966.

Miller, Elinor M. and E. D. Genovese (Eds.). *Plantation, Town, and County: Essays on the Local History of American Slave Society.* University of Illinois Press, 1974.

Miller, William D. "The Narragansett Planters," *Proceedings of the American Antiquarian Society* (April, 1933), 49–115.

Mintz, Sidney W. "The Culture History of a Puerto-Rican Sugar Cane Plantation, 1876–1949," *The Hispanic American Historical Review* (May, 1953), 224–251.

———. "Labor and Sugar in Puerto Rico and in Jamaica," *Comparative Studies in Society and History* (March 19, 1959), 273–280.

———. *Worker in the Cane.* Yale University Press, 1960 [Puerto Rico]

Mitchell, Margaret. *Gone With the Wind.* The Macmillan Co., 1936. [Fiction]

Moore, Wilbert E. "Slave Law and the Social Structure," *The Journal of Negro History* (April, 1941), 171–202.

Myers, Robert M., Ed. *The Children of Pride; a True Story of Georgia and the Civil War.* Yale University Press, 1972.

Niebor, Herman J. *Slavery as an Industrial System.* The Hague: Martinus Nijhoff, 1910.

Norbeck, Edward. *Pineapple Town: Hawaii.* University of California Press, 1959.

Novack, George E. "The Colonial Plantation System," *The New International* (December, 1939), 343–345.

Olivier, Sydney H. *White Capital and Coloured Labour.* London: L. and V. Woolf, 1929.

Olmstead, F. L. *The Cotton Kingdom; a Traveller's Observations on Cotton and Slavery in the American Slave States.* Knopf, 1953.

Oppenheimer, Franz. *The State; Its History and Development Viewed Sociologically.* Trans. John M. Gitterman. Bobbs Merrill Co., 1914.

Paisley, Clifton. *From Cotton to Quail; an Agricultural Chronicle of Leon County, Florida, 1860–1967.* University of Florida Press, 1968.

Percy, William A. *Lanterns on the Levee; Recollections of a Planter's Son.* Knopf, 1941.

Phillips, Ulrich B. *American Negro Slavery; a Survey of the Supply, Employment, and Control of Negro Labor as Determined by the Plantation Regime.* D. Appleton and Co., 1940.

———. "An Antigua Plantation, 1769–1818," *North Carolina Historical Review* (July, 1926), 439–445.

———. "A Jamaica Slave Plantation," *American Historical Review* (April, 1914), 543–558.

———. *Life and Labor in the Old South.* Little, Brown and Co., 1929.

———, Ed. *Plantation and Frontier Documents: 1649–1863, Illustrative of Industrial History in the Colonial and Ante-bellum South.* Cleveland: A. H. Clark Co., 1909.

———. "The Plantation as a Civilizing Factor," *Sewanee Review* (July, 1904), 257–267.

———. "Plantations East and South of Suez," *Agricultural History* (July, 1931), 93–109.

Pim, Alan W. *Colonial Agricultural Production: The Contribution Made by Native Peasants and by Foreign Enterprise,* New York: Oxford University Press, 1946.

"Plantation." *Encyclopaedia Britannica,* 1911, XXI, 726–727.

Plantation Systems in the New World. Papers and Discussion Summaries of the Seminar Held in San Juan, Puerto Rico, November 17–23, 1957. Washington: Pan American Union, 1959. English and Spanish editions.

Potter, David M., Jr. "The Rise of the Plantation System in Georgia," *Georgia Historical Quarterly* (June, 1932), 114–135.

Prunty, Merle, Jr. "The Census on Multiple-Units and Plantations in the South," *The Professional Geographer* (September, 1956), 2–5.

Ragatz, Lowell J. *The Fall of the Planter Class in the British Caribbean, 1763–1833.* Century Co., 1928.

Ramachandran, N. *Foreign Plantation Investment in Ceylon, 1889–1958.* Colombo: Central Bank of Ceylon, 1963.

Raper, Arthur F. and Ira de A. Reid. *Sharecroppers All.* University of North Carolina Press, 1941.

Reed, Stephen W. *The Making of Modern New Guinea, with Special Reference to Culture Contact in the Mandated Territory.* American Philosophical Society, 1943.

Rice, John A. *I Came Out of the Eighteenth Century.* Harper and Brothers, 1942.

Robert, Joseph C. *The Tobacco Kingdom; Plantation, Market, and Factory in Virginia and North Carolina, 1800–1860.* Duke University Press, 1938.

Rodway, James. *History of British Guiana.* Georgetown: J. Thomson, 1891–1894.

Rogers, Sam L. *Plantation Farming in the United States.* U.S. Department of Commerce, Bureau of the Census, 1916.

Rubin, Morton. *Plantation County.* University of North Carolina Press, 1962.

———. "Social and Cultural Change in the Plantation Area," *Journal of Social Issues* (January–March, 1954), 28–35.

Ryan, Bryce. "The Agricultural Systems of Ceylon," *Rural Sociology* (March, 1955), 16–24.

Sale, Edith Tunis, Ed. *Historic Gardens of Virginia.* The James River Garden Club. William Byrd Press, 1923.

Sanders, Charles R. *The Cameron Plantation in Central North Carolina and Its Founder Richard Bennehan, 1743–1973.* Durham, North Carolina: Privately Printed, 1974.

Saxon, Lyle. *Children of Strangers.* Houghton Mifflin Co., 1937. [Fiction. Louisiana]

———. *Old Louisiana.* The Century Co., 1929.

Schul, Norman W. "Philippine Sugar Cane Plantation: Land Tenure and Sugar Cane Production," *Economic Geography* (April, 1967), 157–169.

Scisco, L. D. "The Plantation Type of Colony," *The American Historical Review* (January, 1903), 260–270.

Shaffer, Edward Terry Hendric. *Carolina Gardens . . . The History, Romance and Tradition of Two States Through More Than Two Centuries.* Huntington Press, 1937.

Sheridan Richard B. "The Plantation Revolution and the Industrial Revolution, 1625–1775," *Caribbean Studies* (October, 1969), 5–25.

———. "The Rise of a Colonial Gentry; a Case Study of Antigua, 1730–1775," *Economic History Review* (April, 1961), 342–357.

Shugg, Roger W. "Survival of the Plantation System in Louisiana," *Journal of Southern History* (August, 1937), 311–325.

Silvermaster, Nathan G. and Melvin M. Knight. "Plantation Wares," *Encyclopaedia of the Social Sciences*, 1937, XII, 153–158.

Sitterson, Joseph C. *Sugar Country; the Cane Sugar Industry in the South, 1753–1950.* University of Kentucky Press, 1953.

Smedes, Susan (Dabney). *Memorials of a Southern Planter.* Knopf, 1965.

Smith, Alice R. H., Herbert R. Sass, and D. E. Huger Smith. *A Carolina Rice Plantation of the Fifties; Thirty Paintings in Water-colour, by Alice R. Huger Smith, Narrative by Herbert Ravenel Sass, With Chapters From the Unpublished Memoirs of D. E. Huger Smith.* New York: W Morrow and Co., 1936.

Smith, Henry A. M. "The Upper Ashley; and the Mutations of Families," *The South Carolina Historical and Genealogical Magazine* (July, 1919), 151–198.

Smith, Julia Floyd. *Slavery and Plantation Growth in Ante-bellum Florida.* University of Florida Press, 1973.

Smith, Raymond T. *British Guiana.* New York: Oxford University Press, 1964.

Sorrenson, Maurice P. K. *Origins of European Settlement in Kenya.* Nairobi: Oxford University Press, 1968.

Stein, Stanley J. *Vassouras, a Brazilian Coffee County, 1850–1900.* Harvard University Press, 1957.

Stewart, Watt. *Chinese Bondage in Peru; a History of the Chinese Coolie in Peru.* Duke University Press, 1951.

Stoney, Samuel G. *Plantations of the Carolina Low Country.* Eds. Albert Simomons and Samuel Lapham, Jr. Charleston, S.C.: The Carolina Art Association, 1938.

Sydnor, Charles S. *Gentleman Freeholders; Political Practices in Washington's Virginia.* University of North Carolina Press, 1952.

Székely, László. *Tropic Fever; the Adventures of a Planter in Sumatra.* Harper Brothers, 1937.

Taylor, Paul S. *An American-Mexican Frontier: Nueces County, Texas.* University of North Carolina Press, 1934.

———. "Plantation Agriculture in the United States: Seventeenth to Twentieth Centuries," *Land Economics* (May, 1954), 141–152.

———. "Plantation Laborer Before the Civil War," *Agricultural History* (January, 1954), 1–21.

Taylor, Wayne C. *The Firestone Operations in Liberia.* Washington, D.C.: National Planning Association, 1956.

Thompson, Edgar T. *The Plantation: A Bibliography.* Washington, D.C.: Pan American Union, Social Science Monographs, IV, 1957. [Also a printing in Spanish. A joint publication of the Research and Training Program for the Study of Man in the Tropics, Columbia University and the Pan American Union]

———. "The Plantation as a Social System," *Plantation Systems of the New World.* Papers and discussion summaries of the seminar held in San Juan, Puerto Rico, November 17–23, 1957. Washington, D.C.: Pan American Union, 1959. Reprinted in *Revista Geografica,* XXV, No. 51.

———. "The Plantation System and Problems of Typology," *Caribbean Studies: A Symposium.* Ed. Vera Rubin. Institute of Social and Economic Research, University College of the West Indies, Jamaica, B.W.I. in association with the Research and Training Program for the Study of Man in the Tropics, Columbia University, New York, 1957, 29–33.

——— and Alma Macy Thompson. *Race and Region.* University of North Carolina Press, 1949.

——— and Everett C. Hughes. *Race: Individual and Collective Behavior.* Glencoe, Illinois: The Free Press, 1958.

———. "The South and the Second Emancipation," Change in the Contemporary South. Ed. Allan P. Sindler. Duke University Press, 1963.

Thompson, Virginia. *Labor Problems in Southeast Asia.* Yale University Press, 1947.

Tilley, Nannie May. *The Bright Tobacco Industry, 1860–1929.* University of North Carolina Press, 1948.

Tschan, Francis Joseph. *The Virginia Planters, 1700–1775.* Ph.D. Thesis, University of Chicago, 1916.

Udo, R. K. "Sixty Years of Plantation Agriculture in Southern Nigeria, 1902–1962," *Economic Geography* (October, 1965), 356–368.

Ukers, W. H. *All About Coffee.* New York: The Tea and Coffee Trade Journal Co., 1935.

United States, Bureau of the Census. *Plantation Farming in the United States,* Census Bulletin, 1916.

Vance, Rupert B. *Human Factors in Cotton Culture; a Study in the Social Geography of the American South.* University of North Carolina Press, 1929.

Wagley, Charles. "Plantation America: A Culture Sphere," *Caribbean*

Studies: A Symposium. Ed. Vera Rubin. Institute of Social and Economic Research, University College of the West Indies, B.W.I., 1957.

Waibel, Leo. "The Climatic Theory of the Plantation: A Critique," *Geographical Review* (April, 1942), 307–310.

————. "The Tropical Plantation System," *The Scientific Monthly* (February, 1941), 156–160.

Ward, Robert. "A Visit to the Brazilian Coffee Country," *National Geographic* (September, 1911), 908–931.

Weber, Max. *General Economic History.* Trans. F. H. Knight. New York: Greenberg, 1927.

Welch, Frank. *The Plantation Land Tenure System in Mississippi.* Mississippi State College Experiment Station Bulletin 385, 1943.

Wertenbaker, Thomas J. *Patrician and Plebeian in Virginia; or, The Origin and Development of the Social Classes of the Old Dominion.* Charlottesville, Virginia: The Michie Co., printers, 1910.

————. *The Planters of Colonial Virginia.* Princeton University Press, 1922.

Whitaker, Herman. *The Planter.* New York: Grosset and Dunlap, 1909. [Fiction. Mexico]

Wickizer, V. D. "Plantation Crops in Tropical Agriculture," *Tropical Agriculture* (July, 1958), 171–180.

————. "The Plantation System in the Development of Tropical Economies," *Journal of Farm Economics* (February, 1958), 63–77.

Wolf, Eric R. and S. W. Mintz. "Haciendas and Plantations in Middle America and the Antilles," *Social and Economic Studies,* Jamaica, University College of the West Indies (September, 1957), 380–412.

Wolf, Howard and Ralph Wolf. *Rubber; a Story of Glory and Greed.* New York: Covici-Friede, 1936.

Woofter, Thomas J., Jr. *Landlord and Tenant on the Cotton Plantation.* Works Progress Administration, Division of Social Research, 1936.

———— and A. E. Fisher. *The Plantation South Today.* (U.S. Work Projects Administration, Social Problems Series, no. 5) U.S. Government Printing Office, 1940.

Yeo, C. A. "The Rise of the Plantation in Ancient Italy and Modern America," *The Classical Journal* (May, 1956), 391–395.

Zeichner, Oscar. "The Legal Status of the Agricultural Laborer in the South," *Political Science Quarterly* (September, 1940), 412–428.